# Five Epochs of Civilization

William McGaughey wrote several books while pursuing a career as an accountant with a transit agency. His first, *A Shorter Workweek in the 1980s*, appeared in 1981. This was followed by *Punchdrunk Man Reader* (1988), *Nonfinancial Economics: The Case for Shorter Hours of Work*, coauthored with Eugene McCarthy (1989), and *A U.S.-Mexico-Canada Free-Trade Agreement: Do We Just Say No?* (1991). Since 1993, he has owned and managed an apartment building near downtown Minneapolis. He regularly takes part in sessions of a multicultural singing group with Robert Bly.

# Five Epochs of Civilization

## World History as Emerging in Five Civilizations

William McGaughey

 Thistlerose Publications,
Minneapolis, MN, USA

Thistlerose Publications

Printed in Canada

Published by Thistlerose Publications,
1702 Glenwood Ave., Minneapolis, MN 55405; or
100 Sawkill Ave., Milford, PA 18337 U.S.A.

LCCC No. 99-094008


**Publisher's Cataloging-in-Publication Data**

McGaughey, William.
    Five Epochs of Civilization /
by William McGaughey. -- 1st ed.
    p. cm.
    Includes bibliographical references and index.
    ISBN: 0-9605630-3-2
    1. World history. 2. Forecasting. 3. Mass media
and culture.    I. Title.

D21.M34 2000                         909
                                     QBI99-912

# Acknowledgment

Thanks to Ben Hunnicutt, Jean Helliesen, Mark Welter, Lily Dong, Andrew Nowicki, Joel Kramer, Sheila McGaughey, Gervaye Parent, and Robert Müller, who have read all or part of the manuscript and made useful comments.

Thanks also to Mark Stanley for computer assistance, to Kathy Kruger for the cover design, to Jim Nelson and Joe Schwartzberg for their help, and to several publishers who have granted permission to reprint materials.

To my parents, who together have lived 178 years in the 20th century, 120 of them as a married couple; and to my recently departed brother Andrew.

# Table of Contents

Summary of Book Content

# Illustrative Tables

# SUMMARY OF BOOK CONTENTS

## General Description

A controversy exists as to which events ought to be included in history. For world history, the question is even more difficult. If history consists of a set of stories, the issue might be resolved by considering which story or stories best describe the transition of society from small tribal communities to the large pluralistic communities that we have today in the United States and similar nations. It may be that this story does not lead straight from one situation to another but is a story divided into parts tending in different directions. The problem of world history then becomes one of determining the parts, of deciding where the historical turning points are, and so splitting the mass of human experience into epochs that are associated with successive world civilizations.

This book finds the following pattern in world history:

Civilization as we know it began with the rise of primitive city-states in Egypt and Mesopotamia during the 4th millennium, B.C. For the first three thousand years, the dominant theme of social development was the accumulation of power in the hands of political rulers with authority over particular territories. These rulers gained power through exercise of military might. They built kingdoms from city-states, and empires from kingdoms. The culmination of the first civilization was the formation of four world empires which dominated the Old World in the 2nd century, A.D.: the Roman, Parthian, Kushan, and Han Chinese empires. (The Mayan culture meanwhile was poised to enter its classical phase in the New World.) Then barbarians overran the civilized empires and this epoch came to an end.

The second historical epoch began in the middle of the 1st millennium, B.C., when an extraordinary group of philosophers, prophets, and religious thinkers lived. From them proceeded schools of philosophy and systems of philosophically based, creedal religion. The story of this epoch is mainly the story of the three world religions - Buddhism, Christianity, and Islam - and of other religions that interacted creatively with them. In the end, the world religions fought one another, militarily as well as ideologically, mimicking political empires. This epoch came to an end in the middle of the 2nd millennium, A.D., when religious warfare and coercion turned public sentiment against them.

The third epoch began with the territorial and cultural outburst of European civilization that is associated with the Renaissance. During the 14th and 15th centuries, A.D., modern commercial institutions were established, new standards and practices of secular scholarship were brought to the universities, and once-isolated societies around the earth were connected by sea. The early voyages of transoceanic discovery gave way to political and commercial rivalries between the Atlantic nations, to colonization and enslavement of non-European peoples, to scientific-industrial and democratic revolutions, and to wars with technologically advanced weaponry culminating in World Wars I and II. In the end, the whole world was caught up in this European adventure, producing a backlash.

As relief to serious purposes, civilization in the fourth epoch turned to popular entertainment. Working men and women caught in the cogs of industrial society wanted lighthearted diversions to help them relax in their spare time. With the invention of electronic devices to preserve and disseminate sensuous images, this culture became connected to the "mass media". Live performances in opera houses or vaudeville theaters were replaced by motion pictures and by radio and television broadcasts. Rock 'n roll music created an international youth culture. The new system of electronically delivered news and entertainment transformed the political process, subverted organized religion, competed with schools for children's attention, and took over the merchandizing of commercial products.

Now in the fourth epoch, humanity stands on the brink of a fifth civilization sparked by computer technology. Its history, being mostly in the future, is speculative.

A second thread runs through this book. That is the assertion that each civilization began with the introduction of a new dominant cultural technology. The first civilization began with systems of primitive or ideographic writing; the second, with alphabetic writing; the third, with printing in Europe; the fourth, with electronic technologies of communication; and, the fifth, with computer technology.

In addition to short histories of each of the four civilizations that have appeared in a fully developed form, this book includes a history of the cultural technologies themselves, discusses the relationship between cultural technologies and personal or social values, describes the process of society's development into a system of increasingly complex and pluralistic institutions, identifies changing beliefs and models of personality in the successive civilizations, and speculates upon the future course of historical events in the fifth civilization, known also as the Quintepoch.

## Summary of Individual Chapters

**Chapter One:**     An important part of historical study is the task of finding a design in the mass of human experience. World history is embodied in a set of stories. The stories tell how humanity has progressed from one situation to another - from a less to a more complex type of society. The crux of the matter is to determine the turning points of history. They are times which mark a dividing line between two fundamentally different types of culture. In contrast with histories centering in the experience of particular nations or groups, this book follows changes in the values and structure of society. The introduction of new cultural technologies creates a space for new types of public experience. Their transition defines the successive epochs of world history. Civilizations are not societies which rise and fall in recurring cycles but cultural systems which build upon the work of their predecessors. Curiously, civilizations appear to be worldwide. That makes it possible to view world history with a single focus.

**Chapter Two:**        The flow of world history follows the creation of an increasingly complex society with ever more specialized institutions. When civilizations first appeared in the eastern Mediterranean area, civilized societies were embodied in institutions which combined political and religious authority. During the first historical epoch, the political function split off from the religious. Royal governments went on to create territorially extended empires by force of arms. However, the experience of military violence, cruelty, and injustice produced a yearning for a more rational and peaceful world whose ideals philosophers expressed. In time, philosophy found an outlet in the personal imperatives of religion. There followed an age of idea-based religions which transcended nationality - the so-called "world religions". Subsequently, these religions became contending empires which fought for worldly power. Then it was time for a movement away from spiritual militancy and toward a more secular, sensuous, and commercial set of pursuits. This epoch of European exploration and colonial expansion, beginning in the 15th century A.D., transmitted values centered in wealth and in the cultural trappings of wealth. Western expansion brought all the world's people in touch with each other for the first time. After two bloody wars, this third civilization began to dissolve in the new culture of popular entertainment. Making people have fun became a serious business. Gaining and keeping their attention became the road to power and wealth.

**Chapter Three:**        The institutions of government, world religion, commerce and education, and popular entertainment have a spiritual dimension which is tied to their belief systems and perceptions of attractive personality. Each has its own "religion" in a broad sense. Religion expresses beliefs concerning fundamental questions. It also promotes certain models of personality. The nature worship of tribal peoples gave way to "the worship of one's own collective human power." Civic religion in the service of governments marked the form of earlier worship. Then prophets and philosophers challenged this type of authority. They created a new kind of religion which could be formulated in creeds. Fidelity to those creeds offered a way to gain admission to Heaven. Religion in the epoch of commerce and education focused more upon things of this world. Its adherents believed in money acquired through successful careers and in the greatness of artists and musicians. The invention of electronic technologies capturing the sensuous images of human performers has created a culture of immediate spectacles which the entire community can share. The world of big-time entertainment offers fame and fortune to the lucky few who find a place in its shows; but, as the gossip columns reveal, these glamorous individuals have their share of problems, too.

**Chapter Four:**    The history of the first civilization would be a history of government, which includes the experience of wars and of changing imperial dynasties. This is history as it is commonly understood. Monarchical government began with the institution of city-states which grew to the size of empire when the localities came in conflict with each other. Certain kings prevailed in these wars. Certain peoples were defeated and enslaved. Like a pair of book ends to frame the period, the multi-millennial reign of autonomous governments in Egypt and China presents a model of imperial rule at the beginning and end of this epoch. Western peoples look back to Rome, first seen in the political consolidation of Italy and later in an empire divided between its eastern and western halves. Before that, bloody empires rose and fell with some frequency in the Middle East: Hittites, Assyrians, Babylonians, Medes, Persians, and Hellenistic Greeks. The Persian empire was revived under Parthian and Sasanian kings before succumbing to the armies of Islam. India had two short-lived indigenous empires before foreign Mogul and British rulers unified the subcontinent. This epoch reached its peak in the 3rd century, A.D. By the 7th century, only the Greek Byzantine and Chinese imperial dynasties had survived in the Old World. Balance-of-power diplomacy prevented a revival of empire in Europe. Only religion could bind diverse peoples in a single community.

**Chapter Five:**        The history of the second civilization began with that remarkable intellectual and moral awakening that occurred in several Old World societies during the 6th and 5th centuries B.C. Several spiritually advanced persons who lived then have left their teachings to posterity. The culminating event of this epoch was the establishment of three world religions - Buddhism, Christianity, and Islam - and the transformation of religions such as Judaism and Hinduism which belonged to an earlier tradition. In league with political power, these religions staked out territories of influence. This type of religion was driven by ideas rather than ritual. Besides the founder's teachings, the development of religious doctrine reflects the work of interpreters who evaluate doctrinal positions, codify, and explain. Religion has, however, a worldly side in the hierarchies of clergy who govern its institution. Here ideological zeal and ambition sometimes lead to a result at variance with the beneficial and peaceful attitude at the core of the religion. Toward the end of this epoch, Christian crusaders went to war against Moslems who held the Holy Land. Moslem and Hindu rulers fought for control of India. Buddhists, Taoists, and others cultivated the martial arts. Apart from worldly strife, communities of mystics, monks, and others practiced the hard disciplines of a spiritually centered life. Their quiet experiences, too, are part of the history of this second civilization.

**Chapter Six:**        The third civilization began with another kind of awakening which has been called the Renaissance. Its culture originated in north Italy where commercial prowess was combined with a taste for classical scholarship and exquisite art. European influence spread with the Portuguese and Spanish voyages of transoceanic discovery. West Europeans colonized lands in the New World which Columbus had "discovered" during a trip to the Orient. Rival nations bordering the north Atlantic fought for control of the trade in oriental spices. Later, a brisk trade in rum, coffee, and tobacco developed between Europe and its colonies in North America and the Caribbean islands. Slaves imported from Africa were put to work producing commodities for export. The savage warfare between Protestants and Catholics caused European intellectuals to shun religious controversies and instead pursue secular learning. Scientific discoveries inspired technological innovations that transformed industry and transportation. Industrialized societies gained immense wealth while developing social rifts. The laboring class asserted itself through strikes. Parliamentary governments challenged the authority of kings. Wars and revolutions advanced ideals of progress against the old order. Having defeated Spain on the seas and France in land battles fought in India and North America, Great Britain became the world's leading colonial power. Challenged by Prussian Germany, this sea-based nation threw the flower of its youth into a continental war from which it never fully recovered. Its former colony, the United States of America, filled the power vacuum. Anticolonial movements in the 19th and 20th centuries brought political independence to peoples in South America, Asia, and Africa.

**Chapter Seven:**    It may seem strange to suggest that entertainment is the basis of new civilization replacing that of the past five hundred years. Yet, the signs of its cultural dominance in the late 20th century are compelling. This historical epoch began with the minstrel shows, freak shows, and circuses of the previous century and with popular sporting events such as horse races, boxing matches, and baseball games. Spectacular exhibitions such as the Crystal Palace in 1851 added to the excitement. However, it was the invention of electronic devices to record and transmit images of sight and sound which created a new popular culture. After political alliances, commercial rivalries, and serious ideas had led to the carnage of two world wars, people wanted something a bit lighter. Some Americans enjoyed themselves at Broadway theaters or in clubs featuring jazz music. Others followed the exploits of Babe Ruth and Joe DiMaggio on the baseball diamond. Acquiring sound, movies came of age in the 1920s. Commercial radio stations began broadcasting music, news, and light entertainment. The creative ferment at the juncture of black and white people's entertainment brought forth an international youth culture centering in rock 'n roll music. Television broadcasts, begun after World War II, became an all-consuming presence in many households. The lure of easy money dangled before mass audiences fueled a gambling craze. Entertainment tastes became more diversified: some went in for shows that were suitable for "families" and others for ones appealing to "adults". Computer-generated images created new vistas of visual excitement and new opportunities to have fun with illusion-producing machines.

**Chapter Eight:**     The reason that the introduction of new cultural technologies is linked to the emergence of new civilizations is that, in extending an image or message to broad segments of the population, these technologies create their own type of experience, coloring it in certain ways. Certain institutions would not have been possible without their communicative service. Government bureaucracies employ the technology of writing. The invention of the alphabet put written language into the hands of merchants and others leading active lives. The exposure to visual symbols suggested to some that these symbols had an independent existence; and that insight fueled many a philosophy. Printing brought literacy to the masses of people. It fostered a more precise way of thinking, so important to modern scholarship and science. Well-known authors came to acquire cult-like followings. That changed when the technologies of film production, music recording, and radio and television broadcasting brought the personal images of performers into full view, making them "stars". Famous people were packaged and sold as personal commodities. With the advent of computers, the culture is again set to change. Perhaps the individual experience of  connectedness and interactivity will bring about a new set of public values.

**Chapter Nine:**     Written language was invented in ancient Mesopotamia as a means of recording commercial transactions. The same set of symbols was used to express numbers and words. Ideographic writing began when scribes chose different symbols for the quantities and types of commodities. Phonetic elements crept into writing driven by a need to express abstract concepts. In some scripts, the symbols expressed syllabic sounds. The alphabet, whose letters represent the pure sounds of speech, first appeared in the Middle East during the 2nd millennium B.C. Two Semitic peoples, the Phoenicians and Aramaeans, carried its technique to distant places in the course of trading expeditions. The Phoenician alphabet gave rise to the Greek and Latin alphabets, parent of most European scripts. Far Eastern societies have retained the earlier ideographic or syllabic system of writing. Printing came to the West from China. Gutenberg's pioneering use of movable type sparked an explosion of printed literature. Mass-circulation newspapers appeared in the 19th century. Photography and telegraphy, invented in the 1830s and 1840s, were among the first technologies to use chemical processes or electrical signals to capture or express visual images and words. The phonograph and motion-picture machine presented a series of images in time. Radio and television broadcasting sent messages through the air waves to persons with receivers tuned to particular frequencies. There came to be a culture of live images connecting a small group of performers with mass audiences. The computer, developed for use in World War II, has grown in speed and processing capacity while becoming physically miniaturized.

**Chapter Ten:**     Can world history be used to predict the future? If the future resembles the past, perhaps so. Otherwise, a way to anticipate coming events might be through analogy with other civilizations in a similar phase of development. Each of the four world civilizations whose history is already known exhibits a pattern of events in its life cycle. Generally, its period of exuberant, creative expansion is followed by a maturing phase of empire. This leads, in turn, to use of violence and coercion in an attempt to retain worldly power. One also discerns a pattern by which institutions developed in one period are fundamentally altered two epochs later. Historians are wanting to distinguish history's true turning points from ephemeral changes in the culture. Besides the appearance of major new cultural technologies, this book identifies other conditions that tend to be present in places and times of fundamental change: First, the new civilizations arise in an environment of political parochialism and vigorous commerce. Second, this environment produces important innovations in mathematics and commercial practice. Third, it brings expanded geographical horizons when people's creative imaginations are excited by perceptions of a wider world.

**Chapter Eleven:**    The computer age is upon us. Though in its infancy, this epoch will bring distinct changes to the society that we know. To predict the future of this civilization, one can anticipate impacts that arise from the nature of the technology. Already there is much interest in the commercial application of computers. One can envision a powerful new mode of selling and distributing commercial products which gives consumers much more information, choice, and control. Education is another area which foreseeably will be transformed. Computers give students increased ability to interact individually with the teaching source. They also have an unlimited capacity to duplicate lessons. Shortages of high-quality education could be a thing of the past; and this has immense social implications. The most profound result may be man's use of computers as a tool to remake himself. Computers can handle the extensive information contained in the structure of DNA molecules. They have the potential to replicate processes of the human mind. In this "Frankenstein civilization", man and machine will forge a common future which is at once dangerous and exciting in its far-reaching possibilities.

# Part I

**Chapter One**

# IN SEARCH OF A PATTERN
# IN WORLD HISTORY

## About Historical Knowledge

In reflecting upon its past, humanity is aware of times when life was different than it now is. The artifacts of those times are still to be seen in stone monuments, pottery shards, tools, and other physical remains. History is a collection of stories from the past which explain how the world that we know came to be. Unlike fiction, the stories of history are considered to be literally true. That brings other scholarly disciplines into the process of establishing historical truth. While our memories of history are forever receding into the past, its knowledge therefore increases as new facts come to light. Research techniques developed within the natural sciences, such as carbon dating, have improved the accuracy of information accepted as historical fact. Because the Babylonian, Chinese, Indian, Mayan, and other peoples kept records of astronomical events observed in their times, we are able to date stories found in ancient literature mentioning them. Archeological excavations, the discovery of manuscripts or carved inscriptions, and the deciphering of previously unknown languages increase our knowledge of long-lost civilizations.

One might say that the writing of history extends only so far as historians have knowledge of its events. What may once have happened will, of course, be excluded if the experience has been forgotten. Since stories include an interior consciousness of events, our knowledge of them will necessarily depend upon preserving them in a medium which can express human thoughts. Such a medium is, of course, written language. Some stories have come to us in the form of folklore handed down within tribal societies. While the stories may be based on actual experiences, their long process of oral transmission from one generation to another poses a risk of corruption. Writing, on the other hand, holds together in the same form so long as the material in which it has been expressed can weather processes of natural decay.

Conventionally one associates the experience of preliterate societies with "prehistoric" times. Arnold Toynbee has written: "Nomadism is essentially a society without a history. Once launched on its annual orbit, the Nomadic horde revolves in it thereafter and might go on revolving for ever if an external force against which Nomadism is defenseless did not eventually bring the horde's ... life to an end. This force is the pressure of the sedentary civilizations round about." Malidoma Somé, an African ritualist living in the United States, has compared the preliterate culture of his native village with the culture he found in the West. Westerners, he observed, are always in a hurry to go somewhere, and, in the process, they lose touch with their spiritual roots. Malidoma noted that the people of his tribe, the Dagara people of West Africa, do not have a conception of history. Their world view is timeless. What happens now is important, not what has happened. If an important event takes place, it quickly passes into the realm of mythology.

In the western view, human societies improve through the contributions of creative individuals. There is also destruction as once-healthy institutions become corrupt. Yet, world civilization is always moving towards an expanded state of consciousness. Human societies have changed. Fewer people live in tribal societies and more in those urbanized societies which are called "civilized." World history tells the story of humanity's changing from one situation to the other. The situation at the beginning of the story is different than at the end. Significant history is that which leaves an imprint upon the structure of society. It is the story of how the most advanced types of society came to be. There is not a single story to describe this process but several stories. That is because modern society consists of a plurality of institutions to handle its various functions. They emerged in different times.

The purpose of this book is to take the confused themes of world history, separate them into their different strands, and present each in a clear and coherent set of images. It is analogous to inserting a prism into a stream of white light. Such light is a mixture of variously colored rays with distinctive wave lengths. A prism inserted into its beam breaks the colors apart so that a person can see the separate spectral components. Likewise, world civilization as it exists today is a mixture of several different civilizations. Each has a story to tell. Since these civilizations overlap in time, their combined history is murky and confused. Historical understanding requires that one separate out the events connected with these different civilizations so that the direction behind each set of experiences becomes plainly seen.

## Competition for Space in Books of History

World history, being the accumulated record of past human experience, might consist of a large collection of personal biographies in the form of books, letters, notes, photographs, and other effects. Each person who has ever lived had a story to tell. If history were the sum total of all such stories, world history would not be contained in books but in large warehouses or computer files. Such a massive amount of information would make this history quite inaccessible. No one would have time to review more than a tiny part of it. Traditionally, history has never been a narrative of people's lives but of important people's lives. Some persons are more prone to being historical figures than others. To be lifted to that plane, one needs a device of personal magnification. Government office has placed certain individuals in positions of authority over others. The early histories were, therefore, chronologies of royal dynasties. Democracy has broadened the cast of historical characters. Besides kings and prime ministers, historians now record the lives of philosophers, saints, writers, scientists, entertainers, and other public figures.

The writing of history has lately become a matter of some controversy. That is because, as historical personalities have become democratized, people's expectations have increased that they will find representation in historical writings. It is understood that individuals are included in books of history because of some accomplishment or creative work. It is therefore an honor to be mentioned in history, and the amount of space given to describing a person's life would be a measure of that honor. If the average person is not mentioned, he or she aspires to assume historical importance through surrogates who are of a similar demographic type. People expect that history will provide attractive role models for themselves. Therefore, a political battle is raging about the kind of history textbook which ought to be used in the schools. Histories which give insufficient attention to the accomplishments of certain groups are challenged on the grounds of historical bias: Since "the victors write history", they reflect merely the views of the politically strong in an age when those histories were written.

Opponents of that view accuse its adherents of rewriting history in a partisan way. Arthur Schlesinger, Jr. has compared contemporary efforts to give African-Americans, women, and others greater historical prominence with a similar struggle waged by Irish-American zealots at the beginning of the 20th century. He noted that "John V. Kelleher, for many years Harvard's distinguished Irish scholar, once recalled his first exposure to Irish-American history - 'turgid little essays on the fact that the Continental Army was 76% Irish, or that many of George Washington's friends were nuns and priests, or that Lincoln got the major ideas for the Second Inaugural Address from the Hon. Francis P. Magehegan of Alpaca, New York, a pioneer manufacturer of cast-iron rosary beads.' John Kelleher called this 'the there's-always-an-Irishman-at-the-bottom-of-doing-the-real-work approach to American history.' About 1930, Kelleher said, those 'turgid little essays' began to vanish from Irish-American papers. He added, 'I wonder whose is the major component in the Continental Army these days?'"

Does such a thing exist as a truly objective world history? Probably not. Each selection of facts involves someone's preconceived point of view. Subjectively, many or most people want to believe that historical trends culminate in their own situation. However, a world history is written for all humanity. In a pluralistic world, one must accept that this history will include experiences of persons unlike ourselves. One needs to organize the writing of history by idea or theme rather than by types of persons given space in its works. World history is not centered in anyone's parochial experience.

## An Example of a Biased History

In the late 19th century, western peoples had a strong sense of self-confidence. In the United States, the focus upon European civilization was combined with a jingoistic appreciation of U.S. national strength. Historical textbooks of that era reflected ethnocentric values. A leather-bound book in my great-grandparents' collection, *Illustrated Universal History*, exemplifies historical thinking at the time. Published in Philadelphia in 1878, this book divided world history into three parts: "Ancient History", "the Middle Ages", and "Modern History". Ancient history began with Adam's life in the Garden of Eden and ended with the fall of the west Roman empire in 476 A.D. The Middle Ages followed Rome's fall and continued until 1517 A.D., the year that Martin Luther challenged papal authority. Modern history covered the subsequent period up until the time that the book was published. In a preface, the author informed readers that "(t)he greatest prominence is given to the annals of those nations of ancient and modern times which have acted a leading part on the stage of the world's history."

It is revealing to see the number of pages assigned in this 685-page book to the histories of various nations. The first two pages deal with "Antediluvian History" and the "Dispersal of Mankind." The history of "Oriental Nations" occupies the next thirteen pages. Histories of China, India, Assyria and Babylonia, Egypt, and Phoenicia each claim one page. Persian and Hebrew history together have seven pages. Nearly thirty pages are devoted to the history of ancient Greece, and fifty to Roman history. The 78-page section on the Middle Ages chronicles royal dynasties in Europe between the 5th and 15th centuries A.D. Mohammed's "Saracen Empire" is covered in four pages. India and China are mentioned as destinations of European exploration. "Modern History", focused on post-Reformation European dynasties and U.S. political administrations, claims the remaining pages. Wars and revolutions are the most heavily covered events. They include the "Thirty Years' War", the "English Revolution" and the "War of the Austrian Succession". Tucked away in this history are one-page summaries of events in India and Persia and a brief description of Spanish conquests in America. The history of the United States between 1776 and 1876 takes up sixty-five pages.

Today such a book would not be considered a "universal history". While it is interesting to know, for instance, that a Roman emperor named Heliogabalus was assassinated in 222 A.D. and that rude behavior by the Duke of Buckingham upset plans for Charles I of England to be married to a Spanish princess, such events of western political history shed little light upon fundamental issues affecting those societies. While the history of governments has served as a proxy for general history, human societies do involve more than their political aspect. A more serious deficiency is the book's preoccupation with western Europe and North America. It may have seemed in 1876 that the whole world was moving toward domination by the western powers. Events of the last century have corrected that impression. Much has been omitted from this book concerning the experiences of peoples in the nonwestern world who did leave a complete written record. If the scattered societies on earth each have separate histories, the question then becomes how much space to give each people's experiences in a book of world history.

## Population as a Guide to Historical Coverage

One approach might be to assume that each person's experiences are as deserving of historical coverage as another's, and, since all individuals have an equal claim to this coverage, the amount of space given in world history to the various national histories should follow the size of national populations. The nation with the largest population in a given time period should have the greatest historical coverage for that period, the second most populous nation should have the second most coverage, and so on. If the size of populations drives historical coverage, historians need to review population statistics over a period of time. Colin McEvedy's and Richard Jones' book, *Atlas of World Population History*, provides data concerning world population between 10000 B.C., when the Neolithic revolution began, and 1975 A.D. This information has been updated to the present.

Tables 1-1 and 1-2 show the earth's total population and its percentage breakdown by region in years between 400 A.D. and 1997 A.D. China and India together have accounted for about half the total population for much of this time. The European share of world population increased between the 17th and 19th centuries and then declined. The population of North and South America plus Oceania (Australia and the Pacific islands) gained a sharply higher share of world population between 1850 and 1997. This surge in population roughly corresponds with the emergence of the United States as a world power. European power and influence in the world reached a peak in the 19th

Table 1-1

### Total World Population in Selected Years

| Year | Population (in millions) | Year | Population (millions) |
|---|---|---|---|
| 10000 B.C. | 4 | 1100 A.D. | 320 |
| 5000 B.C. | 5 | 1200 A.D. | 360 |
| 4000 B.C. | 7 | 1300 A.D. | 360 |
| 3000 B.C. | 14 | 1400 A.D. | 350 |
| 2000 B.C. | 27 | 1500 A.D. | 425 |
| 1000 B.C. | 50 | 1550 A.D. | 480 |
| 500 B.C. | 100 | 1600 A.D. | 545 |
| 200 B.C. | 150 | 1650 A.D. | 545 |
| 0 | 170 | 1700 A.D. | 610 |
| 200 A.D. | 190 | 1750 A.D. | 720 |
| 400 A.D. | 190 | 1800 A.D. | 900 |
| 500 A.D. | 190 | 1850 A.D. | 1,200 |
| 600 A.D. | 200 | 1875 A.D. | 1,325 |
| 700 A.D. | 210 | 1900 A.D. | 1,625 |
| 800 A.D. | 220 | 1925 A.D. | 2,000 |
| 900 A.D. | 240 | 1950 A.D. | 2,500 |
| 1000 A.D. | 265 | 1975 A.D. | 3,900 |
| | | 1999 A.D. | 6,000 |

Source: *Atlas of World Population History, Penguin, 1978*

Table 1-2

Percentages of World Population by Area and Date

| date | China | India | Other Asia | Europe | Africa | other |
|---|---|---|---|---|---|---|
| 400 B.C. | 27 | 24 | 21 | 18 | 7 | 3 |
| 200 B.C. | 28 | 21 | 23 | 18 | 7 | 3 |
| 0 | 30 | 21 | 18 | 18 | 10 | 3 |
| 200 A.D. | 32 | 22 | 15 | 19 | 9 | 3 |
| 400 A.D. | 27 | 25 | 17 | 17 | 10 | 4 |
| 600 A.D. | 23 | 26 | 24 | 13 | 10 | 4 |
| 800 A.D. | 23 | 29 | 18 | 13 | 13 | 4 |
| 1000 A.D. | 23 | 30 | 17 | 14 | 12 | 4 |
| 1100 A.D. | 31 | 26 | 14 | 14 | 11 | 4 |
| 1200 A.D. | 32 | 24 | 14 | 16 | 11 | 3 |
| 1300 A.D. | 23 | 25 | 15 | 22 | 11 | 4 |
| 1400 A.D. | 21 | 28 | 18 | 17 | 12 | 4 |
| 1500 A.D. | 23 | 25 | 18 | 19 | 11 | 4 |
| 1600 A.D. | 28 | 25 | 17 | 18 | 10 | 2 |
| 1700 A.D. | 25 | 27 | 16 | 20 | 10 | 2 |
| 1750 A.D. | 30 | 24 | 15 | 19 | 9 | 3 |
| 1800 A.D. | 35 | 21 | 13 | 20 | 8 | 3 |
| 1850 A.D. | 35 | 19 | 12 | 22 | 7 | 5 |
| 1900 A.D. | 28 | 18 | 14 | 24 | 7 | 9 |
| 1950 A.D. | 21 | 18 | 19 | 21 | 8 | 13 |
| 1975 A.D. | 18 | 20 | 21 | 16 | 10 | 15 |
| 1997 A.D. | 21 | 21 | 18 | 13 | 13 | 14 |

Source: *Atlas of World Population History, Penguin, 1978*

century, as did Europe's share of world population. The main reason for gains in population has been the spread of agriculture. Some societies develop agricultural economies sooner than others. Other factors supporting population increases have been industrialization, medical advances cutting the death rate, and migration into underpopulated territories. War, famine, pestilence, and disease bring sudden drops in population. Another cause of population decline is the reduced fertility of women in affluent societies.

Changes in world population can mask conflicting trends between nations. The surge in population growth during the first millennium B.C. took place primarily in Asia, north Africa, and Europe. Greek peoples settling the coastal regions of the Mediterranean, Aegean, and Black seas were major contributors to this growth. Because of their increasing numbers, the Greeks were able to withstand the Persian emperor Xerxes II's invasion of their homeland in the 6th century B.C. and provide muscle for the army of Alexander the Great two centuries later. However, the Greek population stagnated during Hellenistic times. Rome's population of 5 million persons around 200 B.C. gave it an advantage in the war with Carthage, whose population then numbered about 1.5 million. A Jewish population boom during the 1st century A.D. brought Judaism and Christianity to cities throughout the Roman empire. Table 1-3 shows the three largest cities in the world in years since 2000 B.C. The names of those cities evoke the memory of kingdoms and empires which have left their mark upon world history.

The population of both the Roman and Han Chinese empires hit a peak in the 3rd century A.D. The Roman empire then had a total population of 46 million, and the Chinese empire more than 50 million people. China's population declined after the fall of the Han dynasty in 220 A.D. Europe's population, which totaled 36 million persons in 200 A.D., fell to 26 million in 600 A.D. At both ends of the Eurasian continent, nomadic tribes from central Asia with population of perhaps 5 million persons were infiltrating and defeating empires ten times as populous. In China, population growth resumed when imperial rule was reestablished. Its population rose from 60 million persons in 1000

Table 1-3

## Three Largest Cities in the World

| date | first | second | third |
|------|-------|--------|-------|
| 2000 B.C. | Ur | Memphis | Thebes |
| 1600 B.C. | Avaris | Babylon | Setabul |
| 1200 B.C. | Memphis | Khattushash | Dur-Kurigalza |
| 1000 B.C. | Thebes | Sian | Loyang |
| 800 B.C. | Thebes | Sian | Loyang |
| 650 B.C. | Nineveh | Lintzu | Loyang |
| 430 B.C. | Babylon | Yenhsiatu | Athens |
| 200 B.C. | Chang'an | Patna | Alexandria |
| 100 A.D. | Rome | Loyang | Seleucia |
| 361 A.D. | Constantinople | Ctesiphon | Patna |
| 500 A.D. | Constantinople | Ctesiphon | Loyang |
| 622 A.D. | Ctesiphon | Chang'an | Constantinople |
| 800 A.D. | Baghdad | Chang'an | Loyang |
| 1000 A.D. | Cordoba | Kaifeng | Constantinople |
| 1200 A.D. | Hangchow | Fez | Cairo |
| 1350 A.D. | Hangchow | Peking | Cairo |
| 1500 A.D. | Peking | Vijayanagar | Cairo |
| 1600 A.D. | Peking | Constantinople | Agra |
| 1700 A.D. | Constantinople | Yedo | Peking |
| 1800 A.D. | Peking | London | Canton |
| 1850 A.D. | London | Peking | Paris |
| 1900 A.D. | London | New York | Paris |
| 1950 A.D. | New York | London | Tokyo |
| 1975 A.D. | Tokyo | New York | Osaka |

Source: Chandler, Tertius. *Four Thousand Years of Urban Growth.*
(Lewiston, NY: The Edwin Mellen Press, 1987.)

A.D. to 115 million in 1200 A.D. thanks to fuller rice cultivation in the Yangtze valley. The population of Europe began a similar recovery, starting in 1000 A.D. Its center of gravity began to shift from the Mediterranean region to countries bordering the Atlantic Ocean and North Sea. The population of India, centered in the Jumna and Ganges valleys, rose steadily from 41 million in 200 A.D. to 79 million in 1000 A.D., before settling into a more gently rising pattern for the next five centuries.

This period of population growth came to an abrupt end in China when Mongol hordes led by Genghis Khan overthrew the Sung dynasty in the 13th century. Those barbarian tribes set about to destroy China's agricultural infrastructure which they saw as a threat to the nomadic way of life. It is estimated that three fourths of the people in China's northern provinces died from the Mongol violence. Similar attacks against the Islamic and Byzantine empires and kingdoms in eastern Europe also brought great loss of life. The population of western Europe reached a plateau in this period as agricultural technology ran up against the limit of available land. Then, in 1347, a terrible plague hit Europe which had originated in a caravan unloading its cargo at Kaffa in the Crimea. The "bubonic plague", which raged for six years, killed between one third and one fourth of Europe's population.

Perhaps the most unusual event in the history of world population took place with European colonization of the Americas. The native population declined by a fifth during the century which followed Columbus' arrival in the Western Hemisphere. While Spanish rule was brutal, the main cause of the decline was disease. The American Indians lacked immunity to measles and smallpox germs brought from Europe. The colonists, who had originally used Indians to mine silver and gold, needed to find new sources of labor. First Portuguese, then Dutch and English merchants found it profitable to bring captives from east Africa across the ocean to sell as slaves. Between 1500 and 1850, 9.5 million Negro slaves were brought to the Americas, mostly to Brazil and the Caribbean islands. After the slave trade was abolished in the 19th century, voluntary emigration from Europe drove population gains in the New World. About 41 million persons arrived in the great migration that took place between 1845 and 1914. Population growth in all parts of the world has accelerated during the 20th century.

Because so many more people are living today than in previous periods, our sense of historical "space" should take into account not only numbers of years but the weight of populations attached to those years. The quantity of historical experience - if this concept has any validity - should follow man-years of human life. Table 1-4 shows the cumulative man-years at selected intervals of time between 10000 B.C. and 1997 A.D. By this reckoning, more "history" has been packed into the last half century than into the ten thousand years before Christ. If one wishes to divide world history between 10000 B.C. and 1999 A.D. into two equal population-weighted periods, the dividing line would be drawn at 1577 A.D. While this approach has obvious limitations, it does underscore the fact that historical experience has accelerated. One should not underestimate the importance of modern times in any scheme of world history.

## A Division into Parts

History is a great mass of experiences awaiting interpretation. The first step in understanding an unintelligible mass of phenomena is to articulate it in some way. So we divide the mass of historical experience into civilizations. Times and places where human culture was fundamentally different from our own we say belonged to a different civilization. World civilization has existed in many different places on earth. The peoples living in those societies may or may not have had contact with each other. If isolated from one another, they would not have had a common history. In that case, world history would be a plurality of histories proceeding on separate tracks. Each society would have its own recollection of memorable events. Now that the world's people are aware of each other's existence, the concept of world

Table 1-4

Cumulative Man-Years of History
10000 B.C. to 1999 A.D.
by Percentage of 1999 Total

| | | | |
|---|---|---|---|
| | | 600 A.D. | 24.5 |
| 7500 B.C. | 1.7 | 700 A.D. | 26.1 |
| 5000 B.C. | 2.1 | 800 A.D. | 27.9 |
| 4000 B.C. | 2.6 | 900 A.D. | 29.8 |
| 3000 B.C. | 3.7 | 1000 A.D. | 31.9 |
| 2500 B.C. | 4.5 | 1100 A.D. | 34.4 |
| 2000 B.C. | 5.6 | 1200 A.D. | 37.3 |
| 1500 B.C. | 7.1 | 1300 A.D. | 40.1 |
| 1000 B.C. | 9.1 | 1400 A.D. | 42.9 |
| 500 B.C. | 9.9 | 1500 A.D. | 46.3 |
| 400 B.C. | 10.7 | 1550 A.D. | 48.2 |
| 300 B.C. | 11.6 | 1600 A.D. | 50.3 |
| 200 B.C. | 12.8 | 1650 A.D. | 52.5 |
| 100 B.C. | 14.1 | 1700 A.D. | 54.9 |
| | | 1750 A.D. | 57.8 |
| 0 | 15.4 | 1800 A.D. | 61.3 |
| | | 1850 A.D. | 66.1 |
| 100 A.D. | 16.9 | 1875 A.D. | 68.7 |
| 200 A.D. | 18.4 | 1900 A.D. | 71.9 |
| 300 A.D. | 19.9 | 1925 A.D. | 75.9 |
| 400 A.D. | 21.4 | 1950 A.D. | 80.9 |
| 500 A.D. | 22.9 | 1975 A.D. | 88.6 |
| | | 1999 A.D. | 100.0 |

Source: *Atlas of World Population History,* Penguin

history has become important. Historians face the challenge of finding a coherent scheme to describe their past experience.

World history is a form of story-telling on the highest level. There is not just one story to cover all events in this world. Stories describe movement from one situation to another. In the case of world history, one finds that events move in one direction in one period and then reverse themselves in the next. Therefore, the broad narration of world history is divided into parts, called "epochs", to increase narrative coherence. These are large periods of time when people's experiences of the society and culture and historical events run in the same direction. The division of world history into epochs is like the division of a book into chapters. Such organization increases understanding. A key to understanding world history is to know how to split it by epoch or, in other words, to tell one civilization from another.

## Toward a Definition of Epochs

The early Christian community had a clear sense of the world coming to an end. This apocalyptic expectation established the idea of a dividing point between two historical epochs which could not have been more different. On one side of the divide was a period of human turmoil and wickedness when Satan seemed to be in control of the world. On the other was the establishment of God's kingdom on earth when justice and mercy would reign forever. The one period would pass over to the other in the "twinkling of an eye" once the necessary conditions were fulfilled. Because Christians believed that Jesus was the Messiah who was associated with this process, his appearance on earth assumed epochal importance. The western world has adopted the convention of dividing world history into the periods before and after Christ's birth. The years before Jesus lived are designated "B.C.", or "before Christ". Those after his birth are designated "A.D.", or "Anno Domini", which in Latin means "in the Year of the Lord."

This scheme of epochs was first proposed in the 6th century A.D. by a Greek-speaking Scythian monk named Dionysius Exiguus. Prior to that time, people were not conscious of living in a Christian era. The early Christians expected Christ's imminent return. The Disciples met weekly in the room where Jesus had shared his "last supper" with them. This meal was symbolic of the messianic banquet. Christians believed that Jesus's "Second Coming" would take place on such an occasion, when his followers were gathered in one place. After the Christian community became too large to meet in a single room, it became important to establish a single time when Christians in scattered places could meet to share a communal meal. Because Jesus' return was thought likely to occur on the anniversary of his resurrection, the problem of establishing a common date for Easter became a concern for the church. The Council of Nicaea in 325 A.D. decided that Christians in all places should celebrate this holiday on the first Sunday after the vernal equinox.

After western society had existed for more than a thousand years after Christ's birth, a Cistercian monk named Joachim of Fiore speculated that a third phase of the Christian era was fast approaching. Its period corresponded to the third member of the Holy Trinity, he said. The first epoch, the age of the Father, covered the time before Jesus appeared on earth. The second epoch, the age of the Son, covered the time when the Christian church was active in the world. The third epoch would be an age of the Holy Spirit. Direct experience of God's spirit would then become more important to Christianity than the sacraments. This doctrine, which appealed to Franciscan monks and other spiritually sensitive persons, was a challenge to the institutional church. Joachim's predictions centered on the year 1260 A.D. No cataclysmic events occurred then which triggered waves of spirit. It was, instead, a year of interregnum in the succession to the office of Holy Roman Emperor. Emperor Frederick II, seen by some in the church as the Anti-Christ, had died ten years earlier. The next emperor, Rudolf I of Habsburg, would not be chosen until 1271.

Joachim's prediction may have helped to prepare western peoples for thinking in terms of three historical epochs: ancient, medieval, and modern. That scheme came into fashion during the Renaissance, although the term "medieval" had previously been used to identify the time between Christ's first and second comings. Before the Renaissance, Europeans had tended to see a cultural continuity between the Romans and themselves; they were near the end of a long age extending back to Augustus Caesar and Christ. Before Christ was another age, which was an age of darkness. At some point in the 14th or 15th century, people began to realize that a full millennium separated them from Roman times. Their society had evolved into something quite different than what existed then. The old culture of classical Greece and Rome was through; it had the completed look of another culture. Renaissance scholars who studied the Graeco-Roman texts were aware of a civilization comparable or, perhaps, superior to their own, separated by a large number of years. They gave the name "medieval" to that intervening period and associated modernity with themselves. Today, much later, we are still living in "modern" times.

Renaissance historians looked at the ancient civilization of Greece and Rome as a superior culture and their own culture as a revival of classical learning. That left the "medieval" period as a time when culture went into decline. Where Christianity had once represented historical progress, its influence was now seen as narrow, ignorant, and backward. This disdain of Christian culture deepened during the 18th century Enlightenment. Medieval society became associated with the "Dark Ages". Yet, the Christian religion had played an important role in shaping western culture. Its epoch of dominance, occupying the middle position in European history, touched both the ancient and modern in a defining way.

The relationship between Christianity and the Roman empire has been a key element in western history. Its epochs changed when those institutions were fundamentally affected: The dividing point between ancient and medieval times has been variously defined as the year when the Roman emperor Constantine decided to tolerate Christianity (313 A.D.), when Constantine founded the city of Constantinople as the empire's second capital (330 A.D.), when emperor Theodosius I was baptized into

the Christian faith (380 A.D.), and when the last emperor of the
west Roman empire, Romulus Augustulus, was deposed by the
Heruli king Odoacer (476 A.D.). The dividing point between
medieval and modern times has been defined as the year when
the Ottoman Turks extinguished the east Roman empire by capturing Constantinople (1453 A.D.), when Columbus first set foot
in America (1492 A.D.), and when Martin Luther caused a split
in western Christianity by posting his "95 Theses" on the door
of the castle church in Wittenberg, Germany (1517 A.D.).

### Nonwestern Peoples' Histories

The division of world history into three parts - ancient, medieval, and modern - may describe the experience of peoples in
western Europe, but not in the rest of the world. Most of the
world's population is not Christian, and only the westernmost
part of Eurasia belonged to the Roman empire. Therefore, the
experience of a collapsing empire followed by a universal but
empireless religion and then its fracturing and replacement by a
secular order is peculiar to western society. The histories of other
societies show a different pattern.

Even the society most closely related to western
Christendom, the Orthodox Christian society, had a different historical experience. In its case, the original empire lived on until
1453 A.D. Byzantine society engaged in prolonged wars against,
successively, the Sasanian Persians, Umayyad Moslems, Frankish crusaders, Saljuq Turks, Mongols, and Ottoman Turks before Constantinople fell. The Orthodox community then led a
dual existence. After the Duke of Moscow accepted its faith,
imperial religion shifted locations to Russia. Meanwhile, in Asia
Minor and the Balkan peninsula Orthodox Christianity was allowed to continue within an Islamic society. Following World
War I, the Ottoman empire dissolved and the Czarist empire in
Russia was replaced by an atheistic political regime.

In China, religion (in the form of an ethical philosophy) was
subservient to a system of imperial government which domi-

nated that society for two thousand years. The first epoch began with the unification of the Chinese nation in 221 B.C. Thereafter, the succession of imperial dynasties provides a framework for organizing Chinese history: Ch'in, Han, Sui, T'ang, northern and southern Sung, Yüan, Ming, and Ch'ing. These dynasties rose and fell and were sometimes followed by periods of interregnum; but always, until the 20th century, hereditary monarchies were reestablished with administrations staffed by Confucian scholars. Only the Yüan (Mongol) dynasty differed in that respect. The Ch'ing (Manchu) dynasty ended in 1912 when the last emperor was quietly deposed by Chinese nationalists.

India has a completely different history. Only two indigenous political dynasties - the Maurya and Gupta - have ruled over the Indian subcontinent, both for a relatively short time. Instead, Indian society has coped with a series of foreign invaders: Aryan nomads, Macedonian Greeks, Ephthalite Huns, Turkish Moslems, Timurid Moslems, and European merchant-adventurers. India has also been a principal battleground between religions. The original religion possessed by its Aryan conquerors was challenged in the 6th century B.C. by two religious philosophers, Buddha and Mahavira. The Gupta dynasty brought a resurgence of Hinduism, which succeeded in expelling Buddhism from India. Moslem armies from the northwest later took the subcontinent by force as Hindu kingdoms in the south were extinguished. Conflict between Moslems and Hindus marks the latter part of Indian history.

In the case of Islamic society, a single religion created and sustained an enduring network of political empires. Its first epoch might have begun with the message delivered by the archangel Gabriel to Mohammed and ended with the prophet's death in 632 A.D. The next might include Islam's rapid conquest of territory by Mohammed's successors and the reign of the Umayyad caliphate in Damascus. The Abbasid rebellion in 747-750 A.D. replaced Arab with Iranian ascendancy as the caliphate moved to Baghdad. This epoch brought a fracturing of political rule. New kingdoms affiliated with the Abbasid dynasty appeared in north Africa while an Umayyad refugee ruled the Iberian peninsula. Islam came under attack from western Christian crusaders and, more importantly, from the Mongols during the 12th and 13th centuries. After that threat had subsided, three new Islamic empires appeared: the Turkish Ottoman empire, the Persian Safavi empire, and the Mogul empire in India.

The Moslem calendar begins with the hegira, Mohammed's journey from Mecca to Medina in 622 A.D. The Christian era begins at the time of Christ's birth. Before world religion took charge of such matters, it was customary to begin chronologies with important political events. The Roman calendar began with Rome's founding in 750 B.C. The Greek Seleucid empire used a chronology that began with Seleucus Nicator's occupation of Babylon in 311 B.C. The Babylonian Era of Nabonassar, used by the Greeks of Alexandria, began in 747 B.C. If the United Nations had the same degree of influence within the world community as these ancient empires had in their regions, we might have renumbered the dates of world history with a base line set in 1945 A.D. However, government is no longer such a dominant institution, and neither is religion. Other institutions share the power with them in society. It becomes more difficult to find a focal event to represent the society's collective experience.

According to a traditional Christian view, world history began with God's creation of the world in six days. Studying the Biblical lists of generations, Archbishop Ussher of the Anglican church came to the conclusion that the world had been created in 4404 B.C. The Greek and Russian Orthodox church set the date of creation at 5509 B.C. Millennial anniversaries have raised expectations of epochal change. When mankind approached the end of the 1st millennium A.D., many expected the world to end. Clergy of the Russian Orthodox church had a similar expectation in 1492 A.D., which was seven thousand years after the supposed date of creation. Because God had created the world in seven days and one of God's days might have been equivalent to one thousand years, it was thought possible that the world would end on August 31, 1492. Only after that date had safely passed did the Orthodox clergy do their calculations for Easter in the eighth millennium. Now, as humanity approaches the end of the 2nd millennium A.D., its doomsday thoughts center upon the possibility that a massive computer glitch may occur because an earlier generation of programmers failed to provide for more than two digits in the year's field. Many predict an economic recession or worse in the impending Y2K catastrophe.

## Religious Histories

There is a reason why the best-known models of world history are rooted in religious traditions. That is because religion gives history a basis of universality. The natural tendency would be for each society to have its own history. Each society's history would have its own developmental dynamic. World history, if it existed, would be a compilation of diverse experiences described in separate sections of a book. However, religion includes the concept of a God (or gods) who created the entire world. Judaic religion asserts that Jehovah, the tribal God of the Hebrews, is synonymous with this universal God. Therefore, the story of Jehovah's relationship with his chosen people is also humanity's story. If Jehovah is God, then he has power over the earth and holds in his hand the fate of all its inhabitants. God's plan for the world is the basis of a truly universal history.

Since diverse peoples on earth have had experiences apart from encounters with this God, religious history must be oriented towards the future. Eventually, God will reveal himself to all humanity. The apocalyptic element of Judaic religion gives it a future-looking vision. Although Judaism is a tribal religion, it projects a universal message through its two daughter religions, Christianity and Islam, which extend God's promises to all people. Judaic history is highly personalized and thus agreeable to human sensibilities. It incorporates the idea of historical progress. Each epoch has a clear theme.

Starting with Adam's creation on the sixth day, the Judaic religious history might be divided into the following epochs:

The first epoch began with Adam and Eve, progenitors of the human race. From Adam until Noah, the earth's people lived without divine guidance.

A second epoch began with God's promise to Abraham that he would become the father of a great tribe whose descendants would possess the land of Canaan forever. The offspring of Abraham, Isaac, and Jacob did become numerous during their sojourn in Egypt.

In the third epoch, Moses organized this increasing people into an independent nation. He led the Hebrew people on a migration back to their ancestral homeland and gave them a set of divine laws to obey.

The fourth epoch began with David's anointment as king of this nation. The Hebrew people acquired their own political empire. After Solomon's reign, the empire fell apart in a period of more or less unrighteous kings. This epoch ended with the fall of Jerusalem in 586 B.C. and the exile of Jewish leaders to Babylon.

A fifth epoch began with Jewish prophetic writings during the Babylonian captivity and with the subsequent return from exile and restoration of the Temple cult. This was a period of Messianic expectation that God would restore the Jewish nation to its former prominence. The epoch ended with the destruction of Jerusalem in 70 A.D.

The sixth epoch encompasses Jewish experience during the Diaspora. It began with rabbi Johanan ben Zakkai's establishment of a religious academy in Jamnia shortly after the destruction of Jerusalem.

The seventh epoch began with the success of Theodor Herzl's Zionist movement which restored a Jewish state in Palestine in 1948 A.D.

Starting with the fifth epoch, the record of past events was mixed with an idealized history projected onto the future. Jewish prophecies written at that time presented a scenario of coming events which culminated in the time when the Messiah appeared and God's Kingdom was established on earth. The next part of the story would be the Messiah's appearance; and that has not yet happened. Therefore, this history is essentially on hold. Many interesting things may have happened in the meantime but nothing of religious consequence. Christianity shares these expectations, with a twist. Christians believe that the Messiah has already come in the person of Jesus. However, he did not come in the glorious manner that was foretold in prophecy. Consequently, the Christian community now looks forward to a "Second Coming" when Jesus, arisen from the dead and revealed as Son of God, will return to satisfy the full range of Messianic expectations.

The Messiah was a character in a story. It was a story of future history which Jesus knew and self-consciously worked to complete. In the coming day of the Lord, wrote the prophets, God would bring vengeance upon the enemies of Israel and restore the Jewish nation to the glory it had possessed in the days of David and Solomon. One of David's descendants, the Messiah, would act as God's agent in the course of those events. When Jesus said in the Gospels, "the kingdom of God is upon you", he meant that the scenario of events foretold in Messianic prophecy was about to happen. Jesus was himself stepping into this story to fulfill its conditions. (Already the prophet Elijah had returned in the form of John the Baptist.) However, God's timetable is different than man's, so that human expectations are easily deceived. Jesus spoke of the Son of Man, or the Messiah, "coming on the clouds of heaven with great power and glory." He spoke of wars, earthquakes, famines, and other "birth-pangs of the new age." The apocalyptic event to which Jesus referred would mark the dividing point between two historical epochs. The preceding epoch would consist of events in ordinary history. That which followed would be a post-historic time when God's perfect Kingdom would come down to earth.

The prophet Mohammed appeared on earth six centuries after Jesus's death. Moslems believe that he, like Jesus, was a prophet in the Judaic tradition. Such divinely appointed figures periodically deliver new messages from God. Historical epochs run in the times from one major prophet to another. Yet, the messages delivered by God's prophets are often considered heresies by followers of the previous tradition. The Jews rejected Christian teachings. Christians and Jews both rejected Moslem teachings. The reverse was not true. Christians accepted the religious validity of Judaism up to the time that Jesus lived, but afterwards they condemned the Jewish people for rejecting God's son. Likewise, Moslems acknowledge the divine origin of both the Christian and Jewish faiths while faulting their adherents for rejecting the message delivered by the last and greatest prophet, Mohammed. One perceives in this the idea of historical progress. The last of God's messengers is best because, assuming that his inspiration comes from God, he is delivering a more suitable and complete message for the times. Then, once again, living history is closed. God does not speak.

Long after the time of Jesus and Mohammed there appeared another kind of prophet, a political economist named Karl Marx. Proclaiming that religions were "an opiate of the people", this economist nevertheless embraced the historical view of Judaic religion. Marx argued that the forms of economic relationship in a society control its political, cultural, and spiritual life. Social progress occurs when the relationships change. So humanity has advanced in successive epochs from savagery to barbarism and to civilization. Civilization has advanced from societies with slave-based economies to feudal societies and then to those based upon the capitalistic system. A further and final progression was expected from capitalism to the socialist order. Violent insurrections and social upheavals marked the points of change. As the French revolution brought society from feudalism to a capitalistic economy, so a bloody revolution would take place when capitalism gave way to a socialist society. Its peaceful activities would fill history's final epoch.

A revolutionary event did take place when Lenin and his followers seized political power in Russia in 1917. The Bolsheviks liquidated the old order and remade society according to socialist principles. This was the Marxist equivalent of apocalypse. In theory, a "kingdom" of everlasting perfection had been created in the form of a society whose government was committed to managing the economy according to scientific principles. The certainty of science, rather than God's will, guaranteed that history would unfold as Marx and Engels had prophesied. A tumultuous change in governments, rather than divine intervention, brought about a change in the world order. Lenin, as a secular Messiah, presided over this process of epochal change. Unfortunately for Marxist believers, the Russian revolutionaries had an opportunity to put their theory into practice. Lenin found it expedient to revive the sagging Soviet economy by introducing capitalistic incentives. Stalin resorted to terror to enforce the socialist program. The system bogged down in production inefficiencies, militarism, and spiritual decay. Seventy five years later, the communist state came to an end in Russia. Socialism was revealed to be, not society's final stage, but a place on the way back to capitalism.

## Hegel's Scheme of Historical Progress

An important influence upon the Marxist history was Georg Wilhelm Friedrich Hegel, a German philosopher who lectured at the University of Berlin in the 1820s. His work added a historical dimension to western idealistic philosophies. Like Plato and Aristotle, Hegel held that reason controlled worldly events. Unlike them, he envisioned that ideas, or their worldly representations, turned into something else during the process of being realized. World history exhibited progress in ideas. Hegel believed that the various institutions in society were produced through rational processes driven by historical necessity. World history proceeded by a dynamic of institutional development which followed dialectical logic. By this logic, purposes which have been realized bring into existence new purposes which pull in the opposite direction. While an idea of purpose is being fulfilled in the world, it tends to create its opposite, which is the antithesis of this idea. The two movements together then create a synthesis which reconciles their conflicting tendencies in a more complex form. Believing that society's material conditions governed ideas, Karl Marx converted Hegelian dialectics into the philosophy of dialectical materialism.

Hegel's thoughts on world history are expressed in *The Philosophy of History*, based on lectures first given in 1822. In his view, the major figures of history were persons "whose own particular aims involve those larger issues which are the will of the World-Spirit." They knew which historical possibilities were "ripe for development" in their own time. Hegel saw world history as a process of developing towards an ever increasing state of freedom in human society. "The history of the world is none other than the progress of the consciousness of freedom," he declared. A German chauvinist, Hegel wrote that "the History of the World travels from East to West, for Europe is absolutely the end of History, Asia the beginning." He divided world history into epochs associated with: (1) Asia, (2) Greece, (3) Rome, and (4) Germany. The "Roman", or Christian, era was divided into the periods between the time of Jesus and Charlemagne and between Charlemagne and Martin Luther. The "German" era comprised the period between Martin Luther's time and the 19th century. Hegel believed that German culture was superior to the previous types of culture because it exhibited the highest degree of freedom. While the slave-based societies of Greece and Rome were aware of freedom for some people, contemporary Germans were first to realize that "man is free" and freedom is the end of all history.

Hegel's philosophy assumes that a universal mind controls the world, ever spinning out new forms. These forms have a permanent existence somewhere. In that respect, Hegel's scheme is like Plato's. However, Plato had little interest in the changing nature of human societies. Hegel was first to recognize the social dynamic underlying history. His philosophy conveys the idea of historical progress. Since the Hegelian world mind is universal, its processes are equally valid for the Chinese, Peruvian Incas, and west Europeans. Like God, this mind is capable of creating a unified world history. Since ideas are indestructible, the world fills up with more of them as new ideas are created. Development occurs in a single direction. There will be turning points when the force of newly created ideas begins to be felt within human society. There will be historical epochs describing the times when one or another idea system holds sway. While cloaked in objectivity, Hegel's history is, however, really another form of religious history. As such, it is prone to ethnocentric bias.

## Theories of Historical Recurrence

If the historian does not believe in God or in the idea of a universal mind creating worldly institutions, then the mechanism to ensure that world history will follow a single course is missing. The idea of historical progress stands on shaky ground. All that the historian can do is report the histories of separate cultures that have come and gone in the past. "Vanity, vanity ... all is vanity ... What has happened will happen again, and what has been done will be done again, and there is nothing is nothing new under the sun," said the worldly wise preacher in *Ecclesiastes*. Only fools believe that what they now see is being experienced for the very first time. If one studies history, one finds precedents in earlier society for nearly every idea or type of behavior that one observes today. On the other hand, the conditions of contemporary life do seem to be different than in the past. Which theory is correct? Does human society continually develop new and more sophisticated and complex kinds of institutions or does worldly experience repeat in predictable cycles?

In the view of eastern religion, a person's earthly existence is but a single incarnation of soul. Life goes round like a wheel, which is the wheel of delusion and suffering. The object of religious practice is to escape the karmic cycles of incarnation through personal enlightenment or direct experience of God. World history is not a major concern of persons with this outlook. If worldly events repeat in cycles, nothing which happens in a particular cycle can have much significance. The most interesting thing in life would be the possibility of jumping off its revolving treadmill to merge with the cosmic being.

Edward Gibbon's *The History of the Decline and Fall of the Roman Empire*, which was published in six volumes between 1776 and 1788, advanced the idea that worldly empires inevitably become corrupt and fail. When people refer to "the lesson of history", they are normally suggesting a parallel between past societies like Rome's which have collapsed and disappeared and their own society which they believe has entered into the stage of moral decay. Presumably, contemporary society might heed the historical warning and take steps to avoid disaster before it is too late. The fact that Gibbon believed that Christianity had undermined Roman morals and faith does not stop Christian moralists from lamenting today's decline in religious faith. However that may be, Rome's example of a civilization that has disappeared has impressed upon western minds the impermanence of earthly cultures. World history has become a kind of garden in which past and present civilizations can be seen and compared.

## Spengler's History

A German historian, Oswald Spengler, popularized historical recurrence in the early 20th century. He believed that human cultures have a life cycle like those of natural organisms. As an individual person matures and grows old, so entire cultures experience a state of ripeness and then die when they have exhausted the possibilities inherent in their type. His theory, presented in *Decline of the West*, proposed that western culture had reached that stage. Spengler's aim was to create a new method of analyzing history which he called the "morphology" of history. That technique implied that human societies could be understood, and their futures predicted, by recognizing the cultural forms which appeared at certain times in their development. Though the particular forms might be different for the different cultures, they could also be chronologically analogous, or "contemporary", in terms of life cycle. "It is a matter of knowledge," wrote Spengler, "that the expression-forms of world-history are limited in number, and that eras, epochs, situations, persons, are ever repeating themselves true to type."

Spengler was contemptuous of historians who held that world history exhibits progress. They were, he said, "a sort of tapeworm industriously adding onto itself one epoch after another." Instead, human cultures were like the various species of plant or animal life. Spengler declared: "I see in place of that empty figment of one linear history, the drama of a number of mighty Cultures, each springing with primitive strength from the soil of a mother region to which it remains firmly bound throughout its whole life-cycle; each stamping its material, its mankind, in its own image ... Each Culture has its own new possibilities which arise, ripen, decay, and never return. There is not one sculpture, one painting, one mathematics, one physics, but many, each in its deepest essence different from the others, each limited in duration and self-contained, just as each species of plant has its peculiar blossom or fruit, its special type of growth and decline."

The idea of organic life cycles led Spengler to make distinction between culture and civilization. "A culture", he wrote, "is born in the moment when a great soul awakens out of the proto-spirituality of ever-childish humanity, and detaches itself ... It blooms on the soil of an exactly definable landscape, to which plant-wise it remains bound. It dies when this soul has actualized the full sum of its states, sciences, and reverts into the proto-soul ... The aim once attained, the culture suddenly hardens, it mortifies, its blood congeals ... and it becomes **Civilization**, the thing which we feel and understand in the words Egypticism, Byzantinism, Mandarinism. As such it may, like a worn-out giant of the primeval forest, thrust decaying branches toward the sky for hundreds or thousands of years." Spengler's assessment of the West's future arose from his belief that European society had entered into the phase of civilization. Its creative potential had been realized. This was not classical Greece or Gothic Europe, but a time of moribund empire. With cold and calculated decisions, London banks were tightening their grip upon society. All else had been pushed to the limit. Extinction remained the only unrealized possibility.

## Toynbee's Theory of Civilizations

Spengler's was not an ethnocentric history. Western culture was merely one of several cultural types that had appeared in world history. Spengler did not consider this to be better than the others or unique, just different. Arnold Toynbee, British author of *A Study of History*, admitted to having once been in awe of Spengler's "firefly flashes of historical insight" and have wondered "whether my whole inquiry had been disposed of by Spengler before even the questions ... had fully taken shape in my own mind." He agreed with the idea that different cultures might have parallel histories, but disagreed with Spengler's practice of treating preconceived metaphors as if they were ironclad historical principles. Toynbee supposed this to reflect a difference in national traditions of scholarly thinking. "Where the German a priori method drew blank, let us see  what could be done by English empiricism," he declared.

Toynbee proposed that "the intelligible unit of historical study is neither a nation state nor mankind as a whole but a certain grouping of humanity which we have called  a society." A society, he said, provides "common ground" for communities of people to engage in various  pursuits. Civilizations were societies that had advanced to a certain level. In *A Study of History*, Toynbee set about to identify and examine societies of that kind. He found twenty-one different examples. (See Table 1-5.) Of the twenty-one civilizations, eight still exist while thirteen have become extinct. Toynbee acknowledged that world history also includes societies which have not become civilizations. Some, such as the Irish or Nestorian Christian cultures, were "abortive" civilizations. Others, including the Polynesian and Eskimo cultures, were "arrested" civilizations. Numerous other societies were what Toynbee called "primitive societies." In 1915, a team of anthropologists counted 650 different cultures of that type.

Initially, one might suppose that the more advanced and successful kinds of societies were blessed with richer soils, more

Table 1-5

## Toynbee's Twenty-one Civilizations

| name | place | when began |
|---|---|---|
| Egyptiac | Egypt | before 4000 B.C. |
| Sumeric | Iraq | before 3500 B.C. |
| Minoan | Crete & Cyprus | before 3000 B.C. |
| Hittite | Turkey | before 1500 B.C. |
| Babylonic | Iraq & Syria | before 1500 B.C. |
| Syriac | Syria | before 1100 B.C. |
| Hellenic | Greece & Turkey | before 1100 B.C. |
| Western Christian | Western Europe | before 700 A.D. |
| Orthodox Christian | Turkey & Balkans | before 700 A.D. |
| Russian Orthodox | Russia | 10th Century A.D. |
| Arabic | Arabia | before 1300 A.D. |
| Iranic | Persia | before 1300 A.D. |
| | | |
| Sinic | China | c. 1500 B.C. |
| Indic | India | c. 1500 B.C. |
| Far Eastern | China | before 500 A.D. |
| F.E. - Japanese | Japan | after 500 A.D. |
| Hindu | India | before 800 A.D. |
| | | |
| Mayan | Central America | before 500 B.C. |
| Andean | Peru | c. 1st Century A.D. |
| Yucatec | Mexico | after 629 A.D. |
| Mexic | Mexico | after 629 A.D. |

Source: Arnold Toynbee, *A Study of History,* Oxford Univ. Press, 1956
Reprinted by permission of Oxford University Press.

intelligent people, more advanced technology, or some other advantage. Having studied the matter, Toynbee concluded that societies did not prosper through natural advantage but through the experience of successfully meeting a challenge. For example, the early civilizations of Egypt and Mesopotamia faced the challenge of desiccation in the waning years of the Ice Age, as once lush grasslands turned to desert. In response to that challenge, they constructed irrigation works which provided water for agriculture. Likewise, communities on the frontier with barbarian peoples or in a buffer zone between two different societies are often stimulated to superior achievement. Primitive societies, on the other hand, tend to be satisfied with doing things in the same way as before. Lacking a reason to change, they let custom settle upon them with a thick crust. If the society experiences too much hardship, though, it might become retarded or destroyed.

Prehistoric conditions describe life in a state of nature. Allegorically, this may be identified with the Garden of Eden where life is balanced and perfect. A new element enters into this world to upset its balance and set in motion a process of recovery. Such an event represents "an intrusion of the Devil into the universe of God". If God's prehistoric world is balanced and perfect, then historical times are unbalanced and evil. They exhibit a dynamism born of the need to correct error. Yet, the less perfect, civilized societies invariably prevail in confrontations with primitive peoples. That is because their long experience of creative struggle has given these societies the knowledge and power both to tame nature and conquer other human communities. The Biblical story of Cain and Abel personifies this process. "Though the Lord may have respect for Abel," wrote Toynbee, "no power can save Abel from being slain by Cain."

Toynbee offered an analogy to describe humanity's "advancement" from a primitive to a civilized state. "Primitive societies," he wrote, "may be likened to people lying torpid upon a ledge on a mountainside, with a precipice below and a precipice above; civilizations may be likened to companions of those sleepers who have just risen to their feet and have started to climb up the face of the cliff above ... Starting with the mutation of primitive societies into civilizations, we have found that this consists in a transition from a static condition to a dynamic condition." It was a process known to ancient Chinese philosophers: "This alternating rhythm of static and dynamic, of movement and pause and movement, has been ... described ... (by Chinese sages) ... in terms of Yin and Yang - Yin the static and Yang the dynamic ... In the Chinese formula Yin is always mentioned first, and, within our field of vision, we can see that our breed, having reached the 'ledge' of primitive human nature 300,000 years ago, has reposed there for ninety-eight percent of that period before entering on the Yang-activity of civilization."

Toynbee, like Spengler, believed that civilizations pass through life cycles that bring certain events. Their societies typically begin with nomadic tribes who wander into a territory and settle there. Alternatively, they may be resurrected from the social rubble of a fallen civilization. There is generally a "time of troubles" when the new society is put under stress. Civilizations then achieve a "universal state" in the form of a political empire which is able to keep the peace for many years. Finally, the empire decays and falls. A new period of disorder then ensues; and then a new order. A religion created from within the fallen society may provide a cultural structure from which the next civilization can emerge. Toynbee compared this process with a chrysalis connecting moribund insects with larvae that appear in the next generation. The Christian church was such a link between the moribund society of the late Roman empire and the one subsequently ruled by Frankish kings. A similar event took place in China as Mahayana Buddhism penetrated and converted the Han dynasty.

According to Toynbee, the twenty-one civilizations were related to each other generationally, as if arranged in a family tree. (See Table 1-6.) "The continuity of history is not a continuity such as is exemplified in the life of a single individual," he wrote. "It is rather a continuity made up of the lives of successive generations ... in a manner comparable ... with the relationship of a child to its parent." Toynbee noted that all known civilizations have existed within the span of three "generations". A first-generation society would be one which arose, without precedent, by its own efforts. After existing for a time, such a society would typically fall prey to marauding barbarians and disappear. Second-generation societies emerge from the rubble of this collapse, often comprising the same barbarian tribes that were responsible for it. With third-generation societies, the process is repeated.

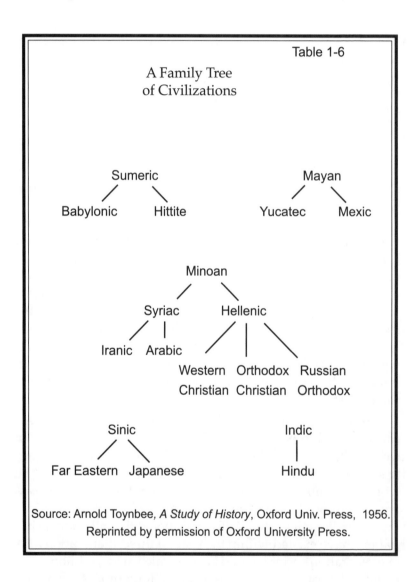

Table 1-6

A Family Tree
of Civilizations

Source: Arnold Toynbee, *A Study of History*, Oxford Univ. Press, 1956.
Reprinted by permission of Oxford University Press.

In such manner, the Hittite and Babylonic civilizations took the place of the Sumeric, their parent, after it collapsed in the 16th century, B.C. A satellite of Sumerian society, the Minoan, was parent to the Syriac and Hellenic civilizations. The Minoans were a seafaring people on Crete and neighboring islands who were overcome by an avalanche of uncivilized peoples around 1200 B.C. Hellenic society was formed from descendants of these people settling along the coastal regions of the Aegean sea. Syriac society was formed from peoples who settled at the eastern end of the Mediterranean sea about the same time. It included the Hebrew kingdom of David and Solomon, Phoenician settlements in Lebanon and North Africa (Carthage), and the Persian Hebrew empire established by Cyrus. Belatedly this society achieved a universal state in the empire created by Mohammed and his successors. Hellenic civilization was spread through Asia and Africa by the conquests of Alexander the Great. The Romans later embraced it.

Syriac society was parent to two third-generation societies which were created through Islamic religion. The Syriac and Hellenic (or Graeco-Roman) societies together gave birth to Christianity, which, in turn, spawned three third-generation societies. These were the Orthodox Christian, Russian Orthodox and Western Christian societies. The remaining Old World civilizations which exist today, located in Asia, are offspring of two other first-generation societies, the Indic and Sinic. Both are products of world religions that had contact with Hellenic civilization at critical points in their development. Mahayana Buddhism, prevalent in China and Japan, was a variant of the Buddhist teaching which developed in the Greek kingdom of Bactria and its Kushan successor state in northern India. The modern Hindu religion is also a product of that cultural cross-fertilization. In the New World, the Andean (Inca) and Mayan societies were first-generation civilizations. Mayan society was parent to the Yucatec and Mexic civilizations overthrown by Spanish conquistadors in the 16th century.

A devout Christian, Toynbee envisioned that Christianity might last forever, syncretistically absorbing new influences and being influenced by them. Since western society was culturally linked with this religion, it, too, might continue indefinitely. The repetitious rise and fall of civilizations suggests historical recurrence. The cumulative wisdom of religion suggests cultural progress. Toynbee found a way to reconcile these different elements in the model of a chariot on wheels. Toynbee compared world religion to a chariot which "mounts towards Heaven ... (through) ... the periodic downfalls of civilizations on Earth." If, as Aeschylus said, wisdom comes from suffering, then the immense suffering that accompanies a fallen society adds to humanity's fund of moral knowledge. Progress will occur in spiritual understanding even if the material structure of society is bound to life cycles: Turning wheels move the chariot ahead.

## A Critique of Toynbee's Scheme

If civilizations are analogous to plant or animal life, a society in a later generation could not advance much beyond its parent. Locked into this model, historians could not admit that contemporary society appears to be quite different than societies were in the past. Human culture seems obviously to be advancing toward new and better forms of knowledge, organization, and material equipment. We have airplanes, automobiles, and television sets while our remote ancestors had suits of armor, shields, and spears. According to Toynbee, our "western Christian" civilization has existed for nearly 1,400 years. Begun at some time during the 6th century A.D., it is still going strong. To suppose, however, that Europeans and Americans in the late 20th century belong to the same civilization as the one which existed in the time of Charlemagne taxes belief. Then, warrior kings and Popes ruled society; today, kids watch Saturday-morning cartoons on television. While Christianity is an element connecting the two cultures, many other influences also touch modern life.

Toynbee associated changing civilizations with the process of their military and political overthrow. The critical event would be a barbarian invasion of the civilized societies, which resulted in destruction of the old order and creation of a new one. Yet, as Toynbee himself observed, the Christian church was a more important factor in shaping western society than the barbarian invaders. Rome's state religion, Christianity, brilliantly survived the wreck of the Roman political structure. There was a continuity of beliefs and values between the Roman and Frankish societies. If the Christian religion was the principal force holding this civilization together, then perhaps one should say that the civilization went back farther than the 6th century A.D. Perhaps it began at the time when Constantine embraced Christianity? Better still, it might have started at the time of Jesus' death and resurrection; or, perhaps, at the time of his birth? Or perhaps this civilization actually began when Jewish prophets first started writing about the Messiah?

The problem may be that Toynbee has equated civilizations with societies. Civilizations he considered to be a subset of societies; they were ones culturally more advanced. By another definition, however, societies may be said to embrace a community's material organization - its government, its economy, its physical infrastructure - while civilizations pertain to the cultural aspect. Accordingly, a civilization would encompass the dominant set of images, ideas, and values in the society; it would be its fabric of consciousness. If that is so, then a single civilization like Christianity's might pass ghost-like through several different societies and not end when those societies came to an end. Conversely, a single society might contain several different civilizations. What determines a civilization's beginning and end may have to do with its pool of consciousness rather than with dynastically continuous governments. Civilization is formed of a people's historical memory. It constitutes an unbroken awareness of experiences. Society is like the structure of cell tissues in a body.

From the perspective of societies, the turning points of world history would be important battles, successions of rulers, and other elements affecting political organization. However, that approach to history is today making less sense. It used to be that the fortunes of nations were tied to the success of wars waged by their political rulers. If wars were lost, the defeated peoples were slaughtered or taken into slavery. But now, peoples have become morally separated from their governments. We can condemn an Adolf Hitler while helping the German people to recover from the war which he conducted in their name. The history of political empires will be interesting to people if, in some way, they can identify personally with those behemoth-like structures. Otherwise, accumulations of worldly power follow what used to be called "the vain repetition of the Gentiles." Nothing much is accomplished by their ceaseless rise and fall.

## Common Elements in World Culture

Even if the world's people grew up in separate places on earth, one finds evidences of a common culture. For example, all of Toynbee's civilizations except for the Inca mastered the technology of writing. One might suppose that, in the Old World, the knowledge of written language spread from Mesopotamia, its first known location, to other lands. It appears less likely that the pre-Columbian Indians had contact with literate societies of the Old World. How then did the Mayans, Aztecs, and other American peoples acquire a script? If their scripts were original, it suggests that some uncanny force drives human cultures. Something in the nature of an organic imperative required that the Mayan people invent written language, as the Sumerians had done, when their society reached a certain stage of development.

Primitive cultures throughout the world have many similar characteristics. They are tribal societies held together by ties of blood kinship. They lack a knowledge of writing. Their practices include, in Arnold Toynbee's words: "the religion of the annual agricultural cycle; totemism and exogamy; tabus, initiations, and age-classes; segregation of the sexes, at certain stages, in separate communal establishments." When civilization first appears, society acquires a different set of characteristics. According to Roger Lewin, its institutions include: "sedentism, elaborate burial and substantial tombs, social inequality, occupational specialization, long-distance exchange, technological innovation, (and) warfare." These characteristics apply to societies throughout the earth. Whether or not the societies had contact with each other, there seem to be a universal process at work as civilizations emerge from tribal society. One finds the same stone-faced pyramids, hierarchies of priest-kings, and wars of conquest in pre-Columbian Mexico as in Shang China and Pharaonic Egypt. One finds the same transition to written language.

We can therefore begin to see the outlines of a world history in the process of moving from one type of culture to another. The adoption of a new cultural technology such as writing would be an element in this process. So would a change in the nature of the society's power structure. Comparing Toynbee's description of primitive society with Lewin's description of the earliest civilizations, one finds a change in the type of society as a relatively small and homogeneous tribal community governed by custom gives way to a large-scale society governed by a bureaucratic hierarchy of kings and priests. The "civilized" society is characterized by this new form of government. Its kings wage wars, use jewelry and fine clothing, facilitate trade, require large burial structures, etc. The technique of writing is useful in transmitting the king's message to scattered communities of people. The two elements - cultural technologies and institutions of power - go together in certain ways.

The cultural technology is the easier of the two to place within a historical context. If history is a record of events in public life, then the mechanism that transmits awareness of high-level events to the public will be a fundamental part of the process. When a new type of cultural technology is introduced, it creates a new kind of public space. Its own qualities as an expressive medium affect the kind of expression that people receive. Public life changes in a certain way, and history is affected by that change. Our own culture appears to be undergoing a transition away from the use of written language and toward communication through electronic devices such as films, audiotapes, radio, and television. As a reversion from written to spoken language, some would say that this revival of non-literate culture denotes the "end of civilization". Let us say only that it denotes a different kind of civilization. The communications technology will have a profound impact upon the society and its scheme of values.

## Changing Cultural Technologies as a Guide to Historical Epochs

Although cultural technologies and institutions of power are both determining factors in civilization, it might be well to start with a review of cultural technologies. In simplest form, one might envision a three-part scheme of history to describe the progression from (1) preliterate to (2) literate and (3) postliterate societies. Prior to the 4th millennium B.C., all societies had a preliterate culture. Such cultures were based upon oral transmission of the ancestral knowledge. The first literate cultures, which we call "civilizations", appeared in Egypt and Mesopotamia between 3500 and 3000 B.C. Written language came to the Harappan culture of India during the 3rd millennium B.C., and to the Minoan and Chinese cultures around 2000 B.C. Meanwhile, preliterate societies continued in places where the people pursued a nomadic or tribal way of life. In the 20th century A.D., a postliterate culture emerged first in the affluent western societies and then in other societies as the technologies of electronic recording and communication became widely used. However, that did not mean that people ceased to read and write.

Looking at Arnold Toynbee's list of twenty-one civilizations, one is struck with a sense that the civilizations which Toynbee called "first-generation" societies were different in type than those which he called "second" or "third" generation societies. The first-generation societies included the Egyptiac, Andean, Sinic, Minoan, Sumeric, Mayan, and Indic civilizations. Second-generation societies included the Syriac, Hellenic, and Hindu civilizations, among others. The third-generation societies were offshoots of religious culture, descended from the Syriac and Hellenic civilizations. Apart from their more ancient appearance, the first-generation societies are distinguished from the others by the fact that their societies used pre-alphabetic systems of writing. Admittedly, some second-generation societies - the Yucatec, Mexic, Babylonian, Hittite, Far Eastern, and Japanese civilizations - also possessed this kind of writing. However, the transition from ideographic or syllabic writing to alphabetic scripts is an important element of historical change.

Alphabetic writing first appeared in the middle of the 2nd millennium B.C. It was effectively introduced in the eastern Mediterranean region and in India between the 11th and 7th centuries, B.C. The Phoenician, Hebrew, Persian, Greek, and Roman societies all had alphabetic scripts while the earlier Mideastern societies used cuneiform or hieroglyphic ideographic writing. Therefore, a dividing line might be  drawn in world history at some point during the first half of the 1st millennium B.C. That line would divide the earliest civilizations from those which are familiar to us from reading the Bible or works of classical literature. Perhaps this literature helps to explain why the Hittites seem alien and cruel while the Greeks seem culturally advanced. The Greek and Roman alphabetic literature creates a cultural bond between these ancient peoples and ourselves. We connect with them through a literate tradition which conveys their philosophies, myths, and religions.

In the middle of the 15th century A.D., the technology of printing was introduced in western Europe. This was another cultural technology which changed society. Printing greatly increased the number and variety of books in circulation. It made printed newspapers possible, and, with them, advertising and the prompt dissemination of news. The age of printing was, therefore, a third epoch within the period of literate culture. In the first epoch, which ran from the 4th millennium B.C. to the first half of the 1st millennium B.C., pre-alphabetic scripts produced a primitive type of literature. In the second epoch, which ran from the first half of the 1st millennium B.C. to the late 15th century A.D., the literate tradition begun in Biblical and classical times continued through handwritten manuscripts written in alphabetic scripts. In the third epoch, which ran from the late 15th

century through the end of the 19th century, printed texts dominated the culture.

The postliterate culture of the 20th century is driven by inventions which record and transmit visual and aural images. Its
dominant technologies include photography, sound recording,
motion pictures, and radio and television broadcasting. In the
late 20th century, the computer has also come into popular use.
This is a radically different type of device than the others. While
computers also work through electronic circuitry, they allow the
sensory images to be changed. Two-way communication can take
place between the sender and receiver of messages. A whole
range of information processing becomes possible with computers that the earlier devices could not handle. Therefore, one might
place a dividing line within the history of the postliterate culture to create two epochs, one dominated by the earlier set of
communications technologies and the other by computers. However, since the computer age has begun so recently, its epoch is
more potentially than historically developed.

Summing up, we have a five-part scheme of world history
which would include the following civilizations:

| Civilization | Approximate Dates |
|---|---|
| Civilization I | 3000 B.C. to 550 B.C. |
| Civilization II | 550 B.C. to 1450 A.D. |
| Civilization III | 1450 A.D. to 1920 A.D. |
| Civilization IV | 1920 A.D. to 1990 A.D. |
| Civilization V | 1990 A.D. to the present |

The beginning and ending dates are a bit misleading. World-
historical epochs are not marked by clean-cut events which bring
one period to an end as another begins. Historians cannot pinpoint such changes in time, saying that one civilization replaced
another on a certain date. Regarding the first civilization, only a
small fraction of the earth's population lived in the Sumerian or

Egyptian societies. Most still lived in tribal societies. When alphabetic scripts took hold in the middle part of the 1st millennium B.C., many peoples continued to use the older system of writing. The Chinese still do to this day. Handwritten manuscripts did not cease to be produced when printing became available. Literacy has not become a lost skill since radio and television came along. A more complicated model of history is required to describe the process of change.

When a new cultural technology is invented and adopted, it does not altogether replace the older technologies. Neither does its type of culture replace the preceding culture. Rather, the technology and its cultural product join what went before. Society fills up with an increasing variety of elements. At the same time, the new cultural technology, being new and unrealized, tends to project itself more energetically than the old ones. It tends to stamp itself more vigorously upon the culture. Perhaps historical epochs are like the different phases of vegetal growth after a forest fire has charred a section of land. First the ferns return, then shrubs of various types, then small trees like poplar and birch, and finally the taller pines which dominate a forest in its period of mature growth. When a certain type of plant appears in a later phase, the other types do not disappear. The forest simply fills up with a broader mix of vegetation.

This book uses the terms "epoch" and "civilization" quite interchangeably. They are different aspects of the same thing. A civilization is a kind of cultural presence. An epoch is a period of time. Our scheme of world history maintains that epochs change when the civilizations associated with them change. Although a new cultural technology may be the triggering agent, we are concerned more with the effect. It would be convenient for historians if societies in all parts of the world simultaneously switched from one type of culture to another. We could then have clean-cut epochs presented in simple diagrams. However, the reality is that civilizations arrived in the earth's societies at different times. For example, the nascent city-state arrived in Egypt and Mesopotamia at least a millennium sooner than it did in China. That means that the beginning date of the first epoch is at least one thousand years earlier in the two Middle Eastern societies than in the Far Eastern society. Even if the same sequence of events is experienced by all or most cultures, the timetable of world history applies differently to the different geographical segments. The civilization itself follows the type of social structure that embodies its relations of power.

## Chapter Two

# INSTITUTIONS DIFFERENTIATING
# WITHIN THE SOCIAL MASS

---

### An Analogy

Human societies resemble living organisms that have evolved from simple one-cell creatures to more advanced forms of plant and animal life. Life itself began in the form of simple organisms. All functions were handled within a single cell. The higher species consist of multi-cell organisms in which the cells have specialized functions but work together to maintain life in the whole. The functions are handled more efficiently due to their specialization. One finds on earth today an immense variety of living creatures, ranging from primitive microbes to human beings. Each species developed at a particular time through a process of differentiation from common ancestors.

In primitive societies, the community is organized in extended families or clans. Tribal government rests in the hands of a council of elders. A primary chief, who may also be a shaman, makes important decisions for the tribe. The shamanic priest communicates with the spirit world on its behalf and conducts rituals. Besides being a religious leader, he may function as a healer, historian, weather forecaster, poet, judge, and military leader. This arrangement works well for a small tribal community but not for one more highly developed. Then it becomes dangerous to put so much power into a single set of hands. As the society becomes larger and more complicated, it becomes difficult for an individual to master all the arts involved in its functioning. The various arts require specialists who can perform their tasks competently and work cooperatively with others.

Each major function in society has a specialized institution to handle it. The institution has a time in world history when it developed its characteristic form and experienced the most vigorous growth. In terms of an analogy with living creatures, we can think of this as a time when the institution split from the social mass and became a separate entity. Like cells detaching from one another, the institutional structures emerged from the matrix of primitive society. A kind of mitosis took place as the society in successive historical epochs split into sectors. First one institution detached from the social amalgam, then another, and another, until society came to include the range of institutions that we have today. Historical progress thus mirrors the process by which the more advanced societies acquire a pluralistic structure.

A characteristic of each epoch is that it takes its historical flavoring from the institution most recently detached. Before then, the society had a different structure and a different social-cultural quality. It belonged to a different civilization. World history reports the progress of civilizations. Each has a birth, a period of youthful growth, and a stage of maturity which reveals its form of empire. Development also continues in the old sectors out of which the new ones were created; but these new sectors, being younger, are more vigorous and dynamic. It is they which dominate the age. For, the detachment of a new institution carries with it a momentum of creative energy that drives worldly events along on a certain course. Historically significant events tend to be concentrated in that sector.

In today's world, human societies are found at many levels of cultural development. There are still primitive tribes living in the jungles of South America, in Siberian forests, or on Micronesian islands. Feudal principalities yet exist in Europe and on the Arabian peninsula. In mid Manhattan and Beverly Hills, society is immersed in the electronics age. A community will tend to stay at the same level of development so long as it remains small and isolated from other communities. It will advance to another level when exposed to different cultures. The more primitive societies are stuck in a "time warp". They remain at a level where most of humanity was at an earlier point in its history. The more advanced cultures emerged at a later time. And so, each cultural advancement is associated with a particular set of events that can be dated historically. The progress of history is seen in the structure of societies.

## Division into Castes and Classes

Starting with tribal communities, human society has acquired new institutions which broke apart from the others and became separate power centers. Society thus came to embody a system of divided power. The institution of royal government detached from the temple cultures of Sumer and Egypt in the 4th millennium B.C. Philosophically based religions, whose conceptions date to perhaps the 6th century B.C., then challenged the imperial state. In Renaissance times, commercial institutions became a separate sector apart from church and state. Finally, in the 20th century, the entertainment industry began to take shape. Each of these developments marked the history of its epoch.

Ancient writings tell how societies formed separate classes of people to handle the different functions. According to Genesis, Jacob's twelve sons each had offspring who became populous tribes. Each tribe received its own portion of land when this

people returned to Canaan. Moses and his brother, Aaron, belonged to the tribe of Levi. Because Moses was "slow of speech",
God appointed Aaron to do the talking. The sons of Aaron became hereditary priests of Jehovah's cult. One would suppose
that Moses, adoptive son of Pharaoh's daughter, might become
a king. However, another tribe, Judah, became associated with
the Hebrew royal household when David supplanted Saul as
king in the 11th century, B.C. Thus, descendants of two tribes,
Levi and Judah, exercised hereditary functions in the religious
and political sectors respectively.

When Aryan nomads from central Asia invaded India
around 1500 B.C., they imposed a system of social castes to maintain their superiority against the numerically superior, dark-
skinned Dravidian peoples whom they had conquered. Strict
rules forbade marriage with persons outside one's caste. At first
racially defined, this system became a scheme of occupational
functions that was hierarchically arranged. Because the Aryan
chiefs were warriors, the top rank was initially assigned to the
Kshatriya warrior caste. The warrior chieftains presided at religious ceremonies, and the priests assisted. However, the Brahmin priests had control of the sacred literature. Their caste gradually assumed the top position during the many years of peace.

As presented in writings from 200 B.C., the castes were arranged as follows in descending order of rank:

| name | function |
|---|---|
| Brahmin priests | holding religious power |
| Kshatriya warrior-kings | holding political power |
| Vaisya farmers and merchants | holding economic power |
| Sudra laborers | other economic contributors |
| Untouchables | beneath the caste system |

Plato presented a scheme of social division in his dialogue,
*the Republic*. His idealized society divided people into occupa-
tionally based castes. Because those in the lowest caste might be
dissatisfied with their rank, Plato proposed that the rulers of

society concoct a myth to suggest that the gods had created the different kinds of persons out of different metals. Precious metals would correspond to persons of higher rank; base metals, to the working class.

Plato's three-tiered scheme of society is as follows:

| metal | occupation |
|---|---|
| gold people | "guardians" (philosophers) |
| silver people | "auxiliaries" (soldiers/police) |
| bronze people | farmers and artisans |

During the 3rd century B.C., Chinese society developed a system of imperial government in which the emperor ruled as "son of Heaven". In this case, there was no political class because the Ch'in emperor in consolidating his empire had crushed the lesser nobility. There was also no religious class. Its place was taken by a cadre of Confucian scholar-administrators which managed the imperial government.

In descending order of prestige, this society contained the following classes:

(1) scholars, teachers, and public administrators
(2) peasant farmers
(3) artisans
(4) merchants

At the time of the Revolution, France was ruled by a strong monarch who consulted a parliamentary body, the States-General, when he wished to raise additional revenues. This body was divided into three "estates", representing the different classes that comprised French society. Its convocation in 1789 led to a series of turbulent events culminating in the death of the monarch and reorganization of society.

The three estates represented in the States-General were:

| estate | class/function |
| --- | --- |
| first estate | Christian clergy |
| second estate | lesser nobility |
| third estate | commercial and laboring people |

It is remarkable that the same trinity of institutions - government, religion, and commercial enterprise - has comprised human societies for over two thousand years. Recently, one has also heard reference to a "fourth estate", which is the press. And, if our theory is correct, the emergence of computers as a dominant cultural technology may bring a new set of institutions associated with a "fifth" estate. Humanity in the past has valued religious and political functions more highly than the economic though the latter is essential to human life.

During the French Revolution, the social order was turned upside down. Christian clerics lost their possessions and privileges, while aristocrats went to the guillotine. Commoners, including merchants, assumed the chief place in society. This regime gave way to Napoleon's reign and defeat and restoration of the monarchy. Yet, the idea of a French-like revolution that would overturn the established order appealed to the European imagination.

The Russian revolution of 1917 was a conscious imitation of the French. In fact, the new society created by the Bolsheviks resembled Plato's republic except that, due to its materialistic philosophy, the ruling class nominally served the interests of workers and peasants at the bottom. The Communist Party enforced its policies through the secret police and Red Army. Lenin, the first head of state, was a professional philosopher. The society's "bronze people" were despotically ruled by Stalin, whose name means "man of steel".

The class structure of the "classless" Soviet society is conceived in these terms:

| institution | function |
| --- | --- |
| Communist party | political philosophers |
| KGB and Red Army | policy enforcers |
| workers and peasants | economic support |

Contemporary U.S. society exhibits an even more pluralistic structure of power. Its sectorial division would follow institutional rather than class definitions. In June, 1996, *Time* magazine identified the ten most powerful persons in the United States. It is interesting to note their institutional affiliations. Three of these men - the President of the United States, Speaker of the House, and Federal Reserve Board chairman - were affiliated with the institution of government. Two - the chief executive officers (CEO) of General Motors, General Electric, and Fidelity Fund - represented business and finance. Two - the CEOs of News Corp. and Disney - represented the business of news and entertainment. Two - CEOs of Microsoft and Intel - represented the emerging computer industry. The field of religion alone had no representatives.

Western society incorporates power-sharing arrangements more than others. To some extent, that is due to its history. This model of society follows the historical experience of peoples living in the western half of the Roman empire after it fell to barbarian tribes. The religious and secular authorities shared power. The "checks and balances" system built into American government reflects that tradition. Chinese society, on the other hand, mirrors its historical experience which is based on a succession of imperial governments exercising centralized control. Therefore, apart from Marxist centralization, the totalitarian tendencies inherent in Chinese and other Far Eastern societies can be explained in terms of historical antecedents. The totalitarian society that existed in the Soviet Union can be explained by the theory of the "Three Romes": Rome, Constantinople, Moscow. Its unified power structure reflects an inheritance from imperial Rome via the Byzantine empire. In this case, religion remained firmly under the control of the political state. When the center of the eastern Orthodox faith shifted from Constantinople to Moscow in the 15th and 16th centuries, the Czarist government of Russia inherited the Byzantine system.

## A Summary of this History

World history gives clues to the origin of contemporary society. Its knowledge will help to explain things that may seem illogical or obscure about the world in which we live today. Throughout history societies have become ever more complicated. New technologies have been invented and human knowledge has increased though spiritually we may not have advanced much, if at all, beyond the level of our primitive ancestors. Violence and coercion have been present throughout recorded time. Yet, for better or worse, humanity has embarked upon a great adventure called civilization. World history describes that process.

World history describes the process of society's growing increasingly complex as successive institutions have become detached from one another in differentiated sectors of function or activity. In a nutshell, it has progressed in the following ways:

The first civilization began when the institution of government detached from the temple societies in primitive city states and, through military conquest, built political empires. We call this "Civilization I", or "CivI" for short.

The second civilization ("CivII") began when philosophy impregnated religion with the spirit of truth and, detaching from the state, created world religions.

The third civilization ("CivIII") began when a new spirit of commerce, art, scholarship, and worldly discovery infused the culture of western Europe. The pursuit of money and education became its cultural focus.

The fourth civilization ("*CivIV*") began when entertainment became a serious business and news reporting came to shape public opinion.

A fifth civilization ("*CivV*") has begun with the arrival of computers; however, it may be too soon to identify its characteristic institutions.

## Detachment of Government in the First Epoch

Society's political institutions are related to its war-making function. When tribes go to war, their military leaders often assume dictatorial powers for the duration of the emergency. Wars create a need for government. The governments of "civilized" peoples are formed as a result of one tribe or nation defeating and enslaving another. This brings persons of diverse origin into close proximity with each other, creating a more rigid system of social stratification and more sharply defined property rights. In peace time, tribal leadership concerns itself more with performance of rituals upon which the community's health and prosperity is thought to depend. Shrines to the gods or ancestral spirits are established in particular places. The priests who attend these shrines are responsible for cultivating the arts and transmitting ancestral wisdom to the next generation. The common people carry out economic functions. After society has advanced beyond the hunting and gathering stage, agriculture becomes the dominant form of economic activity although some persons herd cattle and sheep or engage in metalworking and other crafts.

As agriculture became more widely practiced and human populations increased, small city-states began to  appear. Usually these urban settlements were established in a river valley where the land could be irrigated or reclaimed from the swamp. The Sumerian city of Uruk flourished between 4300 and 3100 B.C. in the lower valley of the Tigris and Euphrates rivers. More than a dozen other cities including Ur and Eridu sprang up in its vicinity. In Egypt, human settlements called "nomes" appeared in several places along the Nile river around 4000 B.C.

Their inhabitants were generally of one tribal stock. They acknowledged the same totem, obeyed one chief, and practiced the same rituals. Recent excavations at Mohenjo-daro and Harappa near the Indus River have revealed an advanced urban culture that existed between 2500 and 1900 B.C. in present-day Pakistan. The first Chinese city-state, Erlitou, was founded around 1900 B.C. in the valley of the Yellow river. Minoan kings on Crete maintained elaborate palaces and temples at Knossos on the island of Crete in the 2nd millennium B.C. The first-known American city was established at Monte Alban in southern Mexico around 200 B.C.

When the earliest civilizations appeared in Mesopotamia and Egypt, most of the world's population lived in tribal communities. Nomadic peoples followed their grazing herds from place to place in search of better pastures. Sometimes they carted their household goods in wagons or traveled by boat. When they

ploughing and sowing

went to war, the heads of families gathered in councils to appoint a king. Tribal customs and taboos dictated acceptable behavior. Punishment of crime was a private matter between the affected families. In the irrigated valleys and swamps of Egypt and Mesopotamia, as well as in Syria and Turkey, a new kind of society arose in the city-states. The irrigation works supporting agriculture in those places required a larger social organization. A ruling elite, which had access to written records, arose to administer the communal projects. Laws inscribed on tablets replaced unwritten customs. The increased productivity of agriculture created an economic surplus, which went disproportionately to the ruling elite. The society became highly stratified. Its rulers required luxuries such as jewelry and perfumes. After death, they were buried in elaborate rituals accompanied by attendants who had committed suicide.

Sumerian society originally consisted of a dozen small cities located in present-day Iraq. The temple was the embryonic institution from which civilization developed. In the land of Sumer, temples consisted of a large brick structure known as a ziggurat, built up on several levels to a towering peak. A community of priests, often assisted by female attendants, inhabited this building which housed a shrine to the local god. The god typically appeared in the form of a gigantic statue with animal or human features. This god owned much of the land surrounding the city, and farmers had to pay rent. High priests, called "patesi" or priest-kings, ruled the cities in the name of their local god. It was the priest's function to represent the people before the god, who protected their community. However, the temples were also centers of commerce where grain and other commodities might be stored. While the priests were primarily concerned with performing rituals to ensure a successful crop, temple functionaries also kept astronomical records to determine the best times for planting. They performed public ceremonies, adjudicated disputes, treated illness, encouraged handicrafts, and administered civic affairs. One can imagine that this small temple community handled most of the specialized functions carried on in society.

The priest-kings who ruled Sumerian cities as servants of the gods combined religious and political authority. Society was yet in a unified state. Gradually the royal function became separated from the religious. As the city-states expanded territorially and encroached upon each other's domain, they clashed militarily. So long as the city-states remained small and scattered, the military function was relatively unimportant. However, conflict developed between the separate communities over land and water rights. One of the first known conflicts occurred between the neighboring Sumerian cities of La-

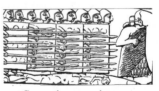

Sumerian warriors in phalanx

gash and Umma over the possession of a canal that bordered both states. King Eannatum of Lagash won that contest. A bas-relief celebrating his victory shows Eannatum's troops in phalanx formation, equipped with helmets and shields. Sometimes disputes arose internally and someone had to mediate on the community's behalf. The kings, while illiterate and uneducated, also tended to be more practical than the priests. Their residential palaces appeared beside the temples. A dual system of justice, royal and religious, was established.

The detachment of royal government from the temple is the critical event which began the first civilization. It may be that monarchy resulted from a naturally increasing need for military services as neighboring city-states expanded. Alternatively, this type of governance might have been imposed upon the settled communities as nomadic kings raided them and took control. Many a ruling dynasty began as leaders of marauding barbarian tribes that swooped down upon agriculturally based societies. The Egyptian priesthood, adept in rituals and magic, grew rich from the offerings made to the gods and income from temple lands. Its members were exempt from the requirements of taxation, forced labor, and military service. Even so, many priests resorted to selling charms and prescriptions for immortal life. The Pharaohs, considered sons of Amun-Re, were living gods whose cult conflicted with other religious traditions. As military leaders, they had need of resources squandered on priestly privileges. As law givers, they felt a need to treat all parties equally. King Urukagina of Lagash issued an edict that the high priest should no longer "come into the garden of a poor mother and take wood therefrom, nor gather tax in fruit therefrom."

At his best, the monarch became a righteous protector of organized society and preserver of peace. "At that time," states the preamble of the Code of Hammurabi," (the gods) Anu and Bel called me, Hammurabi, the exalted prince, the worshipper of the gods, to cause justice to prevail in the land, to destroy the wicked and the evil, to protect the strong from oppressing the weak ... to enlighten the land and to further the welfare of the people." At his worst, he was an oppressive tyrant who taxed the people to indulge his own fancies or waged cruel war against other nations. The prophet Samuel warned the Hebrew people who were clamoring for a king that this person would "take your sons and appoint them for himself, for his chariots, and to be his horsemen ... and to make his instruments of war ... And he will take your daughters to be confectionaries, and to be cooks, and to be bakers. And he will take your fields, and your vineyards, and your oliveyards, even the best of them, and give them to his servants. And he will take your menservants, and your maid-servants ... and put them to his work. He will take the tenth of your sheep."

Unlike the barbarian chieftain who plunders the wealth of others, the ruler of a civilized society has the responsibility to maintain a community that can prosper by its own works. Fundamentally, this involves marshaling an army to defend the society at its borders against external enemies. It also means waging internal war against disorderly or criminal elements. Waging war against foreign cities, the monarch would ride a chariot into battle armed with bow and arrow. A phalanx of foot soldiers would follow in formation. Often the goal was to plunder goods. War bred war, and soon political empires appeared. Around 3000 B.C., King Narmer of Upper Egypt conquered the delta region in the north. He become the first Pharaoh, wearer of a double crown. During the 24th century B.C., Sargon I, king of Agade, established the first known empire in Mesopotamia. Military service became a means of personal advancement for young men who might distinguish themselves by courage and strength. The Roman general Marius developed an army of paid professionals loyal to himself, who shared the plunder of battle and received pensions in old age.

One can imagine that the monarchy won people's hearts and minds through its awesome power to persuade by force. Kings commanded mighty armies that slew the enemy, enslaved defeated peoples, and seized their wealth. Pride in military victory cemented loyalty to the state. Yet, kings and emperors were careful to respect the authority of the gods. Those who conquered other cities often placed statues of the conquered peoples' gods in the pantheon of local deities erected in their capital city; for statecraft then included a good measure of religious diplomacy. Kings ruled as much through structures promoting habits of obedience as through application of force. In ancient Egypt, there were no police to control the population. Public safety depended upon Pharaoh's prestige, reinforced by public ceremonies, monuments, and presumed access to the gods. In the Egyptian cult of the dead, Pharaoh held the key to the afterlife. His own expectations of personal immortality were extended to his loyal subjects.

The internal administration of government depends upon an efficient system of taxation and the rule of law. Both require written records. Priests in ancient Egypt taught writing to upper-class children in schools attached to the temples. Their main function was to produce scribes for clerical work of the state. Government clerks kept track of the census, examined tax records, and handled wills and accounting documents. Legal arguments were made in writing rather than through oral presentations in court. It would not have been possible to conduct governmental functions on this scale without written documents. Once writing appeared, codes of laws replaced the tribal customs that had governed personal behavior. These laws eliminated the need to pursue justice through personal revenge. They prescribed penalties and procedures for resolution of grievances in court. The head of government became a law giver as well as a judge. In China, early attempts to issue codes of law met resistance from a population used to following custom. A compromise was reached which allowed government to decide questions of national policy while popular custom controlled everyday matters.

During civilization's first epoch, the king's role grew to embrace the various functions that have become associated with government. While the military function remained paramount, the king also had a responsibility to strengthen the society during peace time. He administered justice, organized public works, carried on diplomatic relations with foreign governments, collected or paid tribute, and maintained religion by conducting public ceremonies. Monarchs also set the official weights and measures. They devised official calendars. King Urukagina of Lagash stimulated foreign trade by issuing an edict that merchants visiting his kingdom not be molested. Shulgi, king of Ur, initiated reforms in the areas of law, taxation, calendars, and weights and measures. Hammurabi of Babylon built temples and fortifications, dug canals, and compiled a famous legal code, while enlarging his empire. Alexander the Great imposed the Greek script on lands that he conquered. Kuan Chung, an advisor to the ruler of Ts'i, replaced bronze with iron weapons and established state iron and salt monopolies. "But for Kuan Chung," said Confucius, "we should now be wearing our hair disheveled, and the lappets of our coats buttoning on the left side."

The first Persian empire built an extensive network of well-maintained roads. Emperor Shih Hwang-ti standardized axle-gauges in China so that carts from all regions could travel through the soil in ruts of the same width. He also ordered construction of the Great Wall and improved the Grand Canal, which runs along the eastern coast. The Roman emperors Titus and Vespasian built the Colosseum to entertain the public with gladiatorial fights. As many as 10,000 persons perished during one particular festival. Imperial governments have issued coined money. They have collected taxes to finance their own upkeep or else have delegated this function to tax farmers. Governments have stationed garrisons of soldiers in remote places. They have maintained a postal system to dispatch messages throughout their realm. They have supervised bureaucracies of aristocrats or civil servants to carry out these various functions. In the Roman roads, walls, baths, and aqueducts, in Egyptian or Mayan pyramids, in the ruins of Assyrian or Minoan palaces, and in China's Great Wall, one finds enduring evidence of the grandeur of civilization in the first historical epoch.

## Detachment of World Religion in the Second Epoch

In the middle of the 1st millennium B.C., as alphabetic writing spread across Europe and southwest Asia, a remarkable change took place within human culture. This was a time when the peoples of the earth became aware of reason and truth. Karl Jaspers has called that period of intense rationality "the axis age". It was an age which, Arnold Toynbee explained, was "a hinge on which human history has turned." Historians point out that a disproportionately large number of the world's great philosophers and spiritual leaders lived during the 6th and 5th centuries, B.C. (See Table 2-1.) In India, this was the time when Buddha and Mahavira were discovering new paths to personal enlightenment. In Persia, the prophet Zoroaster was developing a cosmology of good and evil. In Judaea, the prophets Jeremiah, Ezekiel, and Second Isaiah were writing of God's plan to redeem the Jewish nation. In Greece, philosophers such as Pythagoras, Heraclitus, and Socrates were seeking to know ultimate truths. In China, Lao-tse and Confucius were expounding the ways of virtuous living.

The Hebrew religion, which had practiced sacrificial rituals, suddenly changed course. Amos, who was the first writing prophet, quoted God: "I hate, I spurn your pilgrim-feasts; I will not delight in your sacred ceremonies ... (instead) ... Let justice roll on like a river and righteousness like an ever-flowing stream ... Hate evil and love good; enthrone justice in the courts." The prophet Micah wrote: "What shall I bring when I approach the Lord? ... Am I to approach him with whole-offerings or yearling calves? Will the Lord accept thousands of rams or ten thousand rivers of oil? ... God has told you what is good; and what is it that the Lord asks of you? Only to act justly, to love loyalty, to walk wisely before your God." In India, Buddha was meanwhile challenging the authority of priests who used their control of ritual for selfish ends. "Learn to distinguish between Self and Truth," Buddha said. "Self is the cause of selfishness and the source of evil; truth cleaves to no self; it is universal and leads to justice and truth." Righteousness and justice were ethical concepts declared pleasing to God. Right knowledge and belief were a foundation of religious practice.

A new civilization was beginning which would end in the establishment of world religion. This was not the religion of the hereditary temple priests but religion infused with philosophy. Buddhism, Christianity, and Islam are its principal representatives. One should not be confused by the fact that the same word, "religion", is used to describe both kinds of practice. There was little continuity between the ritualistic, polytheistic cults found in the earlier period and the so-called "higher religions" which

## Table 2-1
## Philosophers, Prophets, and Theologians by Date and Place

| name | date | place |
|------|------|-------|
| Ikhnaton | 1375-1358 B.C. | Egypt |
| Moses | 13th century B.C. | Egypt |
| Elijah | 9th century B.C. | Israel |
| Amos | 8th century B.C. | Israel |
| Jeremiah | 628-586 B.C. | Israel |
| Thales | 636-546 B.C. | Greece |
| Zoroaster | 628-551 B.C. | Persia |
| Lao-tse | 6th century B.C. | China |
| Ezekiel | 6th century B.C. | Israel |
| Second Isaiah | 6th century B.C. | Israel |
| Pythagoras | 582-507 B.C. | Greece |
| Buddha | 563-483 B.C. | India |
| Confucius | 551-479 B.C. | China |
| Mahavira | 540-468 B.C. | India |
| Heraclitus | 535-475 B.C. | Greece |
| Mo-tzu | 5th century B.C. | China |
| Socrates | 469-399 B.C. | Greece |
| Plato | 427-347 B.C. | Greece |
| Aristotle | 384-322 B.C. | Greece |
| Mencius | 371-288 B.C. | China |
| Jesus | 4 B.C.-30 A.D. | Israel |
| St. Paul | 1st century A.D. | Israel |
| Johanan ben Zakkai | 1st century A.D. | Israel |
| Plotinus | 205-270 A.D. | Egypt |
| Mani | 216-276 A.D. | Persia |
| St. Augustine | 354-430 A.D. | North Africa |
| Mohammed | 570-632 A.D. | Arabia |

belonged to Civil. The institution of imperial government had intervened. Humanity had a fully developed model of organization in front of it when the world religions were conceived.

A clue to the nature of the world religions may be found in the tribes from which their founders sprang. Siddhartha, the Buddha, was born a prince in the royal household of the Sakya clan in Nepal. He was not a Brahman priest but a member of the Kshatriya warrior caste, which is associated with royal government. Buddha renounced the throne at an early age to search for personal enlightenment. Likewise, Jesus did not belong to the priestly tribe of Levi. He was descended from King David, who belonged to the tribe of Judah. A sign was hung above Jesus on the Cross which read in three languages: "Jesus of Nazareth, King of the Jews." The Gospel of John pointedly remarks that the Jewish high priests tried to persuade Pontius Pilate to change the sign to read, "He claimed to be King of the Jews", but that Pilate refused. Mohammed belonged to the Quraysh tribe, which was the ruling class of Mecca. They were not monarchs or priests but Bedouin camel drivers and caravan guides. Mohammed himself was a merchant who actively pursued that trade before receiving messages from God.

The fact that none of these three religious leaders came from the priestly class suggests that they were no reformers of existing religion but creators of a different type of religion. Arriving at a later time in history, the religions of Buddha, Jesus, and Mohammed had more in common with the institution of imperial government than with traditional priesthoods. The new religions showed the influence of the philosophical revolution that had taken place during the 6th and 5th centuries B.C., which was, in turn, related to the introduction of alphabetic writing. Philosophers developed the concept of generality whereby a single entity represents many specific instances. Governments were structured in a similar way: A single monarch governed many people. This all worked together to promote a new way of thinking about how the world was organized. The idea of a single God who ruled the universe took the place of locally based religions serving a plurality of divinities. As philosophers turned their attention to human affairs, they discussed concepts such as justice and goodness which resembled the legal principles underlying imperial governments.

Archeologists believe that alphabetic writing first appeared in Asian territories of the Egyptian empire around 1500 B.C. Semitic peoples in the Near East were first to use the new system of writing. The first expressions of religious monotheism also appeared in that part of the world. A century before Moses, the "heretic" Pharaoh Ikhnaton (ruled 1372-1354 B.C.) proclaimed that there was only one God, Aton, god of the sun, who ruled over all nations. He wrote poems of praise to Aton but forbade visual images to be made because this God was formless. When Ikhnaton died, the priests of Amun-Re reasserted control and the old religion was restored by his successor Tutankhamen. Despite its failure, this religious revolution, personally engineered by the world's most powerful monarch, could not have failed to leave a deep imprint upon the culture. Religion was ripe for the idea of monotheism. Some have suggested that the conception of One God mirrored Egypt's political unification of the eastern Mediterranean region by Ikhnaton's predecessors, especially Thutmose III. God in this image resembled the person of Pharaoh, a figure to be feared and revered.

Moses gave monotheism a more lasting structure. He bestowed the concept of exclusive divinity upon the tribal god of the Hebrews, asserting that their God, Jehovah, had proved superior to the Egyptian gods through the many conspicuous miracles that had forced Pharaoh to permit the Hebrews' departure from Egypt. A God whom nature obeyed had to be real. While the events of early Judaism predate the philosophical revolution of the 6th and 5th centuries B.C., they show a similar rationality. Written law played a role in Hebrew nationhood from the beginning. The prohibition against worshipping graven images reflects the increasing value placed on ideas. Though the Hebrew religion contained many ritualistic elements, they are not mentioned in the Ten Commandments. These Commandments are general principles which describe acceptable or unacceptable behavior. The first Commandment reads: "I am the Lord your God who brought you out of Egypt ... You shall have no other god to  set against me." Monotheism is itself written into law.

Indian religion began to show a philosophical side in the period between 800 and 500 B.C. The Brahman priesthood was then winning its struggle for social supremacy. An alphabetic script, Brahmi, was being introduced. The priests were educators of the young and preservers of the society's oral culture. Written down, the Vedic rituals and stories became the sacred Sanskrit literature. The earlier parts of this scripture were concerned with the performance of religious ceremonies, hymns, incantations, and prayers. However, the priests later wrote commentaries to explain their meaning. From that effort emerged the *Brahmanas* and *Upanishads*, which were philosophical treatises meant to be studied in the solitude of the forest. These writings explored life's ultimate questions, reaching the general conclusion that the individual soul was identical with the totality of external existence. By the 6th century B.C., when Buddha lived, the religious discussions had turned into a freewheeling philosophical debate that questioned all beliefs and doctrines. As in classical Greece, there were materialists, atheists, and sophists, who would argue any position. Each wanted to discover the truth for himself.

In the *Maitri Upanishad*, there is a story of a king who renounces his kingdom in order to practice austere living in the forest, clear his mind, and solve the riddles of the universe. That was also the vocation of Buddha, Mahavira, and other Indian sages. The story is told that at Buddha's birth it was predicted that this child would become either the ruler of the world or, if he had certain experiences of pain and suffering, the discoverer of a universal path of salvation. After witnessing four kinds of suffering, the young Siddhartha left his family and his royal inheritance. He practiced asceticism and contemplation, had a spiritual insight, and became a wandering teacher. Buddha's religious career dramatizes the choice to be made between worldly power and the pursuit of truth. Both options were available to the Buddha, but he chose to pursue the higher good, which was truth. (Jesus, too, was offered a choice by the Devil to rule earthly kingdoms instead of serving God.) In fairness, it should be mentioned that the institution of imperial government was critical to spreading Buddha's ideas in the world. India's greatest political ruler, the emperor Asoka, made Buddhism the state religion.

Two other sages of this period, Zoroaster and Confucius, were initially without a connection to worldly power. Having attained wisdom, these men wandered the land in search of a royal patron who would put their ethical principles into effect. The prophet Zoroaster put forth a scheme of monotheistic religion featuring a protracted historical struggle between Good and Evil. Two spiritual forces fought for the souls of men. Zoroaster found a patron in the Persian king Vishtaspa. Zoroastrianism became the state religion of the first (Achaemenian) and second (Sasanian) Persian empires, and had a strong influence on postexilic Judaism. Confucius was a scholar of ancient Chinese history who lived in a period of turmoil. He had distilled the policies and practices of two "good emperors" from the Shang dynasty into a set of ethical teachings which he believed might revive Chinese society. He attracted a following of students while looking for a monarch receptive to his message. Confucius himself held several government

Confucius with his disciples

positions. His philosophy became, in effect, a state religion when the Han emperor Wu-ti decreed that appointments to imperial office be made on the basis of an examination in the Confucian classics.

Philosophers have needed governments to make their ideas effective. Government leaders have needed philosophers to apply their ideas to the betterment of society or gain intellectual respectability for their regimes. Plato proposed that monarchs and philosophers be one and the same person. He wrote: "Unless philosophers become kings or kings take to the pursuit of philosophy and there is a conjunction of political power and philosophical intelligence, there can be no cessation of troubles for the human race." Alternatively, the sons of kings might study philosophy or invite philosophers to be their policy advisors.

For example, the young king of Syracuse, Dionysius II, invited Plato to advise his administration. Still another way to fuse politics and philosophy is for philosophy, in the form of a religion, to gain political power through a mass movement generated by its ideas as Marxism did. In the case of Islam, the prophet Mohammed made his connection with political power by being invited to head the government of Medina. He and his followers then created a political empire through application of military might. It became unnecessary for Mohammed to beg any king to accept his religious program.

Philosophically based religion appeals both to rulers and their subjects. An ethic of universal brotherhood makes it easier to govern by breaking down the barriers of kinship that separate people in an ethnically mixed society. A religion promising admission to paradise motivates people in this life. The Zoroastrian-Hebrew religious ideology looked to divine intervention rather than princely persuasion as a means of introducing a more perfect society on earth. The prophetic writers created a scenario of future events in which the forces of Good and Evil, God and Satan, would do battle. Just when Satan seemed to be winning, God would snatch victory from this desperate situation and establish an everlasting kingdom of righteousness. A divine figure, the Messiah, would assist in this process. Jesus used the term "Son of Man" to describe him. This expression comes from the seventh chapter of *Daniel*. There Daniel wrote: "I saw one like a man coming with the clouds of heaven ... Sovereignty and glory and kingly power were given to him, so  that all people and nations of every language should serve him; his sovereignty was to be an everlasting sovereignty which should not pass away, and his kingly power such as should never be impaired."

Was this person Jesus? The type of kingdom mentioned in Daniel's writings fits the description of the Christian church which has existed under Jesus' spiritual leadership. If Jesus was a king, however, he was a nonviolent one. Isaiah called the Messiah "Prince of Peace."  The phrase, "prince of peace", seems a contradiction in terms since a king's primary function has been to make war. It originally referred to King Solomon whose peaceful reign followed David's. This phrase has also been applied to

Augustus Caesar, who renounced further territorial conquests after Germanic tribes decimated three Roman legions in 9 A.D., and to the emperor Trajan. It was a fit title for Jesus who, accused of seeking royal power, meekly submitted to death by crucifixion. The early church was pacifistic, mindful of the sad fate that armed Jewish militants had met at the Masada in 70 A.D. Christians were forbidden to serve in the Roman imperial army. Starting in the 3rd century, this policy was gradually relaxed.

Religious communities were incipient centers of power in society. To reach that position, however, they had to engage in a prolonged struggle with imperial governments. It is not that religion detached from the institution of government; for government in that epoch was already a religion. It is rather that a different kind of religion detached from the religious structures based on worldly power. Some think that Christianity overcame the pagan or nature-based religions worshiped in Roman society. But the gods of local communities had long been more important than they. The prevailing type of religion at that time was what one would call "civic religion". Like patriotism in today's world, one did not worship the state so much as exhibit loyalty to one's community. The warlike societies of Civl had conditioned individuals to identify completely with their community and, if necessary, be willing to die for it. That is why pacifists such as the early Christians were so despised. Being rather reclusive and gloomy individuals who pinned their hopes on another world, they were considered basically disloyal to the community.

A notable clash between the two religious views took place at the trial of Socrates. Members of a political faction in Athens accused him of civic impiety. They said that Socrates had corrupted the youth of that city by his philosophical discussions which caused them to question Athenian values. Socrates was found guilty and executed. But his personal courage in facing death, combined with a distinguished record of military service to the city of Athens, were so exemplary that history has instead convicted Socrates' accusers. It did not hurt that Socrates was the mentor of Plato, who was Aristotle's teacher, and that Aristotle tutored Alexander the Great, whose military conquests spread Greek philosophy through half the world.

Rome had a civic religion in the form of emperor worship. The early Christians, being Judaic monotheists, refused to pay homage to the emperor's divine spirit, which was a capital offense. The Romans also suspected that Christians were engaged in secret cannibalistic rituals that involved eating human flesh and drinking blood. Therefore, the first three centuries of the church's existence were a time of intense persecution. Nero blamed Christians for setting fire to Rome. Numerous martyrs were put to death for persisting in their Christian beliefs. But the church withstood the adversity. Toughened by its ordeal, the Christian community thrived. It had become almost a parallel state within the Roman empire when, in 313 A.D., the emperor Constantine issued a decree of tolerance. Later in the century, Christianity became Rome's state religion.

After Germanic warriors destroyed the western empire, the Christian church, of necessity, detached from the corpse-like state and became a freestanding institution. Barbarian kings now held the reins of military power. The Christian bishop of Rome, the Pope, enjoyed prestige through the cultural legacy of the fallen empire. When Pope Leo I persuaded Attila not to invade Rome, it became clear that church officials also exercised some worldly power. Their power increased when kings of the tribes which were occupying Europe converted to Christianity. An alliance was formed between the Pope and Frankish kings. The western Christian church, ruled by the Pope, became like an everlasting royal dynasty, the spiritual equivalent of imperial government. Thomas Hobbes observed that "the Papacy is not other than the Ghost of the deceased Roman Empire sitting crowned upon the grave thereof." This ghostlike structure, detached from yet engaged in the world, was what came in place of the "Kingdom of God".

While Christianity had a monastic component, its main organization mirrored the Roman state. The church's ecclesiastical structure was arranged along the lines of the old imperial bureaucracy. Cities that had been chartered as municipalities within the Roman commonwealth became seats of Christian bishops. The prefectures of the eastern empire were divided among the patriarchates of Jerusalem, Alexandria, Antioch, and Constantinople, while the patriarchate of Rome assumed a role corresponding to the three prefectures in the western empire. Christian attitudes softened toward the military aspect of imperial governments. The physical discipline which Roman soldiers endured resembled the spiritual discipline of Christian martyrs. St. Clement wrote admiringly of "the orderliness, the pliancy, the submissiveness with which they (Roman soldiers) carry out their orders." St. Cyprian compared Christian baptism with enrollment in the Roman army. As Christianity extended its geographical reach, its monasteries established in remote places resembled armed garrisons of the Roman state. Its missionaries sent out to convert the heathen were like soldiers of God.

So long as this was spiritual warfare, the church remained within bounds of its religious mission. It began to cross over the line when in 1095 Pope Urban II proposed that Christian rulers of Europe embark upon a crusade to recover the Holy Sepulcher in Jerusalem from Moslem rule. A series of nine crusades ensued. Seized with worldly ambition, the Roman church was behaving much like a political empire of the old type. In the Sixth Crusade, the Pope excommunicated Emperor Frederick II for failing to begin a crusade promptly. Frederick went through the motions of compliance with the Pope's command. Upon arriving in the Holy Land, he and the Sultan of Egypt sat down together and, after an amiable discussion, concluded a sham agreement for Jerusalem's surrender. In the so-called "Children's Crusade", thousands of idealistic boys assembled for embarkation to Palestine were sold into slavery or else perished from hunger and disease. The church launched a bloody crusade against Albigensian "heretics" in southern France and another against Bohemian followers of John Huss. Now overtly militaristic, Christianity abandoned the peaceful stance it had once assumed. Its true nature as a kind of imperial government was starting to show through.

At the height of the Middle Ages, European society exhibited a dualistic power structure. Religious and secular authorities, with parallel organizations, shared responsibility for governing the community. Roman pontiffs competed with Holy Roman Emperors, elected leaders of the European princes, to become the supreme power. A memorable event in their struggle occurred in 1077 A.D. when Pope Gregory VII kept the Emperor, Henry IV, waiting for three days barefoot in the snow before granting him absolution from excommunication. The issue of lay investiture of clergy was a bone of contention in those days. Church power reached its apex during the papacy of Innocent III. This imperious Pope developed the theory of the "two lights", the sun and moon, which ruled over the daytime and night skies as the Roman church and secular princes ruled over souls and bodies respectively. "(T)he moon," he argued, "derives her light from the sun and is inferior to the sun ... in the same way that royal power derives its dignity from pontifical authority."

spiritual and temporal power

### Detachment of Education and Commerce in the Third Epoch

In the third epoch of civilization, commercial institutions developed into an organized sector of society. Secular education became a means of furnishing these institutions with trained personnel. Economic accomplishments were despised in medieval times. A favorite saying was "Radix omnium malorum est cupiditas", which means "The love of money is the root of all

evil." There was a hatred of rich people, especially the nouveau riche. While the higher qualities of chivalric virtue were ascribed to the nobility, persons belonging to the commercial and laboring class were perceived to have a base nature. "Coming to the third estate," wrote Chastellain, a French court historian, "it is hardly possible to attribute great qualities to them, as they are of a servile degree." The Roman elite had little interest in commerce. They were warriors and statesmen who let slaves manage the household business. Roman emperors tried to squeeze the merchant class. Islamic society had a greater appreciation of the merchant's function since the Prophet himself had practiced it. Commerce flourished in Moslem lands during the European "Dark Ages". Arab traders visited distant places in search of exotic goods and told colorful tales of their adven-
tures. Chinese emperors
coveted the Arabian
horses that they obtained
from the Moslems.

European commercial life began with the religious fairs held next to churches and cathedrals during holidays. Relics of Christian saints would be displayed at the great feasts drawing crowds from near and far. As peasants from the surrounding countryside flocked to these events, Arab merchants set up stalls to display their merchandise. Some of the local merchants placed orders and arranged for artisans to produce goods in exchange. The artisans established small handicraft operations to convert available raw materials into a saleable product. Thus a market was created for various kinds of goods. Towns sprang up near markets, ports and river crossings, or the residence of bishops or local nobility. They were a haven for persons who had freed themselves from feudal obligations. The artisans who congregated in the towns became organized in guilds. They tried to restrict trade in the products that could be locally consumed but allowed free exchange of the surplus. Merchant associations were formed to export this produce. As early as the 10th century A.D., textile manufacturers in Belgium and Flanders were organizing annual trade fairs. Cities along the sea coast became commercial centers which specialized in one kind of merchandise or another.

The city of Venice was such a center, specializing in spices, silk, Damascus blades, and other goods obtained from Islamic and oriental countries. In 1082, it received a charter of liberty from the Byzantine empire which granted its merchants freedom of transit and exemption from taxes and duties in territories west of the Bosphorus. The Venetians were skilled diplomats who, with few military resources, dominated trade between Europe and the eastern lands. As in Florence, a commercial oligarchy ran the city. Trade in the western Mediterranean region was controlled by Genoa and Amalfi. Amalfi, then a large city near Naples, carried on extensive trade with Islamic countries and transported pilgrims to the Holy Land. This city was destroyed in 1131 when the Normans seized Sicily. Genoa, located on Italy's northwestern coast, became a commercial power during the Crusades. In fact, all the Italian trading cities benefited economically from meeting the needs of Christian troops on their way to battle. Venice cut a deal with knights of the Third Crusade to ferry them across the sea to Egypt in exchange for being temporarily pressed into its service. It used this opportunity to conquer the Dalmatian coast and sack Constantinople in revenge for an earlier dispute.

The Crusades were a spur to commerce, especially in northern Italy. The need to equip and provision expeditions to the Holy Land stimulated economic enterprise. Christian military victories in the First Crusade reopened the southern Mediterranean to trade by various routes. Commercial relations with the Moslems continued despite papal warnings. A network of consulates and codes of maritime law protected merchants visiting foreign lands. The Knights Templar and the Knights Hospitalers, created to aid Christian pilgrims, were pan-European military organizations which used their international contacts to amass huge property holdings. The Knights Templar loaned money to kings and princes and ran a thriving mortgage business. Philip IV of France dissolved this order when they refused his request for a loan. Otto of Bavaria kidnapped Richard the Lionhearted on his way home to England from the Crusades. The English crown had to raise a large sum of money for ransom. This money was raised from the nobility, who, resenting it, forced King John to sign the Magna Carta. The nobility persuaded that English monarch to allow a parliament to be convened periodically which would decide how tax monies would be spent.

Christian tradition prohibited lending money at interest. Any amount collected beyond the principal in repayment of a loan was considered usury. Judaic law allowed Jewish money-lenders to charge interest to non-Jews but not to other Jews. So Jewish businessmen dispersed throughout the Christian and Moslem worlds came to specialize in banking. However, the Roman church had also accumulated large sums of money needing to be put to profitable use. The church collected tithes and special offerings as well as monies deposited by individuals for safekeeping. By the 11th century, it had become a practice for monasteries or local parishes to lend money

"Shylock"

to landed nobility and be repaid by a share in the coming harvest. Sometimes the monetary value of the produce repaid would exceed the principal. Moneylenders sometimes disguised the receipt of interest through sham sales of lands producing an annual rent. Starting in the 13th century, church leaders and theologians began to relax doctrines relating to usury. Most European states repealed the laws against interest in the 15th century. The moral stigma attaching to usury was refocused upon charging rates of interest above a certain percentage level.

Wealthy individuals or families were the chief source of capital for large commercial ventures. They would advance funds to a merchant undertaking a voyage to distant lands in return for a share of the profits. Silent partnerships of this sort led to the formation of trading companies in which individual investors received a share of the proceeds proportionate to their investment. In the 14th century, the city of Genoa began to allow the shares to be transferred, creating joint-stock companies. Rich families also engaged in moneylending. The Lombards, especially Florentines, gained a reputation for tough, shrewd dealings. Moneylending families from Arras and Cahors drove a hard bargain with borrowers in Flanders, France, and England. The north Italian bankers developed many of the sophisticated mechanisms used today to finance and protect investments. They accepted banking deposits, recorded transactions to individual accounts, wrote bills of exchange for traveling merchants, took valuables possession to secure loans, and assumed risk in exchange for payment of insurance premiums. Genoese merchants used a system of double-entry bookkeeping as early as the 13th century. Lucas Pacioli published a book on the Venetian method of accounting in 1494.

A second region became commercially important during the 13th century. A confederation of German city-states known as the Hanseatic League conducted trade in commodities such as herring, timber, and salt in ports along the Baltic and North seas. Their commercial association grew out of a treaty concluded between Hamburg and Lübeck for mutual protection. When the Danish King Valdemar IV in 1362 seized the Baltic island of Gothland which included one of its largest ports, the Hanseatic merchants organized a trade boycott against Denmark. An alliance between these German cities and several princes forced the Danish king to withdraw from the island and eventually flee his country. The Hanseatic merchants gained a reputation for honest dealing at a fair price. They maintained "counters", or trading ports, in such places as Bruges, which was a center of finely woven linens, and the Russian city of Novgorod. From London came wool; from Poland, grains; from northern Germany, timber, brewer's yeast, and salt. For over three centuries, the rich "pepper-bags" or merchant traders of the Hanseatic League defended their commercial privileges. Relying on mutual advantage and trust more than force of arms, they became a powerful estate.

During the 15th and 16th centuries, religious and political institutions fought frequent wars to gain or hold territory. Lacking citizen armies, the warring parties had to hire mercenary soldiers. European princes purchased bishoprics from the church. Holy Roman Emperors needed to bribe electors to gain that position. The Vatican state had to defend its territories in Italy against military encroachment by the French. Surrounded by an explosion of artistic  creation during the Renaissance, the Roman church adorned itself richly. Pope Julius II proposed to rebuild St. Peter's church on a much grander scale. Famed artists such as Bramante, Raphael, and Michelangelo worked on this project for more than a century. These undertakings cost money. The mighty ones of Europe turned to bankers for the funds to carry out their various projects. In April 1552, Emperor Charles V, arguably the most powerful European monarch since Charlemagne, had to beg Anton Fugger to lend him the funds to raise an army to oppose his former ally, Duke Maurice of Saxony, who had defected to the Protestant cause. The emerging commercial sector thus gained leverage in society.

Many of the great banking houses in Europe began as financial adjuncts to textiles manufacturing. The city of Florence became a center of weaving and dyeing woolen cloth after the monastic Order of Humble Brethren relocated there from Tyre, bringing with them secrets of oriental cloth preparation. Florentine cloth gained a reputation for high quality. The wool was imported from northern Europe. Its transportation and financing involved risk. Florentine bankers, who handled the Papal funds, worked out a system of purchasing wool from England with monies collected there for the Roman church. Because the profit margin for woolen textiles was less than for luxury goods imported from the orient, cloth manufacturers in Florence had to watch their costs more closely. They had to develop more sophisticated ways to handle credit, to set prices, and cover their risks. They learned how to build a steady business based primarily on trust.

The German House of Fugger began in the 14th century when Hans Fugger produced and marketed a cloth called "fustian" which consisted of linen and wool woven together. His two sons, Jakob and Andreas, continued the family business after Hans' death. Jakob and his sons acquired great wealth in this business. They therefore had money to lend when, in 1488, the Archduke Sigismund of the Tyrol needed to borrow a substantial sum to compensate Venice following an unsuccessful war. As security, Jakob Fugger took an assignment of metal from a silver mine recently opened in the Tyrol. Once in the mining business, he received assignments from other Tyrolean mines and from copper mines in Hungary in exchange for loans to members of the Habsburg family, especially Maximilian I and Maximilian's grandson, Charles V. The House of Fugger also handled Papal funds, earning substantial income from the different exchange rates for receiving and dispersing funds in scattered places. Pope Julius II used the Fugger bank to deposit all incoming funds from the Jubilee Year of 1509, intended chiefly to pay for construction of St. Peter's Church.

The project to build a monumental church in Rome and adorn it with the finest works of Renaissance art seemed to some to reflect mistaken priorities. This was Judaic religion mated with the visual arts, a most unstable combination. To pay for the project, the church had to step up its fundraising efforts in northern Europe. When Johann Tetzel arrived in Saxony in 1517 to announce a new sale of papal indulgences, Martin Luther posted a religious manifesto on the door of the castle church in Wittenberg to protest abuses of the Roman church. Though branded a heretic, Luther received support from powerful German princes. Soon European society was split into two armed camps. The Protestants were religious fanatics in the tradition of Moses, Mohammed, and the Byzantine iconoclasts, who were opposed to worshiping God in the form of graven images. They preferred God's word as presented in the Bible. The worldliness of the Roman church, its wealth and ornate decorations, offended Protestant sensibilities. Ironically, the take from the sale of German indulgences was disappointing. Half of the proceeds went to the Fuggers for commissions and settlement of past debts.

The third epoch of history is characterized by individual enterprise. Its emblem would be that of a talented artist trying to sell his wares to the king, or, in Columbus' case, sell the idea of equipping a transoceanic voyage to Queen Isabella. In the nascent spirit of capitalism, one sees enterprising individuals ready to use their skills for financial gain. One sees go-getters on a mission to achieve something. One sees a willingness to go into the other man's territory to gain or sell something. The vast wealth of this age attracted clever individuals seeking to better themselves by their wits: goldsmiths, musicians, clothiers, portrait painters. In Renaissance Italy, a life of wealth went together with cultivation of knowledge. Power was combined with possession of beautiful objects. In Florence, Venice, and other north Italian cities, it was customary for successful men of commerce to retire early and devote their remaining years to public service. They had their children educated by humanist scholars. They spent money to purchase and copy ancient manuscripts. They commissioned works of art. In this bustling environment, an artist was able to make a name for himself. Risk-taking merchants could become rich.

The 15th century voyages of discovery brought European society in direct contact by sea with the Far East. It brought the destruction of the Aztec and Inca empires, the colonization of foreign lands, and subjugation of various non-European peoples. The motive for this was a mixture of zeal to expand the Christian empire and individual ambition to become rich. The centuries-long struggle between Christianity and Islam had reached a decisive stage. At the eastern end of Christendom, the Ottoman Turks had finally succeeded in conquering and extinguishing the East Roman empire, thereby blocking European trade routes to the East. At the western end, the Christian kingdom of Aragon and Castile had finally expelled the Moors from the Iberian peninsula. Marco Polo's book describing his travels to China in the 13th century had convinced Europeans that the Far Eastern societies possessed huge quantities of gold. Precious spices and silks were to be had in ample supply. Christopher Columbus presented a plan to Spanish royalty to reach this rich region by sailing west. It was approved in the same year that the Christian conquest of Grenada was complete.

When Constantinople fell to the Ottoman Turks in 1453, it unleashed an exodus of Greek-speaking scholars to western Christendom. This reinvigorated a trend, which began with Dante and Petrarch, of studying the artifacts of Graeco-Roman civilization from a realistic perspective. After centuries of looking through the thick lens of Christian dogma, western intellectuals learned to see the classical world as it actually was. Petrarch desired to know the ancient authors as persons. He wrote letters to them as if they were his friends. By the 15th century, such interests had grown into a torrent of humanist scholarship. Men hunted for ancient manuscripts in monasteries or cathedral libraries. Greek emigres from the Ottoman empire brought thousands of volumes with them. They also brought language skills that were in demand. The revival of interest in classical languages had two effects. First, it enabled Biblical scholars to make new translations of original Greek texts and so obtain more authentic knowledge of Christian concepts from their source. Second, it exposed Europeans to the literature of classical Greece. The excellence of those ancient works helped to wean Europeans from their religious heritage.

Petrarch's interest in preserving and studying original texts is regarded as a starting point of the western academic tradition. Martin Luther, who was professor of New Testament studies at the University of Wittenberg, brought scholarship to the service of revitalizing Christianity. Dante had begun the European tradition of writing serious literature in vernacular languages. Its most important application was in translating Biblical texts. John

Wycliffe produced an English-language Bible translated from Latin in the 14th century. Martin Luther translated the Bible from Greek into German. Luther and Wycliffe, as well as John Huss, held positions at universities in Europe. All were critics of the Roman church who, though excommunicated, found official or popular support.

15th century university scene

Today's type of university dates back to medieval times. Of the first dozen universities in Europe, eight were established in Italy. There were twenty European universities in 1300 A.D. That number increased to forty-five in 1400, and to eighty in 1500.

One might suppose that the European cultural ferment of the 14th and 15th centuries was related to the growing number and importance of universities. The  introduction of printing in the mid 15th century was another factor. Ever since the abbot Cassiodorus in the 6th century A.D. had ordered his monks to copy and preserve classical texts, Christian monasteries had been centers of literate culture. The Dominican and Franciscan teaching friars established schools of theology in the 13th century. Medieval universities prepared students for learned professions including medicine, law, theology and the arts. The University of Paris, for instance, was an association of scholars and students who had migrated with Peter Abélard from the Cathedral School of Notre Dame. Originally controlled by the bishop's chancellor, it later operated under a charter granted to the guild of teaching faculty.

The Reformation stimulated European education. Protestants wanted more people to be able to read the Bible. Martin Luther proposed a system of universal education administered by municipal and religious authorities in which students would be taught history, languages, singing, and mathematics. The Scottish Calvinist, John Knox, urged that each church appoint a schoolmaster to teach Latin and grammar. The Jesuits responded to the Protestant challenge with their own kind of intensified education, including a four-year course in theology for preachers. A six-year course in philosophy would train the teachers. A later trend was to include more courses in secular subjects and develop national systems of education. Erasmus believed that studying classical Latin literature would improve moral education. The Port Royalists in France favored courses in French literature. Educational reformers stressed the role of the teacher and the need for children to play. The Bohemian educator, John Comenius, introduced books with pictures. Jean Jacques Rousseau argued that children should receive a "natural education" in which book learning would be delayed. The Prussians, on the other hand, introduced compulsory schooling and use of a professional staff. The state took over schools from the church.

The modern conception of childhood arose in the period between the 16th and 18th centuries. Previously, children were treated like miniature adults. They had no special clothing or toys, and little training beyond observation of parental activities. Many were engaged as apprentices or domestics by the age of seven or eight. Girls married in their early teens. The first schooling was for boys from the better families. The idea of universal education, segregated by age and involving many years of classes with progressively more difficult course work, came later. Another change concerned social classes. European society was traditionally structured by estate rather than by socioeconomic class. Each estate - nobility, clergy, burgher, serf - was bound by a set of legal privileges and restrictions. Except for the clergy, membership in an estate was hereditary. Each individual in society had a role that was fixed for life. Whatever education existed would be directed towards preparing for that role. The French Revolution dissolved social categories. In the new society, anyone was allowed to pursue any occupation or trade.

The "philosophes" of the 18th century Enlightenment were eager to separate European culture from its Christian element. Their feeling was that, while Christianity may once have played a parental role in the culture of Europe, Europeans had now reached the age of discretion and were able to think for themselves. Such attitudes pushed education in a secular direction. The philosophy, literature, music, or art that had been produced under royal or ecclesiastical sponsorship now furnished the basis of a high culture which might be studied in schools. The anticlerical French took the lead in proposing that education abandon its purpose of religious indoctrination  and instead be directed toward preparing for practical occupations. The Marquis de Condorcet proposed to the 1792 Legislative Assembly that French education be reorganized to encourage the cultivation of individual talents regardless of social class. He proposed a universal system of education on five levels:  primary schools, secondary schools, institutes, lycées, and the National Society of Arts and Sciences. An individual might go as far through this system as his abilities permitted. Scholarships would be awarded to the deserving poor.

The idea caught on during the period of the French Revolution that an "aristocracy of talent" should replace the natural aristocracy. Ability alone would dictate how far a student went in the educational process. The idea later took hold that to have gone a long way through the system signifies personal ability. And so, prolonged education became equated with superior intellect. Someone who had graduated from college was thought to be smarter than a high-school graduate, and the graduate with an advanced degree smarter still. The new social contract is based on this kind of reasoning. Employers look for evidence of completed education in employment applications. The applicants expect that their many years of schooling will be rewarded by being offered an attractive job. A new set of lifetime incentives have thus been created to accompany the growth of commercial bureaucracies in the third civilization. As the Roman church once exercised power by controlling the sacraments that offered admission to Heaven, so educational institutions have become gatekeepers to lucrative careers. Education has self-consciously pitched its function in terms of offering social advancement: If you want to "better yourself", go back to school.

## Detachment of News and Entertainment in the Fourth Epoch

World history in the fourth epoch deals with institutions that have existed only in the last two centuries. The sector which has detached from commercial society is associated with news and entertainment. For millennia, human beings have entertained each other and exchanged gossip on topics of current interest. Such activities took place informally. Organized entertainment was used in the past to build a sense of community among sometimes fractious groups. The Greek Olympic games were held every five years to honor the Olympian gods during which a month-long truce was held between the warring city-states. Begun in 776 B.C., the Greeks based their calendar on this event. The Roman government used gladiator sports to pacify the urban masses. "Bread and circuses" became staples of public life. Gladiatorial contests were held year round in the Colosseum and

Circus Maximus before large crowds. Violent fights to the death and dangerous chariot races were the most popular events. Riots sometimes broke out between factions of spectators supporting rival chariot teams.

Though the news and entertainment industries are a subset of commerce, they have become much more. Unlike most other industries, they involve the systematic use of time. They have a potential to influence the society in ways that go beyond a purely economic function. The communications media have a certain ability to determine how people think; and that rebounds in many directions. As a commercial product, entertainment is less essential than housing or food. It is the type of product which is purchased with surplus income. To be commercially feasible, this industry needs audiences with sufficient income and leisure to want the entertainment and be able to pay for it. The industry needs a means of gathering enough people together to make it worthwhile for skilled entertainers to perform. And, finally, the content must be interesting or amusing enough to attract large audiences.

The role of public entertainment would be quite small in a rural society where people worked from sun up to sun down and had little money. It began to increase when they moved to cities and towns that could support traveling shows. Itinerant entertainers began crisscrossing the eastern part of the United States following the war of 1812. Like peddlers of the same era, they roamed from town to town in search of paying customers. The traveling circus came to America from Great Britain in the 1830s. Lyceums sponsoring lectures by cultural celebrities also became popular. Live theater was another fixture of American night life. After a white entertainer named "Daddy" Rice overheard a slave boy in Cincinnati singing a ditty "Jump Jim Crow", he went around the country dressed in rags and with burnt cork on his face doing an imitation of the boy's silly routine. That was the beginning of the minstrel show and vaudeville.

The master showman of this era was Phineas T. Barnum. His enterprise began in 1835 with a single attraction: Joyce Heth, a Negro woman alleged to be 160 years old who Barnum claimed had once been George Washington's nurse. Gawking crowds paid $1,500 a week in admission fees to take a look at her. Barnum broadened his program of attractions to include freak shows featuring such characters as Jo-Jo the dogface boy, Zip the pinheaded man, the gigantic Admiral Dot, and the midget General Tom Thumb. He later purchased

a gigantic elephant, Jumbo, from the London zoo to perform in public. Barnum's "Greatest Show on Earth" merged with James Bailey's competing attraction in 1881 to form the Barnum and Bailey circus. Meanwhile, "Buffalo Bill" Cody organized a "Wild West Show" to recreate scenes from the American West for curious persons living in the eastern part of the United States and in Europe. The show featured cowboys and Indians on horseback twirling lariats and performing gun tricks and even an appearance by Sitting Bull. Queen Victoria became one of its biggest fans when Buffalo Bill brought the show to England in 1888.

Another venue of popular entertainment was the special exhibition or fair intended to celebrate industrial or cultural progress or, perhaps, an important historical anniversary. During the 19th century, a number of international expositions were held for this purpose in Europe and the United States. Queen Victoria and Prince Albert hosted the first such event at the Crystal Palace in Hyde Park, London, in 1851. Its success inspired others including the 1876 Centennial Exposition in Philadelphia (where Alexander Graham Bell ex-

Crystal Palace

hibited the telephone), the Paris Exposition of 1889 (for which the Eiffel Tower was built), the 1893 World's Columbian Exposition in Chicago, and the Louisiana Purchase Exposition held in St. Louis in 1904. World fairs, as they came to be called, were held in New York City, Brussels, Montreal, Seattle, and other cities. State and county fairs, emphasizing agriculture, became an annual tradition in most parts of the United States during the 19th century. In addition, trade associations for various industries have sponsored public shows to introduce their products for the coming year.

Rising incomes and reduced hours of work have given working people in the industrialized countries a greater opportunity to participate in leisure activities, including entertainment-related events. In the early 1800s, it was customary for factory employees in England and America to work twelve or more hours a day. The fledgling trade-union movement agitated to require employers to reduce daily work schedules to a maximum of ten hours. The British Parliament enacted legislation to that effect in 1848. After the Civil War, the goal of the U.S. labor movement was to achieve an eight-hour workday. Average weekly hours in the United States came down by an average of two hours per week per decade - from 68 to 60 hours - between 1860 and 1900. Then, between 1900 and 1940, average hours were reduced by four hours per week per decade: from 60 to 44 hours. Between 1940 and 1980, the average U.S. workweek dropped by an additional 5.5 hours. Since 1980, the trend has been in the opposite direction. Real pay for industrial workers, though fluctuating with the business cycle, has generally increased.

Industrial development brought more people into the cities where entertainment facilities were located. Workers, in their time off, found it convenient to relax in the saloons or attend sporting events. Professional baseball began in the United States not long after the Civil War. Henry Wright organized the first professional team in 1869. In England, rugby football became popular among workers in the northern industrial counties. Workers who played for the teams asked for reimbursement of expenses related to lost wages. Association football, or "soccer", began with the formation of the Football Association in 1863. This English game, also with professional players, spread to the Continent where it became Europe's most popular sport. An international soccer federation, then comprising thirteen European nations, was founded in Paris in 1904. The Tour de France, a marathon bicycling event, began in the previous year. Its sponsor was a weekly newspaper in Paris whose publisher saw an opportunity to gain circulation at the expense of a rival.

The real opportunity for the entertainment industry lay not so much in charging admission for tickets as in building an audience which could be tapped by advertisers. For that to happen, there had to be changes in retailing. For most of European history, goods were sold in public markets convened at particular times and places. A person wishing to buy something when the market was not open went to a shopkeeper who stored various kinds of goods in a cramped room. The most common goods sold in these "general stores" were foodstuffs such as pickled herring, sugar, coffee, tobacco, and tea. Textiles were sold separately by wholesale merchants or tailors. In the early 19th century, stores began to specialize in certain products. There were draper's shops, victualer's shops, hardware stores, and stores selling "home products". Manufacturing firms sent sales representatives to make the rounds of these stores. To display their expanded selection of products, the storekeepers needed to operate in more spacious quarters, preferably on the ground floor. They needed to attract a greater volume of customers to pay the rent. Therefore, the merchants sent people out to distribute handbills on the street, advertising products that they had in stock.

In 1852, a French merchant named Aristide Boucicaut opened the world's first department store in Paris. He called it Bon Marché. Unlike earlier stores where customers haggled with sales clerks to obtain the best price, this store had a fixed price for every item. The merchandise, clearly laid out in racks, was packaged and ready to go. The retailer limited himself to a profit margin of 20 percent, yet allowed customers who were dissatisfied with a purchase to return the item for full credit. Sales clerks were instructed to assist customers, not hassle them to buy something. The new system was a hit with Parisian women. Visitors to the 1867 World Exhibition in Paris learned of this merchandising innovation and took the concept back to their own country. Soon there were department stores everywhere, replacing the small specialty shops. With low profit margins, the trick was to lure numbers of customers into the store. Bon Marché developed attractive window displays to exhibit its products. Since the customers wanted variety, this store offered new styles of fashions each year. It offered promotional "sales" with discounted prices for new or unusual merchandise. All these announcements had to be communicated to the public.

Newspaper advertisements offered the most economical means of reaching masses of potential customers. The basic system of advertising was, of course, well established. Printed broadsheets, combining news and advertisements, had been published in North America since colonial days. The modern newspaper took shape in the 1830s when the technology of cylindrical printing appeared. Newspapers, first in New Orleans, dispatched correspondents to cover the Mexican War. In the mid 19th century, journalists discovered that lithographic pictures could increase popular interest in their publications. *Harper's Weekly* built up circulation by presenting illustrated battle scenes from the U.S. Civil War. Once organs for expressing partisan political

the news reporter

views, newspapers learned to boost circulation by features appealing to the general reader. Large and exciting headlines, halftone photographs, crisply written copy, and sensational news content were found to increase readership. Such efforts reached a peak at the turn of the century in the competition between newspapers owned by Joseph Pulitzer and William Randolph Hearst for the top circulation in New York City. These publications both delighted in reporting garish crimes, wars, and disasters.

Newspapers derive roughly one third of their revenue from paid subscriptions. The other two thirds comes from advertising. Merchants pay newspapers to run advertisements because a certain number of readers who notice the advertisements will be influenced to buy their products. The larger the circulation, the more people who are exposed to a particular advertisement and receive its motivating message. Therefore, advertising rates vary according to a publication's paid circulation. From the reader's point of view, advertisements serving someone else's selling agenda are acceptable because the additional revenue from them helps lower the price of the subscriptions. They come at a cost of having to tolerate unwanted copy next to the features in which readers may be primarily interested. With few exceptions, this material represents junk that must be browsed through to find the parts of the newspaper that they want to read. However, it is a small price to pay.

Some persons read newspapers because they believe it is their civic duty to become informed about current affairs. Presumably, they can cast a more intelligent vote if they often read news articles about public officials or issues raised in political campaigns. In their sociological study of "Middletown", a hypothetical mid-sized U.S. city of the 1920s, Robert and Helen Lynd found, however, that, compared with 1890, newspapers in 1923 provided less coverage of agriculture, education, and politics, and more of organized sports, women's issues, business, and cartoons. While the purpose of newspapers was "ostensibly to give information" about community life, the authors concluded that the press served the additional functions of molding political opinion, creating a favorable image for advertisers, and making money for the newspaper itself. Two thirds of the space in the morning paper was devoted to advertisements. The number of lines of paid advertising had increased sixfold between 1890 and 1923. Advertisements in that day tended to play on feelings of class insecurity, or, as the Lynds put it, "concentrate ... upon a type of copy aiming to make the reader emotionally uneasy, to bludgeon him with the fact that decent people don't live the way he does: decent people ride on balloon tires, have a second bathroom, and so on."

The technology of radio broadcasting inherited the commercial practices that had been created by newspaper advertising. The Radio Corporation of America was established in 1919 to exploit the market for selling radio receivers used in ham-radio broadcasts. This objective proved too modest in view of profits to be made from selling advertising time once commercial radio stations began broadcasting in the 1920s. The broadcasts themselves were necessarily offered free of charge. Yet, because a large audience was tuned to these programs, the radio stations could charge a large sum of money for airing commercials. Listeners could not ignore the radio commercials, which directly interrupted the programs, as newspaper readers could ignore advertisements filling space. When television came along in the late 1940s, it added a visual component to the programming but otherwise continued the arrangement that radio broadcasters had with commercial messages. Television was a perfect instrument for selling consumer products. The corporate sponsors saw big sales increases in return for the money spent on this form of advertising.

Network television in its heyday had a lock on people's attention. Television sets were on for an average of seven hours a day in U.S. households. This pervasive medium captured one in every four waking hours. Such a large audience meant that anyone who needed to communicate with the public had to do it through television. But television commercials were expensive. When televangelists tried to preach the Gospel of Jesus on television, they also had to include a heavy fundraising appeal. The stations were forcing preachers to become pitch men to keep their programs on the air. Although, in theory, television broadcasters cover political campaigns without charge in the context of news reporting, the media have tended to report novelties and gaffes and the horse-race aspect of election contests. The candidates have had to run a gauntlet between reporters asking tough questions. Those wishing more control over their image are forced to purchase time for television commercials. That expense has been the main item driving up the cost of political campaigns, which, in turn, has made it necessary for elected officials to solicit money from wealthy donors and special-interest groups wanting favorable policies in exchange.

More and more, the news is becoming a form of entertainment. There is a feeling that when you tune to radio or television or watch a film, you are wanting to be entertained, not preached at or informed. Sam Goldwyn once said of movies: "If you want to send a message, use Western Union." To a certain extent, then, the entertainment culture has killed serious public discussions. A television consultant who works with politicians described his craft: "We work more with mood and music. We try to create an impression to leave with viewers. We don't care so much about the written word in an era when personalities are more important than issues." Television uses a sequence of carefully selected pictures to produce an emotional effect. A montage of visual snippets and sound bites creates an impression of personality which, hopefully, viewers will find attractive. Television commercials do not sell consumer products through a rational discussion of their technical merits but by suggesting that the product fits in with an attractive lifestyle. Heavy repetition of a brand name makes the product a familiar item. Having little idea of its comparative advantages or disadvantages, the viewer nevertheless sees herself using it.

Commercial profitability depends on the relationship between prices and costs. Advertising makes it possible for a product which is competing against other similar products to charge a higher price than otherwise without losing customers. If the advertisements consisted of logical arguments related to a product's merits as a consumer item, then the manufacturers would have to compete either on the basis of improving product quality or lowering the price. They would have to convince the public that their product represents superior value. However, technological knowledge is transferable. Anyone who follows its blueprint can replicate the process of manufacture or the product design. That means that any well-financed manufacturing firm can produce an unlimited quantity of this improved product and, given the nature of capitalistic markets, price and profitability will quickly come down. The alternative is, by advertising a brand name, to place in the consumer's mind the idea of wanting only this particular product. Whatever forms a distinct image in the public consciousness, if only a name, becomes a unique product capable of fetching a higher price. Once customers have formed the mental habit of purchasing only the branded product, they will not settle for a substitute even if shown that the two are functionally the same.

However, this process is wearing thin. The cheaper house brands sold in supermarkets and stores have, in fact, gained market share at the expense of higher-priced branded products.

The next step, then, is to sell products which are truly unique. The only type of product that fits this description is one based on human personality. Not long ago the Minnesota Timberwolves signed a six-year contract with a 19-year-old professional basketball player named  Kevin Garnett, who agreed to play basketball exclusively for that team in exchange for $125 million. One would imagine that the Timberwolves might have been able to find another player who could handle Garnett's function at a considerably reduced price. However, athletic performances, depending as they do upon the athletes' personal skills, are a unique commodity on the market. The same is true of professional singers, actors, talk-show hosts, and other performers. The public has become used to seeing or hearing, and wanting, a certain person. Supply is limited to that one individual, while demand has no limit. No wonder the contract price of star performers soars to astronomical levels.

Nike footwear has this process a step further in tying a  famous athlete's image to the sale of manufactured products. The Chicago Bulls' star player, Michael Jordan, appears in Nike television commercials in a manner linking this brand of footwear with Jordan's glamorous image and lifestyle. The fact that its shoes, manufactured in the Far East for small change, can be sold at high prices to young men and women in the United States enamored of Jordan's personality fetches Nike a large profit even after the cost of his multi-million-dollar endorsement fees has been deduced. Disney uses cartoon characters to supply the personal element for commercial tie-ins. This arrangement has the further advantage of avoiding endorsement fees that would have to be paid to human celebrities. A fictitious "personality" owned by a film company gets the payments instead.

# Chapter Three

# PERSONALITY AND BELIEF

---

## Religion in a Broad Sense

Public values change in the course of history. These changing values reflect institutions that were dominant society at particular times. Each institution is associated with its own kind of valuable object. See Table 3-1. While economic and political functions are important, civilization is more concerned with the mental, cultural, or spiritual side of life. Here the softer elements of a culture work their way into people's hearts. As an institution, religion comes closest to expressing this aspect of human experience. Therefore, this chapter will discuss the question: What, in a broad sense, is the religion of each civilization?

Religion speaks to the core of values which a society has. It usually, but not always, includes worship of a God or gods. In his book *An Historian's Approach to Religion*, Arnold Toynbee

| Table 3-1 |
| :---: |
| Epochal Values |

| | |
| :--- | :--- |
| CivI | It's good to be powerful and great. |
| CivII | It's good to be good. |
| CivIII | It's good to be educated and rich. |
| CivIV | It's good to be famous. |
| CivV | It's good to be --? |

wrote: "If we set out to make a survey of the religions that have been practiced at different times and places by the numerous human societies ... our first impression will be one of a bewildering infinite variety. Yet ... this apparent variety resolves itself into variations on man's worship or quest of no more than three objects or objectives: namely, Nature, Man himself, and an Absolute Reality." By the worship of nature, Toynbee meant the ritualistic religions practiced by precivilized peoples. By worship of man himself, he meant the association of religion with political institutions, or with, he wrote, "the worship of one's own collective human power." The worship of Absolute Reality referred to the higher religions which focused upon a transcendent spiritual being or God.

All three types of religion identified by Toynbee included worship of a God or gods. God brought human-like personality to the object of worship. Toynbee's premise was that humanity worshiped what it most feared. When it stopped fearing an object, that object ceased to attract worship and religion moved on to something else that had not been tamed. Nature was worshiped when humanity was at nature's mercy. With the arrival of agriculture, the food problem became less threatening than the problem of dealing with other human communities. Therefore, the object of worship shifted to political entities. The warring city-states worshiped local gods who symbolized their collective power. This epoch ended when the great political empires brought peace to a region. Human society then became less fearsome. It was time to worship life's ultimate reality.

Toynbee's three objects of worship - nature, man's own community, and ultimate reality - are associated with religions of the first three historical periods. However, the first period in this case would be prehistory. Nature worship was the religion of tribal societies that existed before the first civilization began. Toynbee's second object of worship - human communities - would relate to the prevailing religion in the first historical epoch, when governments established civic religions. The third object of worship - absolute or ultimate reality - would correspond to ideas associated with philosophically based religions. They belong to the second historical epoch. Humanity's ultimate reality is approached through theoretical speculation. For many, it has led to the concept of a monotheistic God. Toynbee's analysis ends at this point, when religion appears to have been put into its final form. The third, fourth, and fifth epochs of world history lie ahead, seemingly without further religious progressions. Yet, religion, in its broad sense, has continued to develop beyond the stage of world religion.

## Personality and Belief

Any successful religion achieves a balance between personality and belief. Belief comes first. This is what people think is literally true. It is the conclusions of learned persons, those grey-bearded doctors who are consulted on important matters. In Greek and Roman times, philosophy was on the cutting edge of belief. Philosophers had developed a method for discovering truth which allowed them, as Plato said, to separate true "science" from mere "opinion". God is an infallible source of truth for religious persons. Modern society tends to believe more in the theories proposed by empirical scientists. The universe might have begun with a "big bang". The human race might have evolved from other species of animal life through a process of natural selection. With respect to social phenomena, our society looks for sociologists or psychologists to supply believable answers. Someone who has an advanced degree from an accredited institution of higher learning is believed where the ordinary person's views can be taken with a grain of salt.

Many advancements in knowledge of the natural world have involved mathematics. Alfred North Whitehead has identified the period between Pythagoras and Plato (6th and 5th centuries B.C.) and the 17th and 18th centuries A.D. as times when mathematics penetrated the public consciousness to an unusual degree. The Greek philosophical revolution of the 6th and 5th centuries B.C. was inspired primarily by geometry. Pythagoras believed that the world consisted of numbers. Plato was impressed by the purely theoretical nature of mathematical reasoning. A sign hung over the gate of his Academy: "Let no one enter here who is ignorant of mathematics." Algebraic equations, introduced by the Moslems, became widely used by European mathematicians during the 17th century. Newton's laws of physics were a set of equations describing force, velocity, and acceleration. Mathematical equations related to periodicity supported Kepler's theories of planetary motion. Mathematics is a purely objective description of quantities or relationships in the natural world. It is the branch of knowledge most removed from human personality. Mathematicians tend, therefore, to be somewhat unsocialized.

Mathematically based knowledge has proven itself in dramatic ways. Centuries before Europeans knew of the Western Hemisphere, Eratosthenes of Cyrene calculated the earth's diameter to within one percent of its actual size. Through catapults and other mechanical devices, Archimedes held Roman armies besieging Syracuse at bay for three years at Syracuse. Nuclear physicists in the 20th century created a type of bomb so awesome that its explosion over two Japanese cities forced Japan's surrender in World War II. This was belief as basic as anyone might wish it to be. Religion, on the other hand, does not relate so well to the knowledge of mathematics or of the physical world. Its type of belief is more personal. A critical step in the creation of more sophisticated systems of religion is to apply sciences that began with mathematics and the study of nature to the realm of human behavior. That was Socrates' role in the Greek philosophical tradition. He turned the practice of inquiring about the basic stuff of the world into questions about justice, goodness, and truth. After natural science had made a name for itself in formulating physical laws, the "social sciences" applied its method to studying dynamics of the market place and the human psyche.

This leads to a contradiction. On one hand, human beings are wanting primarily to know about themselves. Religion latches on to beliefs reached by the most advanced methods of acquiring knowledge. Christian theology made use of Platonic and Aristotelian philosophies. The economic theories of Adam Smith and Karl Marx and the psychological concepts of Sigmund Freud and Carl Jung have become the basis of quasi-religious ideologies. On the other hand, impersonal "laws of nature" control events in the physical world. Hippocrates, the father of western medicine, denied that the gods caused disease or that its effective treatment consisted of rituals and prayers to appease their anger. He looked for natural causes of disease and sought treatments guided by his own experience with successful remedies. The scientific method teaches that the scientist should make dispassionate observations of nature and base his conclusions upon observed fact rather than personal intuition. He should leave himself out of his theories as much as possible and become a mere instrument of discovery.

Modern science has tended to displace man from his place at the center of the universe. Copernicus proposed that the sun, not the earth, was the center of the solar system. Darwin saw human beings as a product of evolution from lower species of plant and animal life. Scientists maintain that impersonal laws of nature govern this world. Yet, if the most advanced systems of belief arrive at a purely objective kind of knowledge, it poses a problem for human civilizations. The great mass of humanity cannot accept this type of culture; for man cannot live on ideas alone. While having intellectual credibility, a culture consisting only of ideas is also sterile and cold. This situation creates a spiritual crisis because human beings cannot relate to the purely objective. They need models of personality.

A study was done at the University of California at Santa Barbara which showed that "most people more easily solve a problem when it is cast in social terms than when essentially the same problem is cloaked in abstract numbers and symbols. In one experiment, they reworked a classic abstract logic puzzle into new (social) scenarios ... for instance, subjects were asked to imagine they were a bartender whose task was to make sure there was no one at the bar who was underage ... Fewer than 25 percent of the subjects got the problem right when it was put in terms of numbers and symbols. But about 75 percent answered correctly when the subjects were given the same problem cast in human terms." Authors of the study speculated that the need for personal references in solving theoretical problems illustrates the "Stone Age intelligence" passed along in our genes.

Objective knowledge is based upon proper delineation of abstractions. One follows certain logical procedures to move between the abstract and the specific. Proper classification and processes of reasoning help to retrieve the desired information. Personality, on the other hand, gives people something to imitate. One copies a finished model without thinking. Imitation, which is the original basis of knowledge, comes before reasoning. The use of personal images in religion may be a learned response from childhood in coping with situations beyond one's ability to comprehend. As the child relies upon an adult parent to rescue him from dangerous situations, so the religious devotee cries out to God for help in troubled times. This is a complete and emotionally satisfying kind of response. Objective concepts, while demonstrably true, are less able to arouse the emotional side of intelligence. Therefore, no culture intending to touch a society's larger population can consist of this element alone. Philosophies cannot inspire that degree of personal interest and attachment; only religion can.

## Primitive Religion

Whenever in the dim and distant past humanity has confronted impersonal phenomena, it has turned the incomprehensible whole into human forms. Primitive peoples have seen the elements of nature as old women, young hunters, great fathers, etc. The ancients divided the night skies into constellations bearing human and animal forms. Man's first attempt to understand patterns in nature was through mythological explanations. There were stories of struggle or intrigue between gods and goddesses whose outcome set patterns in the natural world. For example, the Greek myth of Demeter and Persephone, celebrated annually at Eleusis, explains the changing seasons as a covenant which the Gods made with Saturn to keep the lovely Persephone at certain times of the year. So belief and personality were fused into a single structure of knowledge when man first began to try to understand nature.

It is misleading to suggest that primitive peoples believe in the divinity of nature. To believe is our religious posture. Primitive religion began with a fear of nature, not so much in the sense of believing it to be evil as of man's being thrown helplessly into a dangerous world. Man had to cope with the danger, and, as always, that was done with knowledge. Not knowing cause and effect, man projected his own mental outlook upon nature. Natural objects were thought to have personalities similar to his own. Events took place intentionally, as if human minds were directing them. This animistic view, which makes the natural world a mirror image of man's own subjective mind, is characteristic of primitive religion. The Moon, stars, and sky were gods endowed with a human spirit, as were other natural elements. They had different spheres of influence, and had to be appeased or approached individually to win their favor.

Gradually one set of gods became associated with the sky, and another set of gods with the earth. The sky gods tended to be male, and the earth gods female. The gods of the sky exuded masculine energy when the Sun poured out its radiant energy upon the world or when Zeus, the thunder-darter,

Neptune and Jupiter

hurled bolts of lightning down from his throne. The earth gods or goddesses, including trees and the earth itself, were more maternal and nurturing; they were a quiet source of natural bounty.

So the gods became like a human family, with a father and mother, sons, daughters, and other relatives in various roles. The central theme of this religion was the mating of earth and sky, or, in other words, the showering of sky-brought rain upon the earth which would moisten the soil and let abundant crops grow.

Fertility was the central object of this religion. Fertility promised abundance, both in regard to producing numerous offspring and providing plentiful food. As these came from nature, nature became the target of religious pressure. The fertility cults of Egypt, India, and the Middle East included sexual rituals meant to suggest to nature what action should be taken. Animals thought to have sexual prowess, such as snakes and bulls, were worshiped with an eye to improved reproduction. Another religious concern was fertility of the fields. In medieval England, public marriages were performed on May Day or Pentecost to inspire the newly sown crops. In Java, peasant couples copulated in rice fields for the same reason.

Such rites illustrate the ancient practice of "sympathetic magic". The theory was that gods, being like people, sometimes had to be shown what to do. To make nature more responsive to their wishes, men would imitate a certain natural process, or partially perform it, or act as if it had already happened. A barren woman would clutch a baby doll in hopes of becoming pregnant. A voodoo witch would stick pins in the wax figure of a person meant to die. That is why festivals of the harvest were commonly associated with sexual promiscuity. The earth was supposed to accept the scattering of seed and prepare for a bountiful crop. Sympathetic magic gave primitive religion its theory of effectiveness. The magician was thought to be able to tap into nature's immense power by personal gifts or through devices such as amulets or fetishes that had special power. Another magical technique was the use of words in blessings or curses, or other verbal formulations, to cast a spell.

As agriculture became the basis of economic life, a professional priesthood presided over ceremonies intended to produce a successful crop. In order to be effective, these rituals had to be performed by someone with enough knowledge to perform the ceremony properly. The key to its effectiveness was thought to be correct execution. Organized religion became a technocracy of magic designed to manipulate or appease the spirits to achieve certain results in the natural world. Human sacrifice was often an element in ceremonies relating to the harvesting of crops. Sometimes human beings were ritually executed, and sometimes substitute objects such as sheep. Primitive peoples believed it was necessary to bury someone to fertilize the soil. The rites of human sacrifice became associated with the myth of gods who died and were reborn in imitation of grains which annually sprouted from plantings in the ground. The Egyptian cult of Osiris was one of many cults of vegetal regeneration foreshadowing the death and resurrection of Christ.

Religion has a sense of the sacred as distinct from the secular or profane. Originally there were sacred places thought to be inhabited by the gods. Priests kept up the shrines located on those sites. The people of Sumer built temples on sacred ground. There Greeks and Romans observed the cults of their local gods. In many Hindu homes, a room is reserved for the household deity, an image of Vishnu, who watches over and protects the family. Jacob built an altar at Beth-El to commemorate his dream of a ladder extending to heaven; he called that sacred place "the house of God." With the advent of written history, the locus of the sacred shifted from space to time. The Jewish Sabbath is a day in the week reserved for religious worship. Festivals and holidays are times in the year devoted to particular divinities or saints. Also, the idea of a time when the whole world would suddenly be transformed at God's direction grew up in Judaic expectations of the future.

It seems that the concept of an anthropomorphic or manlike God arrived relatively late in religious history. Totemic animals were earlier objects of worship. The selection of particular animals to serve as tribal emblems corresponds to our own use of symbols such as the design on flags to identify different communities. In primitive society, the particular animal which a tribe had adopted as its totem or spiritual emblem was considered taboo. People of the tribe were not allowed to eat its flesh except on rare ceremonial occasions. Afterwards, there was a period of transition when gods might be part human and part animal. The Egyptian sphinx is an example. Ovid's *Metamorphoses* describes in hexameter verse the changing of animals into gods, and vice versa. The prophet Daniel dreamed of four political empires emblematically represented by animal hybrids followed by another which was ruled by "one like a man". The first fully human gods may have been powerful men who had died but whose influence remained. Primitive peoples believed that the ghosts of such persons might return to haunt the living and had therefore to be appeased.

### Religion in the First Civilization

With the first civilization came a shift from nature worship to worship of the politically organized community. The gods of nature were converted into gods of parochial states. The states were not only political entities but also objects of worship. Each city had a deity which looked after the well being of its inhabitants. The local god was nominal master of the human community in whose stead the priest-king ruled. In Sumer, the ranking of a city depended upon the order which its god held in the divine assembly. Eridu was the holiest city because it had the shrine of the god which had created mankind. Shrines were located in the temple, which was also the hub of community life. There was usually a huge statue of the god in half-animal form and an altar to receive sacrifices. The statue was sometimes regarded as the image of the god, sometimes the god itself. A group of temple priests and priestesses, servants of the god, performed the sacrificial ceremonies. The priest-king was both the highest servant of the god and its personal representative.

In becoming identified with political institutions, the new order of religion had to contend with the prehistoric cults of nature worship. The two religious systems managed to coexist. "In Egypt," wrote Toynbee, "we find the worships of the Sun, the Corn, and the Nile surviving side by side with the self-worship of the cantons. In Sumer and Akkad we find the worship of Tammuz and Ishtar surviving side by side with the self-worship of the city-states. In China we find ... an annual agricultural ritual, in which the prince communes with Heaven and ploughs the first furrow of the new agricultural year, surviving side by side with the self-worship of the Contending States ... In this gradual, peaceful, and imperceptible religious revolution, the new religion has not only imposed itself on the old one; in many cases it has actually commandeered one of the old Nature gods to serve also as the representative of the new worship of parochial collective human power."

Toynbee gave examples of nature gods which had been appropriated by cities or tribes. He suggested, on the basis of the covenant delivered on Mt. Sinai, that Jehovah had been a volcano god or weather god before becoming the tribal war-god of Israel. Pallas Athena, Zeus' daughter, was both a war god and patroness of olive cultivation before she became the personal guardian and spirit of the Athenian city-state. The supreme god of Egypt, Amun-Re, was a combination of Amun, "the breath of life", sometimes portrayed as a ram, and Re, who was the sun god. Amun was the chief god of Thebes, capital of the Egyptian empire after the Eleventh Dynasty. Pharaoh was considered to be a living god, son of Re, begotten by immaculate conception.

Prior to the Fifth Dynasty, Pharaoh was a god in his own right, but the cult of Pharaonic worship clashed with the old nature-worshiping religion. A powerful priesthood at Re's holy city of Heliopolis in northern Egypt had organized all the separate nature cults into a pantheon of nine nonhuman gods among whom Re, god of the sun, was chief. The designation of Pharaoh as son of Re, linking his divinity with Re's, was therefore a concession to the Heliopolis priests and a sign of Pharaoh's weakening power.

Conflict later developed between the political cult of Pharaonic sun-worship and a popular cult which worshiped Osiris, god of the Nile river and vegetation. As vegetal life annually dies and is reborn, so Osiris, murdered by an evil brother named Set, was brought back to life through the patient labors of his wife, Isis. The kingdom then was passed on to their son, Horus, represented by a falcon. Horus' victory over Set was politically significant because his totemic representatives, the pharaohs of the First Dynasty who came from the southern part of the coun-

try, had conquered the northern Delta region where worship of Set was concentrated. The myth of Osiris also fed the cult of personal immortality centering upon Pharaoh's funeral arrangements. After his death, Pharaoh was thought to have rejoined the gods and become associated with Osiris, lord of the underworld. Pharaoh himself survived in an embalmed body with a spirit kept alive by unceasing rituals and prayers. Pharaoh's faithful subjects could themselves participate in the afterlife

Osiris and Isis          through his intercessions.

In Mesopotamia, the political rulers were generally content to rule as bailiffs of a god. Neither of the great kings, Lugalzaggisi and Sargon I, who unified this region in the 24th century B.C. claimed divinity himself, although Sargon's grandson did. Egypt was unique in the degree that God was associated with a living man. This man, Pharaoh, was an archetype of God as a Great King. The temple became like a royal court where worshipers petitioned the god for favors. One trembled in his presence, bowed, and offered prayers. If a catastrophe befell the kingdom, it was thought that the king had offended its god in some way. The fortunes of humanity were dependent upon pleasing the gods by means of proper rituals. While earthly kings ruled by divine authority, the deities themselves were understood in terms of the majestic personalities of kings. So gods shed their animal forms and became human.

The Egyptian tradition of living deities influenced religious practice in the Greek and Roman empires. The two greatest military leaders of western antiquity both picked up this idea when they came to Egypt in the course of their conquests. Alexander the Great entered Egypt in 332 B.C. with an invading Greek army. Fascinated with Egyptian religion, he traveled 400 miles to a remote oasis in the western desert to consult with the oracle of Amun-Re. The priests told Alexander that he was Amun-Re's son. Thereafter Alexander and his Hellenistic successors claimed divinity as imperial rulers of Egypt. Julius Caesar, an admirer of Alexander, succumbed to the god-king tradition while consorting with Cleopatra in 48 B.C. A cult worshiping him as a god was established. The Roman Senate, at Octavian's urging, officially confirmed this institution two years after Caesar's death. Although Octavian himself resisted deification, the imperial dynasty which he established fostered a cult of emperor worship. As an expression of their religious patriotism, Roman citizens were expected to offer sacrifices to the emperor's "genius" or divine spirit.

Besides self-flattery, deification of the emperor served a useful political purpose in building religious support for the imperial regime. Belief in the emperor's divinity warded off possible assassinations by ambitious or disgruntled soldiers. Some emperors preferred to rule as vice-regents of a god, reasoning that prospective assassins would be more effectively deterred if they believed that a vengeful god might survive a successful attempt. The emperors also used religion to achieve particular political objectives. For example, Ptolemy I attempted to hellenize the cult of Osiris-Apis in order to create a religious bond between his Greek regime and the native Egyptian population. The god Apis (the bull) was renamed Serapis and given a Greek visual appearance. A temple to the new god was built in Alexandria. Although Greeks were attracted to the cult of Serapis, the Egyptians continued to worship Osiris-Apis as before. The desired integration of cultures never took place. A better known example would be the decision of Antiochus Epiphanes IV to erect a statue of Zeus Ouranios in place of the altar located in the Temple at Jerusalem. His aim was to make Yahweh a local god within the pantheon of gods associated with nations in the Seleucid empire. This infamous act sparked the Maccabean military revolt.

Some Roman emperors, mad with absolute power, proclaimed their divinity in provocative ways. Caligula announced that he was a god equal to Jupiter. He established a temple cult of emperor worship and appointed his favorite horse to be one of the priests. Nero ordered a 120-foot high statue of himself to be erected with solar rays projecting from his head in the manner of Phoebus Apollo. The emperor Domitian deified members of his immediate family, organized a new order of priests to attend to their worship, and ordered government officials to refer to him in official documents as "Our Lord and God". Numerous Christians were executed for refusing to offer sacrifices before his image. Most emperors, however, regarded religion simply as a tool of statecraft. They gave the gods of conquered peoples an honorable place within the Roman pantheon. Heliogabalus introduced the cult of Sol Invictus ("the unconquered sun") based upon a Mesopotamian sun-god. Constantine the Great immersed himself in its divinity even after accepting Christianity. Julian the Apostate, Constantine's nephew, tried to make Neoplatonism a state religion.

In the Far East, emperors continued to exercise the ancient role of priest-king well into modern times. Each year, Chinese emperors led the nation in performing sacrificial ceremonies at the Temple of Heaven which included incantations to produce a successful crop. The supreme god was T'ien, or Heaven, which represented the governing force or order in the universe. Scholars interpreted this in an impersonal way while the masses prayed to T'ien as a god. The emperor, being the "Son of Heaven", represented Heaven on earth. He stood at the top of a social hierarchy extending down through the family. The emperor's decrees were considered an expression of God's will so long as his regime retained the mandate of Heaven. The emperor of Japan symbolized the Japanese nation's unity as a family. His ceremonial role was to pay homage to the spirit of the ancestors. The idea of "kami", or sacred spirit, which the emperor represented in the Shinto tradition, led to a respectful attitude in daily life. Only when militarists seized control of the Japanese government did the emperor become a symbol of its warlike ambitions. Emperor worship in Japan was a type of ancestor worship, expressing the spirituality of a race of people.

Religious belief in the first epoch of civilization was the same as in the prehistoric period. Few questioned whether the gods existed or had real power. Existing belief was merely transferred from the nature gods to gods of cities, nations, or empires. The political religions retained popular consent by respecting ancient traditions and paying homage to the ancestral gods of local peoples. To this was added the respect that comes from demonstrating worldly power. The great kings of the earth had the power to reinforce belief by their splendor and might. In those days, people looked to divine spirits and demons for an explanation of events in the natural world. Disease was thought to be caused by demon possession. Treatment was intended to drive demons from the body. Babylonian astronomers acquired much knowledge of celestial bodies while pursuing primarily astrological objectives. Each planet was a god interested in the affairs of men. Divination and fortune telling was an important occupation at imperial courts. The Shang emperors of China consulted experts who read the cracks in bones. Roman generals sought the advice of augurs before commencing battle.

Personality continued to be exhibited in gods and goddesses who inhabited the natural world and sometimes intervened in the affairs of men. Some human beings such as Achilles were descended from gods or personally interacted with them. Kings and emperors actively promoted their own reputations. In writings carved on temple walls, Egyptian Pharaohs boasted of their great victories in battle. An inscription tells how the Assyrian king, Tiglath-Pileser I, killed 120 lions on foot and another 800 lions from his chariot. Darius I of Persia wrote at Behistan: "Fravartish was seized and brought to me. I cut off his nose and ears, and I cut out his tongue." Civic religion also projected personal images through statues, ornamental carvings, and other pictorial representations. The Greek style of realistic sculpture brought personalities out with unprecedented vivacity. One of the most effective ways to spread the monarch's image was through coins. These visual tokens of his presence circulated far and wide. A Pharisee asked Jesus whether it was lawful to pay taxes to the Roman emperor. Holding up a silver coin, Jesus asked: "Whose head is this?" Told it was Caesar's, Jesus remarked: "Render to Caesar what is Caesar's, and to God what is God's."

## Religion in the Second Civilization

The second civilization brought the infusion of philosophy into religion. Philosophy was the most advanced system of knowledge yet seen. Its uplifting spirit touched societies from China to Greece as a roughly contemporaneous group of great thinkers and seers championed the superior values of goodness, justice, and truth. Yet, this philosophy was working from within a more ancient religious culture. That culture, too, made a creative contribution to the emerging world religions. Like two parents, male and female, revolutionary philosophy and traditional religion merged their separate elements to create a new religious order based on  truth and faith. The belief structure inherited from traditional religion was secure. Christian belief was planted in the concept of a monotheistic God inherited from Judaism. The Hebrew God Jehovah had proved his superior powers through the miracles demonstrated by Moses and Elijah's contest with the priests of Baal. Likewise, the Buddhist and Hindu world religions presuppose a more ancient belief in the gods. Philosophy questioned previous religious practices and even God's existence, but in the end settled down to produce a more sophisticated and ethically focused type of religion.

Greek philosophy had an enormous impact upon human thinking because it won the hearts and minds of an elite class that dominated societies in the far-flung lands ruled by Alexander and his successors. With its mathematical foundation and self-conscious methodology, this philosophy was considered to be the most sophisticated kind of knowledge in the world. It had captured the belief of the world's most powerful and intelligent individuals, who saw in it a key to truth. However, the societies of India and China also went through a philosophical phase during the 6th and 5th centuries B.C. Every school of opinion had its representative. Those whom history remembers most were the moral philosophers and idealists with a definite prescription for what human beings ought to do.

The central figure in the Greek philosophical movement was Plato. Plato founded a school for philosophers in Athens. His theory was that, by their study of geometry, music, and other sublime subjects, the souls of young men would be converted from base interests to a love of goodness and truth. Plato believed that to know the pure idea of the good would make men want to be good. He compared education at the Academy with scaling a mountain and viewing the world from a higher perspective. It was the duty of philosophers, having glimpsed the higher truths, to go back down into society and make use of their vision. "For once habituated (to truth)," he wrote, "you (philosophers) will discern them (worldly conditions) infinitely better than the dwellers there, and you will know what each of the 'idols' is and whereof it is a semblance, because you have seen the reality of the beau-

Plato

tiful, the just, and the good." Plato believed that acquiring correct knowledge of ideas was the key to improving individual lives. It was a matter of immersing oneself in abstract reasoning, developing sublime habits of mind, and exercising them in daily life. Plato maintained that ideas were real - more real, in fact, than physical objects. In the *Timaeus*, he described an eternal realm of existence in which ideas were stored, like patterns to create things in the world.

Plato's student, Aristotle, founded a rival school of philosophy. His treatise, *Nicomachean Ethics*, approached the concept of goodness from another direction. In Aristotle's view, it was good to be happy. However, happiness was not so much the pursuit of immediate pleasure as an activity in accordance with virtue which brought long-term satisfaction. Ethical philosophy became a question of how to pursue happiness in a rational manner. Aristotle allowed that individuals had freedom of choice in setting happiness as an end. Ends he defined as "what we wish for". Means were "what we deliberate about and choose" in pursuing those ends. Happiness as an end represents, therefore, fulfillment of one's true desires. Desire creates value; it is a psychic mechanism which makes certain things personally  important and stimulates the process of seeking to achieve them. If it is "good" to fulfill one's desires, the mission of philosophy becomes to develop a strategy for doing so successfully.

The rational pursuit of happiness comes down to steps that an intelligent person might take to improve the chances of reaching this objective in an uncertain world. One eliminates pursuits

such as immoderate wine-drinking which bring short-term pleasure with long-term pain. Most physical pleasures drop out of one's inventory of desires. One also eliminates activities over whose outcome one has little control. For instance, the pursuit of another person's love involves a high degree of risk and uncertainty. Therefore, no rational person would hope to achieve a goal of this sort. Philosophers would instead seek to fulfill intelligent desires - ones which put a person in the position of being able to will a successful pursuit of happiness. The

Aristotle

most radical solution to this question was Buddha's. He taught that the way to happiness, or avoidance of suffering, was to extinguish desires completely. If one has no desires, one cannot fail to achieve them. Short of that, a rational person might escape the unhappiness of unfulfilled desire by avoiding the kinds of emotional entanglements that bring pain.

By this criterion, the best kind of love is self-love. Having the source of reciprocation under one's control, one can will satisfaction of desire. One is thus able to contain the flow of emotional energy and stay serene. Therefore, a life of equanimity, devoid of pity or joy directed towards one's fellow human beings, was considered the most sensible approach for a philosophically directed person wishing to be happy. Indeed, that was the direction that the Graeco-Roman and Indian schools of philosophy ultimately took. Philosophers cultivated an attitude of mental detachment, suppressing sentiments of sympathy and love. Seneca said: "Pity is a mental illness induced by the spectacle of other people's miseries ... The sage does not succumb to suchlike mental diseases." Epictetus told his disciples: "If you are kissing a child of yours ... never put your imagination unreservedly into the act and never give your emotion free rein ... Indeed, there is no harm in accompanying the act of kissing the child by whispering over him, 'Tomorrow you will die.'"

The excessive rationality of this philosophy had to be tempered by other influences for the culture to survive. These influences came in the form of "superstitious" practices and beliefs encountered in conquered territories. Alexander's armies brought back to Greece, besides booty, an interest in Babylonian astrology. The Romans conquered an immense territory which included the land of Judaea. And from Judaea came the strange tale of a man named Jesus who was crucified but rose again from the dead. That such a creed could meet and overcome the sophisticated philosophies of Rome was totally irrational; yet it happened. The Christian message seemed absurd to the Roman ruling class. Its principles of pacifism and submission to worldly authority were despised as "slaves' virtues." In Christianity, reason was offset by the softer human qualities of mercy and love. The Romans could not see any merit in this. Such doctrines seemed to be encouraging weak and irrational tendencies of character. Yet, the Apostle Paul observed in *First Corinthians*: "Divine folly is wiser than the wisdom of man, and divine weakness stronger than man's strength."

What Christianity gave to Rome's philosophical culture was the element of personality. The masses of Roman society could relate more readily to a message of compassion than to admonitions aiming at mental detachment. This religion was especially popular with women and slaves. In the image of Jesus on the Cross, the suffering masses found a sympathetic model. His subsequent resurrection from the dead delivered a powerful message of hope. The Gospel story of Jesus presents the image of a man, not unlike a philosopher, who is highly intellectual and personally disciplined. Since this was not an image congenial with ordinary people, nascent Christianity borrowed other personal elements from rival cults in Roman society to achieve increased emotional appeal. From the Egyptian cult of Isis, Phrygian cult of Cybele, and others, it added the female image of an adoring mother, which was bestowed upon the Virgin Mary. Jesus' role of saviour was foreshadowed by the Persian god Mithras who slew a bull. Devotees of the Greek god Dionysius, like Christians celebrating the Eucharist, believed that they were drinking the god's own blood when they imbibed wine.

A similar process was meanwhile converting the philosophical religion of Buddha into a saviour cult having mass appeal. Buddha's original teachings, which are preserved in Theravadin Buddhism, showed individuals how they might achieve Nirvana, or blissful escape from recurrent lives, through a shift in attitude. The problem was that, once the teacher had escaped to personal extinction, he was inaccessible to followers of his religion. A new branch of the religion, Mahayana Buddhism, developed in northwestern India during the first two centuries, A.D., before spreading overland to China. The Mahayana teaching held that the Buddha, out of compassion for his followers, had delayed his own departure from earth to help others achieve Nirvana. Buddha was thus transformed from a spiritual philosopher into a personal saviour. Though he was himself an atheist or, at least, a person uninterested in questions concerning dei-

Buddha figures on lintel of western entrance at Ta-yen T'a (China)

ties or eternal life, Buddha eventually became in the religious culture a godlike figure endowed with miraculous, benevolent powers. The "bodhisattvas" were deities of lesser rank who would also respond to calls for help. Mahayana Buddhism, like Christianity, developed a practice of charitable works and a belief in a paradise for virtuous souls after death.

The older Hindu tradition of India became a polytheistic religion with a rich array of male and female personalities. Having survived the Buddhist challenge, it reorganized by incorporating elements from its rival religion. Previously, the Vedic rituals were intended to make the gods help people in some way. The Sanskrit literature had become rather technical. Revived Hinduism featured worship with an emotional bond between gods or goddesses and their devotees like that between the bodhisattvas and Buddhist worshipers. A triune of supreme deities - Brahma, Vishnu, and Shiva - ruled over a universe which balances creation and destruction. Shiva and his female consort, Kali, represented the forces of destruction and death. Vishnu, god of love, was a personal savior who was sometimes incarnated in a human being. Brahma was the original creator of the universe, beyond good and evil. Ganesha, the elephant-headed god of wisdom, was son of Shiva and Parvati, his benign consort. An outgrowth of earlier nature religion, the Hindu pantheon was united in a matrix of family-like relationships defined in literature and myth. Worshipers prayed to the particular gods or goddesses for particular purposes, brought offerings, or went to festivals in honor of them.

Ganesha

The religion of Islam was as austere in its concepts and practices as the Hindu religion was lush. In reaction to the Hellenic influences upon Christianity, Islam reaffirmed the uncompromising monotheism of Moses. There was no trinity of persons in the godhead, only one God. Except for theological refinements, the belief structure of this religion was similar to that of the Jewish and Christian religions. The righteous, who passed the Last Judgment, would be admitted after death to paradise. Islam's prohibition of personal images in religion made it difficult to project personality in Islamic culture to the degree possible in other religions. Still, Mohammed himself had left an historical record which included some of this element. The personal ingredient in Islamic culture also comes from a rich tradition of poetry centered in persons who have submitted completely to God. They would include the great Persian poets Rumi and Hafiz, both members of the mystical Sufi brotherhood. Islam makes strict personal demands upon the worshiper. At the same time, Allah is considered to be a merciful and compassionate God who acknowledges the fact of human weakness.

Chinese religion began with a strong tradition of ancestor worship over which was laid philosophies of the 6th and 5th centuries B.C. Two native Chinese philosophies, Confucianism and Taoism, were joined in the 3rd century A.D. by a full-blown religion imported from India. This was Buddhism in its Mahayana form. Each religion had a literature to support its belief component. The followers of Confucius have the "Nine Classics", which include five books attributed to Confucius himself and four written by others. Confucian literature is a mixture of historical, ethical, ritualistic, and metaphysical writings. The Taoist literature is focused on one book, the *Tao-Te-Ching* or "Book of the Way and of Virtue", which is attributed to Lao-tse. While the Confucians tend to be rationalistic and the Taoists mystical, both philosophies became religious cults which elevated their founder to godlike status. Every large Chinese city had a temple where officials offered sacrifices to Confucius' spirit. The Mahayana Buddhists engaged in a highly personal form of worship. Large statues or carvings of the Buddha adorned its temples and caves. The Taoists concocted magical potions and "elixirs of life" to gain personal immortality.

Belief is well established in all the world religions. An extensive theological literature details doctrinal positions on each aspect of religious life. Councils of clergy have been convened to define orthodoxy. Heretics have been identified and punished. It would be pointless to discuss this aspect further. With respect to personality, the supreme person is, obviously, God. Yet, God is not the main focus of personality in the world religions. What we know about God personally comes from an earlier scripture. When religion became philosophical, God became more like an idea. Aristotle wrote that "God's self-dependent actuality is life most good and eternal." In other words, God personifies eternal Goodness. Toynbee wrote that the higher religions all worship "a Reality that is one and the same behind its diverse aspects." In other words, God's being unifies all existence. The "ontological argument" of St. Anselm defined God as the most perfect being of whom we can conceive; God must therefore exist or else he would lack an essential attribute. This was playing with ideas. The consensus of religious opinion has been that God is beyond human understanding - an all-powerful yet personal being whom we cannot definitively know.

Since God is unknowable, personality in *CivIl* would center, first, upon the prophets or founders of the several world religions and, second, upon a myriad of lesser figures in each religious tradition. Literature would be the vehicle for exhibiting these persons. As presented in the four Gospels, Jesus is a character in an intensely dramatic and intimate story. The lives of Mohammed and Buddha, and of Confucius and Lao-tse, are similarly known. The lives, sayings, and ideas of these great religious personalities come through most clearly in a verbal medium. Yet, religious culture has also made use of personal images. Mahayana Buddhism has been called "the religion of images." Inspired by Greek models of visual art, statues of the Buddha were introduced in China in the 6th century A.D. Typically, this figure would be seated in lotus position, his right palm raised and his left palm lowered, with elongated ears and a fat, contented face. Christianity has, of course, the image of Jesus hanging on the Cross. It has the Madonna and child as portrayed in countless paintings. At Christmas, the creche recreates the scene of the Nativity.

With respect to the lesser personalities, we can start with famous hermits like St. Anthony or with spiritual acrobats like St. Simeon Stylites. Their daring exhibitions of self-discipline won the admiration of the entire Christian world. Indian religion provides holy men who perform conspicuous feats of telepathy or acts exhibiting insensitivity to physical pain. Medieval Europe was obsessed with the Virgin Mary. The period of Roman perse-

cution had produced a large number of Christian martyrs and saints whose bones or other remains became objects of worship. Such relics, kept in a shrine or church, were thought capable of producing miraculous cures. Mass pilgrimages took place to visit the saintly remains. Some saints were heroic missionaries like St. Patrick and St. Columba. St. Francis of Assisi is known for his gentle nature and his way with animals. St. Theresa was a Christian mystic and Carmelite nun. Each holy man or woman exhibited the spirit of God in some personal way.

Madonna and child

## Religion in the Third Civilization

One would be tempted to say that Protestant Christianity was the religion of the third civilization. The cultural impetus for this epoch came from Europe, and the Protestant Reformation was Europe's most important religious event. However, the spirit of this age was secular rather than religious. Renaissance humanism considered man, not God, to be the measure of all things. Its culture proclaimed the dignity and worth of the individual person. There was a revival of interest in pagan arts and letters bequeathed from classical antiquity. The Christian virtue of poverty gave way to rediscovered appreciation of wealth. Where medieval culture had embraced the philosophical tradition of exalting mind and hating the body, the human body became a beautiful object for artists to paint. Although the basic concepts of Christianity did not change, the institutional church faced a challenge to its authority. Religious faith became a matter, first, of royal determination and, then, of individual choice.

It ultimately became a part of one's ethnic heritage, which preserved the morals of a community.

Doubting Thomas would not believe that Jesus was resurrected from the dead until he had put his fingers inside Jesus' wounds. Likewise, the attitude of intellectuals in the late medieval and Renaissance periods was that "seeing is believing." Galileo saw that, contrary to Aristotle's opinion, pendulums of varying widths but equal lengths swung at the same rate. He chose to believe the evidence of his own eyes rather than Aristotle. The scientific revolution of the 17th century took place at a time when Christian convictions had grown coercive and violent. European intellectuals were disgusted by the rancorous theological disputes that had led to the Thirty Years War. They wished to channel their creative energies into an area where reasonable men might agree on some points. Scientific truth in its modern incarnation is not a system of belief derived from a superior intelligence but a working hypothesis designed to fit an observed set of facts. The general pattern of knowledge is determined by these facts. The pattern is freely changed if a new set of facts should appear which contradicts existing theory. Science is therefore more a system of "anti-belief", or a studied policy not to hold fast to its principles in the face of contradictory evidence, than of belief in a traditional sense.

Yet, because of its affinity to the natural world, this type of knowledge has been applied to technologies which visibly affect people's lives. Scientific knowledge has literally changed the earth's landscape. Because people can see its results, science has instant credibility. Although the initial scientific discoveries centered in astronomy, enlightened Europeans soon became interested in increasing agricultural yields through crop rotation and horse-drawn plows. The invention of the steam engine in the 18th century was applied to pumping water from mines and to large-scale textiles manufacturing. This required coal; and, to haul coal from the mines to its place of use, industrial engineers built inland canals and railroads through which steam-driven engines might pass. Discoveries in metallurgy developed stronger grades of iron and steel. Bridges were built of this metal, and then skyscrapers. Electricity lit up the cities and propelled trains in the subways. One could hardly doubt the power of scientific knowledge to create a world of marvelous convenience and wealth. Prosperity itself depended on finding and applying the knowledge more quickly than one's competitors.

The natural sciences were related to a new type of philosophy that emerged during the 17th and 18th centuries. This "empiricist" philosophy, associated with such persons as Descartes, Pascal, Locke, and Hume, saw the world differently than the idealistic philosophies had. Where the idealists held that ideas existed independently and were the source of worldly objects, empiricist philosophers treated the mind as a mechanism which produces ideas. The purpose of philosophy became to discover through introspection how the mind worked. Mental processes were based upon operations of a bodily organ called the brain. The natural world itself was a huge, clock-like mechanism that operated according to causal laws. Locke, Rousseau, Montesquieu, and others were architects of a new system of government based upon a social contract, consent of the governed, and respect for property rights, as opposed to hereditary privilege. The principle of divided power ensured its safety and well being. David Hume and his disciple Adam Smith were pioneers of economic theory who argued that national wealth is maximized by removing restrictions upon commercial and personal freedom. These social philosophers created the belief systems supporting democratic government and free markets.

It is clear that in the third epoch of civilization people believed in money. Money was valuable and real. For all the questioning about God's existence, however, few bothered to ask whether money existed. They just assumed that it did. Gold and silver underlay traditional forms of money, so European adventurers went to the New World to seek this kind of wealth. The Spanish king acquired tons of precious metals from American mines only to discover that his nation was becoming bankrupt. The huge increase in the supply of silver had produced severe monetary inflation. Each ounce of silver bought less than before. So silver money was not quite as solid as people had thought. Another revelation came in the early 1700s when the French state, exhausted from Louis XIV's wars, thought it had run out of money. A Scottish financier, John Law, won support for a proposal to create new money by issuing bank notes backed by his own capital. This scheme succeeded beyond his wildest dreams. Public confidence had made the money real. But then, when Law's bank was combined with a stock company to sell land in Louisiana, a speculative frenzy ensued which drove up the price of the shares to unsupportable levels. When the bubble burst, Law fled the country in disgrace. Another lesson in reality had been learned.

What was the nature of a nation's true wealth? A Scottish economist, Adam Smith, attempted to answer this question in a book published in 1776. *Wealth of Nations* argued that wealth was not quantities of money but useful goods and services freely produced and sold to willing purchasers in the market place. The mercantilist scheme of running consistent surpluses in their trading accounts could not be practiced by all nations. Smith's idea that free markets optimized national wealth and that governments should stay clear of this process to the greatest extent possible became the foundation of capitalistic faith. A half century later, Karl Marx proposed the opposite theory, that national economies would be better off if governments not only meddled in commercial markets but, indeed, took over the entire structure of production and managed things according to principles of economic "science". Two competing ideologies, each backed by political regimes which had missiles and hydrogen bombs, polarized the world's nations in the waning years of CivIII. It was this epoch's equivalent of religious warfare.

The money-centered culture carried with it the additional belief that possession of wealth meant something in society. In ancient Chinese society, it had not. The merchants, though comfortable, were despised. In the post-Renaissance European and American societies, the stigma against money was largely removed. To be rich was an important qualification for high social standing. Still, the nouveau riche did not quite belong in a class with the old-money aristocrats who bore their wealth gracefully. Education was useful in repairing that deficiency. Children of the rich needed to acquire the trappings of nobility to make their status secure and complete. So, along with the belief in money went a belief in schools. The first generation might consist of boors or criminals who earned the money, while their children acquired a taste for the finer things in life. Learning to speak and write in grammatically correct sentences, being conversant with some of the civilization's best works of literature and art, and having the money to do as one pleased - these marked being a gentleman.

Personality in the third epoch did not necessarily follow belief. As Graeco-Roman philosophy led to an ethical position devoid of human warmth, so empirical science lacks the element of engaging personality which mass culture seems to require. Disciplined to be objective, the experimental scientist leaves himself personally out of the picture. While a certain cult has formed around the person of Albert Einstein, scientists are perceived to be rather bland individuals who frequent laboratories and other antiseptic places. Only the proverbial "mad scientist" seems colorful enough to excite the popular imagination. Perhaps, then, we should be looking to the business community for heroes? They are the ones who have assembled the largest amounts of money. However, industrial, financial, and commercial leaders as a group lack the personal color and social appeal to inspire masses of people. They generally work behind the scenes of their commercial empires and have personalities almost as bland as the scientists. Occasionally, an Andrew Carnegie or Henry Ford will excite popular interest by their entrepreneurial boldness and philanthropy, but these are the exceptions.

The beginning period of this epoch was not lacking in heroes. Christopher Columbus, Vasco da Gama, Fernando Magellan, and Ponce de León went boldly to places where no European had previously set foot. The military conquests of Hernando Cortés and Francisco Pizarro were as dazzling as any in history. Still, these great historical figures did not personally excite the culture of CivIII as the founders and saints of religion had in CivII. The problem may be that they lacked a vehicle for exhibiting their personalities. Books of world history are not widely read. Where, then, did the third civilization obtain its personal images? A plausible answer is: from literature and art.

The Renaissance is known as a time when skilled artists and craftsmen produced paintings, buildings, sculpture, and other beautiful objects. Portrait painting became popular. So the art of creating visual images, always an important means of conveying personality, played a big part in *CivIII* from the beginning. To the visual arts were added intimate personal expressions in the form of love poems such as those which Dante wrote to Beatrice or Petrarch wrote to Laura. Shakespeare's dramatic works presented an array of memorable characters. These were literate ways of delivering personality to a mass audience, albeit in a fictional mode. What was not fiction was the artist himself. Artists were persons of developed vision who had a talent for expressing it in a certain medium. They had personality in a different sense.

Raphael once said: "To paint a beautiful woman, I need to see many beautiful women ... But since there is a dearth ... I use as my guide a certain idea of the beautiful that I carry in my mind." The artist's expression is in one sense a naturalistic depiction of an object, but, as Raphael admitted, the artist intrudes with his own images and ideas of style. Since each artist carries inside him a different set of images, an artistic expression is stamped with the personality of its creator. Renaissance painters were aware of Plato's conception of beauty, and it guided them in their art. The profession of artist was, therefore, more than simple craftsmanship. Artists were intellectuals cut from the same highbrow cloth as philosophers. However, unlike the philosopher who presents a universal image of truth, an artist expresses a personal vision through techniques related to his art. He develops a unique craft by patient exercise and experimentation. At the end of this process comes a cultivated habit representing the artist's own style. That makes the artist himself a stylistic commodity which attracts a certain clientele.

After the invention of printing, it became possible to record a writer's exact words and reproduce them in many copies. Numerous readers could thereby become intimately acquainted with the writer's habits of mind. Printed newspapers with large circulations began to serialize the writings of well-known authors. Novelists were paid a certain sum of money for each written line, depending on their popularity. The reading public learned to recognize and appreciate the individual writers. Another kind of artist was the composer of music. Working with musical notations instead of words, he, too, developed personal style. One could recognize the composer from the music. Orchestral concerts made his works known. As visual artists, writers, and musicians over the years produced individually recognizable works, a tradition of artistic, musical, and literary culture appeared. Masterpieces of the visual arts became available to a wide audience through new technologies of reproduction such as chromolithography, photoengraving, and color printing. Player pianos and phonographic recordings reproduced orchestral music. Each self-respecting community acquired institutions of high culture, including symphony orchestras, opera houses, and museums, to display the cultural works in public.

Alexander Selkirk became a celebrity when he told his adventures of having been stranded for four years on the Juan Fernández island in the Pacific Ocean to Richard Steele, a journalist, who wrote up the story and published it in a London-based journal in 1713. Six years later, Daniel Defoe published a novel, *Robinson Crusoe*, based on the same experience. The characters, Tom Sawyer and Huckleberry Finn, which appear in Mark Twain's novels of the same names, are notable personalities in

Mark Twain

American fiction. However, the authors themselves rather than characters appearing in their writings have been the main focus of CivIII personality. During the 19th century, books began to include pictures of authors on the title page as well as their names. Novelists such as Charles Dickens, William Makepeace Thackeray, and Mark Twain became cultural idols while touring on the lecture circuit. Serialized novels and the publication of many similar works by the same author created public expectations of him. Literary styles gained a following.

It may have been the English Romantic poets who first inspired the idea that a writer's life could be as colorful and interesting as that of any character found in his writings. In the heady period when England led a coalition of nations to defeat Napoleon's armies, Lord Byron cut a bold figure. A voracious womanizer and gambler who was perpetually in debt, he toured Europe during the French occupation and wrote a poetic account of his adventures, *Childe Harold's Pilgrimage*, which made him internationally famous. Byron's friendship with Shelley, his restless travels, and his heroic fight to liberate Greece from the Turkish empire during the last year of his short life, in addition to his prolific verse, combined to suggest an intellectually and emotionally intense personality which was attractive to youth. Poetry became a source of spiritual excitement with a strong connection to life. Young lovers spoke to each other's hearts through this medium of beauty and truth. Prose literature ripened into the thick 19th century novel. Writers such as Dickens, Balzac, Hugo, and Tolstoy developed a specialty in describing the brutal lives of the poor. Art was in league with powerful political currents which called for the emancipation of humanity from wage slavery and other ills.

Education at the time of the Renaissance focused upon classical literature. Starting in 17th century, the schools paid increased attention to works written in contemporary languages which were both a stylistic model for writing and a source of national pride. Schoolchildren began to study their national literature. College students were encouraged to take courses in the liberal arts which would expose them to, in Matthew Arnold's words, "the best that has been thought and said" in a nation's cultural life. No student of English literature could be ignorant of poets such as Milton, Wordsworth, Shelley, or Keats. The orchestral music of Bach, Mozart, Handel, and Beethoven was familiar to all who had achieved any degree of cultural sophistication. It became a measure of a nation's greatness how many of those creative giants its people had produced. The French led the way with a new style of prose writing

Matthew Arnold

which produced dramatists like Molière and essayists like Montaigne and Pascal. The English could boast of Shakespeare, Milton, and Pope. The Germans were known for their composers of music. The late 19th century French set the pace in experimental painting. Italian, Flemish, and Dutch painters provided more than their share of the "Old Masters" exhibited in museums. And, the nationalistic Americans claimed to have as good as or better than the Europeans in most areas.

Hector Berlioz

Treasured as part of humanity's cultural heritage and exhibited in liberal-arts courses, the works created by famous writers, artists, and musical composers loomed above the horizon of Civ|II like stars in a heaven of beautiful expressions. It became a sign of personal sophistication and intelligence to be a consumer of this culture and to be able to understand and appreciate its exquisite design. To be conversant with names suggesting a high degree of intellectual refinement became the mark of an educated person. One had the worldly yet emotionally detached attitude of the connoisseur who knows excellence in its many forms. The artist, source of that excellence, became the center of cultural attention. Here was genius combined with an often colorful and glamorous personal life. Vincent Van Gogh's bout with insanity, F. Scott Fitzgerald's life in high society, Ernest Hemingway's masculine pastimes, and Jack Kerouac's beatnik lifestyle conveyed an image of living on the edge. (Public interest in Claude Monet increased when it was alleged that he had a mistress.) The idea took hold that one must have personally experienced life at the extremities to be able to write or paint so knowledgeably about it. And so, the hard-living, hard-drinking, womanizing artist or writer of the early 20th century captured the public imagination and helped to satisfy its hunger for personality.

## Religion in the Fourth Civilization

"Fame is really our religion in America," wrote UCLA literature professor Leo Braudy. "And we have a constantly changing calendar of saints whom we encounter in our media churches, especially films and television, which have the largest congregations." To think of television or film entertainment as a religion may seem a stretch since few find their shows to be culturally edifying. Yet, in the fourth epoch of history, popular entertainment sets the cultural/spiritual agenda. The element of belief is barely visible here. Entertainment generally does not present a serious message or, except for the commercials, aim to convert someone to a particular point of view. It is "make believe" - an outgrowth of children's play. From childhood on, people understand the value of this experience. When one is pretending to be someone or be in a particular situation, one safely experiences such things. Entertainment is emotionally stimulating without requiring a commitment of preparation or attention. One can relax, laugh, and have fun.

Personality is the strong suit of the entertainment culture. Films, sound recordings, radio, and television have an unusual ability to capture the sensuous aspect of personality and transmit its images to a large number of people. Radio listeners grow comfortable with the voices they hear at certain times of the day and with the imagined persons behind them. Television viewers are used to having certain individuals in their living rooms. The electronic media have thus extended our personal neighborhoods to include all the people whom we have come to know from their productions. The entertainers' personalities are spread out before us in various roles. On the screen in a movie theater or on television appear the images of familiar persons, their faces and bodies in front of our eyes, close up or distant, in a variety of characters, stories, and scenes. We feel that we are with these people and know them personally.

For all the lonely persons in this world, the electronic image of the performers breaks down their sense of isolation and reconnects them with humanity. These performers have such vibrant personalities yet are accessible to ordinary people. Some like dancers and musicians have obvious talent. The film stars tend to be picked for more elusive personal reasons. Lana Turner reportedly was "discovered" by a Hollywood film mogul while working behind the counter at Schwann's drug store. Mainly, actors and actresses are paid for "being themselves" and acting naturally, although having an attractive body and face helps. That being the case, the idea has taken hold that anyone can be a star. All it takes is being in the right place at the right time, plus a bit of luck.

In the previous civilization, personality appeared in the pale medium of printed words or, indirectly, in the texture of an artist's creative vision. The technologies of electronic recording and communication have filled in the physical presence that was previously left to the reader's imagination. The viewer or listener can now see or hear actual recordings of a scene. The personal image of the performer who stands before the camera or microphone crowds expression in these media. As the night sky disappears with the sun's rising, so the old cult of musical composers, artists, and writers has faded with the arrival of electronic technologies that can deliver the far more vivid images of personality in performing artists exhibited in the full glare of sensuous detail. The focus of personality has therefore shifted from the person who conceives and writes a cultural work to the person who performs it. The performer's direct personal image is so much more powerful than the hints of personality found in the works of pre-electronic culture.

There are still persons who write dramatic scripts serving the same function as ones written in Shakespeare's time. They are the screenwriters for films and writers of scripts for made-for-television drama. Yet, neither the critics nor the general public seems to care about their artistry any more. Budd Schulberg, a screen writer who won a prize at the Deauville Festival of American Films, complained at the awards ceremony that only the film directors, never the screenwriters, were listed in the festival's program. "If the play's the thing, so is the movie script," he argued. In the field of recorded music, the public spotlight falls upon the person who sings and records a popular song rather than the person who wrote it. Jerry Lieber and Mike Stoller, who wrote "Hound Dog" and other songs for Elvis Presley, remarked: "We always thought it was sort of pathetic that the originator of the song ended up with small potatoes and some decal, some imitator, would wind up making a bloody fortune off their efforts."

The star system has conquered Hollywood. Because a performer has personal qualities that appeal to many people, he or she becomes a hot property in the motion-picture industry. Film proposals immediately become viable if one or another performer who had a recent box-office hit can be persuaded to play a leading role in the proposed picture. "If a star is very hot, " said Kirk Douglas, "he can get a film made." For that reason, the talent agents who represent actors and actresses of proven appeal have become top power brokers in Hollywood. In the new era of free agency which replaced the old studio system, they are involved in putting together the packages of talent - performers, direc-

tors, writers, musicians - needed to produce a film. The music industry runs on the injections of personality which recording artists put into their songs. Phonographic or tape recordings, which pick up each inflection in a singer's voice, deliver the unique personal renditions of musical works. Vocal recordings generally outsell instrumental music because the listeners relate to people most of all.

As an intensely personal medium, electronic entertainment provides widely imitated models of personality. Elvis Presley's sideburns and the Beatles' interest in Transcendental Meditation affected personal fashions of their day. James Dean has long been a hero for rebellious youth. Many who cannot relate to other

James Dean

people on the basis of hobby or occupation may share an interest in the movies or television shows that they have seen. Entertainment experiences date people generationally. They are something for strangers to talk about in casual conversation. To have witnessed an important event on live television such as the shooting of Lee Harvey Oswald or man's first steps on the Moon makes one feel connected to history. Professional sports make a ritual of uniting communities behind the home team. To be a rabid sports fan is an acceptable model of sociability - not quite as stuffy as some others. The obituary of a man who had once headed the tax department of a large corporation included this statement: "Despite 60 years in Minnesota, he remained a loyal (Green Bay) Packer fan. He began attending their games in 1925 and always happily recounted how he had a 48 yard line, 12th row seat during the 1929, 1930, and 1931 championship seasons."

As far as belief is concerned, the entertainment industry stands ready to deliver whatever fantasies significant portions of the population might have, be they visions of adventure, easy money, or sexual intimacy. Tourism has changed from travel to places like the Grand Canyon or Williamsburg to what Hal Rothman calls "entertainment tourism". He explains: "You walk through a tourist attraction and you know that you are the most important thing in it. It holds a mirror up to you and says that in this reflection you can be whatever you want to be. Las Vegas is the epitome of this."

Professional sports feeds on the sense of fan loyalty combined with a tradition of "sandlot" baseball, school teams, and families that enjoy recreational pastimes together. Yet, its very success has driven up player salaries, ticket prices, and the cost of sponsoring televised games. When politicians in south Florida refused to build the Florida Marlins a new stadium with taxpayer money, the Marlins' owner traded or sold off virtually every starter on its 1997 World Championship team with the result that the 1998 Marlins finished in last place.    Heretofore, some parity in the playing ability of the two competing teams has been needed to maintain belief in the authenticity of athletic contests. However, the Major League teams located in smaller-sized cities  cannot afford the player salaries which those in the larger cities pay. The Minnesota Twins have slashed player payrolls to achieve profitability at the risk of sacrificing team loyalty. To push the entertainment aspects of the event with special promotions like "Dog Days", blimps, and pregame concerts may or may not overcome that basic deficiency.

David Sarnoff, who unveiled television broadcasting at the 1939 Worlds Fair, believed that this medium would improve the culture of the United States. "It is probable," he said, "that television drama of high caliber and produced by  first-rate artists will materially raise the level of dramatic taste of the nation." This did not happen. Other values than artistic excellence kicked in. One might say that entertainment moguls today believe in the Nielsen ratings, especially viewer ratings within the prime demographic categories. Program producers use every trick in the book to keep viewers from switching channels, especially those who will be likely shoppers for the advertised products. The "eyeballs" must be held together at all costs. If newsworthy or educationally valuable programs attracted viewers, television would certainly air them; but since they do not, programs of lower quality which are cheaper to produce flood the airwaves.

Entertainment is simply entertainment - an attempt to amuse rather than instruct. True or not, whatever engages people's interest and attention will continue to be produced. This is a sector which appreciates the well-done image. While a few stodgy people think that television or film should spread knowledge, George Page, a producer of television documentaries, has said: "Television and film can always only scratch the surface ... If you try to be definitive, you wind up with terrible television and terrible, unwatchable films."

Yet, while movie scripts are basically fiction, the element of belief can also be important. A film such as *Jurassic Park*, which was based upon the implausible premise that dinosaurs were brought back to life, had to convince audiences that the script had a connection with reality. Director Steven Spielberg insisted that the success of this film depended as much upon its "scientific credibility" as the special effects. The idea was that DNA from a dinosaur's blood had been sucked by a mosquito which was trapped in amber and preserved for 130 million years. Scientists extracted the DNA from the amber and used it to clone a dinosaur. In fact, at the same time that *Jurassic Park* was being filmed, biologists were successfully cloning an ancient bee from DNA preserved in amber.

Children learn through play to distinguish make-believe fromreality. Not even this prepares them for the baffling situation that they face when exposed to products of the entertainment industry. A mother took her 3-year-old daughter to see Disney's "Aladdin on Ice". She reported that her daughter's "excitement over 'Aladdin' was so intense that it rendered her speechless ... Midway through the first act, the little one finally spoke.

> 'Mama, is that Aladdin the same one we have at home?'
>
> 'What do you mean,' I asked. 'The Aladdin in our video, or the Aladdin Ken doll?'
>
> 'The movie Aladdin, ding-dong head.'
>
> 'Don't call me ding-dong head,' I said, and explained that the movie Aladdin was a cartoon of an imaginary Aladdin, whereas this Aladdin was a per-

son on skates who was pretending to be an imaginary Aladdin.

'Which one is real?'

Now I was rendered speechless. Which one, indeed. I'm awed by the layers of reality that I must navigate to explain pop culture to a preschooler."

In the early days of live television, part of viewer excitement was knowing that, because the program was live, anything could happen. The performer could forget the lines or make an embarrassing blooper, and the audience was there to watch. There was a sense of anticipation missing in today's taped shows. The experience was real. In those days the television industry stressed its unique ability to communicate with masses of people in the case of civil-defense emergencies. The networks sought respectability in quality news operations to offset criticism of their more profitable but inane entertainment shows. News is a type of programming weighted more heavily towards the "belief" end of the spectrum. The television viewer watches the news partly for the experience of being entertained by new and unusual events and partly for the purpose of monitoring a possibly useful stream of information. Because the news is "unscripted", the public would be outraged if it were disclosed that news reporters simply made up their stories. In an era of staged media events, however, the line between real and fake news can sometimes be hard to detect.

Some types of entertainment depend on the authenticity of not knowing the outcome of a spectacle in progress. Participants in a lottery must have assurance that the winner has not already been selected when they place their bets. Even events such as game or quiz shows which are seen as pure entertainment must have a foundation in belief. When Charles Van Doren confessed that he had been coached to give the right answers on *The $64,000 Question*, it created a national scandal. During an athletic contest, one does not know which contestant will win. To know the final result of a game while watching it would detract from the suspense of experiencing an incomplete event. If the game is shot live, viewers know it could go either way. Credibility was stretched in the 1996 Summer Olympics when the sponsoring network, NBC, failed to disclose to viewers that it was airing a delayed tape of Kerri Strug's gymnastics performance with an injured ankle. The commentators suggested that her points were needed for the U.S. team to win a gold medal. In truth, the commentators already knew the outcome. Strug's routine, while gritty, was not actually needed to win the medal. NBC had decided to stress unfolding personal drama at the expense of reality.

Part of the value of watching an athletic contest is knowing that, because in any such contest there will be both winners and losers, the athletes are under real pressure to win. The uncertainty of victory both adds to the viewing excitement and produces true champions. A champion must learn to discipline himself or herself to perform well at a time when it counts. The performer must learn to control nervousness. The adrenalin must be flowing and the mind be sailing smoothly through a routine. While some talent and much practice are involved, the spectators also realize that a champion performer must be in the right frame of mind. There is an art to achieving this "mental edge". Such concentration is difficult to achieve and the public knows it. Therefore, it is customary for television commentators to interview the winning athletes in the heat of their victory with the object of looking inside their heads. What was the athlete mentally trying to accomplish while making this superb effort? What special thoughts might have inspired it? How, indeed, does it feel to be a winner? The answers to such questions may be the closest that many in our time will come to witnessing divine inspiration.

With respect to scripted entertainment, people realize that its spectacle is mostly illusion. The tapes can be edited to remove blemishes and mistakes so that an artificial degree of perfection is achieved. The performing artist who is "up" for a performance may revert to being a disorganized wreck once the camera is turned off. After all, these are just actors - persons who make a living by pretending to be someone else. Still, people yearn to know the reality beneath the illusion. They eagerly read fan magazines, tabloid newspapers, or anything else that purports to show the real person behind the celebrity performer. The late-night television talk shows present an endless stream of guests from the entertainment industry. These guests make no claim to possessing wisdom or even advanced acting skills whose secret they will now reveal to audiences on the show. The public is interested in them simply as people - seeing the reality behind their public persona. A big thrill lately has been to watch the celebrities fall from a position of storybook success to the depths of humiliation, if not vile criminality. What else would account for the intense interest in Tonja Harding's contract to injure a rival skater or in O.J. Simpson's murder trial?

The world of electronically transmitted entertainment hangs like the Moon before people's eyes, so close yet so far away. Though in some sense real, it cannot be personally touched. There once was a man from New York who regularly attended the live broadcast of a network radio show. Hoping to be "discovered" as a comic talent, he had memorized a number of snappy lines in case the host called upon a member of the audience to say something. He never was called upon. America's premier industry, gambling, is built on the notion that, despite the unfavorable odds, "I can be that one in a million" who wins the lottery or jackpot. Millions of people are each willing to trade a small but real sum of money for the dubious chance of becoming a "big winner". Phineas T. Barnum's adage, "There's a sucker born every minute", sets the tone for this age. The master showman is not exactly deceiving us about his intentions. We are allowing ourselves to be deceived so long as this gives us and the children some good, clean fun.

## Religion in the Fifth Civilization

While it is much too soon to say what will be the religion of the coming epoch, one can identify some of its elements in the computer culture seen to date. It appears that the fifth civilization faces a situation opposite that of CivIV. While the personality aspect is weak, belief is strong. Everyone believes in computers. Computer intelligence is perfect and quick. If a mistake appears in the result of its calculations, this must be the fault of the human programmer or someone who fed faulty data into the system. Wall Street believes in computers. It has valued the stock of a 20-year-old computer-software company, Microsoft, more than General Motors and made its 40-year-old chairman the richest man on earth. Parents buy home computers for their children, hoping that they will pick up skills to ensure future employability. Corporate America believes that computers can improve product quality and customer service while reducing costs.

With respect to personality, the computer has none. Cartoonists may joke about its feelings and thoughts, but even robots have a more people-friendly image. The types of people who work with computers are quite unlike the supercharged, attractive persons who work in the entertainment industry. They are "geeks" and "nerds" who while away their lives at a computer terminal. Those reclusive individuals who are addicted to "surfing the Internet" should come out every once in awhile into the sunlight of real life and meet some people in the flesh. One imagines them, stereotypically, to be rather owlish individuals who click on pornographic Websites for excitement or send hate-filled messages to one another. Alternatively, there are the "cyberpunks" who are a type of juvenile delinquent armed with the technical knowledge to steal from the telephone company or invade corporate data bases. It might be possible to make heroes out of these malicious hackers in a perverse "Robin Hood" sort of way.

If self-made billionaires had an attractive personal image, then the computer industry has delivered more than its share of this commodity. That appears not to be the case. Instead, we must look elsewhere in the computer culture for models of personality. Perhaps this is to be found in Jennifer Ringley's enterprise. She is a 21-year-old woman living somewhere in Washington, D.C., who has installed a Quick Cam camera in her bedroom to record scenes from her daily life. She invites people to log on to her Website for regular photographic updates. Reportedly, this Website receives 100 million hits each week. Although there is some nudity, the chief attraction seems to be simple companionship. The Internet is too diffuse to magnify personal images as the television networks do. Rather, its appeal is one of self-definition. Somewhere in the millions of E-mail addresses a person can find like-minded individuals, perhaps even soul mates, in each area of life. The trick is to know who we are and then learn to express our individual preferences and ideas to elicit a self-affirming response.

## Changing Holidays

As religion changed through the ages, it took on the coloration of institutions that dominated the successive societies. A way to track those changes may be to review adaptations made to institutions of sacred space and time. When the Roman church planned England's conversion to Christianity, Pope Gregory I issued orders to the effect that "the temples of idols ... should on no account be destroyed. He (Augustine) is to destroy the idols, but the temples themselves are to be aspersed with holy water, altars set up, and relics enclosed in them ... In this way we hope that the people may abandon idolatry ... and resort to these places as before." Places sacred to pagan religions were thus converted to serve the needs of advancing Christianity. The Gospels tell the story of Jesus driving the moneychangers out of the Temple in Jerusalem. In this case, Jesus was able to prevent a place sacred to Judaism from being corrupted by the values of money. Now, in CivIII, bingo games operating out of church basements compromise that ideal somewhat.

The advancing epochs have also converted sacred time to new purposes. Jesus may have expelled moneychangers from the Temple, but that has not stopped the holiday which commemorates his birth from being turned into the year's most intense shopping season. It is estimated that purchases of Christmas gifts contribute more than a third of an average U.S. retailer's annual sales, and between half and three quarters of the annual profits. As the Christian holiday of Christmas has been shoved aside by commercial Christmases, so its Christmas once replaced holidays belonging to pagan civilization. (See Table 3-2.) The worshipers of Mithras, a Persian god popular among Roman soldiers, celebrated their god's birthday on December 25. The Roman holiday of Saturnalia, which began on December 17 and lasted for several days, was a festival honoring the god Saturn who had civilized the Italian people. Gift giving was a part of its tradition. In 440 A.D., the Christian church decided to celebrate the Feast of the Nativity at that time of year.

Festivals and holidays have been a part of human culture since prehistoric times. In the age of nature religion, special rituals were performed at the times of the summer or winter solstice and at the vernal or autumnal equinox. Christmas Day comes four days after the winter solstice. May Day was a pagan festival which celebrated the coming of spring. Halloween is related to an ancient Celtic festival which marked the beginning of the new year. Both of these seasonal celebrations were converted into something else in a subsequent age. May Day became an international labor holiday because of a general strike held in the United States and Canada on May 1, 1886 and a bombing that occurred three days later in Chicago. Halloween is the vigil of All Saints Day, a Christian holiday commemorating a group of martyrs from Roman times. Gregory I moved its festival date from May 15 to October 31 to take advantage of the earlier pagan holiday.

| Table 3-2 |
| :---: |
| Christmas in Several Epochs |
| CivI    Saturnalia<br>CivII   the Nativity of Jesus<br>CivIII  the main shopping season<br>CivIV  Bob Hope Christmas special<br>CivV   (stay tuned) |

In the epoch of civic religion, holidays commemorated important events in community life. The Romans designated nearly one third of the 355 days in their calendar as being holidays, when it was unlawful to conduct judicial or political business. The number of annual holidays increased to around 175 in the middle of the 4th century A.D. The city of Venice celebrates the "wedding of the Doge and the Sea" during its annual Ascension Day Fair, commemorating the Venetian doge's victory over Dalmatian pirates in 1000 A.D. The English celebrate "Guy Fawkes Day" on November 5th with bonfires to burn an effigy of Guy Fawkes. He was the leader of a failed conspiracy to blow up Parliament with gunpowder on that date in 1605. Bastille Day in France celebrates the freeing of inmates from the Bastille prison on July 14, 1789. National holidays in the United States include Independence Day (when the Declaration of Independence was signed), Presidents' Day (the birthdays of Presidents Washington and Lincoln), and the Martin Luther King holiday (birthday of the slain Civil Rights leader).

Each major religion has established holidays to commemorate important events or persons. The Jewish Passover remembers the time when God killed each first-born child in Egypt but passed over the homes of Hebrews whose doorposts were smeared with blood. Moslems celebrate Mohammed's birthday and the feast following the fast of Ramadan, the month when the Koran was first revealed. Buddhists celebrate the Buddha's birth and death and the date of his achieving nirvana. The festivals of Holi and of Durga-Puja, in honor of the goddesses Vasanti and Kali respectively, are major Hindu holidays. Easter, which commemorates Christ's resurrection, is the most important Christian holiday. In addition to Easter and Christmas, the calendar of Christian holidays includes days celebrating such events as Christ's Ascension into Heaven, the Pentecost (when the early Christian community was filled with the Holy Spirit), and the Epiphany (revelation of divine power at Jesus' baptism) in addition to commemorations of Christian saints. During the Middle Ages, it was considered a sin to do "servile work" on these holidays. Public worship and merriment instead took place.

When civilization became commercial in the third epoch, opportunistic merchants turned Christian holidays into semiofficial occasions to sell merchandise. The cult of commercial Christmases finds scriptural support in Charles Dickens' *A Christmas Carol*, featuring the character of Scrooge. In the original story, Scrooge is too tight-fisted to give his employee, Bob Crachit, time off from work to celebrate Christmas with his family. Since that theme does not suit contemporary business thinking, Scrooge has instead become someone who is too cheap to spend money on Christmas presents. Santa Claus, today a seasonal employee of department stores, once personified St. Nicholas, a Christian bishop of the 4th century. St. Valentine's Day, which used to honor a saint of that name, has become a day for sweethearts to buy flowers or greeting cards for each other. Halloween is an occasion for giving candy to children or attending ghoulish costume parties. The purely commercial holidays include Mother's Day, Father's Day, Grandparent's Day, and Secretaries' week; they name the person who is to receive gifts. Washington's birthday, no longer a national holiday, remains a day for merchants to offer special sales.

The holiday tradition has carried into the fourth epoch in the form of seasonal entertainment features. As Christmas has had several previous incarnations, it is not surprising to find television shows such as the Bob Hope Christmas Special at this time of the year. Bing Crosby's "White Christmas" was the all-time bestselling record for five decades. Labor Day, transplanted from CivIII, has become known as a time when Jerry Lewis conducts his annual telethon to raise money for children who suffer from muscular dystrophy. New Year's Day has become a time to watch collegiate football games and parades on network television. Superbowl Sunday is an example of a holiday established for purely entertainment purposes.

# Part II

# Chapter Four

# A SHORT HISTORY OF
# CIVILIZATION I

## Prehistoric Times

The human race may be related to a prehuman species, or "hominid", that lived 4 million years ago in east
Africa. A critical distinction between hominids and other ape-
like creatures was the ability to stand upright on two feet, freeing the arms and hands for other uses. Man became a creature
that uses hand-held tools. Modern man, "homo sapiens", was a
creature with enlarged cranial capacity related to a hominidic
race that developed in Africa about 100,000 years ago. The last
Ice Age, which began 75,000 years ago, initially kept most of its
population confined to warm climates. Certain groups ventured
out into the cold, moving north to Europe and east through southern Asia as far as Australia. Most far-ranging were those peoples,
ancestors of the American Indians, who crossed a land bridge

connecting Siberia with Alaska perhaps as early as 25000 B.C. but more likely around 10000 B.C. The last Ice Age came to an end in the period between 12000 and 10000 B.C. The earth's human population, then numbering about 4 million persons, was dispersed to six continents.

The earliest human societies consisted of families and tribal groups engaged in hunting, fishing, and other food-gathering activities. Those late Paleolithic peoples roamed land and sea in search of game. Their garments were made of animal skins and fur. They used chipped-stone tools, including arrowheads and scraping devices, and articles made of bone. The Neolithic revolution, which took place with the waning of the Ice Age, brought the arts of farming, spinning and weaving, pottery manufacturing, bows and arrows, and use of domesticated animals. Agricultural techniques increased the food supply allowing humanity to devote time to other arts. Six to seven thousand years ago, copper implements began to be used instead of implements made of stone. Copper and tin mixed together produced bronze, a more malleable alloy. Iron smelting was introduced about three thousand years ago. With their food planted in the ground, people began to live in settled communities. Population densities increased.

Historians debate whether agriculture was invented in a single place on earth or in several places. Archeologists excavating a site at Abu Hureya in northern Syria have discovered that an abrupt change took place there about 9,500 years ago. Digging into the ground, they found that the soil suddenly changed from brown clay to a mass of black material enriched with plant parts, indicating that a farming village had been built on top of an earlier settlement. The evidence suggests that its inhabitants, returning to this area after a recurrence of cold weather, suddenly possessed a knowledge of more than 150 different species of plant life indigenous to scattered places in the Middle East. Some speculate that the rapid development of agricultural knowledge was due to a "communications revolution" brought on by trade in artifacts and materials including obsidian and marine shells. A site excavated at Catalhoyuk in southern Turkey has revealed a settlement with 5,000 to 10,000 inhabitants which was a center of trade in obsidian. Perhaps 9,000 years old, this bull-worshiping community may have been the world's first city.

## The Earliest Civilized Societies

In the period between 4500 and 3500 B.C., urban settlements appeared in an area reclaimed from the swamp in the lower basin of the Tigris and Euphrates rivers. Another group of cities arose along the Nile. Pressed by natural adversity, these Sumerian and Egyptian peoples drained the swamps, constructed ditches, and irrigated fields. Such an enterprise, requiring a collective effort, produced a ruling class to administer the projects. The governing elite ruled by the authority of a local god; their function was to mediate between it and the community. The earliest Sumerian settlements were the cities of Uruk, Ur and Eridu. Uruk, the oldest, may have been founded around 4300 B.C. It grew sixfold in population between 3500 and 3000 B.C. and came to occupy 1,000 acres. In Egypt, the settlements appeared more suddenly, suggesting Sumerian influence. Settlements appeared both in the lower Delta region and in the Nile valley of Upper Egypt, to the south. The urbanization that began in the 4th millennium B.C. brought the first monarchies, a more stratified type of society, specialized occupations, expanded commerce and trade, ideographic writing, legal and accounting systems, walled cities, large-scale wars, and more elaborate burial arrangements.

brick making in Egypt    (Thebes)

Western historians have taught that Egypt and Mesopotamia were the cradles of civilization. However, it is possible that a sophisticated type of society appeared at an earlier date in India. Several verses in the Rig Veda refer to the winter solstice as beginning in Aries, which would be consistent with astronomical conditions in the 7th millennium B.C. We do know, anyhow, that a highly developed civilization existed in India prior to the Aryan invasion of the 16th Century B.C. Archeological ruins excavated at Harappa and Mohenjo-daro reveal the remains of a technologically advanced culture that existed in the 3rd millennium B.C. Its cities were laid out in a regular grid of streets, with ample provision for water supply, drainage, and public baths. Its people enjoyed a diet of wheat and barley, and wore cotton clothing. Its undeciphered script was perhaps of Dravidian origin. Seals found from this period indicate early Shiva worship. Pre-Aryan Indian society expanded from its place of origin in the Indus and Sarasvati valleys to include territories near the Ganges river. This civilization disappeared in the period between 2000 and 1800 B.C. as the Sarasvati river dried up.

The civilization of China developed around 2000 B.C. on the site of an earlier Neolithic culture. Its relatively sudden appearance suggests contact with other cultures. Rulers of the Xia and, later, Shang dynasties established kingdoms in the basin of the Yellow river where they undertook modest irrigation projects. The first city-state, Erlitou, was founded in 1900 B.C. As in other places, the social classes became sharply differentiated by wealth. Warring kings fought for territory, and the strongest ones gained imperial dominion over territories in northern China. During the Shang period (16th to 11 centuries B.C.), horse-drawn chariots were introduced to the practice of war. A Chinese script was developed; its inscriptions can be found on oracle bones used for divination. Skilled artisans produced bronze vessels with a distinctive three-legged style. Powerful monarchs, accompanied by sacrificed slaves, were buried in lavish tombs. Chinese peasants cultivated rice as well as wheat and millet. They owned pigs and water buffalo. The Shang monarchy was overthrown in 1027 B.C. by the Chou, a vassal state located in the Wei River valley to the west. Continuing the culture of the previous regime, Western Chou kings ruled first from the capital city of Hao (near Xi'an) until 771 B.C. and then, as the Eastern Chou dynasty, from Loyang until 256 B.C.

Roughly contemporary with early Chinese society, the Minoan civilization flourished on Crete and neighboring islands as a satellite of the Sumerian. A forerunner of Greek civilization, it is known for its naturalistic fresco paintings and ceramic art. King Minos, after whom this society is named, built a palace at Knossos about 2000 B.C. The Minoans, rich in copper, conducted an active trade across the Mediterranean sea with the Egyptians, Greeks, and Lebanese until their civilization was destroyed through a series of natural and man-made disasters around 1200 B.C. Another center of commerce was the Persian Gulf, where trade in grain, oil, copper, textiles, precious metals, and pearls flowed between cities in Mesopotamia, northeast Arabia, and western India during the early 2nd millennium B.C. This trade ended with the demise of the Harappan society in India. The Elamite empire, situated to the north of the Persian Gulf in Iran,

Vaphio cup scroll (Achaean)

was a political and commercial power until it was destroyed by the Assyrians in 640 B.C. The Hittites, in present-day Turkey and northern Syria, were an Indo-European people who established a great empire in the 14th and 13th centuries, B.C. They were first to use weapons made of iron. The Minaean and Sabataean kingdoms of southern Arabia were also important civilizations starting in the late 2nd millennium B.C.

Civilization, defined here in terms of the tendency to build political and commercial empires, came to the other continents later than this. In sub-Saharan Africa, a prosperous trading empire arose in Ghana in the 3rd or 4th century A.D. which lasted for more than a thousand years. This was followed, in the 13th and 14th centuries, by the empire of Mali in the bend region of the Niger river; and by the Songhai empire, in the next two centuries. A Nubian dynasty ruled Egypt in the 8th and 7th centuries, B.C. until pushed back into the Sudan by the Assyrians. There, from its capital city of Meroë, the empire of Kush controlled lands watered by the Upper Nile river until the 4th century A.D., when it was conquered by the Ethiopian kingdom of Axum. The art of iron smelting gave it a military advantage over other African peoples. In the Americas, a large ceremonial center was constructed at La Florida in Peru around 1700 B.C. This society had already begun to use irrigation and terraced farming. The Andean culture produced excellent textiles, pottery, and metal tools. The Olmec civilization arose independently in southeast Mexico about this time. This society is known for creating huge stone heads and pottery with jaguar motifs. It developed the first Meso-American script. Both New World societies produced new varieties of foods, tobacco, and other useful plants.

## The First Mideastern Empires

World history in its first epoch follows the course of progress toward larger forms of political organization. A momentous event was King Narmer's conquest of Lower Egypt (near the Nile delta) around 3100 B.C. Then king of Upper Egypt, Narmer became the first Pharaoh, wearer of a "double crown". When we think of Pharaonic Egypt, we envision the massive stone monuments which these people left behind, such as the great pyramids or the Temple of Luxor. The pyramids at Gizah were tombs of Pharaohs belonging to Fourth Dynasty (2613-2495 B.C.). The mummified bodies of these great kings and their attendants were adorned with jewels and were provisioned with food to prepare for eternal life. The pyramids, like the ziggurat temples in Mesopotamia, were artificial mountains whose steps extended towards heaven. They became symbolic of solar rays used by the dead kings to join the sun-god Re. Once considered to be living gods, the Pharaohs later claimed the title "son of Re". Pharaoh was considered to be a god, begotten by Re on a human mother in a nonphysical act. With some interruptions, pharaonic dynasties gave Egypt political unity and stability for three millennia.

| Table 4-1 | | |
|---|---|---|
| Dynasties of the Egyptian Empire | | |
| 3000-2700 B.C. | Dynasties 1-2 | |
| 2700-2200 B.C. | Dynasties 3-6 | Old Kingdom |
| 2200-2100 B.C. | Dynasties 7-10 | interregnum |
| 2100-1788 B.C. | Dynasties 11-12 | Middle Kingdom |
| 1788-1580 B.C. | Dynasties 13-17 | |
| 1580-1090 B.C. | Dynasties 18-20 | New Kingdom |
| 1090-525 B.C. | Dynasties 21-26 | |
| 525-404 B.C. | Dynasty 27 | Persian rule |
| 404-332 B.C. | Dynasties 28-30 | semi-independent |
| 332-323 B.C. | | Alexander the Great |
| 323-30 B.C. | | Greek Ptolemies |

(See Table 4-1.) Pepi II, who ruled for 94 years, was the last Pharaoh of the Old Kingdom. He died in 2184 B.C.

The rites required for each departed king spawned a new contingent of priests who were a drag on the economy. Local princes, who had once been Pharaoh's officers, gained a hereditary right to their positions. They took control of the native Egyptian army and were able to thwart Pharaoh's attempt to regain power with Nubian mercenaries. The local princes reigned until the reestablishment of central government in the Middle Kingdom (1991-1786 B.C.) This pharaonic dynasty, which moved its capital to Thebes, did not revive the burdensome funeral practices of its predecessors. Its rulers built fortresses, not pyramids. However, they were unable to withstand the Hyksos invasion from Syria. Hyksos nomads ruled northern Egypt until 1567 B.C., when Ahmose I reunified the country and established the New Kingdom (1575-1087 B.C.). Egypt became a military power, seeking to control threats from Asia Minor. Pharaohs of the New Kingdom include Ramses II (believed to be the Pharaoh in *Exodus*), "King Tut" (Tutankhamen), and the religious visionary Ikhnaton. In the 1st millennium B.C., a Libyan regime ruled Egypt, followed by Nubians, Persians and Greeks. Cleopatra VII was the last ruler of the Greek Ptolemaic dynasty. With her death by suicide in 30 B.C., Egypt became a Roman province.

Political unification came more slowly in Mesopotamia. King Urukagina of Lagash (2378-2371 B.C.), conquered the neighboring city of Umma and established the first empire of Sumerian city-states. He was overthrown by another king, Lugalzaggisi, who annexed new territories to the north and west. Lugalzaggisi's empire was, in turn, conquered by a Semitic-speaking king, Sargon of Agade (2371-2316 B.C.) Sargon's Kingdom of Sumer and Akkad included most of the territory between the Persian Gulf and the Mediterranean Sea. This dynasty lasted until 2230 B.C., when Gutaean highlanders, infiltrating from the northeast, took control of the empire. Amorite tribes founded the city of Babylon during this period. Gutaean rule (2230-2120 B.C.) came to an end at the hand of a native Sumerian, Utukegal of Uruk. The king of Ur then seized power and established a dynasty which lasted until 2006 B.C. Next, Elamite subjects revolted, sacking the city of Ur. The empire was partitioned among several successor states, including Elam, Isin, Mari, Babylon, and Assyria. King Hammurabi of Babylon (1792-1750 B.C.) reunited most of these provinces in a nine-year military campaign. Though rich in cultural achievements, this Babylonian empire barely outlived Hammurabi's death. Then, Kassite barbarians attacked Babylon and the empire again splintered.

The Middle East was plagued by frequent wars during the millennium that followed the fall of Hammurabi's empire in 1743 B.C. When the Hittite king, Mursilis I, sacked Babylon in 1595 B.C., that gave the Kassites an opportunity to take control of the city. Their revived Sumerian empire lasted until 1169 B.C. After expelling the Hyksos kings from Egypt in the mid 16th century B.C., Pharaohs of the New Kingdom conquered lands in Syria and Palestine to forestall future invasions from that region. The Hittites became militarily aggressive in the 14th century B.C. By 1300 B.C., its empire was as powerful as Egypt's. The two military powers fought for control of Syria. The Hittites defeated Egypt at the battle of Kadesh (1286-85 B.C.) but later reached a peace settlement with the Egyptians partitioning Syria. This may have been the first time in history that two civilized empires went to war against each other. Meanwhile, Assyria was attacking settlements in Babylonia. To the west, Mycenaean Greeks destroyed Minoan palaces on Crete. Though its political structure was weak, the Babylonian civilization which existed during this period was culturally strong. Its mythology, science, and written language permeated the Near East. Even Pharaohs used the Akkadian language when communicating with their Asian subjects.

## Nomadic Invasions

A prominent theme of world history in the first epoch was recurring conflict between peoples living in civilized societies and barbarian nomads who preyed on their wealth. The nomads were remnants of preagricultural society who hunted for their food or tended herds of grazing animals. A thousand years of breeding had given them a new military weapon in the form of horses large and strong enough to support human riders. Used to disciplined migrations from one pasture ground to another, these nomads from the steppe were skilled at waging mobile war. Like a vibrating membrane stretched across the Eurasian continent, their raids and migrations from the unsettled interior touched scattered societies in China, India, Egypt, and the Middle East. In periodic incursions, the barbarians would encroach upon lands belonging to the settled peoples, sack the cities, pillage and steal. After attacking and defeating the civilized societies, the barbarian tribes sometimes settled down among them as a ruling class. It was customary then for the conquering barbarians to absorb the conquered people's culture. If, on the other hand, the civilized society was strong enough militarily, it repelled the invasion.

The barbarian aggression came in waves. There was, for instance, a time of nomadic restlessness in the first half of the 2nd millennium B.C. when Hyksos warriors from Canaan invaded Egypt, Mitanni tribes occupied Mesopotamia, Hittites and Kassites attacked Babylon, and unknown barbarians destroyed the ancient Minoan palaces on Crete. Sanskrit-speaking Aryans invaded northern India, overthrowing the earlier Dravidian society and establishing a caste system. The classical Vedic literature dates from this period. Another wave of barbarian invasion came between 1250 and 950 B.C., as diverse people migrating into the eastern Mediterranean region destroyed the Minoan and Hittite societies and put the Egyptian empire under stress. The attack upon Egypt came from Berbers and Libyans to the west, "seas peoples" from the northeast, Amorites, Philistines, and, perhaps, Israelites. Achaean and Dorian tribes meanwhile attacked the Mycenaean settlements in Greece. The Hittite empire was overrun by Thracians, Phrygians, and Assyrians. There was a third wave in the 8th and 7th centuries B.C., when Cimmerian nomads moved westward and camel-riding Arabs attacked the Assyrian empire. In 6th century B.C., Celtic tribes migrating from northwestern Europe invaded Italy, Greece, and Romania, briefly occupying the city of Rome.

### Militarism in the Middle East

As the settled people grew strong enough to withstand these nomadic pressures, the historical focus shifted to military com-

Sargon II of Assyria

petition between nations. Civilized nations such as the Phoenicians, Chaldaeans, Hebrews, and Greeks were formed from the hordes of people migrating into the east Mediterranean region towards the close of the 2nd millennium B.C. The kingdom of Assyria emerged from the rubble to become the dominant Near Eastern power. With Egypt weakened and the Hittite empire ruined, Assyrian armies in the course of three centuries conquered Aramaean cities in Syria, besieged the kingdom of Urartu (Armenia), destroyed the city of Babylon, and set a puppet ruler on the throne of Egypt. Assyrian treatment of conquered peoples was cruel. A rebellion broke out in Babylonia. Babylonians, Medes, and Persians joined forces against Assyria taking its capital city, Nineveh, in 612 B.C. The Babylonians under King Nebuchadnezzar were briefly the strongest power; then, the Medes. But, before long, a new empire had gained control of the whole region. Cyrus II, king of Persia, supplanted the king of Media in 550 B.C. He then conquered the kingdom of Lydia and, in 538 B.C., the neo-Babylonian empire. Cyrus' son, Cambyses, conquered Egypt in 525 B.C.

The Achaemenian empire of Persia was the largest, richest, and most powerful political empire seen to date. While adopting the religion of Zoroaster, its rulers followed a policy of religious tolerance towards subjected peoples including the Hebrews. Darius I (521-486 B.C.) seized the throne through assassination of Cyrus' second successor, Smerdis. Darius divided the empire into twenty satrapies which were responsible for local administration. He added Thrace and northwestern India to its territories and dug a canal between the Nile river and the Red Sea. A system of well-maintained roads connected cities within the empire. A mistake was Xerxes' decision to invade European Greece in 480 B.C. A coalition of Greek city-states, led by Athens, repelled that invasion. A century and a half later, Macedonian and Greek armies under Alexander the Great, in turn, invaded Persian territory in Asia. Alexander's army defeated the Persian forces under Darius III at the battle of Isis in 333 B.C. For the next

Alexander the Great

decade, Alexander engaged the Persians and other foes in a series of victorious battles, conquering not only Persian provinces in Iran and Babylonia, but in Syria, Egypt, Afghanistan, and parts of northern India as well.

Alexander's generals established royal dynasties in these various domains after their leader's untimely death in 323 B.C. City-states in southern Greece promptly revolted against Macedonian rule but were suppressed. Then the Macedonian generals fought among themselves. Macedonia had to contend both with opposition from the Greek Aetolian Confederation and Celtic migrants from the north before succumbing to the Romans in the 2nd century B.C. Seleucus I acquired most of Alexander's far-flung territories in Asia. His troops were soon expelled from the Indus Valley by Chandragupta, founder of the Mauryan empire. In the mid 3rd century B.C., the Seleucid empire was further reduced by the Parni barbarian occupation of Parthia and the secession of a Greek province in Uzbekistan. Another of Alexander's officers, Ptolemy I, founded a dynasty in Egypt and the southern half of Syria. This was perhaps the strongest of the Hellenic dynasties. Ptolemy's capital at the new city of Alexandria became a center of learning and trade. Seleucid emperors tried repeatedly but failed to wrest southern Syria from Egyptian rule. Conflicts between the southern Greek states and Macedon were equally inconclusive.

Though the successor states to Alexander's empire were weakened by continual warfare, they effectively spread Greek culture within their vast territories. Starting with Philippi in eastern Macedonia, Alexander and his father, Philip II, together founded more than 300 new cities. These cities were self-contained carriers of Greek culture. Typically, each had its own agora (market), theater, and gymnasium, which were public gathering places. The gymnasium housed intellectual as well as physical activities. Greek culture in the form of visual images, philosophy, and written language became associated with the social elite in each community. The common people tended to stick with their local traditions. Tensions between the hellenizers and local religious traditionalists underlay the Maccabean rebellion in Judaea. While Seleucus, like Alexander, encouraged mixing between the Greek and local peoples, the Ptolemaic regime kept important government posts in Greek hands. Social integration went furthest in the eastern part of Seleucus' empire which became the Bactrian kingdom. Athens remained the center of philosophy and drama. In addition to the Aristotelian and Platonic schools of philosophy, the Epicureans and Stoics attracted a broad following in the Hellenic world.

While Greek dynasties controlled the domain of Alexander's conquests, the center of geopolitical gravity meanwhile shifted to the western Mediterranean region. The Greeks had established colonies in Sicily and southern Italy during the 8th and 7th centuries B.C. The Phoenician colony of Carthage in north Africa attacked Greek settlements in Sicily in 480 B.C., but was defeated by an alliance led by Syracuse and Agrigentum. Syracuse made a bid to unify Italy during the reign of Dionysius I (405-367 B.C.). This failed because of conflict with Carthage and other Greek states. Dionysius II invited Plato to Syracuse to apply his political theories. However, in 344 B.C. Timoleon of Corinth overthrew Dionysius II and then forged an alliance between the Greek cities which expelled the Carthaginians from Sicily. After that, Greek fortunes in Italy went into a decline despite military assistance from mainland Greece. The Etruscans, a hellenized remnant of the extinct Hittite civilization, were a rising power in northern Italy during the 7th and 6th centuries B.C. Tarquin kings ruled the city of Rome for more than a century. The Etruscan bid to conquer Italy failed because they, too, were unable to maintain an effective alliance of city states. Additionally, Celtic tribes from beyond the Alps overran their domain.

## Rome's Emergence as a World Power

Once freed of Etruscan rule, Rome concluded peace treaties with Carthage which helped it to wage successful wars of aggression against its neighbors. Roman power doubled through the capture of the Etruscan city of Veii and its territories in 393-88 B.C. A war against the Samnite confederation between 343 and 272 B.C. and defeat of the Latin and Campanian federations in 335 B.C. brought more land under its control. By 264 B.C., Rome had unified peninsular Italy. In the process, the Roman government broke treaties with several states including Carthage. A war between Rome and Carthage between 264 and 241 B.C. brought much destruction but left Italy and most of Sicily in Roman hands. Rome now enjoyed naval supremacy in the western Mediterranean region. A second set of conflicts broke out in 221 B.C. From a base of operations in Spain, Carthaginian armies led by Hannibal marched with elephants across the Pyrenees and Alps mountains into the Po Valley of northern Italy. Hannibal's armies thrice defeated their Roman counterparts in brilliantly executed battles. In the end, however, the Romans successfully defended against the Carthaginian invaders. Roman armies under Publius Cornelius Scipio counterattacked in Spain and, in 202 B.C., captured Carthage itself.

Rome controlled most lands bordering the western Mediterranean sea at the beginning of the 2nd century B.C. By the end of that century, the eastern shores would be added to its territories. A war broke out between the Greek Aetolian League and an alliance headed by Macedon in 220 B.C. Macedon became allied with Carthage, and Aetolia sided with Rome. After Hannibal's defeat, Rome, with Aetolia's help, defeated the Macedonians at Cynosecephalae in 197 B.C. and stripped Macedon of her possessions in southern Greece and Asia Minor. Rome inflicted a similar defeat upon Sparta in the same year. In 192 B.C., Aetolia and the Seleucid empire together went to war against Rome. It took the Romans two years to defeat the Seleucid emperor Antiochus III at Magnesium-under-Sipylus, and three years to defeat Aetolia. The Seleucid empire was forced to cede land to Rome and pay a heavy indemnity. The Aetolian League was effectively finished. Finally, Rome liquidated the kingdom of Macedonia in a hard-fought war lasting from 171 to 168 B.C. Alexander's homeland became a Roman province. Rome's reputation as a military power was now so great that a single warning from a Roman diplomat caused the Seleucid emperor Antiochus IV to vacate Egypt in 168 B.C.

Rome's object then was to cut down potential military rivals; it made no attempt to build its own empire for another hundred years. Rome had won the struggle for geopolitical advantage through a combination of shrewd diplomacy and military might. To gain control of Italian territory, it would make alliances to ensure peace with a powerful adversary while picking off smaller states one by one. Then Rome would jilt the ally when its services were no longer needed. Additionally, its constitution proved attractive to peoples living in politically backward states. The system of dual citizenship helped to harmonize local and imperial interests. Customarily, the Roman oligarchs supported their wealthy counterparts in other states. This assured them of support from a powerful fifth column in enemy nations. Roman society was itself split sharply between the rich and poor classes. The rich acquired their wealth as landowners, tax-farmers, speculators, and government creditors. Increasingly, small farmers joined the ranks of the poor as they were pressed into military service and their neglected farms were picked up by wealthy speculators. To address this injustice, Tiberius Gracchus in 133 B.C. proposed and enacted a law that would limit the size of land holdings. Aristocrats in the Roman Senate assassinated him.

The continuation of plutocratic government led to an economy based on slave labor and private armies comprised of recruits from the poorer classes. The slaves, taken captive in war, were put to work on large plantations that raised cattle and sheep or cultivated olives and grapes. Slave uprisings took place in Sicily, Greece, and on the island of Delos during the late 2nd century B.C. A slave army led by a gladiator named Spartacus overran much of the Italian countryside between 73 and 71 B.C.

While serving as Consul, the Roman general Caius Marius raised an army of paupers with the understanding that he would look out after their interests in exchange for military service. Thus began a period of rule by revolutionary warlords lasting from 108 to 30 B.C. A triumvirate which consisted of Pompey the Great, Julius Caesar, and Marcus Crassus took control of the Roman government in 60 B.C. Pompey completed the Roman conquest of Armenia, Syria, and Judaea before losing out to Caesar in a power struggle.

Julius Caesar

Crassus was killed in a battle with the Parthians in 53 B.C. Julius Caesar extended Roman rule to lands north of the Alps in a successful military campaign. He then became sole dictator in Rome and acted in that capacity for two years before being assassinated by two colleagues in 44 B.C.

A new triumvirate emerged consisting of Mark Antony, Lepidus, and Caesar's adopted nephew Octavian. Octavian defeated Antony and Cleopatra, Egypt's last queen, in a naval battle at Actium in 33 B.C. He located Caesarion, the teenage son of Cleopatra and Julius Caesar, and had him killed. Now possessing absolute power, Octavian became the first Roman emperor. Octavian, or Augustus Caesar, developed a new form of Roman

Augustus Caesar

government based upon a deified state, a professional army, and civil servants. Augustus reformed the system of private armies by employing career soldiers. He replaced private tax collectors and administrators with a "Caesar's household" of slaves and freedmen to serve as his personal staff. Modestly limiting his own title to "princeps of the Senate", Augustus nevertheless tolerated the cult of emperor worship which his uncle had begun. He developed a three-step process by which individuals from defeated nations might become Roman citizens. The Roman Senate, a relic of republican government, was keeper of Rome's traditional ways, but the real power belonged to emperors enjoying the support of the armed forces.

Roman governments had traditionally been reluctant to assume direct responsibility for governing conquered lands. Augustus and his successors organized the Roman empire as an association of autonomous city-states that were restrained from going to war against each other. The central government in Rome provided for their common defense against external enemies. Forsaking further conquests, Augustus sought to establish defensible borders for the empire. His attempt to extend its territory to the Elbe river came to grief when Germanic tribes annihilated three Roman armies at the Teutoburg forest in 9 A.D. The border fell back to the Danube river. Rome's depopulation which had begun in the 1st century B.C. now limited military options. Between 114 and 117 A.D., the emperor Trajan tried to conquer Armenia, Babylonia, and Mesopotamia from the

Parthians. Those expeditions ended in disaster. Trajan's successor, Hadrian, pulled back to the Euphrates river. Military tension continued along the southeastern border after the Parthian king was overthrown by his vassal, Shahpuhr I, who founded the Sasanian dynasty. Shahpuhr thrice defeated Roman armies, capturing the emperor Valerian in 260 A.D. However, a counterattack delivered by Rome's ally, the prince of Palmyra, drove the Persians back. The Romano-Persian wars of 337-60 A.D. were likewise inconclusive.

The Julian dynasty of emperors came to an end in 68 A.D. with the death of Nero. (See Table 4-2.) After three decades of military rulers, Rome was governed by five "wise and temperate" emperors whose combined reign lasted until 180 A.D. The last, Marcus Aurelius, is remembered for a book of philosophical *Meditations*. The reign of his son, Commodus, marked the beginning of a series of despotic emperors and military usurpers who were generally hostile to Christianity. Many lasted for

---

Table 4-2

### Dynasties of the Roman Empire

| | |
|---|---|
| 31 B.C.-68 A.D. | Augustus to Nero |
| 68-96 A.D. | Galba to Domitian |
| 96-180 A.D. | Nerva to Marcus Aurelius |
| 180-305 A.D. | Commodus to Diocletian |
| 305-395 A.D. | Constantine to Theodosius |
| 395-476 A.D. | Honorius to Romulus Augustulus (emperors of the West) |
| 395-618 A.D. | Arcadius to Phocas (emperors of the East) |

Eastern Byzantine dynasties:

| | |
|---|---|
| 610-717 A.D. | Heraclian dynasty |
| 717-867 A.D. | Isaurian dynasty |
| 867-1081 A.D. | Macedonian dynasty |
| 1081-1258 A.D. | Comnenian dynasty |
| 1258-1453 A.D. | Palaeologan dynasty |

only a year or two. The exceptions were Diocletian (284-305 A.D.) and Constantine I (306-337 A.D.) These two able emperors created a mobile army to deal with insurrections and invasions, restored the debased Roman currency, resurveyed the land and adjusted taxes. Constantine I split his vast empire into two administrative districts. He established a new capital city for the eastern half in 330 A.D. It was called Constantinople. The period between 250 and 311 A.D. had seen an intense effort by Roman emperors to suppress Christianity. However, Galerius rescinded an anti-Christian edict on his death bed in 311 A.D. Two years later, Constantine adopted a policy of religious tolerance. Alaric, king of the Visigoths, sacked Rome in 410 A.D. The last western emperor, Romulus Augustulus, was deposed in 476 A.D.

## Hunnish and Scandinavian Eruptions

The western Roman Empire, headquartered in Rome, showed signs of internal weakness in the late 4th century A.D. Big landowners diverted the peasants' agricultural surplus from the tax collector to themselves. The government became a dictatorship under the control of the military high command. After the Visigoths defeated the Roman armies at Adrianople in 378 A.D., Rome's European frontier was severely exposed. The Visigoths had been driven into Roman territory by advancing hordes of Alanic and Ostrogothic tribes who had, in turn, been dislodged from their east European homelands by Huns moving west. East Germanic tribes broke through the Roman defenses on the Rhine river around 406 A.D. The Vandals from Jutland traveled across southern Europe to Spain and, in 429 A.D., crossed over to north Africa where they established a maritime empire. Ostrogoths and Lombards spread havoc in Italy. Angles, Saxons, and Jutes occupied Britain. With the West Roman Empire ravished by other barbarian tribes, Attila and his hordes invaded northern Italy in 452 A.D. Reportedly, Pope Leo I persuaded him not to attack Rome. Attila withdrew from Italy and died a year later.

Chinese society had felt Hun pressure a full century before Rome fell. In 316 A.D., an attacking horde of Hsiung-nu (Hun) barbarians overthrew the Western Chin dynasty and partitioned northern China between several successor states. A half century later, another Hun tribe migrated into the territory between the Don and Volga rivers, dislodging the Visigoths and setting in motion the migration of Germanic tribes across Europe. A remnant of Attila's horde settled down in western Hungary. Ephthalite Huns defeated and killed the Sasanian emperor Peroz in 484 A.D., forcing the Persians to pay tribute to them for almost a century. Then an alliance between Persians and Turks overthrew the Ephthalite empire and partitioned its territories. White Huns attacked and shattered the Indian Gupta empire in 455 A.D. Most of this empire fell within ten years, although a remnant of the Gupta dynasty continued in Bengal until 544 A.D. Descendants of the Hunnish warriors, converted to Hinduism, survived in the Rajput aristocracy which dominates the state of Rajasthan in northwestern India.

The Frankish king Clovis began to build a Gallic empire in the late 5th century A.D. He conquered the Alamanni tribe along the Rhine in 496 A.D., defeated the Spanish Visigoths in 507 A.D., and by the time of his death in 511 A.D. controlled all of Gaul except Provence. His successors annexed Thuringia and Burgundy. Clovis and his heirs embraced the Roman Catholic Christianity unlike most other Germanic kings who had converted to the Arian faith. After acquiring a huge domain, the Merovingian dynasty of Clovis became internally weakened because of its practice of dividing territory among several heirs upon a monarch's death. The Arnulfing family, majordomos in the Merovingian household, effectively ran the government. One of its members, Pippin III, requested that Pope Zacharias recognize his family's claim to the throne. Upon obtaining a favorable response to this request, Pippin deposed the Merovingian king and began his own Carolingian dynasty. When the Lombards captured Ravenna in northern Italy and threatened to take Rome,

Pope Stephen II requested Frankish aid. Pippin sent troops to Italy and defeated the Lombards in 756 A.D.

Pippin's son, Charles, became sole ruler of the Franks in 771 A.D. when his brother, who was co-ruler, unexpectedly died. Charles, today known as Charlemagne, annexed the Lombard kingdom in Italy in 773-74 A.D. He exterminated the Avars in Hungary between 791 and 805 A.D. A more difficult military task was the conquest of Saxony between 772 and 802 A.D. This brought Charlemagne's empire in direct contact with the Danes, who responded by launching naval raids upon its territories. The empire now encompassed most of present-day Germany, France, Italy, and the Benelux countries. For all practical purposes, Charlemagne had revived the West Roman Empire. In recognition of that fact, Pope Leo III crowned him Emperor of the Romans on Christmas Day 800 A.D. Because the East Roman emperors retained the right to that title, Charlemagne made certain territorial concessions to Byzantium to obtain its recognition and consent. His empire lacked a corps of literate administrators, so Charlemagne brought in the Northumbrian cleric, Alcuin, and others to establish palace and cathedral schools. Itinerant inspectors kept a close watch on local officials. After Charlemagne's death in 814 A.D., these officials assumed power. Charlemagne's heir, Louis the Pious, divided the empire among his three sons. Problems grew worse with Viking and North African pirates.

Viking ship

The Viking eruption of the 9th and 10th centuries A.D. was a consequence of Charlemagne's conquest of Saxon territory, which had been a buffer zone between the Scandinavian barbarians and Roman civilization. Its first casualties were Christian monasteries along the coast of Britain, Ireland, and France. In 880 A.D., Rhos adventurers from Sweden on the Baltic Sea navigated the inland waterways of Russia to reach the Caspian Sea. Another group of Scandinavians sailed across the North Atlantic ocean to Greenland, Iceland, and

Vinland in North America. Despite their ferocity, the king of West Francia, Charles the Simple, invited Scandinavian seafarers in 911 A.D. to settle the coast of Normandy on condition that they converted to Christianity. King Alfred of England had made a similar proposition to Danish invaders in 878 A.D. The Scandinavian immigrants proved receptive to the Frankish culture and religion. The seeds of several future European nations were sown in this period. The modern nation of France took shape as the Counts of Paris successfully defended against Scandinavian attackers between 885 and 887 A.D. Rhos Swedes settling at the cities of Novgorod and Kiev gave Russia its name. In 1066 A.D., descendants of the Norman settlers successfully invaded England. English dynastic history usually begins with this event.

## Continuation of the Roman Empire in the East

The East Roman empire, headquartered in Constantinople, did not fall when Germanic barbarians overran the western territories controlled by Rome. This government was staffed with professionals loyal to the state rather than big landowners. It had a citizen rather than mercenary army. The East Roman emperors of the 5th century A.D. were able administrators and legal reformers who kept state finances under control. They built a wall around their capital city and made strategic concessions to the barbarian invaders that allowed them to survive. Among the Byzantine emperors, the best-known may be Justinian I (527-565 A.D.) who built the church of Hagia Sophia and codified Roman law. This emperor also reconquered northwest Africa from the Vandals, drove the Ostrogoths from Italy and Illyricum (Dalmatia), and restored Roman naval superiority in the Mediterranean sea. However, the 26-year campaign against the Ostrogoths drained the imperial treasury. Ruinous taxes were imposed upon the Levantine provinces. Lombard tribes invaded Italy seven years after the Ostrogoths had been expelled. During the war of 572-91 A.D. against the Sasanian Persian empire, Slavs and Avars entered the Balkan provinces unopposed.

Though later expelled, the Slavs returned during the Romano-Persian war of 604-28 A.D. This time, they stayed.

In 633 A.D., Islamic armies led by Mohammed's successor Abu Bakr attacked both the East Roman and Sasanian empires, exhausted from their recent war. The Persian empire was destroyed. The East Roman empire survived with great loss of territory. The Arabs laid siege to Constantinople in 674-78 A.D. and again in 717-18 A.D. but were unable to penetrate its walls. Another military threat came from the Slavic settlers in the Balkan peninsula after Turkish-speaking Bulgars occupying land between the Danube river and Black Sea had founded a rival state. The Romans and Bulgarians competed for the allegiance of Slavic peoples in that region. Constantine V was unable to destroy the Bulgarian state in a twenty-year war but the Byzantine empire did later subjugate most Slavs living on the Greek peninsula. Another lengthy war was waged against Paulician Christians in the northeast. The result of the frequent warfare was depopulation. This worked to the advantage of the peasants who comprised the militia defending the empire against Arab raids. After the loss of Sicily to the Moslems, the East Roman government needed to prevent its Sicilian and Bulgarian opponents from making contact. However, it made few attempts to recover its former possessions in the Mediterranean other than Crete.

Through that turmoil, the East Roman empire developed a distinctive culture that combined Greek and Slavic elements. Its society retained the religion shared with west Europeans but reverted to exclusive use of the Greek language. In the 4th century A.D., the Cappadocian Christian fathers, St. Basil, St. Gregory of Nyssa, and St. Gregory Nazianzene, produced a body of neo-Attic Greek literature which became a model for future writings. A Syrian Jewish convert to Christianity, Romanus the Composer, was instrumental in creating the Byzantine style of music and liturgical poetry. A cultural renaissance took place during the 9th century administration of Photius, Patriarch of Constantinople, who sent scholar-missionaries to Khazar Turks in the Ukraine. They brought with them the Glagolitic alphabet which had been developed for Slavic peoples in Greece. The Khazars were committed to Judaism, so the Byzantine missionaries moved on to the Slavic principality of Great Moravia (Czecho-slovakia). When the Frankish church cracked down on this mission, refugee clergy next went to Bulgaria. Here a new script, Cyrillic, was developed as a simpler alternative to the Glagolitic alphabet. This script was used by subsequent Slavic converts to Orthodox Christianity.

As the first millennium A.D. drew to a close, the Byzantine Greek culture and religion had spread northward into Russia, despite its earlier settlement by Swedes. Prince Vladimir of Kiev was baptized in this faith in 989 A.D. Vladimir then married Emperor Basil II's sister Anna. His religious conversion brought Greek art and liturgy into Russia, along with the Cyrillic alphabet. Meanwhile, high taxes combined with crop failure in the severely cold winter of 927-28 A.D. forced many peasants to sell their land to big landowners. Landlord-aristocrats in Asia Minor, supported by the peasants, engaged in five insurrections against the imperial government between 963 and 1057 A.D. The government launched military offensives against Moslem bases in Sicily and Crete and, with the help of mercenary soldiers, finally conquered Bulgaria. However, this 40-year war was financially ruinous. The peasant militia which had served the empire so well in defensive actions was not motivated to fight for imperial expansion. Not long after the Roman government reoccupied Syracuse, adventurers from Normandy captured key positions in southern Italy. Saljuq Turks who had been menacing Armenia took Emperor Romanus IV prisoner in 1071 and soon controlled most of the empire's former territories in Asia Minor.

The East Roman empire was now under attack from Norman Christians as well as Ghuzz barbarians and Saljuq Turks of the Rum kingdom. The First Crusade (1095-99) brought western Christian armies to Constantinople. Emperor Alexis I tried to enlist their help in ousting the Turks but the European princes were mainly interested in capturing Jerusalem. A Latin Kingdom of Jerusalem was established in 1099. However, Saladin took the city back less than a century later. The Third Crusade (1189-92), undertaken in response to that event, failed to retake the city from the Moslems. After Western businessmen were massacred in Constantinople, the Normans retaliated by sacking Thes-salonica. Serbia and Bulgaria threw off Byzantine rule. The Fourth Crusade (1202-04) was diverted from its original purpose into a scheme to overthrow the imperial dynasty. An army of Vene-tians and French crusaders assaulted, captured, and looted Con-stantinople in 1204. The Venetians took valuable land pos-sessions, while a Frenchman, Baldwin I, became Emperor of Constantinople. Seceding Greek city-states in Asia Minor then set up their own empire at Nicaea. The Nicaean Greeks and Bul-garians together laid siege to Constantinople, which fell in 1261.

The Nicaean Greeks regained Constantinople at the cost of losing most of their Asian lands to the Ottoman Turks. Serbia was also becoming a major power in Europe. If that were not enough, a civil war broke out within the East Roman empire between 1341 and 1347 reflecting both theological disagreements and conflict between large and small landowners. The empire was doomed. Emperor Michael VIII Palaeologus realized that he needed the support of western Christians. He and several successors recognized the Pope's ecclesiastical authority. An Act of Union with the western church was signed by the Emperor and top religious officials at Florence in 1439. However, the mass of Eastern Orthodox clergy and laity rejected this agreement. Most Greeks preferred Ottoman rule to domination by western Christians. The Russian Orthodox hierarchy repudiated the Met-ropolitan who had signed the agreement in Florence and replaced him with a Russian native. The Turks meanwhile tightened their land blockade. The East Roman empire came to an end when the Ottoman Turks captured Constantinople in 1451 A.D. The Turkish rulers gave the Patriarch of Constantinople political au-thority over the non-Moslem communities. Greeks played a lead-ing role in the political and commercial life of the ensuing Otto-man empire.

### Parthian, Kushan, and Sasanian Empires

When Roman power was at its peak in the 2nd century A.D., four contiguous political empires controlled much of the Old World. Besides Rome, there were the Parthian empire in Persia, the Kushan empire in Afghanistan and northwestern India, and the eastern Han empire in China. These four empires extended across north Africa and Europe through southern Asia to the Far East. To their north was a wilderness extending from Scandinavia and Germany to Mongolia and Siberia; to their south, the Saharan and Arabian deserts, southern and eastern India, southeast Asia, and Indonesia. Rome and China, at the extremities, were dimly aware of each other's existence. The Parthian and Kushan empires, occupying a middle position, were in direct contact with the others. Their merchants acted as middlemen for overland trade. This was the culmination of Civl. Each of the four empires was ruled by hereditary monarchs exercising nearly absolute power. Each empire, representing a consolidation of political and military power among warring kingdoms, brought peace and stability to its region. This situation came to an end with the Hun uprisings, which overthrew the Eastern Han dynasty of China in the 3rd century A.D. and destroyed the West Roman empire two centuries later.

Of the four empires, only the Chinese had not been touched by Alexander's conquests in the 4th century B.C. The Roman, Parthian, and Kushan empires were heirs of Greek civilization. All three fell at least partially within the vast territory which Seleucus had inherited from Alexander but could not retain. Long afterwards, Greek culture continued to have a strong influence in those places. Mixed with local traditions, it became an element in the syncretizing process of creating world religions. Bactria (northern Afghanistan) went farthest with the hellenizing process. The Kushan empire, located there, became a cultural cauldron in which Greek philosophy and visual art transformed Buddhism into a religion of personal images. The realism of Praxiteles was applied to images of the divine. It was this Buddhism, in the Mahayana form, which penetrated China beginning in the 2nd century A.D.

As Rome conquered western lands possessed by the Greek dynasties, so the Parthian and Kushan empires began with nomadic invasions in the eastern part of the Seleucid empire. Parni nomads from Türkmenistan, led by Arsaces, freed themselves from Seleucid rule around 250 B.C. and established the Parthian kingdom in northeastern Iran. Kin to the Scythians, they were horsemen and archers of great ability. In 141 B.C., the Parthians under Mithridates I conquered Media and Babylonia from the Greeks. They took the Seleucid emperor Demetrius II prisoner when he tried to regain the lost territory. The Arsacid dynasty

moved its capital to Ctesiphon, a suburb of Seleucia-on-Tigris. The Romans fared no better against Parthian arrows. An army led by Marcus Crassus was annihilated when it invaded Mesopotamia in 53 B.C. Trajan's attempt in 114-17 A.D. to annex Armenia, Mesopotamia, and Babylonia ended in disaster. Neither, however, were the Parthians able to make significant inroads into Roman

Mithradites I

territory. Hadrian set the Roman Empire's eastern boundary at the Euphrates river. The Arsacid Parthian dynasty lasted until 224 A.D. when its last emperor, Artabanus V, was overthrown and supplanted by his Persian vassal, Ardeshir I, founder of the Sasanian (Second) Persian empire.

The Kushan empire was formed in 48 A.D. with the invasion of northwest India by another nomadic people, Kushans or Yüeh-chih, living in Bactria. The process began when a Greek governor of Bactria seceded from the Seleucid empire in 250 B.C. and established a separate kingdom. Exploiting a power vacuum with the collapse of the Mauryan dynasty, the Bactrian Greeks seized parts of northern India around 200 B.C. However, the Greek princes fought among themselves. In a weakened state, their kingdoms were overrun sixty years later by Saka (Scythian) nomads driven southward by the Yüeh-chih from Gansu in western China. Although the neighboring Parthians were also attacked, they managed to divert the Sakas to an area in southern Afghanistan from which they overran Greek settlements in the Indus Valley. The Parthians subsequently imposed their rule upon the Indian Saka states. Around 100 B.C., the Yüeh-chih invaded and occupied Bactria, then under Saka rule. Part of this tribe, the Kushans, moved into the Indus Valley in the 1st century, A.D., conquering both the Partho-Sakas there and an independent Saka state farther south. Their empire thus encompassed

Bactria and northwest India on both sides of the Hindu Kush. During the nearly two centuries of its existence, the Kushan empire was a bridge between the Indian and Chinese cultures.

After Ardeshir I overthrew and supplanted the Parthian Arsacid dynasty in 224 A.D., Sasanian Persia attacked the Roman empire's eastern provinces but was driven back from all but Armenia. The Kushan empire fell to Ardeshir's armies in 241 A.D., though a remnant may have lasted in the Kabul valley until the 11th century A.D. Before gaining political power, the Sasanid family had been hereditary priests of Anahita, an Iranian water goddess later associated with Ahura Mazda, the Zoroastrian chief god, in the Magian cult. Zoroastrianism in Magian form became the official religion of the Sasanian empire. However, another major religion, Manichaeism, appeared during the reign of Shahphur I (242-273 A.D.), when a Persian prophet named Mani was given permission to preach. Kartir, a Zoroastrian priest seeking to uphold

Ardeshir I

Zoroastrianism as the Sasanian state religion, persuaded Shahphur's second successor, Vahram I, to arrest and execute Mani. The Sasanid emperors saw themselves as successors to emperors of the pre-Greek Achaemenian dynasty who had made Persia a world power. Their military aggression directed against the Romans, Armenians, Kushans, and others was intended to restore the Persian empire to its former greatness.

The Sasanian and Roman empires were engaged in a military and religious struggle for nearly four centuries. The Romano-Persian war of 337-60 A.D. ended inconclusively. The Roman emperor Julian was killed while invading Persia in 362. His successor, Jovian, had to cede five Armenian provinces to Persia in order to extricate the Roman forces. Christians living in Persia were suspected of being a Roman fifth column. The reverse was true, from a Roman perspective, of Manichees living in the Roman empire. Shahphur II began persecuting Christians in 339 A.D. The persecution was lifted a half century later. In 440 A.D., Emperor Yazdigerd II ordered all his subjects to convert to the Zoroastrian religion, causing a series of revolts in the Armenian

Varahran II receiving the submission of the Segestani

provinces. In 484, Ephthalite Huns occupied eastern territories belonging to the former Kushan empire. Emperor Peroz was killed in battle, and the Persians had to pay tribute to the Huns. This military disaster caused a social revolution in Persia. A communistic sect of the Manichaean religion, Mazdakism, stirred the poor masses in opposition to the Zoroastrian clergy and wealthy noblemen. When emperor Kavadh I converted to this religion, its program was put into effect.

One of Kavadh's sons, later Khusro I, persuaded his father to disavow Mazdakism. He then proceeded to crush this sect. As emperor, Khusro I (531-79 A.D.) decentralized the military and instituted certain economic reforms to alleviate conditions that had caused the Mazdakite movement. Allied with the Turks, he overthrew the Ephthalite empire in 563-67 A.D. It was partitioned along the lines of the Oxus river. In 572, Khusro began a war with the East Roman empire which lasted for 18 years. The war's unpopularity caused his son and successor, Hormizd IV, to be murdered. The East Roman emperor, Maurice, unseated the Persian usurper and put Hormizd IV's son, Khusro II, on the throne. Emperor Maurice then was killed in a mutiny. To avenge his benefactor's death, Khusro II invaded the East Roman Empire. This last Romano-Persian war, lasting from 604 to 628 A.D., was the bloodiest of all. It ended, upon Khusro II's death, with a treaty restoring territories to the situation before the war. Weakened by this conflict, the Sasanian empire was in no shape to withstand the Arab armies which attacked Persia in 633 A.D. The Islamic conquest was complete by 651.

## India

The Aryan conquerors of India built a new society on the ruins of an earlier civilization when they invaded this region in the middle of the 2nd millennium B.C. A system of hereditary castes determined its class structure. Brahman priests controlled the rituals believed necessary for a prosperous and healthy life. There was a rich religious literature written in the Sanskrit language consisting of hymns, rituals, poetic narratives, and philosophical discussions. A second wave of nomadic immigrants entered northwest India around 600 B.C. The political center of gravity moved eastward from the Indus to the Ganges valley. A group of small kingdoms there was ruled by descendants of the Aryan warriors. The two strongest were Kosala (Uttar Pradesh) and Magadha (Bihar) in the northeast. The ruler of the Magadha kingdom, Bimbisara, attempted to create an empire. It was in this environment of small warring states that the religious thinkers Mahavira and Buddha lived and preached during the late 6th century B.C. In 518 B.C., the Persian emperor Darius I invaded and annexed the western part of the Indus valley. In 478 B.C. Prince Vijaya sailed from Gujarat to the island of Sri Lanka where he founded a Singhalese kingdom. Alexander the Great penetrated deep into the Indus Valley in 327-25 B.C. and left several garrisons.

Around 322 B.C., Chandragupta I, founder of the Mauryan empire, expelled the garrisons which Alexander had left in northwest India. He went on to conquer the kingdom of Magadha. In 305 B.C., Seleucus I attempted to recover the lost Indian territories but was defeated by Chandragupta's army. (After making peace with the Indians, Seleucus purchased 500 war-elephants for use in a forthcoming campaign against Antigonus I of Macedon.) Chandragupta received certain Greek territories in exchange. His grandson, Asoka, conquered the southeastern kingdom of Kalinga in 261 B.C. Asoka's empire now included most of the Indian subcontinent with the exception of the southern tip. After defeating Kalinga, the emperor suddenly repented of further conquests and became a lay member of a Buddhist order. He spent his remaining years promoting Buddhism and issuing moral edicts. His government was an intrusive, authoritarian bureaucracy bent on ethical reform. It tried to curb wasteful rituals and improve economic efficiency. Much of what we know about Asoka comes from multilingual inscriptions in stone slabs which he placed about his realm. The Mauryan empire began to disintegrate not long after Asoka's death in 232 B.C. and was extinguished in 185 B.C.

India was again divided into warring kingdoms during the next five hundred years. During the 2nd century B.C., Greek princes of Bactria occupied a part of northern India until Saka nomads overran their territories. The kingdom of Kalinga regained its freedom and became militarily aggressive. The Sunga dynasty, founded by the general who had assassinated the last Mauryan emperor, took possession of Bihar and Uttar Pradesh including Pataliputra, Asoka's former capital city. Another dynasty, the Andhras, controlled most of the Deccan in south-central India. Saka principalities, satraps of the Kushan empire, occupied the west coast of India, south of the Indus valley. The Kushan empire itself controlled the northwest region. This empire and the Andhra kingdoms were both destroyed around 224 A.D. A period of political instability ensued. During this time, Indian culture and religion were undergoing a major transformation. Sanskrit literature experienced a revival under the Sunga and Kanva dynasties (185-27 B.C.) Mahayana Buddhism, a savior religion, developed from the original Buddhist teaching. The classic Tamil writings on ethics and statecraft were composed. New gods were added to the Hindu pantheon as Brahman authority was affirmed.

During the 4th century A.D., a fortuitous marriage reunited northern and southern Bihar. The Gupta dynasty thus began with the rule of another Chandragupta in 320 A.D. His son, Samudragupta, and grandson, Chandragupta II, enlarged its domain in the Jumna-Ganges basin and conquered the western Saka satrapy with its capital at Ujjain. This empire included northern India east to west but did not extend south beyond the Vindhya mountains. Though territorially less extensive than the Mauryan, the Gupta empire was no less culturally distinguished. The Guptas were Hindu Brahmans who were tolerant of other religions. Samudragupta surrounded himself at court with accomplished artists and scholars. Indian sculpture, literature, and astronomy then reached new heights. The Sanskrit poet and playwright, Kalidasa, lived during this time, as did Vatsyayana, author of the *Kamasutra*. The Laws of Manu, written around 400 A.D., are the classical expression of Hindu law. The game of chess was invented and the so-called "Arabic" numerals were first used. White Hun invasions between 455 and 544 A.D. extinguished this culturally brilliant society although it was briefly rekindled during Emperor Harsha's reign in the early 7th century A.D.

The Gupta dynasty ruled India's last indigenous empire. Thenceforth the prevailing pattern was that of foreign invaders from the north seeking to penetrate the Indian subcontinent and being assimilated by the Hindu culture. The Ephthalite Huns overran territories in the Oxus-Jaxartes basin. When Persians and Turks overthrew this northern kingdom in 563-67 A.D., many Huns migrated to India where their descendants, the Rajputs, became hereditary princes. Emperor Harsha reunited northern India in 606-12 A.D. His bid to expand southward was defeated by Palakeshin II of the Chalukya dynasty in 620, which was, in turn, defeated in 642 by the rival Pallava dynasty of southeast India. The Tamil-speaking Pandya kingdom continued to hold the southern tip of India throughout this period. Indian refugees from the Huns brought Hindu and Buddhist culture to southeast Asia and Indonesia. Tibet came within India's cultural orbit after an Indian script, adapted to the Tibetan language, was used to translate Mahayana Buddhist texts into Tibetan. That happened when a Tibetan army, incited by a Chinese diplomat, successfully invaded India to punish a usurper after Harsha's death in 647 A.D. and was "captured" by the Indian culture.

Table 4-3

## Some Headline Events in the History of Civilization I

| | |
|---|---|
| c. 3000 B.C. | Pharaoh Narmer unites Upper and Lower Egypt. |
| c. 2589 B.C. | Pharaoh Cheops begins reign. |
| c. 2420 B.C. | Pepi II's death ends Old Kingdom of Egypt. |
| c. 2378 B.C. | Urukagina of Lagash creates Sumerian empire. |
| c. 2371 B.C. | Lugalzaggisi conquers Urukagina's empire. |
| c. 2340 B.C. | Sargon I, king of Akkad, conquers Sumerians. |
| c. 2230 B.C. | Sargon's dynasty overthrown by Gutaeans. |
| c. 2100 B.C. | Legal code of Ur-Nammu instituted. |
| c. 2040 B.C. | Egyptian Middle Kingdom begins. |
| c. 1792 B.C. | Hammurabi becomes king of Babylon. |
| c. 1732 B.C. | Kassites found dynasty in Babylon. |
| c. 1720 B.C. | Hyksos tribes invade Egypt. |
| c. 1595 B.C. | Hittites sack Babylon. |
| c. 1570 B.C. | Ahmose I expels Hyksos from Egypt. |
| c. 1500 B.C. | Aryans invade India. |
| c. 1400 B.C. | Mycenaean Greeks destroy palaces on Crete. |
| c. 1270 B.C. | Ramses II signs peace treaty with Hittites. |
| c. 1200 B.C. | Mycenaean palaces in Greece sacked. |
| c. 1087 B.C. | Egyptian New Kingdom overthrown. |
| c. 1027 B.C. | Chou kings overthrow Shang dynasty in China. |
| c. 1000 B.C. | David captures Jerusalem from Jebusites. |
| 753 B.C. | Rome founded. |
| 745 B.C. | Assyrian Tiglath-Pileser III conquers Babylonia. |
| 606 B.C. | Babylonians and Medes destroy Nineveh. |
| 605 B.C. | Nebuchadnezzar defeats Pharaoh Necho. |
| 550 B.C. | Persian king Cyrus II conquers Media. |
| 539 B.C. | Cyrus II founds Persian empire. |
| 525 B.C. | Cambyses of Persia conquers Egypt. |
| 480 B.C. | Greeks repel Persian invasion of Europe. |
| 333 B.C. | Alexander defeats Darius at battle of Isis. |
| 323 B.C. | Alexander dies. |
| 311 B.C. | Seleucus Nicator occupies Babylon. |
| 303 B.C. | Chandragupta defeats Seleucus I in India. |
| 247 B.C. | Arsaces I founds Parthian kingdom. |

## History of CivI  (continued)

| | |
|---|---|
| 221 B.C. | Shih Hwang-ti establishes Chinese empire. |
| 216 B.C. | Hannibal defeats Romans at battle of Cannae. |
| 214 B.C. | Construction begins on Great Wall of China. |
| 197 B.C. | Romans defeat Philip V of Macedon. |
| 146 B.C. | Carthage destroyed after third Punic war. |
| 133 B.C. | Tiberius Gracchus is murdered. |
| 71 B.C. | Romans crush Spartacus' slave rebellion. |
| 53 B.C. | Parthians kill Marcus Crassus. |
| 48 B.C. | Julius Caesar defeats Pompey at Pharsalus. |
| 44 B.C. | Julius Caesar assassinated. |
| 31 B.C. | Octavian defeats Anthony and Cleopatra. |
| 9 A.D. | Germans annihilate three Roman legions. |
| 200 A.D. | Han dynasty overthrown. |
| 227A.D. | Ardeshir I founds Sasanian Persian empire. |
| 320 A.D. | Chandragupta I founds Gupta dynasty. |
| 330 A.D. | Constantine I founds city of Constantinople. |
| 410 A.D. | Visigoth king Alaric sacks Rome. |
| 470 A.D. | Ephthalite Huns raid India. |
| 476 A.D. | Last Roman emperor in West deposed. |
| 581 A.D. | Sui dynasty established in China. |
| 647 A.D. | King Harsha dies in India. |
| 627 A.D. | T'ai-tsung becomes Chinese emperor. |
| 718 A.D. | Süleiman fails to take Constantinople. |
| 1214 A.D. | Genghis Khan captures Beijing. |
| 1368 A.D. | Ming dynasty created after Mongols expelled. |
| 1453 A.D. | Ottoman Turks capture Constantinople. |
| 1644 A.D. | Manchus extinguish Ming dynasty. |
| 1912 A.D. | Last Chinese emperor deposed. |
| 1919 A.D. | First meeting of the League of Nations. |
| 1945 A.D. | United Nations established. |
| 1946 A.D. | War crimes tribunal held in Nuremberg. |
| 1948 A.D. | Universal Declaration of Human Rights |

Indian political history following the decline of the Gupta empire is complicated by regional compartmentalization and a plurality of states. A Chinese Buddhist who visited India in the 7th century A.D. reported seventy different kingdoms. In the southeast, the Pandya and Pallava kingdoms were the dominant powers until the 10th century. The Chola kingdom, which defeated the Pallavas in 897, took control of the south-central region for the next three centuries. They were in the best position to reunite Hindu India in the period when the Moslems were encroaching upon Indian territory from the northwest. However, the Chalukyas, to the north, engaged the Chola empire in a protracted struggle until both sides were exhausted. That left the door open to the Moslems. Rajput clans, descendants of the White Hun invaders, controlled northern India after King Harsha's death. The Chalukya dynasty in Maharashtra governed the Deccan (south-central) region from the mid 6th century until 752, when they were overthrown by the Rashtrakuta, previously a tributary state. This dynasty lasted until it was, in turn, overthrown in 973 by Taila II, who revived the Chalukyan empire. During the 8th century, two new dynasties appeared in northern India, the Pratriharas of Rajasthan and Palas of Bengal, which lasted until the 11th and 12th centuries.

Moslem armies which had overrun southwest Asia reached India in 711 A.D. and seized lands in the lower Indus valley. The Hindu kings made no serious move to evict them. The Turkish Emir of Ghazni defeated a coalition of Indian princes in 991 and extended Moslem rule to include lands east of the Khyber Pass. His successor, Mahmud, pushed the frontier forward to Lahore and conducted raids into the Jumna-Ganges basin and in Gu-

column at Ghazni

jarat. Then, Ghoris from Afghanistan, who had been converted to Islam in 1010 A.D., supplanted the Ghaznavid dynasty. Moslem armies completed their conquest of the Jumna-Ganges basin and Bengal between 1192 and 1202 A.D. Muhammad Ghori appointed a slave-viceroy who ruled his kingdom until a ruler of the Khwarizm, ex-vassals of the Saljuq Turks, ended that dynasty in 1215. Though India escaped Mongol destruction, the Mongols' self-styled successor, Tamerlane, sacked Delhi in 1398-99 and slaughtered 80,000 inhabitants. Previously, the Moslems had conquered the Deccan and attempted to move the capital of their empire from Delhi to that region. Islamic states in the Deccan became an independent empire ruled by the Bahmanid dynasty. These broke up into five states in the period between 1482 and 1512 A.D. Several of these states formed an alliance which overthrew the Hindu empire of Vijayanagar in 1555 A.D.

A descendant of Tamerlane, Babur, invaded northern India from Afghanistan in 1525, where he established the Mogul dynasty. Babur's son, Humayun was evicted from India, but he successfully reentered in 1555. Humayun's son, Akbar, expanded the empire, created an efficient administration, and promoted reconciliation between Moslems and Hindus. Some of Akbar's successors took a less benign view of subjected peoples. Aurangzeb reimposed the poll tax on non-Moslems, put a Sikh guru to death, and provoked a rebellion among the Rajputs. He also imposed Mogul rule upon the independent Moslem states in the Deccan and down to India's southern tip. A Hindu counteroffensive emerged in the form of the Maratha light cavalry which conquered Mogul territory and reestablished a Hindu kingdom under their leader, Shivaji. After Aurangzeb's death in 1707, the Mogul empire rapidly disintegrated. Great Britain and France fought for commercial domination of India. Robert Clive's victory over the French at the battle of Plassey in 1757 decided that contest in favor of the British. The British East India Company became de facto rulers of Bengal, Bihar, and Orissa when they assumed responsibility for provincial revenue collection on behalf of the Mogul empire in 1757-65. A century later, the government of India was transferred to the British crown.

## China

The Far Eastern Chinese society, in contrast to India's, maintained a large degree of political unity during more than two thousand years following the creation of its first political empire in 221 B.C. The Xia, Shang, and Western Chou pre-imperial dynasties, lasting until 771 B.C., were kingdoms in northwest China which enjoyed hegemony over neighboring states. The Eastern

Chou dynasty, headquartered at Loyang, continued until 256 B.C. During that time, a number of large states arose at the periphery of the empire. The Chou ruler was reduced to ceremonial functions. After the central government lost control of its vassals, these states went to war against each other. Their number decreased from three hundred to twenty. By 506 B.C., there were seven large states surrounding the city of Loyang. They fought for control during the three centuries between 506 and 221 B.C.

known as the "period of the warring states." Alliances were formed and broken. After 453 B.C., the states improved their armies by replacing hereditary officers with ones of proven ability. Prince Hien of Ch'in militarized the peasant class. War was transformed from a contest between chariot-riding aristocrats to massive infantry battles. In the final phase, between 230 and 221 B.C., the kingdom of Ch'in conquered its rivals.

Chow Sin's empress

The King of Ch'in, Shih Hwang-ti, became the first Chinese emperor. Embracing the Legalist philosophy, he was determined to improve society by issuing and enforcing laws. This emperor replaced the hereditary nobility with appointed officials, set up a system of provincial administrations, adopted standard weights and measures, standardized the Chinese script, began construction of the Great Wall to protect the northern border, and created a centralized civil service. His government established the legal framework for peasants to own and transfer land. Its army acquired crossbows and replaced chariots with cavalry. In keeping with his strict reforms, Shih Hwang-ti burned books from schools of philosophy other than Legalism and even proposed burying their scholars alive. The result was to create a unified nation which was organized by an unambiguous set of principles. On the other hand, the abrupt creation of a national bureaucracy and suppression of competing philosophies antagonized those who had previously enjoyed favor and power. Its population depleted from war, the peasants were further oppressed by taxes and corvées. The Ch'in empire, too ambitious in its reach, lasted only thirteen years. The first emperor died in 210 B.C. while on an inspection tour. A general insurrection took place a year later, aimed at restoring the old order.

Liu P'ang, founder of the Han dynasty, was the winner in the civil war that followed. Instead of reversing the first emperor's policies, he continued them in a more moderate form. Liu P'ang dismantled the fiefs by requiring that all sons, not just the oldest, inherit their father's lands. Repudiating the Legalists, he promoted first the Taoist and then the Confucian philosophy. In 196 B.C., Liu P'ang ordered the imperial districts to send their brightest young men to the capital to be selected for administrative posts by passing an examination. A subsequent emperor, Wu-ti, based the examination upon knowledge of the Confucian classics. The structure was in place for a system of government that served most subsequent dynasties. Although Liu P'ang reappointed lesser nobility, these titles were rewards for faithful government service and could be revoked. The real power was held by the emperor, on one hand, and the Confucian bureaucracy, on the other. This bureaucracy consisted of many separate departments and overlapping functions, which constituted a checks-and-balances system. Even the emperor's conduct could be criticized by an official known as the "censor". The emperor's household had its Inner and Outer courts, including relatives, eunuchs, harems, and high officials.

A list of the Chinese imperial dynasties is presented in Table 4-4. The Han dynasty, founded by Liu P'ang, is divided into a Western Han (141-31 B.C.) and an Eastern Han (25-220 A.D.) period. The Confucian scholar-administrators established themselves in the first period as a privileged class. They effectively controlled the imperial government and took it upon themselves to decide as well whether a dynasty still enjoyed the Mandate of Heaven. Additionally, the Confucian administrators used their governmental positions to enrich themselves by taking land from the peasants. Under the Han dynasty, peasants could be forced to contribute one month's free labor to the government and was subject to two years' conscription for military service. As in Roman society, peasant-farmers who neglected their land while fighting wars often lost it to rich speculators. The new class of Confucian landlords added to the burden. An imperial decree

Table 4-4

## Dynasties of the Chinese Empire

| | |
|---|---|
| 1500 - 1028 B.C. | Shang dynasty     (preimperial) |
| 1027 - 249 B.C. | Chou dynasty      (preimperial) |
| 481 - 221 B.C. | period of the warring states |
| 221 - 206 B.C. | Ch'in dynasty |
| 206 B.C. - 220 A.D. | Han dynasty |
| 221 - 589 A.D. | six dynasties  (interregnum) |
| 581 - 618 A.D. | Sui dynasty |
| 618 - 906 A.D. | T'ang dynasty |
| 907 - 960 A.D. | five dynasties  (interregnum) |
| 960 - 1279 A.D. | Sung dynasty |
| 1280 - 1368 A.D. | Yüan (Mongol) dynasty |
| 1368 - 1644 A.D. | Ming dynasty |
| 1644 - 1912 A.D. | Ch'ing (Manchu) dynasty |

issued in 6 B.C. proposed to limit individual landholdings, but the administrator-landlords made sure that the decree was not carried out. The Western Han dynasty fell in 9 A.D.

Wang Mang, a relative of the royal family, usurped power and tried to carry out agrarian reform. He, too, was stymied by the Confucian bureaucracy. Peasant armies known as the "Green Woodsmen" and "Red Eyebrows" staged an uprising in the Shandong province. In 25 A.D., a powerful landlord and warlord named Kwang-wu restored the Han dynasty and suppressed the peasant revolt. Since its capital was moved from Changan east to Loyang, this became known as the Eastern Han dynasty. The Confucian bureaucrats remained in power. Not surprisingly, the same problems that had bedeviled the Western Han dynasty resurfaced. Rents were raised on the peasants. The imperial examinations were conducted dishonestly. Many peasants took refuge on the big landowners' estates while others fled to southern China. In 184 A.D., a Taoist physician organized a nationwide peasant revolt known as the "Yellow Turban" rebellion. This lasted nine months before it was crushed by an alliance between big landlords and the regular army. The Eastern Han empire split into three kingdoms controlled by warlords in 220-22 A.D.

A period of civil disorder followed which lasted more than three centuries. Mahayana Buddhism entered China. The warm, marshy southern region attracted an influx of population. The Chinese empire was briefly reunified in 265-80 A.D., but fell apart ten years later. Then nomadic barbarians invaded northern China and established kingdoms there. A branch of the Chin family reestablished the (Eastern) Chin dynasty in southern China. Five imperial dynasties held that region, including north Vietnam, against barbarian attacks from the north. By 439 A.D., the T'o-pa "Wei" dynasty had conquered all the other kingdoms in northern China. Its sinified tribesmen became major landowners. The Wei emperor undertook substantial agrarian reform. Every able-bodied peasant was given a plot of land of minimum size and peasant associations became collectively responsible for tax payments. However, the Wei dynasty was overthrown in 535 after several unsuccessful attempts to conquer southern China. Sui Wen-ti, founder of the Sui dynasty, did reunite the country in 589 A.D.

The Sui dynasty lasted only 37 years. Its second emperor, Sui Yang-ti, undertook construction of the Grand Canal linking the Yellow and Yangtze rivers. His heavy demand for corvée labor led to peasant revolts and civil war during which the emperor was assassinated by his bodyguard. Then Li Yüan and his son established the T'ang dynasty (618-906 A.D.), arguably China's most glorious. The T'ang emperors, like the Han, continued the Sui program but at a more moderate pace. Their capital city, Changan, near Xi'an became a culturally vibrant metropolis of 800,000 persons with a cosmopolitan flavor. T'ang poetry, calligraphy, and sculpture achieved their classic expression. Commercial activities flourished. Silk weaving, porcelain manufacture, shipbuilding, and papermaking were brought to a high level of art. Korean and Japanese intellectuals flocked to the T'ang capital and picked up such cultural elements as chop sticks and kimono dress. The Japanese even built a replica of Changan at Nara in 710 for their own first capital.

In 626, Li Yüan's middle son, later known as T'ai-tsung, murdered his two brothers and deposed his father to assume the imperial throne. However, this filial usurper was an able and intelligent ruler until his death in 649. An ambitious young woman named Wu, who had belonged to T'ai-tsung's harem, managed to become the new emperor's concubine a year later, and then empress five years later. When this emperor died in 683, Empress Wu put her grown son on the throne, then demoted him and put another son on the throne, and finally assumed the throne herself. She was overthrown in 705. The T'ang dynasty reached a cultural peak during the reign of her grandson, Hsüan-tsing, who ruled from 713 to 755. However, its military and political fortunes went into a decline. In 751, Arab armies defeated the Chinese near Samarkand. An Lu-shan, military governor of a northern province, launched a rebellion against the central government in 755 which, lasting nine years, devastated the Chinese population. Though weakened, the T'ang lasted another century and a half. A reform of land taxation in 780 stabilized

Tu Fu, the poet, takes family on a journey

government finances. A revived cadre of Confucian scholars allowed the Chinese nation to survive the brief period of anarchy. Confucian and Taoist partisans attacked Buddhism and other foreign religions.

Heavy taxation and homelessness sparked peasant revolts in the late 9th century A.D. The T'ang dynasty expired in 907 A.D. when a warlord named Zhu Wen entered Ch'ang-an and forced the emperor to abdicate. During the period of Five Dynasties, continual war devastated society. The next dynasty, the Sung, arrived a half century later. Chao K'uang-yin, commander of the imperial guards under the later Chou, mutinied and declared himself emperor. Now threatened by Khitan and Tangut barbarians in the northwest, the Chinese empire made peace by paying tribute. The central government consolidated the regional military commands to prevent future rebellions. An energetic and courageous administrator, Wang An-shih (1021-86), instituted several reforms. He revamped the imperial examinations, provided low-interest loans to peasants, abolished the system of corvée labor, reformed the tax on land, and brought back the peasant militia. The Sung period continued the cultural brilliance associated with the T'ang. When Jürchen barbarians conquered the Sung capital of Kaifeng in 1126, the empire lost all its territory north of the Yangtze river. The Sung dynasty continued in south China until Mongol armies under Kublai Khan conquered its remaining territory in 1273-79 A.D.

The Mongols were the first barbarian tribe to conquer China in its entirety. Kublai Khan moved his capital from Qaraqorum in Mongolia to Peking in 1260-67. Mongol armies overpowered the southern Cempire, taking its capital in 1276. Gunpowder was used in its defense. The Mongols' Yüan dynasty, lasting from 1260 until 1368 A.D., was perhaps the least representative of all Chinese dynasties. Its ruling class remained aloof from the Chinese population. This nomadic people despised the sedentary Chinese and never accepted their culture. During the conquest, they had ruined the agricultural infrastructure of northern China causing mass starvation. Yüan emperors employed foreigners rather than Confucian scholars in top administrative positions. They cordially received diplomats from Moslem countries and the West. The Yüan dynasty was, of course, unusual because its power extended well beyond the frontiers of China. The Mongol territories extended from Manchuria and north Vietnam to lands adjoining Syria and Hungary. Even so, naval expeditions against Japan and Java failed. Local revolts spread through China in the 1340s. The winner among the competing warlords was Chu Yüan-Chang, founder of the Ming dynasty. By 1382, he had evicted the Mongols from China.

The Ming dynasty (1368-1644 A.D.) revived the earlier pattern of Chinese society. Examinations based on the Confucian classics again became the route to top positions in the imperial government. Fearing another Mongol-style invasion, Ming emperors kept a close eye on nomadic tribes in the northwest. Emperor Yung-lo (ruled 1403-24) conducted five military campaigns against them. Briefly, a Mongol leader besieged Peking but could not penetrate its walls. In 1414, Ming armies reconquered Annam (Vietnam) but this nation became independent fourteen years later. Korea and Tibet remained Chinese tributaries. The Portuguese and Dutch established trading posts in southern

China. European missionaries and scholars were received at the imperial court. Emperor Yung-lo commissioned a massive encyclopedia of Chinese culture to be written, which filled 11,000 volumes. He also sent a large fleet of sailing ships to ports throughout the Indian Ocean on seven separate expeditions between 1405 and 1433 A.D. Later emperors turned reclusive and xenophobic. Wan-li (1573-1620) retreated to interior parts of the Forbidden City, effectively leaving the eunuch administrators in control. The last Ming emperor committed suicide in 1644 as Manchu forces attacked Peking.

Manchu official and lady

The last imperial dynasty, the Manchu or Ch'ing, brought to power a sinized group of hunters from Manchuria belonging to the Jürched people. At the beginning of the 17th century, a Jürchen chief, Nurhachi, had united a previously divided group of tribes and conquered much of Manchuria with a tightly organized army. Nurhachi proclaimed himself emperor of the Later Chin dynasty in 1616. Rebellions broke out in Ming China. In 1644, a Ming general enlisted help from the Manchurians to quell the rebellion. Pouring into northern China, they quickly occupied Peking and made it their capital. Between 1675 and 1683, Manchu armies subdued the remaining Ming forces which had retreated to the south. While the new dynasty continued the Chinese form of government, the Jürched people held themselves apart from the Chinese as a ruling class. Two emperors, K'ang-hsi (1661-1722) and Ch'ien-lung (1736-1796), both able military and political leaders, dominated this period. Under the Manchu regime, the Chinese government resisted territorial encroachment from Czarist Russia, conquered Taiwan, and discouraged western influence. However, the Europeans obtained commercial concessions from China. By the end of the 19th century, they had reduced the empire to political impotence. The last Chinese emperor, Henry Pu Yi, who reigned between 1908 and 1912, died under communist rule in 1974.

## East and Southeast Asia

The nations strung out along the perimeter of east and southeast Asia are cultural satellites of the two central powers, India and China. Indian culture spread peacefully to neighboring areas through trade, immigration, and religion. Its sphere of influence spread to southeast Asia with emigration following the Huns' destruction of the Gupta empire in the 5th century A.D. Many fled from the Pallava kingdom taking with them the Grantha script. The spread of Chinese culture was more a projection of China's political power. The lands under its influence were taken by military conquest or the lure of Chinese civilization. China's satellites include Korea, Japan, and North Vietnam. India's include Ceylon, Burma, Thailand, Malaya, Cambodia, and Indonesia. There is an overlay of Islamic culture in Malaya and the southeast islands. Tibet, positioned between the two powers, has been politically annexed to China though it shows the influence of Indian religion.

An ancient Hindu kingdom was founded in Champa (south Vietnam) by Indian adventurers in 192 A.D. The Han emperor, Wu-ti, had annexed Nam-Viet (north Vietnam) in the 1st century B.C. Champa was an independent kingdom until the 12th century when it became a vassal of the Khmer empire. This kingdom was conquered in 1471 by the Annamese empire to the north. The northern Vietnamese people were Mahayana Buddhists under Chinese influence. They had been a part of China until the fall of the T'ang dynasty. Reconquered by the Yüan and Ming emperors, they regained their independence in 1428. The Khmer empire of Cambodia rose to power in the period between the 9th and 12th centuries under a dynasty of god-kings. Its chief monument is the temple complex at Angkor Wat constructed by

a Shan woman

Suryavarman II (1113-1150). The T'ai kingdom on its eastern border destroyed the Khmer state between 1350 and 1360. These T'ais were descendants of a people from Yunnan in western China who had migrated southward and formed a tightly organized state at Ayut'ia in 1350. They conquered Cambodia, lower Burma, and much of the Malay peninsula. East of Thailand, Burmese tribesmen migrating from the northwest overcame the native Mon people of Burma and established the empire of Pagan in 1044.

The Mongols destroyed it in 1287.

Unlike the agriculturally based societies of southeast Asia, the peoples who inhabited the Indonesian islands made a living primarily from trade. Sea vessels traveling between India and China had to pass through the Straits of Malacca or Sunda, located at opposite ends of Sumatra. The Sumatran empire of Srivijaya prospered by intercepting and taxing ships in its territorial waters. It was the strongest power in the region between the 7th and 9th centuries A.D. The Indian Cholas and the Javanese were important rivals. Kings of the Shailendra dynasty ruled Java until the 8th century. They have left a Buddhist monument carved in a hill at Borobudur. These monarchs were replaced by the Hindu Sanjaya dynasty. The Singosari kingdom of east Java, which arose next in the 9th century, ruled over an expanded part of the Indonesian archipelago until the late 13th century. The Mongols attacked Java in 1293 during an internal rebellion. The late king's son-in-law, Vijaya, welcomed their help in defeating the rebels and then treacherously turned on them. After the Mongols were defeated, Vijaya founded the Majapahit empire, which dominated a broad area in the 14th century. In 1403, a Shailendra prince named Paramesvara married a Majapahit princess and founded the city of Malacca. After he converted to Islam, Malacca became a base for propagating this religion.

The Chinese emperor Han Wu-ti first established military outposts on the Korean peninsula in 109-08 B.C. They were destroyed after the East Han empire fell in the 3rd century A.D. However, the northern Korean state of Koguryo adopted Mahayana Buddhism and Chinese-style public administration around 372 A.D. Numerous Koreans claiming Chinese ancestry emigrated to Japan in the 5th and 6th centuries. In the 7th century, T'ang emperors conquered the states of Koguryo and Paekche with the aid of Silla kings. Silla then expelled the Chinese. The unification of Korea under local rule did not prevent Chinese culture from continuing to gain influence there. Mahayana Buddhism and the Chinese script both took root during that period. The Silla kingdom was overthrown at the end of the 9th century. The Koryo dynasty, which suppressed Buddhism in favor of Confucianism, then ruled Korea until the Mongols arrived in 1231. Finally, the Yi dynasty came to power in 1392. This regime lasted until 1910. A vassal of Manchu China, the "hermit" kingdom of Korea existed in nearly total isolation from the rest of the world.

Japan became sinified during the period of the T'ang dynasty. Its imperial government, headquartered first at Nara and then at Kyoto, copied the Chinese model. However, Japanese society did not have enough educated persons to staff a central government effectively, so the power devolved to provincial governors. Also, the powerful influence of the Fujiwara family and of Buddhist priests encroached upon the emperor's authority. Provincial gentry opposed to the Fujiwaras set up their own feudal governments around the country. After prolonged civil war, the Minamoto family defeated their rivals. Their leader, Yoritomo Minamoto, established a military dictatorship at Kamakura known as the shogunate in 1185. He did not seek to become emperor but the leader of a parallel government which exercised the real power. This new dynasty of warriors reformed the courts and restored peace to society. It presided over a cultural blossoming and repelled the Mongol naval attack against Japan in 1274 and 1281. Emperor Go-Daigo attempted a coup d'état in 1331. The shogunate was then transferred to the Ashikaga family in Kyoto. Their rule broke down after two centuries. Civil war took place in the streets of Kyoto.

Beginning in the middle of the 16th century, three warlords restored the shogunate and brought peace to the country. The first, Oda Nobunaga, seized power after winning a battle with another warlord who had marched on Kyoto. After ruling for twenty years, he was assassinated in 1582. One of Nobunaga's lieutenants, Toyotomi Hideyoshi, sought to avenge this death. After becoming shogun in 1590, he invaded Korea intending later to attack the Ming dynasty. The invasion was repelled. Hideyoshi used shrewd strategies to foil potential opponents. He ordered all non-samurai to turn in their swords to make a gigantic metal statue of Buddha while also using Christian missionaries to fight Buddhist soldiers. Hideyoshi wanted his son to succeed him, but, after his death in 1598, an associate, Tokugawa Ieyasu, gained the upper hand. As shogun, Ieyasu moved the capital to Tokyo. He kept the other samurai in check by forcing them to maintain two residences and so incur a great expense. Finally, Ieyasu expelled the Portuguese missionaries from Japan. This arrangement preserved the peace for 250 years while Japan was closed to the outside world. Then, in July 1853, the American admiral Matthew Perry brought a fleet of gunboats into Tokyo bay, forcing the shogunate to reopen this nation. The imperial dynasty was restored in 1868.

## Pre-Columbian America

When Hernando Cortés conquered the Aztec empire of Mexico in 1519-21 A.D., he arrested the growth of a militaristic state in an expansive phase. The main civilizations of the Americas were concentrated in Mexico and Central America, on one hand, and along the Pacific coast of South America, on the other. The Olmec and Chavín societies unified those two regions in the first half of the 1st millennium B.C. The first great empire of the Americas, the Mayan, flourished in Guatemala and the Yucatán peninsula of Mexico beginning at the time of Christ or, perhaps, in the next three centuries. In its classical period, this culturally rich society lasted about four hundred years. Its capital at Teotihuacán was the largest Meso-American city existing before the Spanish conquest. The Mayan people were distinguished by their mathematical and astronomical knowledge and their art. Teotihuacán was violently destroyed around 600 A.D. The Mayan culture continued in outlying jungle areas even after its ceremonial centers were abandoned. In South America, two cities - Huari in Ecuador and Tiahuanaco in Bolivia - began forming their own empires around 600 A.D. Between them, they controlled two thousand miles of coastal territories from Ecuador to northern Chile. These empires lasted about two centuries.

The classical Mayan civilization of Meso-America fell around 900 A.D. The next significant society in that area was the Zapotec society, located in the Oaxaca province of southern Mexico. The Toltec people gained political ascendancy in the Valley of Mexico around 900 A.D. Their capital city was Tula, just north of Mexico City. Toltec in the Aztec language means "skilled worker", suggesting architectural prowess. Many ruins of temples, palaces, and pyramids adorned the Toltec capital. The founder of Tula, Topíltzin, was expelled by political opponents. He fled towards the eastern coast. Legend had it that this exiled Toltec king would return some day from the sea as the feathered serpent god Quetzalcoatl. In fact, a conqueror by the same name in the Mayan language founded a small empire on the northwest coast of the Yucatán peninsula in 987, which lasted until 1224. The Aztecs migrated from the desert of northern Mexico in the late 12th century. Around 1325, they settled on the west edge of Lake Texcoco, where, for defensive reasons, they created a Venice-like city on piles in the middle of the lake. This became Tenochtitlán, or Mexico City. In South America, a number of large cities including Chanchán and Cuizmanco exercised political power in the "urbanizing age" between 1000 and 1430 A.D.

The Aztecs took the first step in building an empire around 1430 when their leader, Itzcoatl, formed a military alliance with two neighboring city-states. During the next ninety years, the Aztec confederation conquered thirty city states. The purpose of these wars was to loot, exact tribute, and gather captives for religious ceremonies involving human sacrifice, not to create a politically integrated society. For, the Aztecs believed that the

Cortés confronts Aztecs

gods needed to be liberally fed with human hearts to maintain the universe. By 1519, this military machine controlled a territory extending from the Atlantic to Pacific oceans between southern and central Mexico. The Incas of Peru had begun to build their empire around 1438 when the ruler of Cuzco repelled an attack from the Chanchas. His son, Pachacuti, then set about to conquer the Chanchán territory as well as that of other Andean peoples. A hundred years later, the Inca empire between the Andes mountains and Pacific ocean was so large that a second capital, Quito, had been added to administer the northern part. A civil war was in progress between royal brothers in these two capitals when Francisco Pizarro arrived in 1532, which the Spaniard shrewdly exploited. Likewise, Cortés' war of conquest in Mexico was materially aided by provincial peoples who hated the Aztecs.

## Chapter Five

# A SHORT HISTORY OF CIVILIZATION II

## A Change in Religion

The second civilization, introduced by alphabetic writing, began with a change in the nature of religious worship which took place in the 1st millennium B.C. Primitive religions, one may recall, typically include rituals intended to increase the fertility of agriculture. They acknowledge and feed a community's ancestral spirits. They may involve animal or even human sacrifice as a means of pleasing the gods. These religions are polytheistic, reflecting the diverse elements of nature. They are instituted in cults of particular gods or goddesses which function under the supervision of hereditary priests possessing the knowledge to perform the rituals correctly. These priests also exercise political power. Later, the nature gods become associated with the collective identity of tribes, city-states, and king-

doms. The gods and goddesses become patrons of particular
peoples. Their totemic characters are adapted to express these
people's communal identity. The different deities are arranged
in hierarchies mirroring tribal or national relationships within a
political empire. The emperors are considered to be divine figures or be uniquely endowed with divine authority and power.

All this changed with the wave of philosophical thinking
that swept through societies of the Old World during the 1st millennium B.C. Hereditary priesthoods gave way to a more democratic and meritocratic method of selecting religious leaders.
Sacrificial rituals mattered less than maintaining ethical conduct.
An open-ended brotherhood of believers replaced stratified
castes. Ideas began to play a dominant role in religion. Divine
spirit, once confined to particular places or persons, became a
universal presence. And so it was possible for anyone who con-
sented or believed to adopt the religion, regardless of nation.
Like law, the principles underlying the religion could be applied
anywhere. These principles could be expressed in creeds.
Learned doctors could ponder and dispute the finer points of
God's truth. Those who bucked the general consensus of belief
could be branded heretics. The inner attitude or direction of heart
would become the criterion of correct religion, not expertise in
performing a ritual. In the West, correct religion also involved
worship of the right God, who was right because he was the
only real God. Religious worship changed with the concept of
monotheism.

### The Monotheism of Ikhnaton and Moses

It may be that the first "prophet" of this new religion was
the Egyptian Pharaoh Ikhnaton, who reigned between 1367 and
1350 B.C. He was first major historical figure to advance a program of monotheistic religion. A century before Moses, Ikhnaton proclaimed that the religion of Amun-Re, his ancestral religion, was false and there was only one God, Aton, god of the
sun, who ruled over all the earth. Aton gave life to all living

creatures. Ikhnaton wrote poems of praise to Aton but forbade visual images to be made. He moved the capital north from Thebes to Akhetaton ("City of the Horizon of Aton") and ordered monuments to be defaced in which the name of Amun was inscribed. While antagonizing Amun-Re's powerful priests, Ikhnaton also neglected affairs of state. The Hittites invaded Egypt's Asian dependencies and tribute stopped. The imperial treasury became empty. When Ikhnaton died, the priests of Amun-Re regained control and the old religion was restored by his successor Tutankhamen.

Ikhnaton

Moses, who lived in Egypt in the 13th century B.C., was Pharaoh's adopted son. He would likely have been aware of Ikhnaton's religious crusade. Whether or not Jewish monotheism derives from that source, Moses firmly embraced the concept of One God. The First Commandment states: "I am the Lord your God who brought you out of Egypt ... You shall have no other god to set against me." None of the Ten Commandments had to do with performing rituals. All were concerned with right conduct and belief. Moses transformed the Hebrew tribe from being one of a common nomadic type to being a nation which lived in accordance with God's law. He forced this society to conform to a particular set of ideals. Though not explicitly philosophical, his instructions delivered in God's name were ethical precepts like those of philosophers. Moses railed against the Hebrews for fashioning a golden calf as an object of worship. His God, Jehovah or Yahweh, was an invisible or spiritual being rather than a "graven image". It required a certain intellectual discipline to worship a god whom one could not see and whose existence, from a common perspective, might therefore be in doubt.

The God of the Hebrews, known to Abraham, Isaac, and Jacob, was identified as the God who had delivered his people from captivity in Egypt. This God had demonstrated earthly power in overcoming the will of Pharaoh. Powerful rulers like Pharaoh were thus coming under the yoke of a new kind of God, believed to be universal and omnipotent. A threat to monotheistic religion was the marriage of Hebrew kings to foreign women who brought other gods into the royal household. After Solomon's death, the Hebrews took to worshiping Canaanite fertility gods such as Baal and Anath to seek increased agricultural productivity. A religious faction arose, led by the prophets Elijah and Elisha, which claimed that Yahweh alone should be worshiped. For the Hebrews to worship other gods was like being unfaithful in a marriage. A rebellion broke out in the northern part of Israel in 840 B.C. against the infidelity of the royal household. It spread to the priesthood of the Temple at Jerusalem. However, the Yahweh-alone party was unable to impose its views upon the nation. A group of religious writers, including Amos and Hosea, began to interpret God's will in light of current events. A picture of God emerged as being jealous yet merciful and desirous of justice for the poor.

After Assyria conquered the northern kingdom of Israel in 722 B.C., the Yahweh cult served to rally nationalistic sentiments in the yet unconquered southern kingdom of Judaea. Around 630, an unknown person in Jerusalem wrote a new set of laws and divine instructions, building upon older traditions, which was "found" by the high priest in the Temple at Jerusalem a decade later and judged to be authentic by King Josiah. These writings form chapters in the book of *Deuteronomy*. They take an uncompromising stand against worshiping Gods other than Yahweh. The Deuteronomy texts, embraced by the Yahweh faction, strengthened legalistic tendencies within Judaism. A later crisis occurred with Jerusalem's capture by the Babylonians in 586 B.C. This event raised doubts that Yahweh was all-powerful and real if this God would let his own people become subjected to foreign empires. However, the Yahweh-alone party, through the prophets, argued that God had devised this painful experience to punish the Hebrews for their previous apostasy and teach them a moral lesson. After the lesson was learned, God would restore the nation of Israel to its previous glory. Then it would be seen that God had sent his people into captivity for the purpose of revealing himself to other nations. Yahweh would be revealed as God of Jews and Gentiles alike, a universal God.

In the meanwhile, because Deuteronomy restricted sacrificial rites to the Temple in Jerusalem, Jewish exiles living in Babylon were denied this means of practicing their religion in traditional ways. A type of nonsacrificial worship centered in such activities as praying, singing hymns of praise, and reading the Law was developed in its place. The core of Jewish religion lay in refusing to worship Gods other than Yahweh and in observing the purity laws. The Yahweh faction produced a body of historical writings to support its interpretation of divine will. These, along with works of the prophets, were compiled in books of the Old Testament. The final version was not completed until the end of the 5th century B.C.

## Zoroastrian Influence

When the Persian emperor Cyrus II in 538 B.C. issued a decree allowing the Jewish exiles to return to Jerusalem and rebuild Solomon's temple, it seemed to confirm the theory that Yahweh was a universal God. Cyrus, the most powerful monarch in the world, had been compelled to do this God's bidding. In fact, the time spent in Babylon and Persia had been beneficial for Judaism as a religion. It had transformed the religion of a once provincial people into a religion with advanced cosmological features. This was largely the work of the Iranian prophet Zoroaster (628-551 B.C.). His teaching, Zoroastrianism, was the state religion of Persia. Because the Persian government treated Semitic peoples in a benign manner, the Hebrews were receptive to Persian cultural influences. So postexilic Judaism included many elements that can be traced to Zoroastrian teachings.

Zoroaster was an original thinker who lived in a  society that was in transition between agricultural and nomadic ways of life. The industriousness, honesty, and trust implicit in the agricultural life were qualities which he identified with goodness. In contrast, the nomads who raided settled communities and stole their livestock were identified with evil. Conflict between good and evil was the central feature in Zoroaster's religious philosophy. Ahura-Mazda, the supreme god, led the forces of good. Lower gods, daevas or whom one might call fallen angels, comprised the forces of evil led by Ahriman. The world was a battleground between these two camps. Animals such as dogs and oxen, which helped man, were good, while such creatures as snakes, scorpions, and toads were evil. Zoroaster taught that blood sacrifices should be abolished while such virtues as humility, cleanliness, and compassion should be cultivated in daily life. Yet, human beings were to show unrelenting hostility towards those persons, creatures, or beings aligned with the forces of evil. A battle was raging continually both within the cosmos and the human heart. In the end, good would triumph over evil to win an everlasting victory. Before then, evil would be seen gaining the upper hand. A redeemer figure would snatch the victory from Ahriman just when he appeared to be winning.

The Jewish prophetic writers who lived after the Babylonian exile wove Zoroastrian elements into their scenario of future events related to God's restoration of the Hebrew nation. The idea of national restoration began to be replaced by that of a supernatural kingdom which God would establish on earth. As in the Zoroastrian scheme, the forces of good and evil first would do battle to control the world. There would be a period of tribulation in which the righteous would suffer greatly. Then, God would intervene at the last moment to ensure victory for the good. A captain of evil, Satan, would take part in these events. A Messiah, elevated from the ranks of humanity, would appear as God's agent at the moment of victory. He would be delegated the task of judging human souls and either allowing or denying them entrance to God's perfect kingdom. The idea that the souls of departed persons might be resurrected for the Last Judgment comes from the Zoroastrian cosmology. So do concepts relating to angels and the hierarchy of heavenly beings. The stark duality between evil and good, darkness and light, is, however, Zoroaster's main contribution to religious thinking. God had created the material world to give it over to Satan, trap him in a finite structure, and then destroy him. Man's duty was to assist in that process.

## Jews under Foreign Rule

In the tolerant atmosphere of Persian society, Jewish intellectuals readily absorbed these religious ideas. Then, suddenly, Alexander the Great conquered the Persian empire. The ensuing Greek culture was alien to Semitic peoples. Adherents of the traditional Judaic religion were thrust back into a hostile environment. In 167 B.C., Emperor Antiochus Epiphanes IV, an ardent hellenizer, desecrated the Temple at Jerusalem. A priest named Mattathias, together with his five sons, launched a campaign of guerrilla warfare against the Seleucid empire. One of those sons, Judas Maccabaeus, led the rebel armies to a series of speedy victories against the Syrian Greek dynasty. He captured Jerusalem and restored Jewish worship in the Temple. The Maccabee family, as the Hasmonaean dynasty, ruled Judaea for about a century. At last the Jews had their own nation. Judaism became a missionary religion which forced male converts to become circumcised. However, the Hasmonaean rulers in ruling their worldly empire also became more hellenized. In 63 B.C. the Roman general Pompey intervened in a civil war and captured Jerusalem. Rome then ruled Judaea through proconsuls while the Herodic dynasty, hellenized Jews allied with Rome, ruled the northern part of Palestine, including Galilee.

As first the Greek Seleucid and then Roman power asserted itself in Judaea, themes of national redemption enunciated at the time of the Exile took on new urgency. Messianic fervor ran high in hope that the House of David might be restored. The prophetic writings, anticipating the end of the world order, continued in a more intense and fantastic form. A tension existed between this spiritualized religion and Jewish political militancy. Jewish society in the 1st century B.C. was split into several factions, based upon their attitude toward foreign occupation. The Pharisees were extreme anti-Hellenists. Known as the "Party of the Righteous", they had endured much persecution in their attempt to keep Jewish religion free of foreign influence. The Sadducees were upper-class Jews belonging to the Temple establishment who did not accept religious innovations such as belief in the Messiah. A political faction known as Zealots favored armed resistance. The Zealots did mount a guerrilla offensive against Rome, but it was brutally crushed by Titus' armies in 70 A.D. The last of this faction died in a mass suicide at the Masada fortress. Jerusalem was utterly destroyed. Sixty years later, another group challenged Roman rule following Simon Bar Kokba, believed to be the Messiah. It, too, was defeated.

In the debacle of 66-70 A.D., more than a million Jews may have died of starvation and other causes. Another one hundred thousand were taken to Rome as slaves. The leader of Jerusalem's Pharisees, Johanan ben Zakkai was smuggled out of the city in a coffin. He later received permission from Emperor Vespasian to settle in Jamnia and establish an academy of Jewish studies there. Now that the temples in Jerusalem and Egypt had been destroyed or closed, this institution became the center of Jewish religious authority. There Judaism was reorganized around worship in synagogues. Its practice focused upon study of the Torah and observance of laws and rituals. The canon of sacred literature was determined. After Jewish uprisings in Cyprus, Egypt, and Palestine during the first half of the 2nd century A.D., the Roman government considered banning Judaism. Instead, a commission investigated Jewish law and suggested changes. Rabbi Judah the Prince published a code of laws, known as the Mish-

Jewish scrolls

nah, which spread through the Graeco-Roman world. The Palestinian patriarch Hillel II published procedures for regulating the Jewish calendar in 359. After Christianity became the Roman religion, Jews experienced a period of increasing hostility. Theodosius II abolished the Jewish patriarchate in 425. The East Roman emperor Justinian proscribed rabbinic law and exegesis.

Conditions improved for the Jewish population in western Europe and Persia during the 8th century. The new Frankish and Arab rulers tolerated them as minority peoples within their large, heterogeneous empires. Christian kings often granted charters to their Jewish subjects guaranteeing their right to exist as a self-governing community in exchange for collection of special taxes. In the Ukraine, a Turkic dynasty established the Khazar empire with an army drawn from Iranian Moslems. Rejecting both Christianity and Islam, its rulers converted to Judaism in 750 and made this the state religion. The Khazar empire played an important role in commercial contacts between east and west until Prince Sviatoslav of Kiev conquered it in 970. Jews also thrived in the cosmopolitan culture that developed in Baghdad under the Abbasid dynasty. In the 10th century, the Moorish city of Córdoba became a similar cultural magnet for Jews. The Berber Almohade dynasty that swept across North Africa and Spain in the 12th century brought an end to this culture. Meanwhile, the Christian crusaders' calls to rid Europe of "Christ-killers" gave vent to anti-Jewish campaigns, leading to the formation of ghettos. In once tolerant Spain, the Jewish population in 1492 was ordered to convert to Christianity or leave the country.

## Early Christianity

Jesus, who was a rabbi, self-consciously assumed the role of Messiah that had been created in Jewish prophetic scripture. He began his religious career by submitting to baptism by John the Baptist, a ritual designed to remove sin and bring salvation in the Final Days. Jesus preached a simple message: "The Kingdom of God is at hand." The apocalyptic scenario would unfold momentarily. In this scenario, the Messiah was a divinely appointed figure who would bring human history to an end and introduce God's kingdom on earth. The three-year period of Jesus' active ministry was devoted to preparing his followers for the Kingdom and fulfilling the scriptural conditions by which its arrival might take place. According to the Gospels, Jesus separated himself from the anti-Hellenic spirit of contemporary Jewish religion. He criticized the Pharisees, the most zealous anti-Hellenists, while he counseled cooperation with the Roman authorities in such matters as paying taxes. Railing against Jerusalem as a city notorious for killing prophets, Jesus himself broke specific religious laws. In some respects, his critique of Pharisaic legalism resembles Plato's idealistic philosophy in its focus upon essential truths.

Yet, Jesus, a descendant of King David through Joseph, was a character positioned squarely within the Jewish religious tradition. His earthly role was defined by scriptural references to the Messiah, which were linked to expectations of the coming of God's kingdom. Jesus was crucified before any such event took place. When, two days later, followers discovered that his dead body was missing from the tomb, this was taken as a sign that Jesus had been resurrected from death by God's power and was therefore in a state like that of the supernatural Messiah. Heart-

Christ of the Andes

ened by the news of his resurrection, Jesus' circle of disciples launched a spirited missionary movement to spread the good news. One not originally in this circle, the Apostle Paul, devised a new interpretation of Messianic events. Paul wrote that, in dying innocently upon the Cross, Jesus had atoned for the sins of others. His self-sacrifice would pay the price of admission to God's kingdom for all believers, however sinful they might be. Yet, the early Christian community also awaited Jesus' return to earth. The earlier Messianic expectations were transferred to Jesus' Second Coming, when his glory and power would become visible. The book of *Revelation*, written by John of Patmos near the end of the 1st century A.D., provided a mystical view, from a Christian perspective, of events in the Final Days.

Paul rationalized the failure of God's kingdom to arrive promptly by suggesting that, starting with Jesus' resurrection, the world was in the process of transformation from a temporal to spiritual state. As with the dawning of a new day, the change was not initially evident. Slowly the degree of spirituality would increase in the world and then, at some point, people would see plainly that God's kingdom had come. Every once in awhile, as at Pentecost, one could see an outpouring of divine spirit, but mostly it was imprisoned within the material world. In language reminiscent of Plato, Paul urged Christians to fix their "eyes ...

not on the things that are seen, but on the things that are unseen; for what is seen passes away; what is unseen is eternal." He urged Christians to cultivate chastity so as to liberate themselves from bondage to the flesh. The inquiring spirit of the age also focused upon the person of Jesus. The Gospel of John begins with the idea of Logos, or God's word. Jesus was believed to personify this word. In a philosophically intense society, Christians began then to question what kind of person, or God, Jesus was. Was Jesus a man with a physical body or was he a god, who was pure spirit? Or, perhaps, Jesus was both?

In places like Alexandria, with large Jewish and Greek populations, such questions were often on people's minds. Diverse religions and systems of philosophy coexisted and freely mixed to form new theological hybrids. Philo, the Jewish Platonist, conceived of Logos as a mediating agent between the eternal and the temporal. Given the heavily philosophical disposition of this culture, it was likely that many arguments would take place concerning religion and many different conclusions would be reached, some of which would be considered heresies. The heretical position associated with Gnostic Christianity showed the influence of Neoplatonism. The Gnostics denied Jesus' human nature and the historical record presented in the Bible. God only seemed to be involved in human affairs, and Jesus only seemed to be a man. Arian Christians, on the other hand, doubted Jesus' divinity. Jesus the Son was subordinate to the Father, who was the one and only God. Marcon, an advocate of pure love, saw the Law of Moses as an evil influence. The Welsh heretic, Pelagius, believed sin was a result of misdirected free will. Montanus claimed to be the Paraclete or Spirit of Truth promised in John. Expecting the end of the world, the Montanists practiced speaking in tongues.

In 325 A.D., Constantine I convened the Council of Nicaea to resolve questions raised by the teachings of Arius. The Arian point of view, then dominant, was opposed by Athanasius, a church deacon from Alexandria. A key question was whether Jesus' nature was "like" God's, the Arian position, or "the same as" God's. The Council decided to condemn Arius and his supporters and, instead, adopt the formulation of the Trinity. The

Nicene Creed stated that Jesus was "the Son of God .. begotten not made, of one substance with the Father." The Council of Ephesus, convened in 431 A.D., condemned the teachings of Nestorius, who opposed the designation of Mary as "Mother of God" and upheld Christ's dual nature as man and god. In 451, the Council of Chalcedon condemned the Monophysite heresy which held that Christ had a single divine nature. Such questions were important for political as well as religious reasons. Several of the Germanic tribes whose kings had converted to Christianity embraced the Arian version of the faith. The Franks, on the other hand, won the Pope's backing by supporting the orthodox version expressed in the Nicene creed. Elsewhere, Christians holding heretical views comprised important religious communities.

Nestorius, then Patriarch of Constantinople, called the wrath of the Christian community upon himself by attacking the idea that the Virgin Mary could give birth to a divine son. After the Council of Ephesus condemned his teaching, the Christian community at Antioch became deeply divided. Many of Nestorius' followers emigrated to Iraq in the Sasanian empire where Nestorianism became the dominant faith of the Persian Christian church. Rebuffed in Europe, this doctrine became a missionary religion which spread to India, China, and Central Asia. According to Marco Polo, Nestorian chapels lined the trade routes between Baghdad and Peking. Monophysite Christianity arose in reaction to Nestorianism. That faith was strong in Syria, Egypt, Armenia, and Abyssinia. Monophysitism is derived from the teachings of Eutyches. When Jacob Baradaeus became Bishop of Edessa in the mid 5th century, he organized the Jacobite church to serve Syrian Monophysites. The Coptic church was its counterpart in Egypt. The East Roman emperor declared the Council of Chalcedon invalid in 476, but later emperors vacillated. The excommunication and persecution of Monophysite Christians alienated members of this religious community from the Roman empire, paving the way for the Moslems' quick and easy military victory in Syria and Egypt.

## Development of the Western Church

The monastic life had its origin in the rejection of worldliness which some believed was infecting the Christian church after it became Rome's state religion. It reflects the spirit of Neoplatonism and Gnostic Christianity with their dark ruminations concerning body and mind. Considering that Asoka had sent Buddhist missionaries to Egypt in the 3rd century B.C., the idea of monastic communities might also have come from India. St. Anthony, an Egyptian hermit, pioneered this type of Christian life. In 285 A.D., he withdrew to the desert wilderness to live in solitude where he was tempted by womanly apparitions, demons, and desires of the flesh, and attacked by wild beasts. His brave example attracted imitators, and a number of other hermits settled around him. After ignoring them for twenty years, he emerged from his solitude long enough to organize these people into a monastic community. The "anchorite" monks who followed St. Anthony were given to extravagant feats of self-deprivation. St. Simeon Stylites, for instance, sat for thirty-five years atop a stone pillar. Asceticism eventually gave way to religious communities which, isolated from the world, allowed individuals to grow in a holy state. In the 6th century, St. Benedict founded a monastery at Monte Cassino in Italy, which stressed a life of service to God. Irish monasteries were centers of evangelical advance.

By developing attractive models of Christian personality, these monks helped the church to win human hearts long after the age of Roman martyrdom had passed. Christianity was also advanced by church doctors and theologians, who, combating heresies, posed answers to tough moral questions. It was advanced by brave and able administrators such as St. Ambrose, Bishop of Milan, who refused communion to emperors when their policies went against the interests of the church. Such efforts succeeded in enlisting the power of the state to suppress rival religions. Pope Leo I was instrumental in establishing the Roman church as a power separate from the Byzantine empire and ecclesiastical authority separate from secular authority. After Europe was invaded by barbarian tribes, the Christian church represented the cultural legacy of the fallen empire. It persuaded the barbarians that only through baptism could they join civilized society. In the beginning, the church evangelized areas that had fallen within the boundaries of the Roman empire. Later, its missionaries went beyond those limits to extend God's spiritual empire to heathen lands. St. Patrick converted Ireland to the Christian faith, and Irish missions were then sent to northern England. An English missionary, St. Boniface, who was martyred in Holland, established the first German see in the 8th century.

As the Hebrew prophets had once turned Jerusalem's fall to spiritual advantage, so, when Rome fell, Christianity profited from the writings of St. Augustine. The greatest Christian theologian since Paul, Augustine had once been a Manichee and a Neoplatonist. His *Confessions* told of riotous living as a young man in Carthage. He had converted to Christianity through the influence of St. Ambrose and his mother, St. Monica. From his later theological writings came the orthodox teaching of salvation by grace and the doctrine of original sin. Augustine wrote *The City of God* during the barbarian devastations of Italy and North Africa explaining why, after Rome had abandoned pagan gods and embraced Christianity, this great city fell. In answer, Augustine drew a distinction between worldly cities such as Rome and the "City of God", which could never be destroyed. This City of God was a spiritual community, created through divine love, which was eternally unchanged. It stood in contrast to earthly cities, built from selfish desires and pride, which inevitably would pass away. So, as Rome's secular empire crumbled, humanity clung to that which was safe from corruption and decay.

Perhaps the church's ablest administrator was Pope Gregory the Great, who is credited with rebuilding the Roman church in a dark hour. Born to nobility, Gregory instead chose the hard life of a monk and later ascended the ladder of ecclesiastical offices. As Pope, he strengthened church discipline, reorganized the properties of the church, sent missionaries far and wide, negotiated with the Lombard kings for Rome's political independence, and kept in check the rival claims of Byzantine bishops. A notable accomplishment was his role in converting England to the Catholic faith. In 597 A.D., Gregory recruited a Benedictine monk named Augustine for a mission to the British isles. Augustine and a retinue of forty monks were received cordially by King Etherbert and given land at Canterbury to build a church. His timely arrival in Britain helped stop the spread of Irish Christian civilization which might have challenged Catholicism for leadership of Western Christianity. An agreement reached at the Synod of Whitby in 664 A.D. regarding the method of calculating the date of Easter and the shaving of monks' heads tipped the scales decisively in favor of Rome.

## Power of the Roman Church

Technically, the Pope was Bishop of Rome, leader of Christians in that city. He later assumed leadership of the entire church due to the apostolic origins of that position. The church at Jerusalem had initially assumed the leadership role. Jesus' brother James was its leader. Rome replaced Jerusalem as the center of Christianity because the apostles Peter and Paul had moved to that city and been martyred there. The Roman church became a kind of spiritual government whose authority rested upon a continuous line of succession back to Peter, who was the first bishop of Rome. A famous passage in the Gospel of *Matthew* quotes Jesus: "You are Peter, the Rock; and on this rock I will build my church ... I will give you the keys of the Kingdom of Heaven; what you forbid on earth shall be forbidden in heaven, and what you allow on earth shall be allowed in heaven." In medieval art, St. Peter was frequently shown with a set of keys in his hands, which were the keys to Heaven. In the Biblical quotation, Jesus was entrusting to Peter and, by implication, to Peter's ecclesiastical successors the power to decide who would be permitted to enter Heaven.

When Christianity became the state religion of Rome, the Church received an additional boost to its authority. During the

Table 5-1

## Some Headline Events in the History of Civilization II

| | |
|---|---|
| c.1375 B.C. | Pharaoh Ikhnaton begins heretical reign. |
| c.1250 B.C. | Hebrews start to invade Palestine. |
| c. 925 B.C. | Solomon dies and Hebrew empire splits. |
| c. 600 B.C. | Zoroaster has religious revelations. |
| 586 B.C. | Nebuchadnezzar captures Jerusalem. |
| c. 530 B.C. | Buddha experiences enlightenment. |
| 399 B.C. | Socrates is tried and executed. |
| 261 B.C. | Emperor Asoka converts to Buddhism. |
| 250 B.C. | Buddhist convocation adopts Pali canon. |
| 30 A.D. | Jesus is crucified and resurrected. |
| 45 A.D. | St. Paul begins missionary travels. |
| 67 A.D. | St. Peter executed in Rome. |
| 70 A.D. | Jerusalem is destroyed by the Romans. |
| c. 100 A.D. | Kanishka promotes Mahayana Buddhism. |
| 242 A.D. | Mani begins preaching new doctrine. |
| 313 A.D. | Constantine legalizes Christianity. |
| 323 A.D. | Council of Nicaea adopts doctrine of the trinity. |
| 411 A.D. | St. Augustine writes *The City of God* |
| 431 A.D. | Council of Ephesus condemns Nestorianism. |
| 432 A.D. | St. Patrick begins mission to Ireland. |
| 496 A.D. | Clovis, king of Franks, is baptized a Christian. |
| 529 A.D. | Benedict founds monastery at Monte Cassino. |
| 590 A.D. | Gregory I becomes Pope. |
| 596 A.D. | Gregory sends Augustine on mission to England. |
| 610 A.D. | Mohammed has vision at Mt. Hira. |
| 622 A.D. | Mohammed moves to Medina. (the hegira) |
| 632 A.D. | Mohammed dies. |
| 650 A.D. | Official version of *Koran* is determined. |
| 658 A.D. | Mu'awiyah establishes Umayyad dynasty. |
| 661 A.D. | Caliph Ali is murdered. |
| 664 A.D. | Synod of Whitby binds England to Rome. |
| 691 A.D. | Dome of the Rock built in Jerusalem. |
| 726 A.D. | Byzantine emperor Leo III attacks icons. |
| 732 A.D. | Franks defeat Moslems at battle of Tours. |
| 749 A.D. | Abbasid dynasty is established at Baghdad. |
| 751 A.D. | Arabs defeat Chinese near Samarkand. |
| 800 A.D. | Charlemagne crowned Holy Roman Emperor. |

## History of Civ II    (continued)

| | |
|---|---|
| 841 A.D. | Foreign religions persecuted in China. |
| 910 A.D. | Monastic reform movement begins at Cluny. |
| 960 A.D. | Qarluk Turks converted to Sunni religion. |
| 969 A.D. | Fatimid caliphate established in Egypt. |
| 989 A.D. | Vladimir of Kiev baptized in Orthodox faith. |
| 1054 A.D. | Schism between Constantinople and Rome. |
| 1055 A.D. | Saljuq Turks capture Baghdad. |
| 1086 A.D. | Almoravid dynasty established in Spain. |
| 1087 A.D. | Gregory VII absolves penitent Emperor Henry IV. |
| 1095 A.D. | Pope Urban II launches First Crusade. |
| 1187 A.D. | Saladin recaptures Jerusalem from Crusaders. |
| 1206 A.D. | Moslem state established at Delhi. |
| 1273 A.D. | St. Thomas Aquinas writes *Summa Theologica* |
| 1309 A.D. | Papacy moved from Rome to Avignon, France. |
| 1377 A.D. | Papacy moved back to Rome. |
| 1417 A.D. | Martin V's election as Pope ends Great Schism. |
| 1439 A.D. | Byzantine emperor accepts papal authority. |
| 1453 A.D. | Ottoman Turks capture Constantinople. |
| 1492 A.D. | Moors expelled from Spain. |
| 1517 A.D. | Martin Luther posts 95 Theses on church door. |
| 1525 A.D. | Babur founds Mogul dynasty in India. |
| 1534 A.D. | Henry VIII becomes head of Church of England. |
| 1538 A.D. | Nanak, first Sikh guru, dies. |
| 1540 A.D. | Ignatius Loyola founds Society of Jesus. |
| 1565 A.D. | Hindu kingdom of Vijayanagar falls to Moslems. |
| 1582 A.D. | Mogul Emperor Akbar announces new religion. |
| 1827 A.D. | Joseph Smith discovers Mormon tablets. |
| 1859 A.D. | Charles Darwin publishes *Origin of Species.* |
| 1948 A.D. | Israel reestablished as a Jewish state. |
| 1965 A.D. | Paul Twitchell brings Eckankar to West. |

Dark Ages, the prestige of the fallen state passed to it as Rome's legimate heir. The Roman church was the remnant of a glorious empire that was no more. Popes used their prestige and authority in alliance with worldly rulers to create a dual system of governance. A universal church, whose spiritual jurisdiction covered the western half of the fallen empire, was paired with a multitude of secular states that were formed by the barbarian peoples involved in Rome's collapse. The idea of reconstructing that empire was to become an enduring theme of European political history. The Frankish dynasty, supporters of the Roman church, acquired secular power in much of western Europe during the 8th century. It seemed that imperial rule might be revived when, in 800 A.D., Pope Leo III crowned Charlemagne emperor of the Holy Roman Empire. However, the secular government became divided again when Charlemagne died and, later, his three grandsons inherited the kingdom. The power in medieval society was shared by two institutions, church and state. The church looked after people's spiritual needs and secular governments provided physical security.

While church and state worked cooperatively, there was also a power struggle. The head of the Roman church, the Pope, struggled to gain an advantage over secular governments by exercising its powers of recognition and, more forcefully, by excommunicating disobedient rulers. History records the contrite appearance of Emperor Henry IV before the pope after Gregory VII excommunicated him in 1076. If the Church wished to punish a king, it could deny the sacraments to the king and his subjects, thus denying them entrance to Heaven. Kings and emperors, on the other hand, fought the Church through use of their earthly power. A particular point of contention was the struggle

between Popes and European monarchs over the right to "invest" (appoint) local church officials. The Concordat of Worms resolved this question in the Pope's favor but kings were allowed to supervise church elections. The administration of justice was divided between ecclesiastical and secular courts, each having certain powers and scope of authority. Pope Boniface VIII called ecclesiastical and secular governments the "two swords" of the church. Symbolizing the dual power structure, coins of the period often exhibited the Pope's likeness on one side and the Holy Roman Emperor's on the other.

investiture of a bishop

On a personal level, the Roman church exercised its authority through the sacraments. These were rituals conducted by priests which were thought necessary for salvation. Seven sacraments were believed most important: baptism, confirmation, the Eucharist, penance, extreme unction, orders, and matrimony. Church doctrine asserted that sacraments were the means by which God transmitted his grace to humanity. Grace meant undeserved forgiveness of sins. The institution of the sacraments was based on the principle that all men were sinners in need of forgiveness who were unable to obtain this by their own powers. The Eucharist, which was patterned after Jesus' last supper with the Disciples, was the greatest of the sacraments. The early Christian community especially cherished this ceremonial meal because it was believed that Jesus would return during its celebration. In the 9th century, A.D., a Benedictine monk named Radbertus wrote a treatise arguing that the bread eaten during celebration of the Mass was the flesh of Jesus and the wine which was drunk was his blood. Another monk suggested that these two substances were only symbols of Christ's body and blood. The literal interpretation, more in tune with the spirit of the medieval church, was accepted at the Fourth Lateran Council in 1215.

The Church claimed competent authority to decide theological questions through its firm connection to Jesus and the Apostles. The historical record of God's word presented in the Bible became a criterion of truth. At the same time, the Roman church put much emphasis upon traditional church teachings. Such doctrines, being inspired by the Holy Spirit, were considered to have equal authority with the sacred scriptures. "The Church has never erred and will never err to all eternity," a papal declaration of the 11th century maintained. An earlier declaration held that "the Popes, like Jesus, are conceived by their mothers through the overshadowing of the Holy Spirit ... All powers in Heaven, as well as on earth, are given to them." With such attitudes, it is not surprising that leaders of the Roman church instituted the Inquisition and burned heretics at the stake. Disbelief, in the form of rational inquiry, began to creep into the culture despite the Church's best efforts to enforce its monopoly of faith. Given the importance of papal links to St. Peter, the Great Schism of 1378-1417, in which two rival popes each claimed authority, produced a severe crisis of confidence in the Papacy.

Perhaps the best evidence that the Roman church was becoming a worldly empire lay in its advocacy and use of military force. The church itself controlled certain territories in northern and central Italy. In 756, Pippin III gave the Pope temporal control of certain lands conquered from the Lombards as a reward for his support in recognizing Carolingian claims to the Frankish throne. The Papal States were drawn into a long struggle with Holy Roman Emperors and local powers to control this and other territories. However, the Church was also responsible for launching and maintaining the Crusades which were directed against the Islamic rulers of Palestine between the 11th and 13th centuries. Responding to complaints from Peter the Hermit and others that the Turks were harassing Christian pilgrims to Jerusalem, Pope Urban II issued an appeal in 1095 for European Christians to recapture the Holy City from the Moslems. A huge army led by Godfrey of Bouillon was assembled in Constantinople to carry out this mission. "Deus volt" - God wills it - was their battle cry. The Christian crusaders did capture Jerusalem in 1099 after a battle in which 70,000 civilians were massacred, and set a French king upon the throne in that city. The First Crusade was followed by eight others, progressively less successful. In the end, Moslems retained control of that region.

### Orthodox Christianity

The East Roman empire, which had survived the barbarian onslaught of the 5th and 6th centuries A.D., was continuously associated with the See of Constantinople. A church council held in 381 A.D. had declared that it ranked second after the See of Rome. The church council convened in  Chalcedon in 451 A.D. gave Constantinople spiritual authority over western Turkey and the eastern part of the Balkan peninsula. In this realm, political rulers tended to dominate the religious institutions, following the principle which Justinian laid down in the 6th century: "Nothing should happen in the Church against the command or will of the Emperor." The church became like a department of government in charge of religious ceremonies. The Metropolitan of Constantinople could make no claim similar to the Roman Pontiff's of having authority that ran back to the Apostles. He merely exercised geographical jurisdiction. His scope of authority followed the lines of imperial power. Consequently, the center of power in the eastern church drifted toward Moscow after Constantinople fell to the Turks in the 15th century.

Orthodox Christianity put less emphasis upon the authority and structure of the church, the sacraments, priestly celibacy, and other worldly aspects of religion than the western Church, and more on theological questions. The Eastern church did not accept the solution of Chalcedon regarding Christ's being: one "in two natures .. without change, without division..." It did not accept the filioque clause in the Nicene creed: that the Holy Spirit had proceeded "from the Father and the Son." Orthodox theology tended to stress a single nature, accepting the divinity of Christ at the price of neglecting his humanity. An issue peculiar to the Orthodox church was the controversy concerning iconoclasm. Visual representations of divine subjects, long tolerated in the Christian church, went against the grain of Judaic religion. Hoping to increase support among his Jewish and Moslem subjects, Emperor Leo III in 726 launched a personal crusade against the use of icons in the church. He demanded that the icons be destroyed and removed church officials who resisted. Leo's iconoclastic program met with stiff resistance, especially in the monasteries.

John of Damascus argued that icons helped religious understanding. "When we set up an image of Christ in any place," he wrote, "we appeal to the senses. An image is, after all, a reminder; it is to the illiterate what a book is to the literate; and what the word is to the hearing, the image is to the sight." Leo remained unconvinced by such arguments. He continued with the idol-smashing campaign despite strong opposition and a growing rift with the western church. His son, Constantine V, was an even more ardent iconoclast. The Synod of Hiera in 753 A.D. formally supported the emperor's position. Three decades later, Constantine's grandson, Constantine VI, became emperor but was too young to rule so his mother, Irene, assumed power. When it became apparent that the young emperor too favored the iconoclastic program, Empress Irene took steps to block this. She convened a general council of the church to repeal previous decisions. To thwart opposition within her own family, she had the young emperor, her son, blinded and deposed. The use of religious images was again permitted. A revival of the iconoclastic campaign took place during the reign of Leo V. It was again stifled through the intervention of another icon-loving empress and regent, Theodora. Ultimately, a compromise was reached, banning three-dimensional images but tacitly permitting two-dimensional ones.

The furor concerning icons was one of several issues which drove a wedge between the eastern and western branches of Christianity. While the worldly power of the eastern patriarchs was limited by the Byzantine state, the head of the western church was becoming steadily more powerful. As the Roman pontiff claimed primacy within the church on the basis of his succession from Peter, so the Metropolitan of Constantinople claimed authority based on his relationship to the surviving Roman state. In that regard, the Pope's coronation of Charlemagne as emperor of the Holy Roman Empire posed a direct challenge to the claims of the Byzantine Empire and its captive church. The issue of Photianism, an eastern declaration of independence from Rome, became the immediate cause of a rupture between the two branches of the church. Theologically, they were divided by the fact that the eastern church did not accept the "filioque clause". The Great Schism officially took place in July 1054 A.D. when Pope Leo IX excommunicated Michael Cerularius, an eastern patriarch. After Frankish crusaders sacked Constantinople in 1204 A.D., reconciliation between the two domains of Christendom became all but impossible. The Byzantine emperor did accept Rome's spiritual authority in the 15th century, but it was too late the save the empire from conquest by the Ottoman Turks.

The salvation of the Byzantine church was its outreach to Slavic peoples. In the 9th century, the Patriarch of Constantinople sent a pair of scholarly brothers from Thessalonica, Constantine and Methodius, on a mission to neighboring peoples. They went first to Khazaria, but its rulers decided instead to convert to Judaism. Next the brothers received an invitation to the Slavic principality of Great Moravia (Czechoslovakia and Hungary). Constantine, also known as Cyril, brought with him the Glagolitic alphabet which he had invented for Slavs living in Greece. The brothers adapted this script to the local idiom and established a mission. Although they were driven out of Moravia through pressure from Frankish German priests, some of the remaining Orthodox clergy made their way to Bulgaria, carrying the Glagolitic script. Bulgaria had converted to the Eastern Orthodox faith in 863. Its ruler, Khan Boris-Michael, received the Moravian refugee clergy with the idea that their Slavonic-language script would enable Bulgaria to develop its own national church and remain politically independent of Constantinople or Rome. In 885, Bulgarians simplified the Glagolitic script, naming it "Cyrillic" after Cyril. It was this script primarily which brought Slavic peoples such as the Russians into the Orthodox fold.

Bulgarian peasants reacted to their nation's adoption of Orthodox Christianity by embracing a religious creed known as Bogomilism, which an Orthodox priest, Bogomil, had devised between 927 and 954. This was an anticlerical doctrine adapted from Paulician Christianity, a Thracian heresy. Bogomilism held that the world had been created by Satan, who was God's older son, and that Jesus, God's younger son, was sent to earth to overthrow Satan and rescue mankind. Another version put good and evil on a parity. While rejecting Christianity, the Bogomils practiced celibacy and asceticism perhaps to distinguish themselves from the loose habits of the Orthodox clergy. Bogomil missionaries spread this religion to other parts of the Balkan peninsula, especially Bosnia, where the ruling family embraced it as an alternative to the Hungarian Catholic and Serbian Orthodox faiths. The French Albigenses belonged to the same movement. The Bogomil heresy was fiercely suppressed and died out with the expansion of Islam in the Balkan region.

Eastern Europe was a battleground between the Roman Catholic and Greek Orthodox faiths at the close of the 1st millennium A.D. Poland and Bohemia broke with Slavic peoples elsewhere in affiliating with the Roman church. To forestall Teutonic encroachment upon Polish territory, Duke Mieszko I (960-

992) placed his realm under the Pope's direct protection and control. The Polish Piast dynasty subsequently conquered territories as far east as Kiev and blocked the Teutonic German advance along the Baltic sea. Russia's conversion to Eastern Orthodox Christianity coincides with the baptism of Prince Vladimir of Kiev in 987. The prince made his selection of religions from among several competing types after receiving the hand of Emperor Basil II's sister, Anna, in marriage. Vladimir ordered his subjects to be baptized en masse. Missionaries from

Bulgaria brought the Old Church Slavonic liturgy and the Cyrillic alphabet to Kiev. The Mongols conquered the Ukraine in the 13th century and held it for over two centuries. When Mongol power sub-

the Kremlin in Moscow

sided, the Dukes of Moscow began annexing territories in what later became the Russian state. After Ivan III married the last Byzantine emperor's niece and took the title of "Czar", Moscow became the new center of the Orthodox faith. The Patriarch of Constantinople was given civil authority over Christians living in the Ottoman empire.

## The Later Persian Religions

The religion of Zoroaster supported the first (Achaemenian) Persian dynasty. Like most other philosophical religions, Zoroastrianism had to be softened by personal features to make it suitable for devotional worship. Although Zoroaster was a monotheist, a later version of his religion turned the separate aspects of Ahura-Mazda into goddesses. The Magi were hereditary priests of this religion. Christians know them as the three wise men who, following the Star of Bethlehem, brought gifts to the infant Jesus. The Arsacid dynasty which ruled the Parthian empire for more than four centuries personally embraced Magian Zoroastrianism but was tolerant of other religions. The Sasanid family, which supplanted the Arsacids in 221 A.D., were priests of the pre-Zoroastrian water goddess, Anahita, whose cult had been incorporated into the Zoroastrian religion. Its rulers were therefore more zealous in promoting that religion.

In 240 A.D., a Persian prophet named Mani began preaching that he was a reincarnation of the Holy Spirit. A self-styled successor to Zoroaster, Buddha, and Jesus, he had received the final and most complete revelation of God. Emperor Shahpuhr I gave Mani permission to preach his new religion throughout the empire. Missionaries spread Manichaeism, as well, to Egypt, Central Asia, and the Roman empire. Like Zoroastrianism, its theology centered upon the opposition of evil and good, darkness and light. Man needed to be redeemed from his material nature through Christ's divine light. After Shahpuhr died, priests of the Zoroastrian state religion persuaded Emperor Vahram I to arrest Mani and put him to death. Like Jesus, however, this prophet's death and subsequent persecution of his followers had a stimulating effect upon the religion. In north Africa, the future St. Augustine was briefly a Manichee. The Manichaean faith became the national religion of the Uighur Turks living west of China. It also influenced the Paulician, Bogomil, and other Christian heresies.

coin of Shahpuhr I

Since Christianity was the Roman state religion after Theodosius I's ban on pagan religions in 391 A.D., Sasanian emperors tended to view Christians living in Persia as a potential fifth column. Likewise, Roman emperors mistrusted Zoroastrians. In 297, Diocletian denounced Egyptian converts to Manichaeism as Persian sympathizers even though Persian emperors had put Mani to death and persecuted his followers. After the Council of Ephesus condemned Nestorian Christianity in 431, Roman Nestorians moved across the border to Nisibis in Persia where they were welcomed as refugees. Their persecution in Rome cleared them of suspicion. However, in 440, Emperor Yazdigerd II ordered all his subjects to convert to Zoroastrianism. This provoked a rebellion in Christian Armenia, which was crushed. The

Persian military defeat by the Ephthalite Huns in 484 forced the Sasanian government to back down and tolerate non-Iranian Christians.

The same disaster produced a social crisis that was accompanied by a religious movement led by Mazdak, head of the Drist-Den Manichaean sect. It was a communist movement formed in response to the economic inequality of Persian society. Emperor Kavadh I became a convert and put through its program of reform. The Persian nobility and Zoroastrian clergy together opposed the Mazdakites. Ultimately, the emperor himself disavowed them at the urging of his son and heir, Khusro I, who later crushed this movement. In 572, Khusro I began a war with the East Roman empire, which lasted until 590. Another war between the Christian Roman and Zoroastrian Persian empires broke out in 604. It was not settled until 628. The Arabs attacked both empires simultaneously five years later. Exhausted from its Roman wars, the Persian empire was extinguished. The Sasanid capital of Ctesiphon fell in 637.

Most Zoroastrians in Persia readily accepted Moslem rule. A few fled to northwestern India where they were granted asylum on condition that they refrain from proselytizing. They became known as the Parsee sect, numbering today less than a million persons. Another group fled westward to China through a part of Turkestan which Khrusro I had annexed to the Persian empire. A Sasanid prince reached Ch'ang-an, the Chinese capital, as a refugee in 674. All three of Persia's principal religions - Zoroastrianism, Manichaeism, and Nestorian Christianity - penetrated China from the west during the early T'ang period. Manichaeism, being the Uighur Turk's national religion, made perhaps the greatest inroads. However, Kirghiz nomads defeated the Uighurs in 840. In 841-845, the Chinese government conducted a crackdown against foreign religions at the instigation of Taoist clergy. While the Buddhists suffered mainly economic losses, this campaign of xenophobic persecution was fatal to the Persian religions established in China.

## The Religion of Islam

Religious and political conflict beset Arabian peoples in the beginning part of the 7th century, A.D. The last war between the East Roman and Sasanian Persian empires took place between 604 and 628, A.D. Arabs served as mercenary soldiers for both sides. In the process, they acquired valuable experience in making war and the latest military equipment. These Arabs were immersed in religious controversies as Christians, Jews, Zoroastrians, and Manichees struggled for dominance. A large number of Jews lived on the Arabian peninsula in cities such as Yathrib (Medina) and Khaybar. Yemen in the south was first a Christian kingdom and then a state controlled by the Persian empire. In the 3rd century, A.D., Mani had claimed to be a prophet in the lineage of Zoroaster, Buddha, and Jesus who put a "seal" on prophecy. Later the same idea was taken up with greater effect by Mohammed, founder of the Islamic religion.

Islam means self-surrender or submission to God. God, whose name is Allah, is the same as the Jewish or Christian God according to Moslem teachings. However, these earlier religions had become corrupted so that a new prophet had been commissioned to deliver a revelation that would set humanity straight. The prophet Mohammed lived in the city of Mecca which was situated on the trade route between Yemen and Syria in western Arabia. He conducted caravans between Mecca and Damascus for his wife, Khadijah, who was a wealthy widow. While in Syria and Palestine, Mohammed had been exposed to the Jewish and Christian religions. He became ashamed of the polytheistic religion of the Arabs which seemed primitive in comparison with them. In 611 A.D., at the age of forty, Mohammed had a vision in a cave near Mecca in which the Archangel Gabriel commanded him to transmit a new revelation of God to the people of Mecca. This was a message of monotheism confirming earlier Judaic teachings. Gabriel's lengthy dictations to Mohammed were compiled in a collection of Arabic-language writings known as the *Koran*. Mohammed's religion imposed strict personal disciplines such as a prohibition against drinking alcohol or eating pork and religious duties that included daily prayers, annual fasting, and pilgrimages to Mecca. It also forbade usury and abuse of the poor.

For twelve years, Mohammed tried to persuade fellow residents of Mecca to adopt this new religion, but his efforts met with limited success. Although a Quraysh tribesman, he was not part of the inner circle that controlled the city. Also, Islam's monotheistic principles conflicted with the polytheistic cult of the Ka'bah, a large black stone whose annual festival was economically important to Mecca. Mohammed's fortunes suddenly changed when, in 622 A.D., he received an invitation to head the government of Medina, a neighboring city torn by political rifts. Mohammed proved to be an able administrator. His theocratic government in Medina united the quarreling factions and grew militarily strong. Its armies waged aggressive war first against Mecca and then other Arabian cities. A factor aiding in their success was that Mohammed allowed his followers to attack caravans and plunder defeated enemies. The rich Jews of Medina, who refused to convert to Islam despite its acceptance of a single God, were a particular target. By the time of Mohammed's death in 632 A.D., his Islamic empire controlled most of the Arabian peninsula.

Ka'bah shrine in Mecca

After the prophet's death, local Arabs revolted. The cities of Mecca and Medina, controlled by the newly converted Quraysh clan, opposed them as Islamic loyalists. Mohammed's temporal successor or "caliph", Abu Bakr, persuaded the other Arabs to end their revolt and join forces in conducting military raids against the East Roman and Sasanian Persian empires whose armies were exhausted from more than two decades of war. Their roads intact, the Moslem armies rapidly overran the domain of the Persian empire. They pushed the East Roman empire back into an area north of the Taurus mountains in Turkey. Syria, Palestine, Mesopotamia, and Egypt fell to the Moslems by 641 A.D. The Sasanian empire was extinguished by 651 A.D. During the next half century, Islamic forces took Armenia and Georgia. They conquered all the East Roman territories in northwest Africa and the Visigothic kingdoms in Spain and southwest France. In the East, they captured the Ephthalite Huns' possessions in Uzbekistan and Transoxania (south and east of the Aral Sea), as well as lands adjoining the Indus River. However, the Moslems failed on two occasions to take Constantinople. Their push northward through France was checked at the battle of Tours in 732 A.D.

Contrary to an opinion expressed in Europe, this was not a campaign to force conversions to the Islamic faith. Membership in other religions was tolerated so long as their people submitted to the Islamic government and paid a surtax. These people had their own self-governing communities, civil codes, and religious leaders. Arab military commanders served as governors of the conquered territories. Lacking a literate corps of administrators, they wisely left civil administration in the hands of their hellenized Christian and Persian subjects. Nestorian, Monophysite, and other persecuted Christian sects generally welcomed the change in governments. Many voluntarily converted to Islam because it was financially advantageous to do so. The Arab conquerors wore their religion as a badge of national pride. The Umayyad dynasty, which Mu'awiyah founded at Damascus in 661, established Arab Moslems as a privileged class. Exempted from paying poll taxes, they also received regular payments from the state treasury. When Caliph Umar II (717-20) abolished the poll tax for non-Arab Moslems, it precipitated a financial crisis. Caliph Hisham's subsequent substitution of a land tax upon non-Arabs to replenish the treasury caused much dissatisfaction. The Umayyad rulers were replaced by the Abbasid dynasty in the Arab Civil War of 747-750 A.D.

Theoretically, the Abbasid insurrection was about legitimacy of succession. Their claimant to the caliphate was descended from Ali, Mohammed's son-in-law, whereas the Umayyad rulers traced their lineage back to a Qurayshite tribesman unrelated to the Prophet. After Abu Bakr's death in 634, Umar was elected caliph. A wise and effective ruler, he was assassinated by a Persian slave in 644. The next caliph, Uthman, was less capable. He was assassinated in 656. Ali became the next caliph. Opposed by Aisha, Mohammed's widow, and some of the Prophet's companions, he was assassinated in 661. Ali's eldest son, Hasan, was elected to succeed him. However, Mu'awiyah, governor of Syria, was recognized as caliph in Damascus. Mu'awiyah persuaded Hasan to give up the caliphate in exchange for a royal pension and a harem in Medina. This arrangement held until Mu'awiyah's death in 680. Then Ali's younger son, Husayn, set forth from Medina with a group of supporters to claim the caliph's position. Mu'awiyah's son and successor, Yazid, sent a small army which intercepted Husayn at Karbala. When Husayn refused to return to Medina, Yazid's forces slaughtered him and his supporters. They brought the head of Husayn, Mohammed's grandson, back to Yazid in Damascus.

This shocking event led to a schism within the Islamic community. The Shi'ite Moslems, predominant in Persia, regarded the Umayyad dynasty as usurpers of the caliphate. They supported the rival claims of Ali's descendants on the basis of their blood line running back to Mohammed. For them, Husayn's murder in 680 came to symbolize the abuse suffered by non-Arab minorities under Umayyad rule. Sunni Moslems, on the other hand, represented the Umayyad loyalists. They were the mainstream group during the period of Arab ascendancy. Abbas, a Shi'ite descendant of Mohammed's uncle, became caliph after the upheaval of 747-50, founding the Abbasid dynasty. Abbas' successor, Mansur, moved the capital of the empire from Damascus to Baghdad. There Persians gained political and cultural ascendancy. Meanwhile, an Umayyad refugee, Abd ar-Rahman, escaped to the Iberian peninsula where he founded a Sunni state. Now there were two caliphates - one Shi'ite and one Sunni - and the political unity of Islam was lost. The succession to the caliphate has thus become a greater source of controversy within Islam than questions of philosophical belief. Heresy plays a smaller part in the Islamic than Christian religion. Perhaps that is because, in contrast with Jesus, who preached about another world, Mohammed left specific instructions about many earthly things.

Islamic religion, like others in the Judaic tradition, includes belief in the Last Judgment and in Heaven and Hell. Persons who remain faithful to the religion, especially those who died fighting for it, will be accepted into paradise while infidels will spend an eternity in Hell. Islam attaches much importance to interpretations of law. The *Koran*, which includes many of Mohammed's spiritual teachings and administrative rulings, is a principal source of this law. In addition, scholars have assembled collections of stories about Mohammed and sayings attributed to him. Mohammed once said: "My community will never agree in an error." That statement has given sanction to legal interpretations not found in the Prophet's teachings which have become accepted within Islamic society. This culture is tolerant of doctrinal differences. Within the Sunni tradition, there are four different schools of Islamic law which are considered equally valid. A community is free to pick whichever it prefers. Theological questions are decided by a consensus of learned opinion. The caliph is strictly a political authority. Ibn Taymiyya taught that any state governed in accordance with Islamic law belongs to Islam, whether or not it has a caliph.

the muezzin

The centuries which followed the founding of the Abbasid dynasty in 750 A.D. brought a flowering of Islamic culture. Baghdad in the 9th century A.D. was a cosmopolitan city, exciting both commercial and intellectual activity. While the Arabs had lost official privileges, their language acquired a rich literature as many poems were written in Arabic and works from other cultures were translated into it. New translations of Greek philosophical writings became available during this period. The Islamic religion developed a theology competitive with that of other religions. Mutazilite scholars debated such questions as predestination, free will, and justification by faith. The doctrine of a "created" Koran as embodiment of God's word was analogous to Christ's role in Arian Christianity. One type of religious thinking tended to be legalistic. A second represented the rationalism of theologians like the Mutazilites. A third, which stood in stark contrast with the other two, sought direct experience of God. Persian Shi'ites in the late 10th century formed a fraternity of Sufi mystics who practiced their religion through poetry, ecstatic chanting, and dance.

## Islamic Empires

The Abbasid revolution of 750 A.D. ushered in a period of confusing political events. In 756, a refugee from the House of Umayyad established a new dynasty on the Iberian peninsula where Sunnis comprised a majority of the population. However, this regime was under intense pressure from Frankish Christians to give up territory. Three new Moslem states ruled by Shi'ite separatists were formed in Algeria between 757 and 786 A.D. Morocco became an independent state in 788 under the Alid (House of Ali) king Idris I. In 800, a Sunni state which recognized the suzerainty of the Abbasid dynasty was established in Tunisia by Aghlabid Arabs. Isma'ili (Seven-Imam) Shi'ites denying the Abbasid's legitimacy overthrew this regime a century later. In Iran, where the Abbasid revolution had originated, several insurrections took place after the second caliph, Mansur, put to death in 754 the man who had instigated the rebellion against the Umayyad dynasty. Though fractured, Islam's political empire was continuing to expand. In 751 A.D., Abbasid armies defeated Chinese forces in a battle at Samarkand. Umayyad Moslems evicted from Iberia captured Crete from the East Roman empire in 826 A.D. The Aghlabids from Tunisia conquered most of Sicily. Qarluq Turks, who later occupied the Tarim basin, were converted to the Sunni sect in 960.

The 10th and 11th centuries A.D. were times of tribulation for the Islamic world. Its rulers fought with the East Roman empire and later with western crusaders for possession of Sicily, Syria, and Palestine. Nomadic tribes including Turks, Arabs, and

Berbers overran large areas of the empire. In 945 A.D., Buway-hid rulers of a Moslem state in western Iran overthrew the Ab-basid dynasty. That put Iranians and Berbers of the Tunisian Fa-timid dynasty in control of much of the Islamic world, exclud-ing Spain. Qarluq and Ghuzz Turks, including a band loyal to the House of Saljuq, entered Asia Minor. In 1055 A.D., Saljuq Turks, embracing the Sunni faith, replaced the Buwayhid Shi'ites on the throne in Baghdad. These Turkish Moslems chose to re-tain the Persian administrators. Saljuq Turks in Anatolia estab-lished the Sultanate of Rum in 1057. The Saljuq allowed other Turkish tribes to enter Armenia. En route, they devastated Iran. Arab nomads trekking west through north Africa ruined the ol-ive fields which had dated from Carthaginian times. During this turbulent period, the Islamic religion acquired a softer, personal side thanks to an Iranian scholar, Ghazzali, who introduced mys-ticism into the Sunni tradition. His *Restoration of the Science of Religion* is Islam's best-known theological work.

Under fierce attack from western Christians, Islamic rulers held most of their territory during the 12th and 13th centuries A.D. A Turkish officer of the Saljuq empire drove the Frankish crusaders out of their Syrian strongholds and established a new kingdom in Egypt. Salah-ad-Din (Saladin), a Kurdish officer in its employ, later set up his own kingdom. Saladin recaptured Jerusalem from the Franks in 1187. He later repelled avenging Christian armies of the Third Crusade. Saladin's dynasty was inherited by a consortium of Turkish military slaves, the Mam-luks. A more serious threat than the Christian crusaders was the attack on Islamic territories by the Mongol hordes beginning with Genghis Khan's devastation of Khwarizm in 1220-21. The Ab-basid caliph Nasir created a new chivalric order, the futuwwah, to meet this military threat. Moslem kingdoms in Turkey and Iraq fell to the Mongols. The Abassid caliphate was liquidated in 1258 A.D. However, the Golden Horde was unable to con-quer Syria or Egypt because of Mamluk opposition. Defying earlier expectations that the Mongols and western Christians might form a grand alliance, the rulers of three Mongol succes-sor states in the western part of the empire later became Mos-lems.

Nestorian and Monophysite Christians living in Asia Minor, once in the majority, converted to Islam in large numbers during the 14th century. Afterwards, only a small part of the population continued to profess the Christian faith. On the other hand, Moslems were steadily being expelled from the Iberian peninsula as Christian kings advanced. Political adversity did not prevent a great flowering of Moorish culture before its em-

Santiago
the Moorslayer

pire disappeared. The last Islamic stronghold at Granada fell to the Christian monarchy of Aragon and Castile in 1492 A.D. The religion of Islam began to make inroads into the African population south of the Sahara desert. In Mamluk Egypt, Coptic Christians were a dwindling part of the population. Arabs infiltrating into Nubia from Egypt gradually converted its people from Monophysite Christianity. The Abyssinian kingdom, south of Nubia, remained Monophysite Christian until the 16th century A.D. Islam also achieved peaceful conversions in Malaya and Indonesia, coexisting with the Buddhist and Hindu religions. Some conversions took place in western China.

Turkish nomads from central Asia had been drawn into the sedentary population of Asia Minor during the 11th century when Saljuq Turks captured the Abbasid empire. Between 1261 and 1300 A.D., other, more warlike Turkish people who had been subjects of the Mongols occupied most of present-day Turkey while the East Roman empire was retaking Constantinople from the western Christians and neglecting its Asian provinces. When Mongol rule was extinguished in 1335 A.D., there was a competition among the Turkish tribes to establish a successor state in the area. Waging war in the spirit of jihad, the Ottomans won that contest by capturing several key cities during the first half of the 14th century. They increased their power by recruiting other Turks for their armies and using Christians to perform economic functions. In the late 14th century, a new barbarian scourge appeared in the person of Tamerlane, self-styled successor to Genghis Khan. He led Moslem armies from Transoxania on a rampage through India, Russia, and the Middle East. Tamerlane's horde temporarily seized the Ottoman possessions in Asia. Once this threat had subsided and the Asian lands were reconquered, a new revolt against Ottoman rule broke out in Bulgaria, organized by a Sunni mystic. Another took place in Asia Minor a century later. The Ottoman Turks suppressed both rebellions.

The second rebellion, which occurred between 1511 and 1513 A.D., involved Shi'ite sympathizers of Shah Isma'il, founder of the Persian Safavi empire. This empire grew rapidly between 1500 and 1513, reaching its northeastern limit in territories inhabited by Uzbek nomads and its western limit in the Ottoman empire. In a land once predominantly Sunni, Shah Isma'il required his Iranian subjects to adopt the Shi'ite religion. The Safavi army was comprised of Qizilbash soldiers in red headgear who had once lived under Ottoman rule. A spirited group, they belonged to a Sufi religious order of which the Shah was the spiritual head. The Ottoman Turks defeated the Safavi forces at the Battle of Chaldiran in 1514 and later seized Iraq. After Shah Abbas I recovered Baghdad from the Turks in 1623, he built a beautiful new capital at Isfahan. Another Safavi emperor, Shah Jahan, built the Taj Mahal at Agra in India. This empire was overthrown by Afghan nomads occupying Isfahan in 1722. However, it was resurrected after a short time by Nadir Quli, a Turkish soldier who invaded India. Ruling as Shah of the Afshar dynasty, he was assassinated by officers of his own guard in 1747. An Afghan successor state then took possession of Persia and India.

Nadir Shah

A third Islamic empire, the Mogul, was created in India when a descendant of Tamerlane, Babur, invaded northern India from Afghanistan. Babur defeated the sultan of Delhi at the battle of Paripat in 1526. He seized the cities of Agra and Delhi and soon controlled much of northern India. However, Babur's son, Humayun, lost this territory to the Bengali Afghan emperor Sher Shah Sur. The Mogul dynasty was established on a more solid footing when Humayun reconquered the kingdom of Delhi in 1555. Humayun's son, Akbar, expanded the empire to include Afghanistan, Baluchistan, and lands in India as far south as the Godavari river. His royal court became a center of learning and the arts. Since Akbar's domain included a largely Hindu population, his regime depended on them heavily for military and administrative support. Concerned about the Hindus' loyalty to a Moslem state, Akbar hosted a series of religious dialogues between representatives of the Moslem, Hindu, Zoroastrian, and Roman Catholic Christian faiths, seeking common ground. In 1582, he announced the creation of a new monotheistic religion called the Din-i-Ilahi, of which he, Akbar, was the prophet. This venture provoked a rebellion in Moslem circles and never caught on.

At the start of the 17th century, the Islamic world was divided into three great empires: the Ottoman empire in Turkey, the Safavi empire in Iran, and the Timurid Mogul empire in India. The Ottoman dynasty, which began in the 14th century, was extinguished in the Versailles peace treaty ending World War I. This Sunni Moslem empire, which had conquered both Mamluk Egypt and the East Roman empire, included most of the territory bordering the eastern Mediterranean and Black seas as well as in north Africa, Egypt, Arabia, Hungary, and the Balkan peninsula. Its capital was Istanbul, formerly Constantinople. The Ottoman rulers followed a policy of excluding their free-born Moslem subjects from top military and administrative positions. Their army was staffed by specially selected slaves called "janizaries", who typically were Christians abducted as boys from peasant families. As a result, Greek Christians held the reins of government in this Islamic state. Ottoman power was threatened at sea when Portuguese vessels seized their trading ports along the Indian ocean during the 16th century A.D. Czar Ivan IV cut off the empire's contact with Uzbek Moslems by annexing Kazan and Astrakhan in the 1550s. Currency decline brought on by the Spaniards' silver-mining operations in the Americas produced an economic crisis.

The Moslem empires in Persia and India expired during the 18th century. After Nadir Quli's death in 1747, the Afghan

Zand dynasty founded by Ahmad Shah Durrani took control of Persia while battling the Hindu Marathas in India. A eunuch, Aga Mohammed Khan, overthrew this regime in 1794 and established the Kajar dynasty, which lasted until 1925. Czarist Russia began to encroach upon Persian territories in the 19th century. Afghanistan was detached from Iran in 1857. The last Shah, Reza Pahlevi, was deposed in 1979 by forces supporting the Ayatollah Khomeini. Akbar's Mogul successors in India abandoned his policy of tolerance towards Hindus. When Emperor Aurangzeb sought to impose his rule on the southern tip of India, it provoked a furious Hindu counterattack. However, Afghan Persian forces under the Zand dynasty invaded northern India and defeated the Hindu armies in 1758-61. About the same time, British forces under Robert Clive defeated the French. Weakened by wars with the Hindus and Sikhs, the Mogul empire was ruined. The British East India Company ran the Indian government under a succession of puppet regimes. The British crown took possession of India in 1877 and granted this colony its independence seventy years later. Hindu India and Moslem Pakistan became two separate nations.

mosque of Aurangzeb at Benares

## The Hindu and Buddhist Religions

A most ancient religion developed in northern India during the middle and latter part of the 2nd millennium B.C. The Aryan conquerors of India brought with them a pre-philosophical religion of rituals and prayers intended to achieve practical results. This religion had a pantheon of nature gods and goddesses, not unlike that of the Greeks. The hymns, myths, prayers, and poetic utterances, long carried within the memory of priests, were eventually written down in a collection of Vedic-language literature called the Rig-Veda. This religion had a powerful Brahman priesthood and a caste system which perpetuated social roles. Public ceremonies such as the horse ritual, which dramatized military victories, reinforced Aryan values. Priestly commentaries in the Brahmanas and Aranyakas explained liturgical practice and discussed the mysteries of the universe.

In the last section of the Veda, called the Upanishads, philosophical discussions appear concerning man's relationship to God. The individual person, or soul, was seen to be experiencing a cosmic journey which includes life in this world. This life is a kind of bondage to delusional existence. The soul of each person is actually identical with the universe as a whole. The Hindu cosmology involved a belief that human souls were born

Hindu devotee

and reborn in cycles of reincarnation. One's status in the next life depended upon the moral quality of actions undertaken in this and previous existences. The law of karma stated that each action had a consequence in the soul's future experience. Wrong or hurtful acts might bring lower status or seemingly unjust treatment in a future life, while benevolent actions would be rewarded. Conversely, one's situation in the present life could partly be explained by one's activities in previous incarnations. Such an explanation helped to reconcile individuals to their place in the caste system. It created an incentive to behave. The goal, however, was to escape the treadmill of reincarnations and be released into the cosmic whole. Certain yoga  exercises or other methods known to the priests helped to hasten that process.

Buddhism is one of two Hindu "heresies" of the 6th century B.C., Jainism being the other. The Hindu salvation, "nirvana" or release from the cycle of earthly rebirths, was not available to ordinary people. If one followed the "way of works", it was still necessary to be reborn as a Brahman to achieve nirvana at death. If one followed the path of knowledge through the Upanishads, one needed time for contemplation and study. Buddha and Mahavira, founder of Jainism, offered salvation to everyone. "No Brahman is such by birth ... A Brahman is such by his deeds," Buddha declared. Jainism required strict asceticism and total renunciation of the world. Buddhism offered a "middle way" between asceticism and living in the world. Buddha saw a moral dichotomy between selfishness and love of truth. "Learn to distinguish between Self and Truth," he said. "If we liberate our souls from our petty selves, wish no ill to others, and become clear as a crystal diamond reflecting the light of truth, what a radiant picture will appear in us, mirroring things as they are, without the admixture of burning desires, without the distortion of erroneous illusion, without the agitation of clinging and unrest."

Siddhartha Gautama, the Buddha, was born in Nepal in 567 B.C., son of a petty king. A seer informed his father that Buddha was destined to become the greatest king in history. If, however, he saw four things - disease, old age, death, and a monk who had renounced the world - then he would forgo that destiny to become the discoverer of a universal path of salvation. Buddha's father, wishing to have a royal successor, tried to shield the boy from those experiences, but to no avail. Buddha saw each of the four fateful situations during a ride in the park. He renounced his throne, abandoned his wife and infant son, and spent six years practicing spiritual disciplines including physical self-torture and philosophical study as a wanderer and hermit. Finally, after meditating for seven weeks under a Bo tree, Buddha experienced personal enlightenment in the form of an insight concerning human suffering. He returned to the world to teach this doctrine as an itinerant preacher until his death in 483 B.C. The group of disciples who accompanied him became the nucleus of the Buddhist sangha, a monastic community.

Buddha's followers produced a scripture from the memory of his teachings.

The insights which Buddha had under the Bo tree can be summarized in a set of philosophical principles called the "four noble truths". They include the ideas that: (1) Life is filled with sorrow. (2) Sorrow originates in personal desire. (3) Sorrow ends when desires end. (4) The way to end desire is by following the "eight-fold path." This path consists of the following elements: (1) right belief, (2) right resolve, (3) right speech, (4) right conduct, (5) right occupation, (6) right effort, (7) right contemplation, and (8) right meditation. If one attains complete extinction of desire, one achieves the blissful state of nirvana. This was an attitude of detachment from the world, which brought freedom from pain. Having reached its spiritual goal, the human soul would then be spared of further rebirths.

Though born in Nepal, Buddha spent most of his life in northeast India in the present-day state of Bihar, near the Ganges river. It was the site of the powerful Magadha kingdom. Buddha often preached in a deer park at Sarnath, which adjoined the holy city of Benares. Like Confucius, he and his followers wandered among warring kingdoms without interference. Neither Buddha nor Mahavira belonged to the Brahman class. Both opposed the caste system and filled the ranks of their followers with men and women of all backgrounds. Hinayana Buddhism, which represented Buddha's original teaching, grew out of a council to certify the accuracy of these doctrines and set rules for the sangha. The third council was held during the reign of the Indian emperor, Asoka, more than two hundred years after Buddha's death. He was Buddhism's great patron.

Asoka (reigned 269-232 B.C.) was the grandson of Chandragupta, founder of the Mauryan dynasty. He conquered neighboring kingdoms until his empire included much of the Indian subcontinent. Remorseful after the bloody conquest of Kalinga, Asoka converted to Buddhism in 261 B.C. He announced that he would cease to pursue military conquest and instead seek conquests of religion. Asoka joined a Buddhist lay order and promoted Buddhism within his realm. He sent Buddhist missionaries to Syria, Egypt, Greece, and Ceylon. While Buddhism was the state religion of the Mauryan empire, Asoka tolerated other religious practices. He promoted a strict ethical code, including the humane treatment of animals. In his zealous attempt to remake Indian society, emperor Asoka resembles China's first emperor, Shih Hwang-ti, who lived during the same century. Unlike him, however, Asoka did not leave an enduring model of political empire by which the state might become resurrected after a dynastic decline. Instead, his pacifist policies invited political disintegration. The empire fell apart fifty years after Asoka's death. Yet, his adoption of Buddhism as a state religion set an important precedent for the coming age.

The early Buddhist religion consisted of doctrines, scripture, and traditions associated with the Hinayana branch, sometimes called Theravadin Buddhism. It accepts the Pali canon adopted at the time of Asoka. This philosophically inclined religious path allows only a few persons who strictly follow Buddha's example of worldly renunciation to achieve nirvana. Someone who marries, has children, and earns a livelihood might become a lay follower of Buddhism (as Asoka was), but that person could not attain the ultimate goal of spiritual release and bliss. To become a mass religion, Buddhism had to provide a means of salvation within everyone's reach. The Mahayana or "greater vehicle", which was developed in Bactria

brass image of Buddha

at the time of Jesus, offered salvation through a personal savior. It asserted that Buddha had taught an inner circle of followers a higher teaching which allowed anyone to gain release. The idea was that Buddha, showing compassion for other suffering souls, had delayed the time of his own departure from earth in order to save others. Because this saving help from Buddha is universally available, the devotee can remain engaged in worldly pursuits while continuing on the path to nirvana.

Buddhism spread to the Bactrian empire of northwest India after Asoka's death. The Bactrian king Menander (160-130 B.C.) converted to its religion. Later, the Kushan emperor Kanishka (ca. 100 A.D.) became an ardent patron. There was a strong Greek influence in the Bactrian culture expressing itself through written language, philosophy, and the visual arts. That was the environment in which Mahayana Buddhism developed. Greek philosophy and the Zoroastrian cosmology of Heaven and Hell transformed Buddhism from a philosophical religion into a cult of personal saviors or "bodhisattvas" - Buddha-like personalities embodying the essence of enlightenment. They were ones who had attained Buddhahood but had declined to enter nirvana until other sentient beings preceded them. The Mahayana Buddhist religion readily enlisted the local gods of different regions in that role. Under influence of the Greek visual arts, Buddhism projected itself through statues of the Buddha seated in contemplation; one finds such images in numerous temples and caves. The Mahayana sect taught life after death, which increased its popular appeal. The "compassionate Buddha" aided by other bodhisattvas would arrange passage to that blissful domain for all those who called upon them for help.

The Brahman tradition began to make a comeback in the years after the Mauryan dynasty fell in 183 B.C. The subsequent Sunga and Kanva dynasties brought a Sanskrit revival in Hindustan. Sanskrit, a literary version of the ancient Vedic language, became the sacred language of Hindu texts, while Prakrits, a vernacular-language script associated with Buddhist and Jainist texts, became less widely used. The Gupta dynasty of north India (320-544 A.D.) did much to develop and spread the Hindu culture. Its religion was split into two main branches, Shivaism and Vaishnavism. The former comprised worship of Shiva, a phallic god also associated with death. The latter comprised worship of Vishnu, the Preserver, who has appeared in several human incarnations. Such innovations were made in response to the Buddhist challenge. These gods were like Hindu bodhisattvas. Buddha himself was regarded as an avatar of Vishnu. There was an emotional relationship between the god and his devotees. Sankara, a Hindu philosopher of the 9th century, argued that personal identities were an illusion and so special relationships between persons and gods were unnecessary. Each person was instead identified directly with ultimate reality. Ramanuja, in the 11th century, accused Sankara of being a crypto-Buddhist. In his view, one could still have a devotional relationship with the gods.

The Tamil-speaking part of southern India may have led the way toward this more emotional type of religion. During the 7th century, there was a resurgence of devotional Hinduism in the southern kingdoms of Pandya and Pallava, where Buddhism and Jainism had once been strong. Rock carvings and temples at Mamallapuram and Kanchipuram are among the treasures of Hindu architecture. Sankara, the great theologian, was a native of Kerala in the southwest. Buddhism became extinct in India as a result of devastation inflicted upon its monasteries by foreign invaders beginning with the White Huns in the 6th century. The Pala kingdom in Bengal, which Moslem armies conquered in 1202, was its last stronghold. The Bengalis preferred Tantric Buddhism which emphasized magical rites and worship of divine beings. They passed along this form of religion to the Tibetan people. The Palas dominated northern India during the opening decades of the 9th century but then lost out to the Pratihara dynasty of Rajasthan and central India, who were worshipers of Shiva and Vishnu. Jainism, also patronized by this regime, survived the purging of Buddhism; there are today about two million Jainists in India. However, the revived Brahman religion, Hinduism, gained a firm hold on the vast majority of India's population.

a Maratha Brahman

After Muhammad Ghori defeated an alliance of Rajput kings in 1192, the religion of Islam was added to the Indian religious mix. Possessing a highly developed religion, these Moslems were unable to be absorbed into the Indian culture; but neither was the Hindu population willing to convert to Islam. Consequently, India presented the paradoxical case of a state whose rulers professed one religion and whose people observed another. Out of respect for a superior civilization as well as political expediency, Moslem rulers of India felt obliged to designate their polytheistic Hindu subjects as "peoples of the Book". Emperor Akbar formed an alliance with the Hindu Rajput kings to keep the power of his Turkish commanders in check. He abolished the special taxes on Hindus and gave them permission to build Hindu temples. Moslem clerics regarded this as apostasy. A Mogul successor, Aurangzeb, undid these concessions and, in the process, provoked a furious counterattack by the Hindu Marathas. Religious teachers or poets such as Nanak and Kabir synthesized elements of both religions. Their doctrines appealed to lower-caste Hindus as did Islam. Higher-caste Hindus were recruited into the armed forces and civil service of the Persian-style Moslem governments, following a practice of Islamic administrations everywhere.

## The Spread of Indian Religion to Lands outside India

The Kushan empire, which united Bactria and northwest India in the 1st and 2nd centuries A.D., was the epicenter of emerging Mahayana Buddhism. It included lands in western Afghanistan and Uzbekistan abutting the eastern part of China. Mahayana Buddhism was adaptable to local creeds and traditions. There was a ripe combination of circumstances for this religion to penetrate Chinese culture starting in the 2nd century

Tibetan boy with
prayer wheel

A.D. Trade routes from western China to the Middle East and Europe ran through the Tarim basin and Soghd, southeast of the Aral sea, which were located just north of the Kushan empire. Buddhism may have seeped into China from that region in the form of neo-Sanskrit documents and works of visual art in the Gandharan Greek style. The Chinese and Indian modes of thinking were quite different. Chinese thought was expressed concretely and in a monosyllabic language. Indian thoughts were more abstract. Of the Chinese philosophies, the Buddhist mentality came closest to Taoism, so the early Buddhist writings frequently used Taoist concepts and terminology. Numerous scholars were at work translating Buddhist scriptures into Chinese.

When the eastern Han dynasty fell in the 3rd century A.D., there was a spiritual vacuum in China which Mahayana Buddhism filled. The Confucian ideology was discredited by its close association with the former corrupt imperial administration. The Taoists were discredited by their passivity in the face of public need. Zealous Buddhist missionaries were met by Chinese willing to listen to new ideas. Between 399 and 414 A.D., a Chinese pilgrim named Fa-hsien traveled to India to study Buddhism at its source. An Indian scholar named Kumarajiva, taken captive in 382 by a Chinese raiding party, spent his remaining life in China translating Buddhist classics. The Chinese Buddhists created their own sects. One was the "pure land" school which offered escape to a western paradise through faith in the bodhisattva Amitabha. Another was the Ch'an (Zen) school which stressed contemplation and personal discipline. The Buddhist monasteries acquired wealth. Emperors of the Sui and T'ang dynasties were personally attracted to Buddhism though they tolerated other religious philosophies. However, in a time of troubles the Confucians and Taoists conspired to curtail Buddhist activities. Between 842 and 845 A.D., the Chinese imperial government cracked down on Buddhist institutions. Monks and nuns were defrocked in large numbers. Property was seized from the monasteries.

Mahaparinirvana
sutra of Pei-chi

Buddhism became the dominant religion in lands outside India which were influenced primarily by Indian or Chinese culture. The civilization of India began to spread towards southeast Asia and Indonesia during the 1st century A.D. That trend accelerated in the 3rd century as the Gupta society radiated cultural influence. Tibet came into India's cultural orbit when a Tibetan king who invaded northern India after the death of emperor Harsha in 647 developed a script in the Indian style for the Tibetan language. That script was used to translate Mahayana Buddhist scripts from Sanskrit. Tibetan or Tantric Buddhism later became the religion of nomadic peoples living in Manchuria and Mongolia. It tamed the warlike spirit of those peoples, eliminating them as a threat to civilized societies. Buddhism first came to Ceylon in the 3rd century B.C. Missionaries from the Pala kingdom brought the Mahayana religion to Java in the 8th century A.D. In 1190, monks who had visited Ceylon introduced Hinayana Buddhism to Burma and Cambodia. Vietnam's adoption of Mahayana Buddhism, in contrast with other southeastern nations, reflects Chinese influence.

Buddha Hall, Ching-t'ung, Lu-ssu

China also exerted cultural influence upon the neighboring lands of Korea and Japan. Emperor Han Wu-ti established a colonial output in Korea during the 2nd century B.C. Although the Koreans later expelled the Chinese from that outpost, their culture remained. In the 5th and 6th centuries A.D., a large number of Koreans migrated to Japan, bringing with them the Korean version of Chinese Mahayana Buddhism. The Buddhist religion was introduced to Japanese society in the 7th century A.D. Block printing had been invented in T'ang China to mass-produce Buddhist and Confucian texts. Some of this literature made its way to Japan where scholars adapted the Chinese characters to spoken Japanese. The resulting script is based on associations between Chinese visual characters and syllabic sounds in the Japanese speech of that day. Japanese Buddhists developed simplified versions of Chinese religious teachings to appeal to a wider audience. Zen Buddhism, taken from the Ch'an school, was introduced to the samurai court at Kamakura in 1191. Its strict mental and physical discipline was attractive to soldiers. Honen and Shinran Buddhism were mass cults which promised entrance to a heavenly paradise to persons who repeated the name of the bodhisattva Amida. The Nichiren sect taught salvation by chanting praise of the Lotus Sutra.

The rival Buddhist sects established kingdoms of their own. They fought one another employing techniques of the martial arts. Buddhist monks trained squads of Ninja warriors to infiltrate enemy headquarters and kidnap or assassinate individuals. Ieyasu, last of the three great shoguns of the 16th century, once hired these warriors to kidnap the children of a rival warlord so that he would have a bargaining chip to offer in exchange for his own captive children. However, he and his successors promoted the neo-Confucian philosophy because they believed its ethical doctrines would strengthen their regime. Portuguese missionaries brought Christianity to Japan in the 16th century. Nobunaga, first of the three shoguns, tolerated Christianity because it offset Buddhist power. His successor, Hideyoshi, was of another mind. He mistrusted the western missionaries believing that religious conversions might precede a political takeover as had happened in the Philippines. Persecution of Christians began under Hideyoshi in 1597. When a rebellion broke out in the Catholic community of Shimabara in 1638, the government suppressed both Christianity and foreign trade. Buddhism was not suppressed. Indeed, all Japanese were required to register as a lay associate of a Buddhist temple to prove they were not Christians.

Hinayana Buddhism spread from Burma into the neighboring countries of Thailand, Laos, and Cambodia during the 13th century, ousting the Hindu and Mahayana Buddhist religions. The Thai people had come from western China, but they converted to the Burmese type of religion. A dynasty of god-kings influenced by Indian civilization had ruled the Khmer empire in Cambodia for over five hundred years. The Vietnamese carried their Chinese-style Mahayana Buddhism with them as they conquered the Champa kingdom to the south. The Chams then became Moslem. The Srivijaya empire on Sumatra, founded in the 7th century, and the Sailendra empire, founded in Java in the following century, were both Mahayana Buddhist; however a Shaivist Hindu regime, the Sanjayas, arose in east Java in the late 8th century to replace the Sailendra kings. The Empire of Majapahit was founded in Java in 1293 in the aftermath of the Mongols' naval defeat. This far-flung empire was founded by a Mahayana Buddhist prince, but Hindu and animistic religious influences were also strong. In the 15th century, Islamic religion from India poured over Malaya and the Indonesian archipelago to form the last religious layer. Rulers of port cities and coastal principalities found it advantageous to adopt the same religion as the Moslem merchants on whose trade their livelihoods depended.

An alluring religious possibility in the 13th century was that the world's largest political empire might convert as a block to whatever religion managed to win over its Mongol rulers. Although the Mongols were originally shamanists, Kublai Khan's mother was a Nestorian Christian. The great Khan asked Marco Polo's father and uncle to invite the Pope to send a delegation of learned Christians to his court to persuade him of the merits of their religion. Nothing came of that invitation. Kublai himself preferred Buddhism, especially Tibetan Lamaism. The Mongols converted to "Yellow Church" Buddhism, associated with the Dalai Lama, in the late 16th century, although several of their successors in the west converted to Islam. However, a former Buddhist monk, Chu Yüan-chang, led a rebellion against the Mongol dynasty in southeast China and, in 1368, proclaimed himself emperor of the Ming dynasty. Nestorian Christianity was expelled from China. Neo-Confucianism became again the state religion. In the mid 19th century, a religious visionary named Hung Hsiu-ch'üan, who believed that he was the younger brother of Jesus Christ, aroused a horde of peasants and unemployed workers to rebel against the Manchu government and non-Christian religions. These soldiers of the "Taiping Rebellion" controlled the Yangtze Valley for more than a decade but, with western help, were suppressed.

## Chapter Six

# A SHORT HISTORY OF CIVILIZATION III

### Special Circumstances: Its Origin in Europe

The next epoch of world history is focused particularly on western Europe. Its civilization began there before spreading to the rest of the world. The European ascendancy at the beginning of this epoch created an imbalance which produced a backlash at the end; for it was intolerable that one people's history should be the history of all mankind. In terms of our theory, a critical event was the introduction of a new cultural technology in western Europe, which was Gutenberg's invention of printing with movable type. Although the technology of printing had previously been employed in China and Korea, it did not take hold in the East Asian societies to the extent that it did in the West because of differences in script. Printing did not catch on in Islamic society because of religious and cultural restrictions. That left western Europe, a relative latecomer in acquiring the technology, to make full use of it. The particular culture which appeared then northern Italy was the embryo of a future civilization in Europe and the rest of the world. Its direction was secular and commercial.


## Thawing Religious Culture


In the late Middle Ages, European people were caught in the grip of a religious ideology that permeated community life. A thick dogma had settled down upon the society. Philosophical conceptions once incandescent in Greek or Jewish minds had long since cooled in frozen shapes. The eternal truths of Christianity, unchallengeable by reason, were embalmed by faith. Beneath the surface, life yet stirred. It was, in fact, a vigorous, healthy stirring of the human spirit. Despite its spiritual veneer, medieval life was bustling with a lusty materialism. Religious offices, indulgences, and relics of saints were offered for sale. Holy names, places, and things were regularly blasphemed. The church became a "trysting place" for young lovers. Obscene pictures were peddled there on festival days. Johan Huizinga has written that with "an enormous unfolding of religion in daily life ... all that is meant to stimulate spiritual consciousness is reduced to appalling commonplace profanity ... Holy things ... become too common to be deeply felt."

Then, like a glacier, the religious culture of the late Middle Ages, or what would be the springtime of CivIII, began to melt. The solid chunks of dogma, exposed to reason, developed cracks here and there. As some of these cracks became wider, tiny streams of fresh thinking slipped through. In time, the streams became torrents, which burst the dam of faith. One can associate this process with a few persons of strong intellect and determination. Such a person was Peter Abélard (1079-1142), a teacher of theology at the University of Paris. Another was Francesco Petrarca or Petrarch (1304-1374), an Italian scholar and poet. Others include: Emperor Frederick II (1194-1250), a freethinking monarch who defied the Pope; Roger Bacon (1214-1294), an

| Table 6-1 | | |
|---|---|---|
| Renaissance Personalities | | |
| Dante Alighieri | 1265-1321 | poet |
| Giotto di Bondone | 1266-1337 | painter |
| Petrarch | 1304-1374 | poet |
| Filippo Brunelleschi | 1377-1446 | architect |
| Cosimo de' Medici | 1389-1464 | statesman |
| Johann Gutenberg | 1397-1468 | printer |
| Pope Julius II | 1443-1513 | religious leader |
| Sandro Botticelli | 1444-1510 | painter |
| Lorenzo de' Medici | 1449-1492 | statesman |
| Christopher Columbus | 1451-1506 | navigator |
| Leonardo da Vinci | 1452-1519 | painter |
| Pico della Mirandola | 1463-1494 | writer |
| Erasmus of Rotterdam | 1466-1536 | writer |
| Vasco da Gama | 1469-1524 | navigator |
| Niccolò Machiavelli | 1469-1524 | writer |
| Albrecht Dürer | 1471-1528 | graphic artist |
| Nicholas Copernicus | 1473-1543 | astronomer |
| Michelangelo Buonarroti | 1475-1564 | painter |
| Baldassare Castiglione | 1478-1529 | writer |
| Raphael Santi | 1483-1520 | painter |
| Martin Luther | 1483-1546 | religious leader |
| François Rabelais | 1490-1553 | writer |
| St. Ignatius Loyola | 1491-1556 | religious leader |
| Benvenuto Cellini | 1500-1571 | goldsmith |
| John Calvin | 1509-1564 | religious leader |
| Miguel de Cervantes | 1547-1616 | writer |
| William Shakespeare | 1564-1616 | playwright |

English monk who developed the theory of experimental science; and Dante Alighieri (1265-1321) who wrote the *Divine Comedy*. (See Table 6-1.) The Roman church meanwhile was losing its moral credibility. The "Great Schism", which produced rival Popes in Rome and Avignon, struck at papal legitimacy. The public was becoming disgusted with corrupt clergy and the need to raise increasing sums of money. There was an air of violence and coercion about the church, so unworthy of its founder.

## The Seeing Revolution

The idea which we have of the Renaissance is that, being a time of cultural rebirth, it brought forth new discoveries of the world. Like a new-born child, humanity again learned to see. The civilization of western Europe was emerging from its cocoon of medieval piety to embrace the humanist principle that "man is the measure of all things." The Renaissance culture rejected philosophical speculations in favor of a new worldliness which sought knowledge based on natural observation. "Mental things which have not gone in through the senses are vain and bring forth no truth except detrimental," Leonardo da Vinci declared. The previous epoch, begun with a philosophical revolution, had valued "things unseen". Its religious culture considered ideas to be a source of goodness and truth while the body was a source of sinful weakness. Believers were asked to have faith in God's promise and quell doubts born of worldly experience. In contrast, the third civilization began with a revolution in **seeing**. Its redirected attention to things of the world represented a complete reversal of the previous culture.

The first fruit of this seeing revolution was a host of beautiful objects created by artists whose eyes were open to new possibilities of color, shape, and composition. The human body as painted by artists became a object of pleasure and grace. Mind was subjected to belief in what could be found in the physical world. Where Byzantine art had produced monochromatic and rather ethereal representations of human figures, the north Italian art pioneered by Giotto fleshed out its subjects. The names of Michelangelo, Leonardo, Raphael, Titian, Boccaccio, Brunelleschi, Masaccio, and others suggest the creation of beautiful colors and shapes in a balanced composition. North of the Alps, another group of talented artists including Jan van Eyck, Pieter Brueghel, and Albrecht Dürer were creating works rich in realistic detail. Realism was the theme of Renaissance art. Leonardo studied human anatomy to create more realistic visual representations of his subjects. Alberti, Brunelleschi, and others developed the technique of perspective to suggest how objects at various distances might appear in real life.

In literature, the veil was lifted from works of classical authors known by reputation or in translations from Arabic. Petrarch taught himself Latin and Greek to be able to read ancient manuscripts in the original. He came to feel that he knew their authors personally. His famous love poems dedicated to Laura abandoned medieval courtly traditions in favor of presenting the image of a real woman. Petrarch's example inspired a revival of interest in classical Graeco-Roman texts. Where medieval scholars had been careless in copying or compiling texts, Petrarch respected the integrity of original compositions. He was concerned with the authenticity of texts and with discovering an author's real intentions. Dante wrote the *Divine Comedy* in his native Tuscan language rather than in Latin, which made poetry accessible to many more people. Vernacular translations of the Bible were a revolutionary event. They challenged the authority of the Roman church by allowing the masses of people to read God's word for themselves and seek salvation in truths of the Bible rather in church-controlled rituals.

Petrarch

Medieval society had sought truth about nature in the scientific writings of Aristotle. Roger Bacon challenged this attitude in promoting the alternative approach of experimental science. "Cease to be ruled by dogmas and authorities; look at the world," he said. Following Bacon's prescription, empirical science finds truth in observed patterns in the natural world and in theories that can be experimentally tested. Alchemists and astrologers had long been gathering facts about nature. This empirical orientation, combined with mathematics and a willingness to give up beliefs contradicted by natural observation, led directly to modern science. The Polish astronomer Nicholas Copernicus conceived the modern scheme of the solar system, which contradicted the earth-centered scheme of Ptolemy. Galileo conducted an experiment to see if Aristotle's teaching was true that objects would fall to earth at different rates depending upon their weights. He found, to the contrary, that differently weighted balls dropped at the same time from on top of the Leaning Tower of Pisa hit the earth at the same time.

Leaving behind a religious culture laden with symbolic or invisible meanings, Europeans in the Renaissance period discovered the physical world. An Italian navigator, Christopher Columbus, persuaded the Queen of Spain to finance a voyage across the Atlantic to reach what he supposed would be east Asia. But, instead of the Indies, he reached the shores of a strange new land. There, in the western hemisphere, Columbus and his European companions found a different race of people, new types of food, unknown diseases, tobacco, furs, timber, inland waterways, deserts, silver and gold in abundant supply. Columbus had heard that Japan had inexhaustible supplies of gold. A Florentine map, badly underestimating the size of the earth, placed Japan just west of Europe. Magellan's voyage around the earth revealed the existence of a new continent which could be traversed at its southernmost point. The Spanish and Portuguese voyages of global exploration were another manifestation of the spirit of worldly discovery feeding the new civilization.

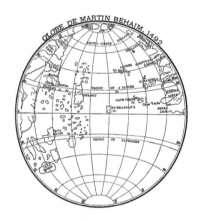

globe of Martin Behaim   1492

The spirit of commercialism drove this age of discovery. There was a strong market in Europe for oriental nutmeg and spices, which could preserve meat and add exotic flavoring, and for the Chinese silk used in princely garments. When the Ottoman Turks captured Constantinople in 1453, a hostile empire blocked the overland trade routes to China that were previously available to European merchants. Portuguese navigators found an alternative route by sea around the southern tip of Africa and soon captured Moslem trading posts along the Indian Ocean. Columbus was a native of Genoa. Genoese trade routes ran between Kaffa in the Crimea and ports in the Adriatic and western Mediterranean seas. The Venetians, who dominated trade with the Ottoman empire, also sent ships into the north Atlantic. A third trading bloc maintained a network of ports in the Baltic and North seas. Northern Italy and Flanders, centers of textiles manufacturing, were the most active commercial regions. The great wealth generated by trade, banking, and manufacturing created a demand for various kinds of luxury goods. Money and luxurious objects were no longer something to be despised or feared as a temptation to the soul. The appeal of wealth was visual and immediate, not other-worldly.

## Luther's Protest

The growing concern with wealth and beautiful objects affected the Roman church, which was headquartered in central Italy. The church needed large amounts of money to support its worldly projects. Unable to raise enough funds from management of its lands and other properties, it resorted to such fundraising methods as selling church offices and papal indulgences. The Renaissance popes had frequent need of moneylenders; Innocent IV called them "the peculiar sons of the Roman church." The Papal fortunes became intertwined with those of the Borgia and de' Medici families. Pope Callistus III openly practiced nepotism. Pope Alexander VI, his nephew, was the father of Cesare Borgia, Machiavelli's model of a ruthless prince. In the

1490s, the worldliness of the church found a determined oppo-
nent in a Dominican monk, Girolamo Savonarola, who urged
his fellow Florentines to forsake artistic images, abandon luxuries, and return to simple Christian living. Alexander VI ordered
him to desist in his anti-Roman preachings. Savonarola refused.
For this he was excommunicated and burned at the stake.

Julius II launched a massive project to rebuild St. Peter's
church. This project, which required a century and a half to complete, engaged artists of such talents as Bramante, Michelangelo,
Raphael, and Bernini. Such an undertaking required new fundraising efforts. In 1509, the Pope instituted a special Jubilee in-
dulgence. A Dominican preacher named Johann Tetzel arrived
in Saxony in October 1517 to promote a new dispensation of indulgences granted by Leo X. This was the event that inspired
Martin Luther to post the "95 theses" on the church door at Wit-

tenberg. His manifesto was widely distributed.
While Luther was branded a heretic, the pressure to reform the Christian church was now
too strong for him to be treated as a politically
isolated monk such as Savonarola had been.
In 1521, Pope Leo X issued a bull condemning
Luther's views and threatening him with excommunication within sixty days if he did not
submit to Roman authority. Luther and his

Martin Luther

friends burned a copy of it in a bonfire. The Saxon elector Frederick III gave Luther sanctuary in his castle at Wartburg.

A new Christian faith, supported by a powerful group of
north European monarchs, took shape along the lines of Luther's
religious arguments. Among its tenets were disbelief in the supernatural powers of the Mass and other church sacraments, in
the ability of sinners to win salvation by good works, and in the
presumed power of Roman priests to mediate between God and
humanity. "Justification by faith" was, in Luther's view, the sole
means of salvation; however, some persons were predestined to
believe and be saved while others were not. While the Roman
church claimed authority on the basis of ecclesiastical succession, Protestants maintained that "scripture alone" was the basis of religious authority and truth. The ability of each believer

to read and interpret passages in the Bible kindled a spirit of individualism. Individual believers could go straight to the source of Christian teaching and **see** what Jesus had actually said. Thomas Hobbes observed that "after the Bible was translated into English, every man, nay, every boy and wench that could read English, thought they spoke with God Almighty." An age of vigorous public discussion followed as pamphlets were printed to defend the Protestant or Catholic cause. Still, individuals were not free to choose their own religion. The temporal rulers of Europe had the power to decide what faith their subjects would adopt.

As strong-minded individuals preached their own versions of Christian truth, western Christianity became hopelessly split into denominations. By 1650 A.D., there were at least 180 different Protestant sects. Luther's own followers, concentrated in Germany and Scandinavia, were a conservative group compared with the Calvinists, Zwinglians, Anabaptists, Mennonites, and Quakers. Zwingli differed with Luther over interpreting the Mass. The Anabaptists repudiated infant baptism. The most important Protestant figure after Luther himself was John Calvin, theocratic leader of the city of Geneva. His teachings are presented in a treatise, *The Institutes of the Christian Religion*. Theologically, Calvin believed in the moral depravity of the human race, which would lead to eternal damnation but for Jesus' saving grace. The Calvinist doctrine of eternal damnation held that from the beginning of time God had ordained that a person's soul after death would be either saved or damned. Regardless of one's efforts, nothing could be done to change that determination.

Forces working within the Roman church might have prevented the Protestant rupture had they acted more promptly to restore its commitment to poverty and Christian service. Bishop Caraffa, later Pope Paul IV, led a group of Italian prelates seeking to reform church practices even before Luther's defiant act. The Council of Trent, held intermittently between 1545 and 1563, reviewed church sacraments and beliefs in light of Protestant criticisms. The so-called "Counter-Reformation" was a conservative movement to revitalize and strengthen the church. Its most important figure was St. Ignatius Loyola (1491-1556), a Spaniard who founded the Jesuit order in 1540. The Jesuits emphasized spiritual discipline and education. Self-styled soldiers of the church, Jesuit missionaries were prominently involved in evangelizing the native peoples of the Americas. They also undertook missions to India and the Far East. Thanks largely to the Jesuits, Spanish and Portuguese colonization always retained a hard religious edge. English and Dutch colonists were more willing to limit themselves to purely commercial objectives. It is ironic that the spirit of commercialism was stronger in Protestant than Catholic countries considering that Luther's complaint had concerned excessively commercial practices within the church.

St. Ignatius Loyola

Scholars have noted a correlation between Calvinism and commercial progress. Perhaps the best-known explanation is that presented in Max Weber's treatise, *Protestant Ethic and the Spirit of Capitalism*. Weber argued that persons such as the New England Puritans, who were raised in a strongly Protestant culture, were more likely than others to regard money-making as a worthwhile pursuit. Theirs was an ethical imperative to achieve wealth. Weber speculated that, although Calvinist dogma held that good works were ineffectual in achieving salvation, the Calvinists craved reassurance that they were among God's elect. While strength of faith or spiritual conviction would be for any Protestant a sufficient means of salvation, Calvinists believed that "faith had to be proved by its objective results."  One increased the sense of conviction in one's own salvation by experiencing at each moment a life of "systematic self-control". Therefore, the righteous persons  of this religious persuasion were ascetics actively engaged in the world - Christian businessmen like John D. Rockefeller - driven to make money not for the sake of enjoying physical comforts but deriving satisfaction from the money-making itself.

## Commercial Rivalry
## between the North Atlantic Nations

The European voyages of discovery beginning in the 15th century introduced an era of exploration and colonization in distant lands on earth. Each nation developed territorial interests. Portugal and Spain made the first claims to new territory by virtue of their navigational feats. In 1493, Pope Alexander VI divided the entire world outside Europe between the two Iberian nations on condition that they convert the native peoples in their respective possessions to Christianity. A Papal bull (later adjusted by treaty) gave Portugal lands east of a longitudinal line running through present-day Brazil, and Spain lands west of that line. In the west Pacific region, a similar line assigned the Molucca (Spice) islands to Portugal and the Philippines to Spain. That gave the two Iberian nations a big head start in the race to colonize and commercially exploit the non-European world. The focus of political rivalry shifted from the Mediterranean area to the North Atlantic and to the larger-sized nations located along its shores.

Portugal made the first significant discovery when, in 1488, ships commanded by Bartholomeu Dias rounded the Cape of Good Hope in southern Africa. In 1498, a Portuguese flotilla under Vasco da Gama's command sailed around the Cape and traveled to the west coast of India. The Portuguese found that Arab merchants controlling trade along the Indian ocean were uninterested in the type of merchandise that they carried. So the Portuguese, equipped with muskets, returned several years later and took the Arabs' trade outposts by force. They seized Goa in 1510, Malacca in 1511, and Hormuz in 1515. Portuguese merchants controlled the trade in oriental spices for the remainder of the century. Along with the traders went Jesuit missionaries intending to convert the Asian peoples to Christianity. St. Francis Xavier founded missions in west India, the Molucca islands, and Japan between 1541 and 1552. Matteo Ricci traveled to China in 1582, where for the next three decades he translated Christian scriptures into Chinese, wrote cultural treatises, and became a mathematician and astronomer at the Ming court in Peking. The

Iberian Christians were later expelled from that region when church officials refused to compromise on theology to accommodate local traditions.

In 1492, Christopher Columbus and his Spanish companions landed on the island of San Salvador in the West Indies (mistakenly believed to be a part of India) in search of gold. What little gold they found there gave rise to further explorations and a system of slave labor to work the mines of Hispaniola. In 1519,

Columbus

Spanish adventurers led by Hernando Cortés came in contact with a populous nation in southern Mexico. Greatly outnumbered, they conquered the Aztec empire in less than two years thanks to their boldness, superior equipment, help from peoples hostile to the Aztecs, and the lucky fact that Cortés' arrival on a certain day and year convinced the Aztec emperor, Moctezuma, that he was the reincarnation of the god Quetzalcoatl. Another Spaniard, Francisco Pizarro, conquered the Inca empire in South America between 1532 and 1535. Both empires were rich in silver and gold. The Spanish set about to exploit that resource systematically.

Tons of precious metals from American mines were shipped to Spain each year. Instead of becoming rich from this cargo, however, the Spanish monarch found that he was becoming steadily poorer. Mining and shipping operations, military protection for the galleons, and loss of revenues to private mine owners were costing the crown more than the gold and silver was worth, especially considering that the large increase in the supply of these metals brought a reduction in price. Spanish silver was causing severe monetary inflation not only in Europe but also in the Ottoman empire. In response to growing debts, the Spanish parliament imposed a ban on shipments of precious metals from the country. The king then suspended debt payments, issuing bonds to his creditors. As state finances continued to deteriorate, Philip II and his advisors blamed the situation on foreign merchants, usurers, and speculators. They required that the American colonies buy only from Spain. They imposed duties on goods imported from the Americas, escort fees for the warships, and other new taxes. Meanwhile, attendance at once brisk trade fairs languished. So much land was taken out of wheat cultivation that Spain could not feed its own people.

To protect its interests, the Spanish government tried to exclude English merchants from trade with the New World. Matters came to a head in 1567 when the Governor of Vera Cruz seized English ships filled with African slaves and arrested the crew. Two ships escaped, commanded by John Hawkins, the squadron leader, and a young captain named Francis Drake. Drake and a crew of English pirates later went on a rampage against Spanish towns along the Atlantic and Pacific coasts. Piracy had long been a way of life in the Atlantic. Merchant seamen were given a royal charter to engage in armed piracy against Spanish vessels in the series of wars between Spain and France beginning in 1521. While French pirates plundered at will, their English counterparts held back because the daughter of Henry VIII, the future Queen Mary, was married to Philip II of Spain. After Mary's death in 1558, that constraint was removed. For a time, the new queen, Elizabeth I, steered a delicate course between supporting English seamen and keeping the peace with Spain. Her decision to confer knighthood on Francis Drake aboard his pirate ship in 1580 signaled an end to that policy. Philip II responded in 1588 by dispatching the Armada, a fleet of 130 ships, to conquer England. The smaller but more agile English fleet defeated it.

After ousting the Arabs, Portugal controlled the lucrative trade in oriental spices. The Dutch began to challenge their position at the end of the 16th century. Philip II, who after 1580 was king of Portugal as well as Spain, attempted to punish his rebellious subjects in the Netherlands by ordering Dutch ships seized if found in Spanish or Portuguese waters. Jan Huyghen van Linschoten, a Dutch merchant who had spent five years in Goa, published a book in 1595 suggesting how his fellow countrymen might break the Portuguese monopoly on trade with the Indies. His idea was that the Dutch ought not to challenge the

English and Spanish war vessels   (16th century)

Portuguese military outposts in India but, instead, to set up trading posts in the relatively undefended areas of Indonesia and Malaya where the spice trade originated. In the same year, Cornelius Houtman embarked on a voyage with four ships to Bantam and the Moluccas which succeeded in breaking the Spanish-Portuguese naval blockade. That triggered a series of Dutch expeditions to the South Seas.

In 1602, the Estates General of the Netherlands gave the United East India Company the right to enter into treaties with Indian princes, raise troops, build fortifications, and appoint governors and judges. Its directors promptly sent fourteen sailing ships to Asia. A stone trading post established at Bantam (Java) became a base for further expeditions to neighboring areas. Other Dutch fleets, which were equipped with powerful guns, attacked Portuguese forts, negotiated friendship treaties with Indian rulers, and blockaded Goa. The Dutch defeated Spanish and Portuguese fleets in several naval engagements. The hard-pressed Spanish monarch signed a 12-year armistice with the Dutch in 1609, allowing free trade in Asia. The Dutch used this opportunity to build trading posts and forts throughout Indonesia. They developed a flourishing trade in spices based not on force but on favorable purchases and sales in the open market. The armistice with Spain was not renewed in 1621. Portugal and Spain again barred Dutch merchants from their harbors. The Dutch then imposed a tight naval blockade of Portuguese trading ports in Africa and southern Asia. When peace was established in 1645, Portuguese trade was ruined. The Dutch ruled the seas.

England's interest in the New World began with John Cabot's voyage to North America in 1498 in search of a northwest passage to the Pacific. Failing in that purpose, Cabot discovered what became the world's richest cod fishery off the coast of Newfoundland. In the 16th century, fishing for cod turned out to be more profitable than mining silver. Sebastian Cabot, John's son, made another attempt on England's behalf to reach the Far East by a sea route. In 1553, he set sail on a voyage around the northern part of Norway with a fleet of three ships. Two ships perished in the Arctic Sea but the third reached the current site of Archangel. From there the ship's captain traveled overland to Moscow where Czar Ivan the Terrible received him cordially. The Russians realized that they had found an alternative source of European goods. The English found a source of furs and a potential market for their woolen products. The Muscovy Company, first of England's great colonial shareholders' companies, was formed in 1555 to take advantage of that opportunity.

Several other companies were established to represent English commercial interests in diverse parts of the world. The Levant Company obtained a royal charter to trade with the Ottoman empire in exchange for an annual duty of at least 500 pounds. England set up consulates in Syria and Egypt. Despite official obstacles, its merchants did a brisk and profitable trade with countries bordering the Mediterranean sea. However, the defeat of the Invincible Armada and England's subsequent retaliation against Spanish ports brought an end to lawful trade with the Iberian countries and their colonies in Africa and the Americas. No English ship dared sail past the Straights of Gibraltar into the Mediterranean sea. Therefore, merchants of the Levant Company sought other channels for trade in oriental goods.

Table 6-2

## Some Headline Events in the History of Civilization III

| | |
|---|---|
| 1215 A.D. | King John signs Magna Carta. |
| 1295 A.D. | Marco Polo returns to Italy from China. |
| 1341 A.D. | Petrarch crowned poet laureate in Rome. |
| 1401 A.D. | Ghiberti wins arts competition in Florence. |
| 1454 A.D. | Gutenberg prints copies of Bible. |
| 1469 A.D. | Lorenzo de' Medici rules Florence. |
| 1492 A.D. | Columbus discovers America. |
| 1498 A.D. | Vasco da Gama sails around Africa to India. |
| 1503 A.D. | Leonardo da Vinci paints Mona Lisa. |
| 1506 A.D. | Bramante appointed architect of St. Peters. |
| 1511 A.D. | Portuguese establish base at Malacca. |
| 1513 A.D. | Machiavelli begins writing *The Prince*. |
| 1521 A.D. | Cortés conquers Aztec empire. |
| 1522 A.D. | Magellan's crew circumnavigates the earth. |
| 1530 A.D. | Pizarro invades Peru. |
| 1543 A.D. | Copernicus publishes book about solar system. |
| 1557 A.D. | Spanish crown is bankrupt. |
| 1567 A.D. | Dutch revolt against Spain begins. |
| 1583 A.D. | Sir Walter Raleigh's expedition to Virginia |
| 1588 A.D. | English defeat Spanish Armada. |
| 1600 A.D. | Elizabeth I charters East India Company. |
| 1605 A.D. | Shakespeare writes *Macbeth* and *King Lear*. |
| 1606 A.D. | Virginia Company is founded. |
| 1609 A.D. | Bank of Amsterdam is established. |
| 1620 A.D. | English Pilgrims found New England colony. |
| 1649 A.D. | Charles I of England is beheaded. |
| 1681 A.D. | William Penn receives charter for colony. |
| 1687 A.D. | Newton publishes *Principia Mathematica*. |
| 1694 A.D. | Bank of England is established. |
| 1709 A.D. | Czar Peter I defeats Swedes at battle of Poltava. |
| 1720 A.D. | John Law's Mississippi scheme collapses. |
| 1757 A.D. | Clive wins battle of Plassey in India. |
| 1759 A.D. | Wolfe defeats Montcalm at battle of Quebec. |
| 1769 A.D. | Watt patents invention of steam engine. |
| 1776 A.D. | Americans issue Declaration of Independence. |
| 1789 A.D. | French Estates-General is convened. |
| 1803 A.D. | Jefferson purchases Louisiana from Napoleon. |
| 1815 A.D. | Napoleon defeated at battle of Waterloo. |
| 1819 A.D. | British Parliament passes First Factory Act. |
| 1825 A.D. | Parliament legalizes trade unions. |
| 1842 A.D. | Chinese Opium Wars end. |

---

### History of Civ III    (continued)

| | |
|---|---|
| 1848 A.D. | Gold is discovered in California. |
| 1854 A.D. | Admiral Perry reopens Japan. |
| 1863 A.D. | Lincoln issues Emancipation Proclamation. |
| 1869 A.D. | Last spike is driven in U.S. transcontinental railroad. |
| 1886 A.D. | American workers conduct "May Day" strike. |
| 1888 A.D. | Cecil Rhodes achieves diamond-mining monopoly. |
| 1901 A.D. | Carnegie sells steel company to J.P. Morgan. |
| 1914 A.D. | Henry Ford offers $5-a-day minimum wage. |
| 1917 A.D. | Bolsheviks seize power in Russia. |
| 1929 A.D. | Stock market crashes in New York. |
| 1947 A.D. | British grant independence to India. |

---

John Newbury persuaded its management to send him and five companions on a mission around southern Africa. Though unsuccessful, this expedition gave the English a close look at the riches of India. They learned intimate details of conditions in China, as well as boat construction, by capturing a Portuguese vessel off the Azores in 1592. Queen Elizabeth sent a fleet of ships to explore trade with China which, unfortunately, sank during a storm.

The English persisted in pursuing trade opportunities. The East India Company, an association of English merchants, received a charter from the queen on December 31, 1600, granting them a monopoly on trade in the Eastern Hemisphere. At first, this venture was hindered by falling prices for pepper and spice, by opposition from its European rivals, and by the fact that south Asian peoples had little use for English woolen goods. After the Dutch made it clear that they would not tolerate an English presence in Indonesia, the East India Company decided to concentrate on trade with India where it was hoped they might acquire goods to be traded later for Javan spices. An Englishman named Midnall had made friendly contact with the Mogul emperor, Akbar the Great. Officials of the East India Company followed up on that visit by sending another fleet to India. The Portuguese, entrenched at Goa, blocked English efforts to establish trading posts in western India. However, the English commander, Hawkins, traveled to Agra to plead his case with the Indian emperor. Emperor Jahangir, Akbar's successor, granted the English all the commercial privileges that they requested. This was the beginning of a long and fruitful association between the British East India Company and the Mogul dynasty.

Although the papal bull of 1493 had granted Spain all American lands except for Brazil, the Spanish crown was too busy with administering its Mexican and South American colonies to pay much attention to North America. Other European nations, starting with France, explored the coastal and interior waterways of this continent. English kings in the 17th century granted royal charters which allowed individuals to settle and govern tracts of land in North America so long as their rule did not conflict with English law. One such colony was established at Jamestown in 1607, and another in Massachusetts in 1620. Groups of religious dissenters who felt oppressed by the Church of England flocked to the New World. The first major influx brought more than 20,000 Englishmen, mostly Puritans, to colonies in New England before the English Civil War erupted in 1642. Other religious minorities, including Quakers and Roman Catholics, were given opportunities for exile to American colonies. During the reign of Charles II, the English government began to tighten its regulation of those colonies. The Navigation Acts, enacted between 1660 and 1696, required that American commerce be transported in ships built and operated by English nationals. The Crown also altered or revoked many colonial charters, placing its North American subjects under the control of appointed governors.

The Spanish possessions in America were on a still tighter leash. From the beginning, the King of Spain ruled his American empire by a thick, detailed code of laws. Persons wishing to emigrate to the Americas had to apply for a permit. A Supreme Council of the Indies, headed by the king, made the major administrative decisions in Spain, while viceroys, judges, and other bureaucrats carried out its mandates on site. The Pope gave the Spanish monarch authority over religious as well as political matters in return for a commitment to maintain the church. Special attention was paid to the treatment of native peoples. Generally, the church acted to protect them from severe exploitation and to gain conversions by persuasion rather than by force. On the other hand, the native population declined precipitously during the first century of Spanish rule. In Portuguese Brazil, the colonial government was more loosely organized. The real power lay in the hands of the large plantation owners. The European and native American peoples mixed more freely in Latin America than in the English colonies to the north, producing a hybrid race. By 1800, the population of Spanish America had reached 18 million. Its cities rivaled those of Europe both in size of populations and in culture and wealth.

French settlements in the Americas were concentrated along the St. Lawrence river in Quebec. French fur traders in the Great Lakes region obtained beaver pelts from Indian trappers in exchange for rifles, knives, and steel implements. These pelts were used for the high-priced beaver hats worn by European nobility. Louis XIV of France, who set the pace of fashion in Europe, had his eye on European conquests rather than overseas colonies. He built ornate palaces such as the royal residence at Versailles. The king's finance minister, Jean Baptiste Colbert, had ambitious ideas about making France an economic power. His memorandum written in 1664 recommended the creation of a French East and West Indies Company. Colbert was the architect of a planned economy aiming to make France economically self-sufficient. French textiles and other manufactured goods were prized objects of trade. Colbert hoped to obtain American silver from Spain in payment for its trade deficit with France which could be used to purchase spices in Asia. However, the Spaniards hoarded their silver. Colbert's mercantilist strategy of restricting imports and pushing exports became self-defeating when other nations followed suit. Ultimately, his micromanagement ran the French economy into the ground. France was bankrupt when Louis XIV died in 1715.

## Colonial Trade

Wars impose heavy costs upon national economies. To raise money for its protracted wars against France, the English government in 1694 gave a group of merchants the right to issue bank notes to the extent of their invested capital. This bank immediately loaned the government its entire capital of 1.2 million pounds sterling. It then issued paper money good for purchasing precious metals and foreign bills of exchange. That is how the Bank of England began. After Louis XIV's death, a Scottish financier named John Law convinced the Duke of Orleans to allow him to establish a similar institution in France. The French economy was then facing a severe monetary squeeze. Law proposed to restore money and credit by issuing bank notes backed by his own capital. The Banque Générale Law et Cie was created for that purpose in May 1716. While acceptance of the bank notes was voluntary, Law's scheme was successful. The French government took over the bank in 1718. Law, as controller general of finances, merged the royal bank with a stock company which he had formed to promote land sales in Louisiana. There was a frenzy of speculation which increased the price of the stock to unsustainable levels. When the price collapsed in December 1720, Law fled the country. The English "South Sea Bubble" burst about the same time.

While financial speculation had brought Law's downfall, the idea behind his Mississippi Company was basically sound. Law intended to attract European settlers to the French Louisiana territory where they might cultivate crops that could be marketed in Europe. The chief crops were coffee, sugar, and tobacco. Law would encourage the settlers to grow these crops on plantations and would extend credit to them to purchase necessities from Europe while the crops matured. He would also use credit for the settlers to purchase African slaves to work the plantations. Law consolidated all the French overseas trading companies into one, purchased the colony of Louisiana, secured the tobacco monopoly, and expanded the French slave trade. Although his Mississippi Company operated for only two years, those years marked a shift in the direction of European commerce. Previously, European merchants had focused upon the trade in spices from the East Indies. Law's enterprise diverted attention to the West Indies. Europeans acquired a taste for those exotic goods which, Ernst Samhaber wrote, "introduced into the chilly West the whole seductive warmth of the tropics and the sweet ease of life in a sunny climate."

France and England were now on a collision course. Once united in opposition to Spanish power, the two nations clashed when England joined the "Grand Alliance" against Louis XIV. In North America, the French had a long-standing alliance with the Huron tribe of Indians who supplied them with beaver pelts taken from interior waters. The Iroquois Indians attacked the Hurons, forcing the French to take sides.

smoking tobacco in America

Dutch fur traders stationed in New Amsterdam, and later the British, sided with the Iroquois, who promised to divert the fur trade from the St. Lawrence river to the Hudson. Thus, the European powers were drawn into conflict for trade dominance. This struggle was resolved a century later with the English general Wolfe's capture of Quebec in 1759 which ended the "French and Indian War". When England's American colonies broke away from their mother country in the mid 1770s, the British and their Iroquois allies fought the colonial rebels then aided by the French. George Washington, an English officer in their earlier conflict, was commander in chief of the American colonials. After this war was concluded, Canada remained a British possession with a sizable French-speaking minority in the Quebec province.

Both England and France had trading companies in India. As the Mogul empire weakened during the 18th century, these companies formed strategic alliances with Indian princes and became militarily engaged. Robert Clive's victories over the French and Dutch between 1748 and 1760 put England in a dominant position. The British East India Company took over the administration of provincial governments in northern India on behalf of the Mogul empire. Its representatives grew rich from exercise of their official duties. To combat corruption, the British Parliament assumed joint control of the Indian government in 1774, ruling through a series of governor generals. Public administration was actually an unprofitable undertaking for the East India Company. Its money was made in the tea trade. A publicity campaign in the 1720s had persuaded the English public to drink tea rather than coffee. Whenever the British government needed money, it raised the tax on tea. This strategy back-

fired when in 1774 a band of American colonials disguised as Indians dumped a shipload of tea into the Boston Harbor to protest the increased taxes. The British retaliated, bringing on the American war of independence.

During colonial times, North America participated in a highly profitable three-cornered trade. Ships from England carrying textiles, beads, and metal wares sailed first to the coast of

Boston tea party

west Africa, where they exchanged these goods for human slaves. The ships then sailed across the Atlantic ocean to the Caribbean islands, Brazil, or England's North American colonies, which needed the African slaves for plantation laborers. In the Americas, merchants purchased such products as sugar, coffee, and tobacco from the plantations, as well as timber and fish. Those commodities went back to England to complete the cycle. The West Indian products, especially rum distilled from the sugar, had greater commercial appeal for Europeans during the late 18th century than the traditional eastern luxuries of spices and silk. There was also an assured demand for slaves in the New World. The key to this trade was finding items which the slave-hunting chieftains of west Africa would accept in exchange. Each chieftain preferred certain products.

Later, leaders of the Dahomey and Ashanti tribes from the interior of west Africa offered to furnish the white merchants an unlimited number of slaves in exchange for firearms which they could use to subdue their rivals. They organized regular man-hunts nabbing a greatly increased number of captives. Portuguese navigators had begun the slave trade in the 15th century, and the Dutch had expanded it. The English brought this trade to a peak. An estimated 900,000 slaves were shipped from Africa to America in the 16th century. That number rose to 1.7 million slaves in the 17th century, and to over 7 million in the 18th century, before dropping off in the 19th century. Slavery was abolished in the British West Indies in 1833; in the United States, in 1865, following the U.S. Civil War; and in Brazil, in 1888. Most black African slaves were brought to islands in the West Indies and to Brazil; less than a million went to the United States. Many others died during the Atlantic passage.

Liverpool was the center of the English slave trade as well as trade in manufactured products. Over 300,000 slaves were brought across the ocean on ships sailing from that port between 1783 and 1793. However, the cargo carried back to England had changed. Instead of coffee, bales of cotton were starting to appear. There was not enough land in the West Indies to grow this crop, so cotton began to be cultivated in the southern part of the United States. Unfortunately, the variety of cotton which grew well in that region was difficult to gin. Eli Whitney's cotton gin, invented in 1793, solved this problem. Another problem was the lack of labor to weave cotton cloth. Again, mechanical inventions came to the rescue, including Hargreaves' spinning jenny and Crompton's "mule" machine, both powered by steam engines. Cheap textiles made of cotton replaced woolen goods as England's leading export product. In India, once an exporter of cotton textiles, machine-produced goods imported from England underbid the local product and threw millions of weavers out of work. Much of England's wool business moved to Australia. Twenty-nine merino sheep shipped there in 1787 multiplied into today's herds.

## Trade Competition in the Industrial Age

The Industrial Revolution resulted from technologies that came from the natural sciences. According to Arnold Toynbee, the religious wars which raged in Europe during the 17th century were so hateful and intense that men of intelligence turned their attention instead to the natural world. While theological questions were clearly divisive, men could be friends as fellow students of nature. "Before the close of the (17th) century," wrote Toynbee, "Religion had been replaced by Technology ... as the paramount interest and pursuit of the leading spirits in the Western society." The Royal Society of London, proposed first by Sir Francis Bacon in *The New Atlantis,* was established in 1660 by a group of men who, tired of religious controversies that had led to the English Civil War, wished instead to discuss the physical world. Earlier in the century, Galileo had built a telescope which allowed men to study celestial objects. A Dutch lens grinder, Anton van Leeuwenhoek, used the microscope to observe cell tissues, bacteria, and other minute objects. Sir Isaac Newton, a president of the Royal Society, worked out mathematical equations describing fundamental relationships that underlay gravitation, optics, and physical motion.

It took about a century for this interest in science to be translated into technological improvements affecting daily life. A system of crop rotation introduced from Holland in the late 17th century helped to increase wheat yields in England and so supply foods that would keep livestock alive during the winter. Starting in the 1760s, inland canals began to be used to transport coal from mines to industrial centers such as Manchester. James Brindley of Staffordshire designed and built almost four hundred miles of canals. A new generation of ironmongers built iron bridges across rivers. Men such as Joseph Priestley, Josiah Wedgwood, and Benjamin Franklin conducted scientific experiments with gases, metals, ceramics, and electricity which had practical applications. The most important technological advancement may have been James Watt's invention of the steam-driven engine, which was installed in an English cotton mill in 1785. A steam engine was attached to a boat in 1802, and to a railroad locomotive in 1804. Steamboats were in use both in England and the United States by the first decade of the 19th century. The age of railroads began in the 1820s.

What is called the Industrial Revolution started in the English cotton mills. Production techniques were improved not only by Watt's steam engine but by a host of other mechanical inventions including the spinning jenny, spinning frame, mule, and power loom. Samuel Slater's theft of English technology brought this industry to America in 1790. The use of special machines to weave cotton and produce cotton cloth allowed much more cloth to be produced in an hour of operation than before. Cloth produced this way could be sold for lower prices than cloth produced in the traditional manner. Business shifted to the new mode of production. Textiles factories required people to tend the machines. Some came from villages whose cottage industries and local handicrafts were meanwhile being ruined by competition from factory-made products. Others came from the farm. The development of commercial law made it possible for business managers to have legally enforceable contracts to buy and sell various commodities including labor. Because the factory system was based on commercial contracts, its enterprises did not employ slave labor but workers whose had agreed to sell their effort and skill for a certain time in exchange for wages.

Trevithick's locomotive

Most nations, including the United States, adopted a policy of protecting their infant manufacturing industries by high tariffs, even at the risk of killing their shipping business and foreign trade. Napoleon Bonaparte tried to choke British commerce with the "Continental System", which prohibited trade with England in any lands under his control. The effect was to deprive European consumers of the coffee, sugar, and tobacco which the British had once supplied and to ruin French agriculture. Napoleon was forced to grant numerous "licenses", excepting one or another special situation. Trade was resumed after

the war; however, Europe was impoverished from its devastation and had become used to making do with homegrown products. That situation bred policies of trade protection. In 1815,
English landed gentry persuaded Parliament to ban wheat imports when the price was below a certain level. Wheat prices
rose in England, increasing hunger in its cities. They fell in France,
where the farmers suffered. As protectionism spread through
Europe, trade and employment plummeted. Although the French
Revolution had established the individual right to choose a career, this meant little to people working in a depressed economic
environment.

British manufacturers, who enjoyed a comparative advantage in most kinds of products, supported a campaign for "free
trade" which would open foreign markets to them at the cost of
accepting more competition from imported goods. Richard Cob-
den, a former cotton merchant from Manchester, led the  fight
for repeal of the corn laws in 1846. He persuaded the French
emperor Napoleon III to enter into an agreement with Great Britain for a mutual reduction of tariffs in 1860. Two years later,
France signed a similar agreement with Prussia. The volume of
world trade expanded enormously. In contrast with previous
periods, this trade included foodstuffs, steel, and other necessities, not just luxury goods. In the Far East, the campaign to liber-
alize trade was accompanied by military force. Admiral Matthew Perry of the United States opened Japan to foreign commerce and cultural influence after centuries of isolation. Recognizing their own backwardness, the Japanese eagerly modern-
ized their society along western lines. British gunboats forced
China to accept opium imports from India after the Chinese government banned this narcotic in 1839. The reason was that the
East India Company needed a product to trade for Chinese tea.

During the 19th century, the new industrial order of Europe and North America marched triumphantly over the rest of
the world. The old plantation system was in retreat; slavery was
finished. The large Jesuit plantations in South America which
had produced agricultural exports with Indian labor had been
swept away in the previous century. The King of France banned
the Jesuit Order in 1764 when the Society was unable to pay its

debts from speculative ventures in Martinique. In the late 1860s, cotton plantations in the southern United States fell into ruin as the Confederacy met with military defeat. American wheat farmers, cultivating large acreages with mechanized harvesting equipment, shipped huge quantities of grain by railroad to urban markets in their own country and abroad. New mineral discoveries were made in remote parts of the earth. A transportation network consisting first of inland canals and then railroads allowed inexpensive shipment of commodities from their point of production to distant markets. Electric telegraph lines communicated information instantaneously. New alloys and processes of production improved the cost and quality of steel.

Giant corporations arose to produce newly invented products. Capitalizing on his ties to the railroads, a Scottish immigrant to the United States, Andrew Carnegie, acquired one quarter of this nation's steel-production capacity by paying close attention to quality and cost and by busting unions. He imported from England the Bessemer process of producing steel from cast iron. John D. Rockefeller created the Standard Oil trust through mergers, efficient production, and aggressive moves against business competitors. In Germany, firms such as Bayer, BASF, and Hoechst captured much of the world's market for artificial dyes. Synthetic drugs such as aspirin and materials such as celluloid were other products of chemical research. Thomas Edison's laboratories in Menlo Park and East Orange, New Jersey, invented and developed a variety of products that used electricity. An American tinkerer and race-car driver, Henry Ford, helped to found an automobile-manufacturing firm that bears his name. He is cred-

on the floor of the stock exchange

ited with inventing the factory assembly line. His "Model T" Ford offered a reliable product which people could afford. Henry Ford also built up the market for automobiles by paying his workers high wages and scheduling shorter hours of work. In the process, he became one of the richest men on earth.

## The Labor Movement

The Industrial Revolution, which began in England during the late 18th century, increased production efficiency and wealth but also increased wealth inequality. Cheap factory-produced goods undercut the market for goods less efficiently produced in handicraft industries. The enclosure and privatization of once public lands by several acts of Parliament closed off the opportunity that rural people might eke out a living in such places. So a multitude of persons, having nothing to sell but their labor, migrated from the countryside into industrial cities. In theory, the new system of contractual labor respected the workers' freedom and dignity. In practice, individual workers were at a disadvantage in bargaining with their employer. Given a lack of alternative employment in the villages, employers could pick and choose among job applicants, play one off against another, and, if necessary, blacklist uncooperative individuals. The dynamics of increasing production efficiency meant that fewer workers were needed to tend the machines so unemployment tended to increase. Employers had a financial incentive to pay workers as little as possible and extract from them a maximum amount of work. This led to an upward spiral in scheduled work hours. Around 1800, people customarily worked 14 hours a day in the factories, and sometimes longer.

A possible remedy for this intolerable situation was for several workers to bargain jointly with their employer so as to obtain more favorable contracts. However, the British Parliament passed a law in 1799 forbidding such "combinations" which were intended to raise wages or prices in restraint of trade. Effectively, some workers could undercut their fellow employees by agreeing privately to a lower wage. It was necessary for workers to communicate with one another, if only in secret. The earliest workers' organizations were therefore secret societies which, being illegal, sometimes resorted to violence. Parliament legalized labor unions in 1824-25 so that collective bargaining could take place in the open. Labor issues also became part of reform legislation enacted during this period. The Factory Act of 1833, introduced in Parliament by the Earl of Shaftesbury, limited the hours that children of various ages were allowed to work. A universal 10-hour bill was passed by the British Parliament in 1848. Factory workers were becoming an increasingly active economic and political force in society. Worker agitation built up to a peak in 1848, when the English Chartists pushed their program of universal male suffrage and other reforms.

Perhaps the most important person in the early labor movement in Great Britain was not a worker but Robert Owen, owner of a textile factory. In 1800, Owen bought his father-in-law's cotton mills at New Lanark, Scotland, which he managed for 29 years. There Owen created a model industrial community where the firm's 2,500 employees enjoyed superior housing and sanitation, stores with fair prices, and free schooling. The work day at New Lanark was 10 1/2 hours compared with 13 or 14 hours in rival mills. Owen was the principal promoter of the Factory Act of 1819, which limited working hours for women and children. He supported trade unions and agricultural-industrial coops and agitated for a universal eight-hour day. In later years, Owen established a utopian community at New Harmony, Indiana, which used labor rather than gold as a medium of economic exchange. The idealism of Owen and others fed a current of labor activity which appealed to intellectuals and ultimately became the socialist movement.

Another force was the trade-union movement itself. After labor unions became legal in 1824, British workers rapidly organized, especially in the mining and textiles industries. The Trade Union Congress was formed in 1868 to coordinate policies on a national scale. Trade unions also arose in Germany and other nations of continental Europe after the revolution of 1848, as well as in North America. Initially, labor agitation was focused upon reducing the length of the working day. In 1825, carpenters in Boston struck unsuccessfully for a ten-hour day. However, a general strike in 1835 over the same issue persuaded the Philadelphia city government to adopt a "6 to 6" daily schedule, including two hours off for lunch. In 1840, President Martin Van Buren signed an order granting all mechanics and laborers in the executive branch of the federal government a uniform ten-hour day. Another burst of activity took place in the United States around the time of the Civil War when a national movement to promote the eight-hour day headed by a Boston machinist, Ira Steward, achieved several legislative victories. These proved to be hollow. The fight for the eight-hour day continued throughout the 1870s. In the summer of 1872, more than 100,000 building-trades workers in New York City struck for three months to win this concession.

On May 1, 1886, U.S. and Canadian unions conducted a general strike in support of the eight-hour day in several large cities. An estimated 350,000 workers participated in this "May Day" strike. It is best remembered for the bombing which occurred in Chicago's Haymarket Square three days after the strike and for the trial in which four labor leaders were convicted of inciting violence and sentenced to death. The American Federation of Labor was organized in Ohio later that year. This organization made plans for another strike on May 1, 1890. When delegates to a conference of the Second International in Paris heard of those plans, they endorsed the event. European trade unions, supported by socialists, staged a general strike for the eight-hour day on the same day as the North Americans' strike, thus turning "May Day" into an international labor holiday. The socialists were a group of political agitators who advocated that labor-friendly governments seize control of productive enterprise. The American Federation of Labor rejected this sweeping program and thereafter confined themselves largely to bargaining with employers to their members' best economic advantage.

The eight-hour day came to pass in most industrialized countries around the time of World War I. Its standard is embodied in the first convention of the International Labor Organization, adopted in 1919. Two years earlier, Marxist socialists had seized control of the Russian state. That brought labor questions to the forefront of world politics. When Russian communism brought other peoples into its political orbit after World War II, the earth's nations became divided into a socialist and capitalist camp, each governed by a quasi-religious economic philosophy. Karl Marx and his associates had founded the International Workingmen's Association, later known as the "First International", in London in 1864. The "Second International", founded after Marx's death, included the leaders of most European socialist parties in the period between 1890 and 1919. Then, with the triumph of Bolshevism, the "Third International" was created to serve the ideological objectives of the Soviet state. The overthrow of the Stalinist empire in the former Soviet Union and eastern Europe represented a major setback to those ideals. Meanwhile, the western labor movement has been weakened by the disparity of incomes between union and nonunion workers and the globalization of labor competition.

## Education

It may be that the western labor movement is a victim of its own success. Its purpose lay in overcoming economic disadvantage. As the unions succeeded in increasing wages and reducing hours, however, the working class graduated into a more comfortable condition of life. Its new middle-class status raised expectations that the workers' children were in a position to seize even greater opportunities for advancement in society. The gateway to this multigenerational improvement was education. Education cultivated the mind, rendering it fit for glorious achievements. Persons trained at the universities might become lawyers, doctors, or prime ministers though their parents were poor. It was so much more satisfying to become associated with such an institution, which promised success through individual effort and intelligence, than to belong to an organization representing people who worked with their backs and hands and, if contract talks were successful, won pay increases regardless of merit. So the prospering trade unionists abandoned their heritage built on claims of disadvantage and went for the brighter future that education held forth.

Western education is rooted in medieval institutions associated loosely with the church. Theological training, along with studies in medicine, law, and the liberal arts, formed the core of the curriculum at the University of Paris. A strong humanist tradition developed with exposure to classical Greek and Roman writings. After 1500, Europeans learned to imitate the styles of Latin authors from the period between Cicero and Augustus. The Protestant Reformation, led by religious scholars, viewed education as a means of acquiring direct knowledge of Christian teachings. Indoctrination in religion was the spiritual equivalent of military training for Catholics and Protestants alike. Mistrusting the educated poor, the princes of Europe later tried to take control of the schools and turn them into devices to attract clever young men for service to society. H.G. Wells observed that "the university was part of the recognized machinery of aristocracy ... A pompous and unintelligent classical pretentiousness dominated them ... The only knowledge recognized was an uncritical textual knowledge of a selection of Latin and Greek classics, and the test of a good style was its abundance of quotations, allusions, and stereotyped expressions ... Such a training ... showed the world reflected in a distorting mirror of bad historical analogies."

Prussia responded to the challenge of defeat by Napoleon's armies in numerous ways, including reorganization of its schools. University education was improved, and the gymnasium became

Balliol College, Oxford

the center of training for a social elite. Applied science was added to the curriculum. Thanks to its academic institutions, Germany became a leader in chemical technologies. When Prince Albert of Saxe-Coburg and Gotha married England's Queen Victoria, he took pains to warn his adopted country of its educational deficiencies. He initiated the university commission of 1850 and, a year later, the first International Exhibition at Hyde Park in London, whose purpose was to show the English what other European nations had accomplished artistically and industrially. Anglo-German rivalry during the second half of the 19th century prompted much soul searching among British educators, especially when the Germans began to compete with Britain for naval power. National competitiveness dictated more rigorous training in the natural sciences. The British public began to see the need for popular education, now that steam power had reduced the demand for persons who worked with their muscles and increased the demand for workers who exercised judgment and skill.

The irony was that Great Britain and France, whose educational systems stressed literature and classical studies, had led the way in making scientific discoveries and developing useful technologies based on this knowledge. The great pioneers of experimental science were, for the most part, persons without much education. Neither Kepler nor Descartes were affiliated with a university. Benjamin Franklin, Michael Faraday, and Thomas Edison were largely self-taught. James Watt lacked a university education although he did consult with Joseph Black, a professor of chemistry at Glasgow. Joseph Priestley went to divinity school. Yet, the German example of academic training in the sciences made a deep impression upon the British public. At first, the idea of popular education was quite humorous to Britain's educated elite. Wells reports that "in the middle Victorian period it was thought to be extraordinarily funny that a shop assistant should lean across the counter and ask two lady customers not to speak French, as he 'understood the langwidge' ... The German competitor later on robbed that joke of its fun. Before the death of Queen Victoria, English shop assistants were being badgered to attend evening classes to learn French."

A western university education had another purpose which, in the long run, had enormous historical impact. With the rise of western science and especially military science, the balance of political power in the world shifted decisively toward the west. Nonwestern leaders realized that, for the sake of self-preservation, their nations needed to modernize along western lines. Specifically, these nations needed to acquire the weapons technology to defend themselves against western aggression. In some cases, they employed westerners as military advisers. Moroccan kings defeated an invading Portuguese army in the 16th century with the help of western weapons technology and recruits. Ranjit Singh in the 19th century employed veterans of Napoleon's army as instructors to fight the British in India. Eventually, however, these nonwestern regimes found that mere possession of technology was not enough. To use it effectively, they needed disciplined troops, good hygiene, adequate public finances, supporting industrial facilities, and other features of western society. They needed a wholesale adoption of western culture. What they did not want, however, was western religion because conversion to Christianity would mean the loss of their own spiritual identity.

Some nonwestern governments decided to modernize completely. Peter the Great of Russia (1682-1725) is an example of this policy. The young czar traveled to the west and even worked as a carpenter at a shipyard in the etherlands to gain experience of western methods before returning to his country and embarking upon a program of modernization. Others, in the 19th cen-

Czar Peter I

tury, include the Ottoman emperor Mahmud II, King Mongkut of Thailand, and the Japanese reformers of the Meiji restoration. The most common way for nonwestern nations to acquire knowledge of western ways was to send young men to be educated in Europe. A barrier was that most western universities had religious qualifications for students. Until 1871, for example, Oxford University required each candidate for a degree to declare personal acceptance of the *Thirty-Nine Articles* promulgated by the Church of England. An exception was the University of Padua, located in Venetian territory, which allowed non-Catholics to be admitted. It became a favorite of Greek students, both in Venice and the Ottoman empire. As religious tolerance spread in Europe, more universities dropped their requirement of assent to the locally accepted version of Christianity, and a western education became more attractive to foreign students. This happened just as western technology was demonstrating its superiority.

What had started slowly became a torrent in the 19th century. A new class of western-educated natives of nonwestern societies appeared in nations around the earth. The name, "intelligentsia", has been given to this group in Russia. Living between two worlds, such  individuals became an interface between westerners and their own society. Many took high government positions where they carried out modernization programs. While the nonwestern governments had generally supported this class, the intelligentsia sometimes pursued its own agenda. Westernized Greeks under Prince Ypsilanti rebelled against the Ottoman empire in 1821. A corps of Russian officers conspired against Czar Alexander I in 1825. Both rebellions were crushed. Foreign students in Europe tended to pick up on intellectual and cultural fashions of the day. The Marxist ideology appealed to European intellectuals during the late 19th and early 20th centuries. Chou En-lai and Ho Chi Minh began their revolutionary activities in Paris just after World War I. Sun Yat-sen was educated in Honolulu. Mohandas Gandhi studied in London. Nehru attended Harrow and Cambridge University. Kwame Nkrumah of Ghana attended Lincoln University in the United States. It is fair to say that the anticolonialist movements of the mid 20th century were products both of nationalism and a western education.

The original lure of western culture had been its technology, especially fire arms and artillery. German-style training in science spurred British education, as, a century later, the Soviet launching of Sputnik inspired increased appropriations for American colleges and schools on the theory that the Russians had more rigorous training in science. In the 1930s and 1940s, it did seem that academic science was the key to technological advance. The atom bomb and electronic computers were first developed in that milieu. Yet, ultimately, U.S. education has been more concerned with building a homogeneous society. It has taken an immigrant population and taught them to be Americans. It has molded farm populations, veterans returning from war, racial minorities, and other irregular types into persons who could live in the cities and hold professional jobs. This function is not unlike that of teaching foreigners how to cope with western society. All the power and wealth that this society has to offer is made available to the one trained to make the right approach.

## National Histories

A political dream in Europe has been to duplicate what was happening in China at the other end of the Eurasian continent. Once the first Ch'in emperor had created a unified empire, it never really came apart. Sometimes a dynasty would fall, barbarians would intrude, and the empire might be split into several kingdoms; but, inevitably, the Chinese empire would be reconstructed. In western Europe, on the other hand, the political fragmentation that began with the Germanic invasions of the Roman empire in the 5th century A.D. has persisted into modern times. Political empires such as Charlemagne's which comprised the bulk of western Europe proved ephemeral. The Roman Popes tried to unify Europe in a quasi-political religious empire, but this enterprise was doomed by the Great Schism of the 14th century and the Protestant Reformation. Ironically, the empire which European monarchs sought to achieve in Europe was collectively built on a global scale during the third epoch of world history. This, too, has come apart in the 20th century.

CivIII political history is characterized by a plurality of nations rather than by unified empires. Its "prophet" was an Italian writer and one-time political advisor named Niccolò Machiavelli who had advised the political ruler of Florence for ten years until the Medici family took charge in 1512. His book, *The Prince*, published posthumously in 1532, tells what he had learned during that time. Machiavelli denied that the object of statecraft was to advance Christian ideals or build a better society. Politics, as it was actually practiced, was about getting and keeping power. Therefore, heads of state ought to pursue their political self-interest without reservation or remorse. Machiavelli also recommended the "balance of power" strategy which guided European diplomacy in centuries to come. This strategy dictated that parochial princes combine to oppose any other prince who became too powerful. For example, Lorenzo de' Medici kept the peace by aligning the power of Florence and Milan against Venice and Naples. In the military struggle between Emperor Charles V and Francis I of France during the 1520s, Charles was supported by the Pope and England's Henry

VIII; Francis, by the Ottoman Turks. Once Charles appeared to be winning, Henry and the Pope abruptly switched sides and supported Francis.

The Carolingian dynasty of Charlemagne and his heirs established the geographical framework within which the European nation states emerged. In 843, Charlemagne's Frankish empire was divided between his three grandsons. Charles the Bald received most of present-day France. Lewis the German received the eastern German territories. The middle strip of land running from Belgium through Italy was assigned to Lothaire, who was also named Holy Roman Emperor. During the 10th century, the German territories and most of Italy were united in the empire of Otto the Great. France was then comprised of a royal domain surrounding Paris and several large fiefdoms, including Burgundy, Normandy, Brittany, and Aquitaine. The Normans conquered lands in southern Italy and Sicily during the 11th century to establish the Kingdom of Two Sicilies. In 1066, Duke William of Normandy defeated the English king, Harold, at the Battle of Hastings. His Norman dynasty unified England. The English and Burgundians together battled the French dynasty of Hugh Capet. In its darkest hour, a peasant girl, Joan of Arc, saved France from destruction, expelling the English. King Louis XI of France (1461-83) later brought Burgundy under control. From that time forth, France was a strong and united monarchy.

At the end of the 15th century, the marriage of Ferdinand and Isabella united the Iberian kingdoms of Castile and Aragon which for centuries had been pushing the Moors back toward North Africa. This task was completed in 1492. Their grandson, Charles V, was also the grandson of the Austrian Habsburg emperor, Maximilian I. Upon Maximilian's death in 1519, Charles became sole heir to a European empire which included Spain, Austria, Hungary, Bohemia, the Netherlands, the Kingdom of Two Sicilies, and, of course, Spain's American possessions. In addition, as Holy Roman Emperor, he indirectly controlled the German states of Central Europe. The French king, Francis I, was Charles' principal rival. Seemingly a child of destiny, Charles had the misfortune to be a Catholic monarch and emperor at the time of the Protestant Reformation. He faced open rebellion from German princes who supported Luther. War broke out in 1546 between Protestant and Catholic forces, and again in 1552.

Charles chose to retire to a monastery. Between 1554 and 1556, he turned over his possessions in Italy, Sicily, the Netherlands, and Spain to his son Philip. The Habsburg possessions in Central Europe he bequeathed to his brother Ferdinand. Charles died two years later.

Charles V

Religious warfare continued into the next century. England had turned Protestant as a result of Henry VIII's quarrel with the Pope over a divorce. The Thirty Year's War, which began in 1618, devastated central Europe. It began with resistance to the Catholic Habsburg king Ferdinand II by Protestant Bohemian princes, and grew to include Denmark, Sweden, France, Spain, and most German states. This war pitted Catholics against Protestants and much of Europe (including France) against the Habsburg dynasty. Rivalry between the two Catholic superpowers, France and Austria, continued into the next century. Catholic Spain, which had been united with Portugal in 1580, made a brief bid to conquer its European neighbors under Philip II. However, its power was eroded by the Dutch Civil War of 1567-1648, disastrous naval expeditions against England and Holland, and the revolt of Portugal and Catalonia. In the late 17th century, it was France's turn, having achieved cultural ascendancy in Europe, to seek corresponding political dominance. Louis XIV, the Sun King, engaged in a series of aggressive wars against his neighbors to the east, but was effectively opposed by the Dutch, Swedes, Spanish, and English. Europe's most populous nation, France was weakened by expulsion of its industrious Protestant minority.

Later, the English and French struggled for dominance. The British evicted the French from North America between 1690 and 1763, and from India between 1746 and 1761. Having survived several Turkish sieges of Vienna, the Habsburg Austrian dynasty recovered Hungary at the expense of the Ottoman empire. It inherited Spanish territories in the southern Netherlands and Lombardy. Leopold I persuaded Serbia to join the Habsburg empire by offering religious freedom. Czar Peter the Great defeated Sweden between 1700 and 1722, annexing territories along the Baltic sea. The Russians conquered Belorussia and much of the Ukraine from the Ottoman empire under Catherine the Great. Then the rising power of Brandenburg-Prussia clashed with the Austrians, Russians, and French. Poland was partitioned between Prussia, Russia, and Austria. The French revolution brought Napoleon to power. His principal opponents were the Germans, Russians, and British. Napoleon's empire encompassed most of continental Europe, but his ill-fated Russian invasion sapped its military strength. By this time, religious motives no longer played a significant role in European warfare. Wars were fought primarily for political and commercial advantage. Instead of involving the civilian populations, the combatants employed uniformed soldiers who furnished their own supplies and fought within limits.

Napoleon's conquests enkindled nationalistic feeling among the German and Italian people. Italy was united as a nation under the monarchy of Victor Emmanuel II in the period between 1859 and 1870. Prince Otto von Bismarck was instrumental in uniting the German states under Prussian rule in the period

Napoleon Bonaparte

between 1866 and 1871. Germany established itself as the strongest military power in Europe by defeating France in the Franco-Prussian War of 1870-71. France and England meanwhile added new colonial possessions in Africa and acquired trade enclaves in China. In Asia, the westernized Japanese empire defeated Manchu China in 1894-95, accelerating its partition by western powers, and then defeated Russia in 1904-05. The United States of America, which had consolidated its North American territories during the first half of the 19th century, evicted Spain from Cuba and the Philippines at the end of that century. The commercial rivalry between Great Britain and Germany was accompanied by formation of military alliances between France, Russia, and Britain. Still, the balance-of-power diplomacy enunciated by Machiavelli remained in effect. Then, a decade and a half into the new century, a bloody "world war" broke out in Europe itself. The civilization self-destructed.

World War I had an evident impact on the European political landscape. Four powerful monarchies disappeared after the war's conclusion. All the monarchies belonging to the Central Powers disappeared: Kaiser Germany, the Habsburg Austro-Hungarian empire, and the Ottoman Turkish empire. In addition, Czarist Russia was replaced by the Soviet Union after, first, the Kerensky provisional government and, then, the Bolshevists seized power. The Americans, who had intervened on the winning side, carried with them an aura of the future. Democracy had triumphed over the old system of European monarchies. Several of the western monarchies which had participated in the war on both sides - the Habsburg dynasty excluded - were genealogically related, mostly through minor German nobility. Germany's Kaiser Wilhelm and King George V of England were both grandsons of Queen Victoria. The Kaiser imagined that the war might be settled by a polite conversation with his royal cousins, the British king and the Russian czar. It was not to be. The war swept away not only his government but a dream held by Europeans since Charlemagne. This last, loose empire of European monarchies was swept away.

## Democracy and Revolution

The political situation at the end of the third epoch was the opposite of that which it had been at the beginning. In the early 16th century, three strong monarchs - Charles V of Germany and Spain, Francis I of France, and Henry VIII of England - bestrode western Europe. Each claimed title to his throne by virtue of a legitimate inheritance sanctioned by God. With the decline of the Papacy, the temporal ruler possessed nearly absolute power within his realm. He even had the power to choose his subjects' religion. At the end of the epoch, the institution of monarchy appeared to be dying. Democratic government (or pseudo-democratic dictatorship) was taking its place. The political rulers were persons selected by the will of the people rather than divine favor. Government, which had arisen as a coercive institution in Ciul, took on characteristics of the marketplace. It replaced autocratic rule with a softer regime whose power is based on the ability to sell itself to the public.

The transition from absolute monarchy to democratic government is another part of the story pertaining to CiuIII. The Magna Carta, which King John had signed to placate rebellious noblemen in 1215, started the trend toward a system of government which was accountable to the people. To build their lavish palaces and wage dynastic wars, the monarchs of Europe needed large sums of money, which had to be raised by taxation or borrowings from wealthy merchants and bankers. Parliaments were formed to facilitate the tax-collecting function. At first these were assemblies of men representing the shires and counties of the realm, who testified as to the tax-producing capacity of their area. The king had to call the parliament into session to seek additional sums of money, and this body enjoyed a certain right of refusal. Parliamentary government began to impinge upon the power of the English crown during the 17th century when Cromwell's armies defeated the Royalists and Charles I was beheaded. A similar process occurred in France in the 1790s as the Estates General, convened by Louis XVI, seized absolute power. A new government was meanwhile being created in the United States of America in which an elected President took the place of the monarch.

As nomadic invasions of settled communities were a recurring theme in the first epoch of world history, so the history of CiuIII is marked by a series of political upheavals which historians call "revolutions". After Czarist Russia and Manchu China had completed their encirclement of the nomads' pastoral homeland in the 17th century, the threat to civilized society from external barbarians subsided and became virtually extinct. The new barbarian threat came from within. The commercially developing societies of Europe had developed disparities between certain classes of people with respect to their economic and social condition. The "lower" classes, economically oppressed and dissatisfied with their lot, became a force threatening social stability. The European empires also came in conflict with colonized peoples who were deprived of their political liberty. These two types of grievance led to a new kind of "barbarian" eruption during the third epoch. Within the heart of the European world empire, masses of dissatisfied people were challenging the society in violent ways. The hordes of political and social revolutionaries turned the civilized world upside down.

Examples of these revolutions include: the Dutch revolt against Spain in the 16th century, the English Puritan revolution of the 17th century, the American and French revolutions of the late 18th century, and the Russian and Chinese revolutions of the 20th century. (See Table 6-3.) All of them involved bloodshed incurred in the course of rebellion against the reigning political authority. All were successful in seizing power. In the case of the English Puritan and French revolutions, however, this power subsequently reverted to rulers of the previous type after the death or defeat of their leader. All revolutions except for the Chinese were directed against the institution of monarchy. In the case of the English, French, and Russian revolutions, the lawful monarch was executed. In some cases, parliamentary government replaced the monarchy; in others, dictatorship. The as-

Table 6-3

Revolutions of the Third Civilization

| name of country | execute monarch? | establish republic? | religious liberty? | anti-colonial? | class warfare? |
|---|---|---|---|---|---|
| Netherlands | no | yes | yes | yes | no |
| England | yes | yes | yes | no | yes |
| U.S.A. | no | yes | no | yes | no |
| France | yes | yes | yes | no | yes |
| Russia | yes | yes | no | no | yes |
| China | no | yes | no | yes | yes |

piration for religious liberty played a part in the Dutch and English revolutions. On the other hand, the French revolutionaries were anti-cleric while the Russian and Chinese Marxists were atheistic. Religious issues generally played a less prominent role in these upheavals as time went by. Economic concerns became increasingly important.

The Dutch, American, and Chinese revolutions were anti-colonial movements. The Dutch revolt against Spain was driven by a desire for tolerance of Protestant religion in a Catholic empire, for constitutional government, and protec-tion of local interests. It resulted in the creation of an independent Dutch republic. The American Revolution opposed autocratic colonial government and "taxation without representation". Its leaders likewise established an independent republic. Both supported and advanced the interests of the merchant class. The Chinese Revo-

Washington

lution, on the other hand, combined the anti-plutocratic themes of Marxist revolution with opposition to western influence in China, including an immediate fight against Japanese imperialism. The other three revolutions were internal uprisings in the mother country. The English Puritan revolution featured a struggle for religious liberty and ad-vancement of parliamentary government, but also included an element of social leveling. The French Revolution brought the emerging interests of the Third Estate - business people, workers, and peasants - to bear against the feudal privileges enjoyed by the nobility and Christian

Robespierre

clergy. The Russian revolution of October 1917 was a coup d'état in a war-weary land instigated by members of an ideologically hardened political party which advocated socialism.

To sensibilities of the previous civilization, the idea that lower-class people would violently rebel against divinely appointed governments was indeed scandalous. It was shocking when such rebellions included executing a lawful king. The Puritan regicides became the worst of criminals once the beheaded monarch's son, Charles II, regained the British throne. Yet, the verdict of history is colored by the fact that these revolutions succeeded. Since the victors write history, their bloody and unlawful acts are mitigated by the revolutionary ideals which they embraced: The English Puritans were fighting for religious liberty. The brave soldiers of the American Revolution were struggling against unjust colonial government. The French revolutionaries were advancing the Rights of Man. It is the combination of those lofty principles with bloodshed and disorder which makes the revolutions seem morally confusing. The social riffraff, who brutally executed their superiors, were also, in a large sense, contributing to human progress.

## The Unraveling of Western Colonialism

Historical epochs often reverse themes on which they began. For example, the third epoch, which began with a trio of strong European monarchs (plus Babur and Süleiman the Great), ended with the abolition of absolute monarchy in Europe. The lusty pursuit of gold and material wealth has given way to an anti-plutocratic spirit in the 19th and 20th century labor movements. This period also began with the European voyages of discovery, establishment of colonial governments, and the subjugation of native peoples. It brought racially based slavery to the New World. If the third epoch of civilization began on a theme of European dominance, one might expect that it would end on an opposite note. And so it is that in the late 20th century resentment of "western imperialism" runs strong in the nonwestern world. Five hundred years after the first African slaves were brought to the Americas, many of the slaves' descendants curse the white society and its culture as historic oppressors of their people. This curse has unleashed a wave of racial hatred and self-hatred that reverberates in many directions.

The anti-European attitudes exhibited today are a consequence of the fact that the history of CivIII is abnormally skewed toward the European experience. White Europeans were once the conquerors and civilizers of peoples around the earth. Their acquisitive and secular culture begun in Renaissance times has become the world's culture. Quite naturally, most of the world's people, being non-European, will see this as something alien to themselves and become antagonistic. The Europeans conquered other people's lands by their superior technology combined with an insatiable greed and a martial spirit built up over centuries of fighting Moslem armies. The Spanish and Portuguese, coming in the first wave of European invasion, tended to be motivated at least in part by religious conquest. Having recently defeated the Moors, they were the ones closest to the front of religious wars. As the initiative passed to the Dutch and English, the commercial element became more pronounced. These were merchants and adventurers unaccompanied by Jesuit missionaries, who sought to grow rich through trade. The commercial culture blossomed under their regime.

Force inevitably followed European explorations and trading expeditions. The European adventurers possessed muskets and cannon, laws, written language, and ocean-going ships. The spectacular conquests of Mexico and Peru were followed by colonization of sparsely populated lands elsewhere in the Americas. The British converted their tax-collection arrangements with the Mogul empire into imperial rule of the Indian subcontinent. They first cut a deal with the Sikh empire-builder, Ranjit Singh, to respect the Sutlej river as the boundary of their respective empires. A generation later, between 1845 and 1849, Britain conquered the Sikh empire in the Punjab. The western-style Russian army was able decisively to defeat the Ottoman Turks in the Russo-Turkish war of 1768-74, which prompted Sultan Selim III to undertake similar measures to modernize his armed forces. After Napoleon's armies conquered and withdrew from Egypt, Muhammad Ali came to power in Egypt as a viceroy of the Ottoman empire. The British and French prevented his conquest of Syria and Palestine at Ottoman expense. The British later established a protectorate in the region including the Sudan. The French had controlled Algeria since 1830. Following the Opium War of 1839-42 with China, the British established a colony in Hong Kong.

The 19th century was a golden age of European nationalism. In the decades after Napoleon's forces had fought English,

Austrian, Prussian, Spanish, and Russian armies, these various peoples derived a sense of national pride from having defeated the great French general. The Germans were especially filled with this proud spirit. German musicians, philosophers, scientists, and poets achieved cultural ascendancy during this period. German literature was said to be best in the original, free of French influence. A similar attitude infected the youthful culture of the United States. Russian novelists and symphonic composers came into their own during this period, producing classics of their genre. Italian nationalism found a voice in the operas of Verdi and

Puccini and a political champion in Garibaldi. Greeks fought for national independence against the Ottoman empire. Early in the century, Haitian guerrillas under the command of Toussaint L'Ouverture defeated Napoleon's crack troops. Símon Bolívar and José de San Martín ended Spanish colonial rule in South America. An attempt to establish a French empire in Mexico during the U.S.

Emin Pasha    Civil War was foiled.
of the Sudan
                    Nationalism caught up with other nonwestern peoples during the 20th century. The Japanese military victory over Russia in 1905 showed Asians that a major European power could be beaten. That became even more clear after European society sacrificed the cream of its youth on the battlefield in World War I. Among Woodrow Wilson's "Fourteen Points" at the Versailles peace conference was a statement affirming all people's right to national self-determination. An immediate result was a resurgence of Turkish nationalism in the "Young Turk" movement led by Kemal Atatürk. Nationalists led by Sun Yatsen attempted to build a democratic nation in China. In India, Mohandas Gandhi agitated nonviolently for an end to British rule. After Europe experienced another bloodbath in World War II, the anticolonial movement began in earnest. Great Britain and France divested their colonial empires. The Philippines received its independence from the United States, as did Indonesia from the Netherlands. India and Pakistan became  self-governing nations in 1947. A year later, an independent Jewish state was established in Palestine. Communist forces ousted the  Chinese

nationalists. Many new African nations were created from former colonies during the 1960s. Vietnamese communists expelled French and American armies from Indochina.

## Materialism and Disintegration

A new kind of philosophy was conceived during the third epoch. This "materialist" philosophy is mother of the modern social sciences. A key figure in this movement was the Scottish philosopher and historian, David Hume, who was Adam Smith's mentor and an important economist in his own right. Hume's philosophy, like that of other materialists, held that the human mind resembled a machine. Where Plato had taught that ideas were real and the natural world was created from them, materialistic philosophers held that ideas were the product of a physical brain. The brain carried on certain processes which explain how people think. The philosophies of Descartes, Spinoza, and Leibnitz, which are sometimes called "rationalist" philosophies, set the stage for the British empiricists' even more devastating attack on objective ideas. For them, sense data were the primary source of knowledge. Ideas were the synthetic product of worldly experience. The wholeness of ideas disappeared.

After the embers of romanticism had cooled, 19th century Europeans pursued realism in literature and art. Gone were sentimental expressions conveying beauty and good. People wanted to see the ugly truth. And so, detailed descriptions of life in urban slums filled the novels of Charles Dickens and Victor Hugo. The French painters, Gustave Courbet and Jean François Millet, were celebrated artists of the realist school. This was the age of Karl Marx and Charles Darwin. In their schemes of creation, design came from the bottom up. When photography was invented, mindless machines were able to produce a more accurate visual representation of worldly scenes than the best artists. Inspired by the camera, painters such as Degas tried to create an image of objects as if seen from unexpected angles. Impressionist painters abandoned any attempt to depict shapely things; they instead placed colored dots upon the canvas to imitate how rays of light might strike the eye. This break with tradition led to other schools of experimental art - cubism, surrealism, Dada.

All this "modern art" came to a head in the period just before the outbreak of World War I. The public could not fathom the presumed excellence that lay in its disharmonious forms. Picasso's grotesque pictures reminded Karl Jung of the "lacerated" thought patterns that he had observed in schizophrenic patients. The poet Yeats complained that "things fall apart; the center cannot hold." Artistic expressions were pieced together in eclectic assemblages lacking form. Not coincidentally, crossword puzzles were  invented during this period. Such games arranged words in mechanical ways without reference to meaning or expressive flow. The artist seemed to be taunting the public, challenging it to make sense of his work. This was the opposite of the beautiful art created in Renaissance times, whose objects were painted in full and round shapes. It signaled the end of an epoch whose culture many today deem synonymous with "civilization."

# Chapter Seven

# A SHORT HISTORY OF
# CIVILIZATION IV

## A Weight Lifted from our Cultural Shoulders

The eldest daughter of England's King George V recalled that her father had an almost pathological aversion to change. "The postwar world was to him an abomination," she said. "He disapproved of Soviet Russia, painted fingernails, women who smoked in public, cocktails, frivolous hats, American jazz, and the growing habit of going away for weekends." After the mind-numbing carnage of World War I, the world's people awoke to a different kind of experience. It had a lighter air. There was a distinct sense of frivolity about this period. Suddenly, a sense of the modern hit public consciousness. Automobiles were replacing horse-drawn carriages. The first radio stations began broadcasting. In years following the Great War, there were vaudeville shows, New Orleans jazz, chorus lines, and a new type of entertainment called the movies. Unserious in its tone, this was an age of popular culture. It was such a relief from the culture of high art that had filled the 19th century.

The fourth civilization came together in the wreckage of the previous culture when western society appeared to be com-

mitting suicide. The bloody world war, sinking of the Titanic, discordant themes in music and art, and overall pretentiousness of the old order created an urge to jump off the historical track and try something different. In Europe, the old antagonisms continued to rage. The harsh reparations imposed upon Germany by the treaty of Ver-

scene from the Roaring 20s

sailles left a bitterness that led to Hitler's assumption of power. Mussolini and his fascist supporters bullied their parliamentary opponents into submission. Claiming that their enemies would be "swept into the dustbin of history", the Bolshevists staged a coup d'état in Russia. Angry ideologies of various types were destroying public civility. Cultural decadence and economic crisis shook society at its roots. In America, on the other hand, people were enjoying an unprecedented level of prosperity, there was a casual disregard of laws prohibiting the use of alcoholic beverages, new dance fashions emanated from Harlem, and the movies began to talk. Americans tuned out the hostile, intellectually overpowering message of Lenin and opened themselves up instead to the lightheartedness of Bing Crosby.

## Some Difficulties in Telling this History

To write the history of *CivIV* presents some special difficulties. By its nature, entertainment appeals in different ways to different individuals. There is such a diversity of interests that historians would be hard pressed to find a single set of events to represent a community's experience. A sensible approach might be to select entertainment experiences on the basis of their size of audience. The history of this culture might therefore include descriptions of the most popular shows. Unlike most historical events, those of the entertainment culture would consist of staged productions experienced by people sitting in movie theaters or in front of television sets at many different locations. For example, on the evening of December 17, 1969, more Americans were tuned to the *Tonight Show* to watch "Tiny Tim" marry "Miss Vicky" Budinger than for any other event in the history of that show. Can, however, simultaneous tunings to a television frequency by a large, but geographically scattered audience be considered an **event** in the same sense that the "Woodstock" rock concert which took place on Max Asgur's farm earlier that same year would be?

The history of entertainment should, of course, include reference to specific images and sounds to which the audiences have paid attention. Each venue has its own set of internal experiences. For instance, the history of Major League baseball might include exciting events such as Don Larsen's "perfect game" in the 1956 World Series or the time when Babe Ruth pointed to the centerfield bleachers during the 1932 World Series with the Cubs and hit the very next pitch to that spot for a home run. Seasoned sportswriters could surely come up with a list of memorable incidents in each sport and write a history which narrates them in some way. Most would agree, however, that a history of Major League baseball should also include events related to its institutional experience. For example, Branch Rickey's decision to add Jackie Robinson to the roster of the Brooklyn Dodgers or the change in the free-agency rule might be considered historically significant events related to the game of baseball which did not happen in the games themselves. One can see that a multi-volume history could easily be written on Major League baseball alone.

The entertainment culture includes much more than this. Some of its categories might be: drama, sports, popular music and dance, stand-up or situation comedy, exotic or pornographic exhibitions, and public demonstrations. In addition, what we consider to be "the news" is increasingly being treated as a form of entertainment. Given the eclectic nature of its content, the progress of entertainment cannot be told in a simple narration like the rise and fall of imperial dynasties. Each type, or venue, would have its own history. The idea that a society as large as that of the United States could have a focused set of entertainment experiences seems quite unrealistic. The problem is compounded by the fact that each society or nation has its own pastimes. The people living in India, Africa, the Middle East, and Latin America may not be interested in the same kinds of music, drama, or sports as those in the United States. They each have their own type of public diversion. Therefore, a world history which makes entertainment a major focus of attention may have less coherence than what people would want in such works.

World history could be presented in a collection of stories, visual images, samples of music, and memorable lines representing the highlights of popular culture. But, if history consists only of a stream of audiovisual vignettes, it may lack recognizable themes. Too much would depends on the historian's judgment as to what is important. Photojournalists often produce a montage of images using time as the unifying element. For instance, a television documentary on events which Americans experienced in 1957 might include these images: President Eisenhower sending federal troops to Little Rock to enforce a school desegregation order; Elvis Presley singing "All Shook Up"; Mickey Mantle hitting a home run in Yankee Stadium; Soviet rockets launching Sputnik; the tail fins on that year's models of cars. History in that mode becomes a kind of generational experience, appealing separately to each age group. Each decade brings its own style in popular music, clothing fashions, and political leadership. It becomes the journalist's function to characterize each period in a meaningful way and anticipate what might come next. So, the "Roaring Twenties" in America were followed by the depressed "Thirties", the wartime "Forties", the bland but prosperous "Fifties", and the turbulent "Sixties" of the youth culture and anti-war rebelliousness.

A book-based history necessarily takes another approach. This book will tell the story of structures supporting entertainment as well as of the entertainment itself. Being a commercial industry, popular entertainment needs to attract enough revenues to pay for the programming. Its events can be financed directly through ticket sales, or, indirectly, through commercial advertising and associated activities such as gambling or the sale of licensed products. Such considerations would partly drive its history. Another aspect would concern the mode of presentation. Are the audiences live, or do people experience entertainment events via radio, television, motion pictures, or cassette tape? Here again, practices have changed over the years. The history presented in this chapter will focus upon entertainment in the United States, both to keep the discussion to a manageable length and to acknowledge the fact that communications technology has spread American entertainment quite broadly to other parts of the world. This more than other national cultures has become the basis of a worldwide civilization.

## Amateur and Professional Sports

Athletic events have been a part of popular entertainment in all countries. Horse racing came to America with the Dutch settlement of New Amsterdam in the 17th century. In 1779, the Earl of Derby instituted a horse race on his property at Epson Downs in England, which became an annual event. A horse-racing event on Long Island in 1823 drew 60,000 spectators. This is believed to be the first large crowd to watch a sporting event in the United States. Regular racing began at Saratoga Springs in 1863 and at Churchill Downs in Kentucky in 1875. Cockfighting was also a popular sport in many American cities until the Massachusetts legislature banned it in 1836. Huge sums of money were wagered on these

winning the Kentucky Derby

fights. Boxing became an organized sport when rules were imposed in the 18th century. An amphitheater owned by Jack Broughton near Tottenham Court Road in London was the center of English boxing. Rules issued there in 1743 governed the sport for more than a century. Then, in 1865, the Marquess of Queensberry issued a new set of rules, giving the contestants gloves, dividing the contest into separate rounds, and providing for a ten-second count before a downed boxer lost the bout.

John L. Sullivan

John L. Sullivan was the reigning world heavyweight champion fighting with bare knuckles. In 1892, he lost to James J. Corbett fighting under the Queensberry rules.

Sports such as boxing, wrestling, fencing, or archery, which involve physical violence or the use of weapons, utilize skills which once had military value. English monarchs between the 11th and 15th centuries required their subjects to practice archery. English proficiency with the long bow helped produce a string of victories over the French in the Hundred Years war. The Asian sports of judo and karate are martial arts with a different twist. Judo, derived from the Chinese Buddhist art of jiu jitsu, exercises mental and physical disciplines that were attractive to the Japanese samurai warriors. It taught the warrior how to win by yielding to superior force. Karate was developed in Okinawa by patriots resisting foreign rule. Because their Japanese conquerors forbad them to possess weapons, Okinawan patriots trained at night in techniques of manual combat that could be employed without weapons. As spectator sports, however, such contests may be too individualistic to attract large crowds. The sports which play the greatest role as entertainment tend to be team sports. Such teams are symbolically linked with communities to which the spectators may belong.

The game of football is one such sport. During the Middle Ages, residents of English villages used to play a primitive version of this game. The whole town was the playing field. An unlimited number of players on both sides would try to kick a ball between goal markers at opposite ends of the town. The sport tended to become rowdy, so King Edward II banned it in 1314. Young people continued to play football on an informal basis well into the 19th century. Then this game was picked up by English public schools such as Eaton, Harrow, and Rugby. Each school had its own version. The first attempt to develop a standard set of rules for football might have been at a conference held in 1848 at Cambridge University. Fourteen different schools were represented. A second conference in 1862 produced agreement on ten rules for football, which became the "Cambridge University Football Rules." In October 1863, football players from the London area gathered at the Old Freemasons Tavern where they formed "The Football Association". Association football, or "soccer", thus became formally organized. (The word "soccer" is student slang for the letters s-o-c in "association".) English players took this game with them to all parts of the world.

In 1823, a young football player at the Rugby School in Warwickshire, England, committed an impulsive act which forever changed the game. Against all rules, William Webb Ellis suddenly picked up the ball and began running with it down the field. Football rules then permitted only kicking and bouncing the ball. Word of Ellis' rules infraction spread to other schools. Some students decided to try the game as it had been played "at Rugby". The Rugby version of football, today known simply as "Rugby", acquired its own participants and rules. In 1872, twenty-one clubs in London partial to this game formed the Rugby Union. Rugby was then an amateur sport. However, the game became popular among industrial workers in northern England. Many who were eager to play for their club could not afford to take unpaid time off from their work. Northern clubs began to pay these workers small sums of money to compensate them for their travel expenses and wage loss. When the issue of paying players came up at the annual meeting of the Rugby Union in 1893, a vote was taken and a decision made not to permit such payments. Two years later, delegates from several Rugby clubs in the North organized their own league on the basis of allowing the payments. This "Northern Union" became, in effect, a league for professional players.

The American game of football is a derivative of rugby. While the first intercollegiate football game took place between Rutgers and Princeton in 1869, these two teams were actually playing soccer, which forbad running with the ball. Rugby-style football came to the United States by way of Canada. In May 1874, athletes at Harvard University invited a team from McGill University in Montreal to play a game of football. Watching the Canadians practice, the Harvard players realized that the teams were playing two different games. So a compromise was reached. The two teams would play the first half of the game under Harvard's soccer rules, and under McGill's rugby rules in the second half. The Harvard players decided that they liked rugby better, so it became a part of American collegiate sports. Walter Camp, Yale's first coach, is known as the father of American football. He developed the concept of eleven-man teams, the scrimmage line, and other features and rules of the modern game. After several college students were killed while playing this sport, President Theodore Roosevelt convened a conference for the purpose of improving safety. To relieve congestion at the line of scrimmage, a committee chaired by Walter Camp decided to allow the forward pass. Notre Dame's Knute Rockne popularized it during an upset victory over Army in 1913.

Venerable tradition has it that Abner Doubleday, a Civil War general, invented the American game of baseball at Cooperstown, New York, in 1839. Soldiers in the Union army played this game for recreation between battles and took it home with them after the war. However, a book published in 1834 presents rules for a game similar to baseball and a woodcut illustration which shows boys playing it on Boston Commons. It seems more likely, then, that American baseball was derived from rounders, a game played by English schoolboys since medieval times. A game called "old cats" used a wooden cat in the shape of a spindle and a stick for hitting this object. As in the British game of cricket, a batter ran between two bases after hitting a pitched ball. He was "out" if an opposing player caught the ball on the bounce or in flight. In American baseball, the number of bases was increased to four. After hitting the ball, the batter ran as far as he could in a clockwise direction without being tagged. The running direction was later changed. In 1842, a group of young men began to play baseball for recreation in lower Manhattan. They became organized as the "Knickerbockers" club three years later. In 1857, a group of amateur clubs formed the National Association of Baseball Players which issued the game's first uniform set of rules.

Basketball was a game started from scratch in the United States. Its inventor, Dr. James Naismith, was a physical-education instructor at the YMCA in Springfield, Massachusetts. He was looking for a sport which young people might play during the winter or at night. Naismith invented basketball after studying other existing sports. He determining what elements were needed and then developed a set of rules. The first basketball game was played in December 1891 in the Springfield YMCA gymnasium. Peach baskets were suspended at either end of the court. They had to be emptied by a man on a ladder each time that a "basket" was made. In 1906, open loops mounted on a backboard replaced these receptacles and the number of players on a team was reduced from seven to five. The game of basketball became an immediate sensation. By the early 1920s, it was the most popular sport in American schools. The annual state high-school basketball tournament became the biggest athletic event in town. In 1923, Robert and Helen Lynd noted in their sociological study *Middletown*: "More civic loyalty centers around basket-ball than any other thing."

The sports of football, baseball, basketball, hockey, and golf, among others, have become important entertainment features on television, appealing especially to men. Because the event is unscripted, it sustains viewer suspense. The tradition of team play includes a moral dimension in suggesting vigorous camaraderie and unselfish cooperation in an endeavor identified with a larger community. These sports are regularly played in American high schools and colleges, where spectator interest is equated with "school spirit". In professional sports, a polite myth is maintained that professional teams represent cities or regions; civic piety obliges residents of those communities to root for the home team. Professionalism came first to baseball. Teams of professional players representing certain U.S. cities formed the National League in 1876, while the American League was created in 1900. The first World Series was played in 1903. The American Professional Football Association, forerunner of the National Football League, was established in 1920, and the American Football

League in 1960. The National Basketball Association was founded in 1949 through a merger of two groups.

Sports competition also takes place between teams representing nations during the International Olympic Games, held once every four years. This worldwide event revives a tradition begun in Greece during the 8th century B.C. Athletes from the Greek city-states competed then in such sports as running, jumping, throwing, and wrestling. While the games were initially held in honor of the Greeks' ancestral gods, they became a force for pan-Hellenic cultural cohesion and peace. Their revival in 1896 A.D. was a result of efforts by the French baron Pierre de Coubertin. The baron had been impressed by the enthusiasm with which rugby was played in English public schools. He was also inspired to revive Olympic competition by the recent excavation of archeological sites near Mt. Olympus and even the controversy regarding free trade. "Let us export our oarsmen, our runners, our fencers, into other countries. This is the true Free Trade of the future," he declared. Baron de Coubertin's proposal to revive the Olympic games won acceptance at an international athletic congress held in Paris in 1894. The first Olympiad of the modern era took place in Athens, Greece, in April 1896.

Greek runners

## Other Entertainment in 19th Century America

An early form of entertainment in the United States was the lecture circuit. Well-known writers, scientists, preachers, educators, and other learned persons would go on tour, lecturing on topics of interest for a fee. The lyceum movement, begun in New England in the 1820s, included more than 3,000 local groups by the mid 1830s. The English novelists Thackeray and Dickens were among the more popular attractions. Ralph Waldo Emerson, Horace Mann, Theodore Parker, and Mark Twain were

American celebrities in demand. While these events appeared to be instructional, the social aspect was also important. They were a suitable form of entertainment for couples while courting. Lectures at the Cooper Union in New York City were vehicles of self-improvement for the working class. Rather less serious were the traveling shows that featured dance companies, acrobats, wax museums, singers, ventriloquists, and comedians such as Artemus Ward. Equestrian acts, combining acrobatic or circus-like features, were popular in the 1830s. Exotic animals or artifacts were exhibited in traveling circuses or in museums, sometimes pretending to serve a moral purpose but always entertaining.

The live theater, which became popular in the United States during the 1840s, was at first considered to be a questionable activity. Religious stigma against theatrical presentations went back to the 1600s. Theaters tended to be located next to billiard parlors and saloons. In addition to the main piece, the performers usually did short routines that featured women in breeches singing bawdy tunes. Italian and French ballet added to the sense of scandal by putting the female dancers in skimpy costumes with a full view of their legs. Many of the early theatrical productions were imported from England. Famous British tragedians such as Edmund Kean and Junius Brutus Booth, father of Lincoln's assassin, regularly performed on the American stage. As it did later in Hollywood, the star system came to dominate the live theater. Edwin Forrest, a melodramatic tragedian, and Charlotte Cushman, who specialized in performing male parts in Shakespearean plays, were among the better-known American performers on tour. The American theater included stock characters such as the villainous Yankee or Davy Crockett-like frontier characters. By the end of the 19th century, most American cities had their own opera house which gave several theatrical performances each week.

In the 1890s, mechanical gadgets became an important part of the American entertainment scene. Besides popularizing Egyptian belly dancers, the World's Columbian Exposition of 1893 included a Ferris wheel which rose 200 feet above the shore of Lake Michigan. The carnival midway made its debut at this event.

In many American cities, the streetcar companies operated amusement parks on the outskirts of town. Families on week-

ends could ride the trolley to the park where they might enjoy a picnic to-gether, experience roller-coaster rides, and listen to concert bands. The penny arcades were filled with mechanical novelties, many of the

scene from Columbian Fair

peepshow variety. A crank-driven "movie machine" spun pho-tographic images on a reel of cards attached to a wooden spool, creating the illusion of motion. A fortune-telling machine pur-ported to read a player's palm and predict his future. Another type of machine tested mens' arm strength and endurance. A coin-operated phonograph developed from Edison's invention emitted recorded sounds. For a nickel, thrill-seeking patrons could experience a mild electric shock by gripping two handle bars. And, of course, the "French postcard" peepshows showed women in various stages of undress.

## Racial Overtones

A theme unique to American entertainment may have been the relationship between black performers - or white perform-ers imitating them - and  predominantly white audiences. Ini-tially, white Americans found the song and dance routines of Negro slaves to be childishly amusing. Daddy Rice's "Jim Crow" act started the craze which blossomed into the minstrel shows. White entertainers by the score, their faces darkened with burnt cork, traveled the country exhibiting the southern Negro's songs, dance steps, humor, and style of speech. This was America's most popular form of entertainment for a half century. The minstrel shows were typically performed in two parts. In the first part, a dozen or so entertainers would be gathered in a semicircle, shak-ing tambourines. An elegantly clothed "interlocutor" standing in the middle would act as straight man to two gaudily dressed comedians, Mr. Tambo and Mr. Bones. This part of the show was a mixture of repartee, banjo playing, ballads, and dancing, smartly performed, until each performer in turn broke away from the circle, did a "walk around" followed by a jig, and then retired from the stage. The second part of the show was an assortment of monologues, comedy skits, songs, and dances, followed by a burlesque in which a male entertainer wearing a wig, brassier, and swishing skirts pretended to be a woman.

The "Virginia Minstrels", starring Dan Emmett of "Jim Crow" fame, opened in New York City in 1843 with great success. It was followed by the "Kentucky Minstrels", "Ethiopian Minstrels", and other minstrel companies comprised entirely of white-male performers. Black entertainers did not perform in these shows until after the Civil War. The first all-black company was the "Plantation Minstrel Company" whose members, although black, darkened their faces and circled their lips with white or red paint to exaggerate the racial features. A similar event occurred with the "Tom shows", which were melodramatic performances based on Harriet Beecher Stowe's book, *Uncle Tom's Cabin*. These shows included such exciting features as bloodhounds chasing Eliza across the ice and the famous whipping scene. The slave girl, Topsy, often played by female impersonators, was a highly memorable character. The scene of Little Eva going to heaven never failed to raise tears. The first performance of *Uncle Tom's Cabin*, took place in Troy, New York, in 1853. While black singers were used in the chorus, whites generally took the acting parts.

Even after the minstrel shows declined in popularity, the routines performed in the "Olio" were continued in the form of vaudeville shows, which offered a complete evening's entertainment. There were both white and black companies. The Theater Owners Booking Association was an important vaudeville circuit for black performers after World War I. Pantages, Loew's, and the Keith Orpheum Combine booked predominantly white performers. Vaudeville was performed both on the road and in big-city theaters. The acts included everything from tap dancing, comedy, and snake charming to demonstrations by heavyweight boxing champions. Bill "Bojangles" Robinson, the tap dancer, was the highest paid black performer. Vaudeville was

Table 7-1

## Some Headline Events in the History of Civilization IV

| | |
|---|---|
| 1823 A.D. | Rules infraction invents game of rugby. |
| 1835 A.D. | Barnum exhibits George Washington's "nurse". |
| 1851 A.D. | Great Exhibition at Crystal Palace in London. |
| 1853 A.D. | Musical drama of "Uncle Tom's Cabin" opens. |
| 1854 A.D. | Millard Fillmore leads boat trip to upper Mississippi. |
| 1859 A.D. | Emile Blondin crosses Niagara Falls on tightrope. |
| 1869 A.D. | First U.S. intercollegiate football game |
| 1871 A.D. | Barnum organizes "Greatest Show on Earth". |
| 1875 A.D. | First Kentucky Derby is run. |
| 1876 A.D. | Centennial Exhibition held in Philadelphia. |
| 1883 A.D. | Buffalo Bill launches "Wild West Show". |
| 1891 A.D. | James Naismith invents game of basketball. |
| 1892 A.D. | Sullivan-Corbett heavyweight boxing match. |
| 1896 A.D. | Olympic games revived in Athens. |
| 1903 A.D. | First baseball "World Series" |
| 1913 A.D. | Notre Dame upsets Army in college football game. |
| 1915 A.D. | D.W. Griffith's *Birth of a Nation* opens. |
| 1919 A.D. | "Black Sox" baseball scandal. |
| 1920 A.D. | First broadcast on commercial radio station. |
| 1922 A.D. | BBC receives license to broadcast on radio. |
| 1923 A.D. | Houdini escapes from straight jacket. |
| 1926 A.D. | First U.S. radio network (NBC) established. |
| 1927 A.D. | Babe Ruth hits 60 home runs in a season. |
| 1931 A.D. | Gambling legalized in Nevada. |
| 1932 A.D. | Hollywood premiere of MGM's *Grand Hotel*. |
| 1933 A.D. | Franklin Roosevelt's "fireside chats" on radio. |
| 1936 A.D. | Jesse Owens wins gold medals at Berlin Olympics. |
| 1937 A.D. | First televised sports match. |
| 1938 A.D. | Orson Wells broadcast creates Martian scare. |
| 1939 A.D. | Atlanta premiere of *Gone with the Wind*. |
| 1943 A.D. | *Oklahoma!* opens on Broadway. |
| 1944 A.D. | Bobbysoxers riot at Frank Sinatra's appearance. |
| 1946 A.D. | First Cannes international film festival. |
| 1947 A.D. | Jackie Robinson signs with Brooklyn Dodgers. |
| 1952 A.D. | Cinerama and 3-D movies introduced. |
| 1953 A.D. | Birth of Lucille Ball's baby on television. |
| 1955 A.D. | Opening of Disneyland park in California. |
| 1956 A.D. | Elvis Presley becomes national singing sensation. |
| 1958 A.D. | The $64,000 Question" quiz show cancelled. |
| 1960 A.D. | Kennedy-Nixon debate on television. |
| 1961 A.D. | FCC  chairman calls television a "vast wasteland". |

## History of Civ IV    (continued)

| | |
|---|---|
| 1964 A.D. | Beatles appear on Ed Sullivan show. |
| 1967 A.D. | Green Bay Packers win Superbowl I. |
| 1969 A.D. | Woodstock and Altamont music festivals. |
| | First television broadcast from the Moon. |
| 1973 A.D. | Billie Jean King-Bobby Riggs tennis match. |
| 1974 A.D. | Evel Knieval tries to jump across Snake River. |
| 1977 A.D. | "Star Wars" movie debuts. |
| 1980 A.D. | Ted Turner starts Cable News Network. |
| 1986 A.D. | Geraldo Rivera opens Al Capone's safe on live TV. |
| 1990 A.D. | MCA sold to Matsushita. |
| 1992 A.D. | Johnny Carson retires from "Tonight Show". |
| 1994 A.D. | O.J. Simpson's "suicide" ride in Ford Bronco. |
| 1998 A.D. | Mark McGwire-Sammy Sosa home run contest. |

an important mode of entertainment from the 1880s until the early 1930s when radio cut into their audiences. Famous radio comedians such Jack Benny and George Burns began their careers as vaudeville performers. Radio's first hit show, "Amos 'n Andy", begun in 1928, continued the American tradition of expressing black people's humor through the mouths of white entertainers. However, the television version which went on the air in 1951 featured a black cast.

Inevitably, black entertainers worked in their own productions and white imitators faded from the scene. As early as the 1820s, a black theater group, the African Company, performed Shakespearean plays in New York City. Ira Aldrich, an actor known as the "African Roscius", toured Europe to great acclaim. The Luca family was a popular group of black singers who performed for Queen Victoria. By the turn of the century, black entertainers were appearing without blackface in their own shows. Singing comedians such as Bert Williams and George Walker starred in the so-called "coon shows" in which a well-dressed male performer flanked by an alluring female chorus would do

a musical routine with a derby and twirling cane. A dance routine known as the "cakewalk" created a sensation in Europe.
Female singers such as Ethel Waters, Florence Mills, and
Josephine Baker, who performed at the Folies Bèrgeres, developed routines which became hugely popular with white audiences in the 1920s. The Harlem Globetrotters entertained crowds
with a burlesque of basketball. More serious presentations of
black cultural themes included Paul Robeson's performance in
*The Emperor Jones* and George Gershwin's social opera, *Porgy and
Bess*.

The impact of black culture on American popular entertainment may be greatest in the field of music. The Negro slaves
brought certain rhythms with them from Africa which many
whites found appealing. In the early 1800s, slaves used to gather
at a place in New Orleans called "Congo Square" to perform
their music for tourists. Black melodies were converted into
popular tunes by white composers such as Steven Foster. A slave
tune originally called "Old Zip Coon" became "Turkey in the
Straw". At the turn of the century, a new kind of piano music
called "ragtime" incorporated a syncopated jazz beat. It was
made popular by Scott Joplin, a white composer living in Mis-
souri. Ragtime opened the door for jazz music performed by
black artists such as  Buddy Bolden and W.C. Handy. The Clef
Club's Syncopated Orchestra brought jazz to Carnegie Hall in
1912. From New Orleans came Louis Armstrong, who, together
with Duke Ellington, Miles Davis, Charlie Parker, Count Basie,
and Ella Fitzgerald, developed this into a distinctively American musical art form. Blues singers supplied vocal accompani-
ment. During the 1920s, the Savoy Ballroom in Harlem was
known as "the Home of the Happy Feet". The Charleston and
the Lindy Hop (named after Charles Lindbergh) began there,
setting off a new dance style in which couples danced apart.

The Big Band era, beginning in the late 1920s, centered on
"swing music" performed in a somewhat less spontaneous way.
White instrumental groups dominated this period. White croon-
ers such as Bing Crosby and Perry Como set the tone of popular
music with their laid-back style. Dancers such as Ginger Rogers
and Fred Astaire projected an image of cool sophistication. Frank

Sinatra became famous as a vocalist with the Tommy Dorsey band. Black musicians were being relegated to a cultural ghetto, albeit one which continued to be a source of new ideas. Bebop music challenged swing in the late 1930s. Mahalia Jackson's Gospel recordings sold more than a million copies. Most hotel supper clubs provided opportunities for black entertainers such as Johnny Mathis, Lena Horne, and Nat King Cole to find work. Black-oriented radio stations played a peculiar kind of music that attracted many white fans. Harry Belafonte's Calypso started a brief musical craze in the 1950s with its Caribbean beat.

## Black-Flavored White Singers

From the 1930s through the mid 1950s, American popular music bore the stamp of Bing Crosby, Frank Sinatra, and other white singers who had mastered the cool style of black jazz musicians. Bing Crosby did not seem to take himself seriously as a singer. He often missed shows and, in fact, could not read a note of music. Though a family man, Crosby liked to chase chorus girls and drink booze. His intimate style of "crooning" softly into the microphone inspired a generation of imitators. He had a smooth and pleasing voice which made singing seem easy. He may have borrowed his habit of "scatting" - substituting sounds for words - from Louis Armstrong. On stage, Bing Crosby projected an image of carefree sophistication and good cheer. He played the part of a wisecracking hustler in light-comedy films co-starring Bob

Bing Crosby

Hope. His breezy, easygoing way captured the spirit of America in the late jazz age. Frank Sinatra combined Crosby's intimate style of singing with overt sex appeal. His boyish intensity excited a generation of bobbysoxers. The young Sinatra precipitated a riot in Times Square on Columbus Day, 1944. In later years, he became pals with Dean Martin and Sammy Davis Jr., making a big splash in Las Vegas. His immense popularity even survived  the coming of rock 'n roll.

Sam Phillips, a Memphis record producer, is supposed to have said in early 1953: "If I could find a white man who had the Negro sound and the Negro feel, I could make a billion dollars." He found such a person in Elvis Presley, a young truck driver who came into Phillips' studio later that year to make a private recording of a now forgotten song, "My Happiness."  Another song, "That's All Right, Mama", which Elvis recorded a year later, attracted considerable attention. It was a fast blues swing piece, like some heard on black radio stations, which had strong country influence. After performing mostly in the South for two years, Elvis broke out of this regional ghetto to become a national sensation. With his sideburns and half-smiling sneer, he presented a rebellious image to Americans of high-school age. Mobs of screaming teenage girls attended his concerts. In an age of social conformity, his stage performances  included sexually suggestive hip  gyrations. Therefore, when Elvis appeared on the *Ed Sullivan Show* in September 1956, television cameramen were instructed to show only the upper part of his body. His songs struck a chord with restless youth and changed the chemistry of race relations in America.

Elvis Presley was drafted into the U.S. Army in 1958. He married, returned to the United States to resume both a singing and acting career, became a headline performer in Las Vegas, and died in 1977 of a suspected overdose of drugs and medications. The rock 'n roll revolution which he began resumed, after a brief interlude of experimentation with folk music, in the early 1960s. A young, fun-loving Harvard graduate then occupied the White House. The black Civil Rights movement, supported by idealistic white students, was raging in the South. Bob Dylan's folk anthem, "The Times, They are a-Changin'", seemed to capture the spirit of this generational and racial change. Then, suddenly, a new wave of rock music came to America from across the seas. Invited to perform on the Ed Sullivan Show, a British band called the "Beatles" arrived at the international airport in New York City greeted by newspaper reporters and a large cheering crowd. More than 70 million people witnessed their American television debut on February 9, 1964. Beatles tunes hit the top of the charts; and then songs by other English groups such as Herman's Hermits and the Rolling Stones. The "British invasion", bringing rock 'n roll back to its homeland from abroad, was in full swing.

During the next five years, a culture saturated with rock 'n roll music became intertwined with drug experimentation, racial protest, the anti-war movement, free love, and other strands of the youth culture. The Beatles were transformed from a clean-cut band which produced ballad-like hit singles into an album-producing group which experimented with marijuana and Eastern meditation. America's youth shared in the Beatles' personal growth, appreciating their political views, their offbeat humor and shaggy appearance, their interest in drugs, and the direction of their music. The '60s rock culture integrated black and white music as never before. Black "Motown" performers including Diana Ross and the Supremes continued the tradition of romantic ballads while Jimi Hendrix appealed to the avant-garde. After the flower children visited San Francisco in the summer of 1967, the mood grew uglier. The anti-war protests intensified, and two political assassinations took place. There were race riots in several large cities. The Chicago police clubbed protesters at the Democratic national convention. Rock fans assembled for a colossal rally at the "Woodstock" concert in July 1969. This peaceful event, which drew one-half million spectators, was followed by another of similar size at Altamont in California which turned violent.

Rock 'n roll music now belongs to an international culture that appeals to young people in Asia and eastern Europe as well as in Britain and the United States. In America, however, it has entered a mature phase. There are no more "hit parades" of Top 40 singles; no more Major Bowes' amateur hours giving a Frank Sinatra his first break, or television variety shows like Ed Sullivan's which would showcase an Elvis Presley. Recording artists today produce albums rather than singles. The corporate managers who control this music are into packaging sounds for different radio audiences and consumer types. The amplified heavy-metal sound of the 1970s had drifted far from the simple

love songs of the previous decade. Punk rock was more auda-
ciously theatrical. Video presentations entered the rock scene.
The biggest-selling album in the 1980s was Michael Jackson's
"Thriller", promoted with the help of MTV. Jackson is the grown-
up version of that small black boy who once performed with the
Jackson Five, now strangely vulnerable, with an innocence which
still appeals to teenagers and preteens. British rock icons such as
Eric Clapton and Elton John are joined by a new generation of
American performer, including Madonna and Prince, who at-
tract young, hip, racially mixed audiences.

## Productions on the Broadway Stage

Traditional entertainment suggests live theater. The center
of this activity in the United States has been a complex of theaters in New York City known collectively as "Broadway". A
street by that name runs the length of Manhattan. Near Times
Square (42nd Street) it becomes the "Great White Way". The tradition of the Broadway theater goes back to the 19th century. Its
spirit has always been entrepreneurial rather than academic,
focused on producing new hits. Yet, a type of academic, the theater critic, is on hand to observe and analytically report each
production on opening night. In March 1915, the Schubert brothers, who controlled the theater market in New York City, tried to
influence this process by refusing to allow a drama critic from
the *New York Times* to enter their theaters after he had written an
unfavorable review of one of their plays. The *Times* retaliated by
refusing to publish advertisements for Schubert productions.
When the Schuberts backed down a year later, it reconfirmed
the critics' independence and enhanced the newspaper's reputation for editorial integrity.

Broadway theaters are torn between the urge to produce
creative works of high quality and the need to stick with productions which appeal to basic human instincts. Plays which
are too intelligent often fail from a commercial standpoint. John
D. Williams, a successful theater producer in the early part of
the 20th century, once said: "Intelligence and good taste are fatal

to successful play producing anywhere in America because, handicapped by either of these, you are apt to produce the kind of play you think other college graduates will go to see." Such productions would fail because "(e)very college graduate ran as fast as he could past the theaters containing these handstitched college graduate plays, put on by a college graduate. And they didn't stop running until they landed in the front row of the 'Follies'; failing that, they ran over to see 'Girls, Girls, and Nothing but Girls', 'Oh, You Girls' or 'The Skidding of Tottie Coughdrop.'" Still, when an intelligent work such as Eugene O'Neill's *Beyond the Horizon* developed new tragic themes or a performer such as John Barrymore brought personal magnetism to a production of *Hamlet*, critically acclaimed works might also enjoy box-office success. O'Neill's genius set the stage for other serious playwrights such as Arthur Miller and Tennessee Williams.

An important element in drama, as in other types of entertainment, is the appeal of individual personality. This fact became clear when the Actors' Equity Association, whose members were individually much better known than their bosses, struck owners of Broadway theaters in August 1919. Threatened with legal action, the striking actors took their case to the public. They did fundraising benefits and free performances in the streets and marched down Broadway waving American flags. The theater owners capitulated after thirty days. Some of the actors, organized in a group called the "Theater Guild", put on their own performances in a rented theater during the strike. This organization became an incubator for daring and original works both by American dramatists and Europeans such as Chekhov, Ibsen, or George Bernard Shaw. Its idea was to create theater in the form of a democratic cooperative that would produce works for subscription audiences. This concept progressed to that of the "Theater Group", a politically inspired company which celebrated America's working class. Clifford Odets' *Waiting for Lefty*, produced in 1935, dramatized a New York taxi drivers' strike of the previous year. The methods developed here to teach acting shaped the careers of Marlon Brando, Paul Newman, Robert De Niro, and others.

Even so, Broadway theaters were in the business of enter-taining customers and making money. The Ziegfeld Follies did this by presenting beautiful women in chorus lines. However, there was always room for a play which became a smashing hit by giving Americans a new look at themselves. *Showboat*, pro-duced by Florenz Ziegfeld in 1927, was among the first Broad-way musicals to explore race relations in a socially conscious way. Based on a novel by Edna Ferber, it employed the creative talents of Oscar Hammerstein and Jerome Kern to depict life and love on the southern stretches of the Mississippi river. A contro-versial musical hit of 1940, *Pal Joey*, starring Gene Kelly, glamor-ized the life of a low-class womanizer who danced his way into women's hearts. In 1943, Oscar Hammerstein teamed up with Richard Rodgers to produce an upbeat view of life on the farm. Considered "corny" by some, *Oklahoma!* dazzled audiences with its western costuming, energetic dance routines, and memorable tunes. It was unapologetically optimistic about heartland America. The same creative team went on to produce such Broad-way favorites as *Carousel*, *South Pacific*, and *The Sound of Music*, until Hammerstein died in 1960.

## The Movies

During the 20th century, a new element entered American entertainment in the form of newly invented technologies to con-vey sensuous images. Edison's pair of inventions, the phono-graph and motion picture, captured fluent sights and sounds in a medium which allowed later retrieval by electrical machines. The earliest film production took place in the East perhaps be-cause Edison's studio was located there. The jump was made from short features for nickelodeons to longer productions that told a story. An eight-reel Alaskan adventure film, *The Spoilers*, drew 40,000 customers to New York's Strand Theater during its first week. D.W. Griffith's *Birth of a Nation*, offered two and a half hours of entertainment on twelve reels. Released in 1915, it provoked black riots in Boston by glorifying the Ku Klux Klan. On the other hand, cinema historians credit Griffith with being the first director to realize the full potential of filmmaking techniques. He greatly increased the number of shots and shifted the camera from one view to another to follow significant events in the story. It was Griffith who pioneered close-up shots and crisscrossing between simultaneous action. While creating a new art form, his works attracted a growing audience for the film industry.

In 1913, a New York vaudeville producer, Jesse L. Lasky set up an independent film company engaging Cecil B. DeMille as its creative director and Samuel Goldfish (later Goldwyn) as sales agent. Its first production was the film version of a western stage play, *The Squaw Man*, starring Dustin Farnum. DeMille proposed making the film in the West to take advantage of the more realistic scenery. After spending an afternoon at Edison's studio in the Bronx to observe filmmaking techniques, he and his colleagues headed west to Flagstaff, Arizona, to shoot the 90-minute film over a period of eighteen days. The editing work was done at a rented laboratory in Hollywood. Hollywood had certain advantages over eastern locations. Its season was longer for shooting outdoor scenes, its labor costs were lower, and, most importantly for independent producers, it was far from film makers whose works were licensed by the Motion Pictures Patent Company. Members of this "trust" used legal threats and violence to discourage independent film production. Being close to the Mexican border offered independents an escape if a U.S. court attempted to shut them down. In DeMille's case, an unidentified vandal broke into his laboratory and destroyed the negative of *The Squaw Man*. Fortunately, DeMille had made a second negative.

Lasky's production company made more than twenty films during the next two years before merging with Adolph Zukor's Famous Players. They became Paramount Pictures in 1917. Sam Goldfish and an associate, Edgar Selwyn, left Paramount to form their own studio, Goldwyn Productions, which merged with Louis B. Mayer Productions in 1922 to become MGM. A third Hollywood studio, United Artists, was created in 1919 through the efforts of a studio manager, Benjamin Schulberg, who convinced some of Paramount's principal actors and directors to form their own company. United Artists was jointly owned by Charlie Chaplin, Douglas Fairbanks, and Mary Pickford - three of the biggest stars of the silent-film era - plus D.W. Griffith and William G. McAdoo, the general manager. It had become apparent by then that the presence of certain actors or actresses in a film was critical to box-office success. Realizing that, the film stars demanded and received higher salaries. Pickford, for instance, negotiated a contract with Paramount to do ten films for $2,000 per week plus half the profits. Charlie Chaplin signed a contract to receive $670,000 for a year's work. The idea behind United Artists was that the stars, in performing for their own company, might keep all the profits.

Starting with Thomas Edison himself, several inventors had envisioned adding sound to motion pictures. The film studios did not push this, however, because silent films were so popular. In 1923, Lee DeForest, a pioneer of radio technology, started the Phonofilm Company to produce and market an optical recording device that would provide synchronized sound for motion pictures. Bell Laboratories developed a similar process called the Vitaphone. In 1926, the Warner Brothers studio produced an experimental film using the Vitaphone technology. Its next venture was a full-length movie with sound. Warner Brothers bought the film rights to Sam Raphaelson's hit play, *The Jazz Singer*, starring George Jessel. Jessel would not come to terms so the studio signed a contract with Al Jolson, the singer on whose life the play was based, to do the film version. Jolson was a veteran vaudeville performer used to wisecracking on stage. What made the film so appealing was Jolson's ad-libbed lines in the scene with his mother. The spontaneous conversation struck a chord with the audience, and Jolson became a national sensation. The film industry could not turn back from sound.

Motion pictures had a huge impact on popular culture. Their increasingly frequent performances cut into attendance at lodges. The cheaper theaters featured western adventure films and comedies. "Society" films were more apt to be shown in the high-class theaters. Young women went to the movies to learn how to handle problems of dating in a modern society. Al Jolson's next film after *The Jazz Singer* was *The Singing Fool*, in which he sang

"Danny Boy" to his character's recently deceased son. Horror films also became a popular genre. The premier of *Dracula*, starring Bela Lugosi, on Friday, February 13, 1931, introduced a theme which appealed to Depression-era audiences. Dracula, the monster, had some human qualities that drew a sympathetic reaction from audiences. Theater operators promoted the film by telling customers to stay away and placing nurses in the theaters to revive spectators who had fainted. This winning formula led to sequels such as *Frankenstein*. Boris Karloff's frightening appearance was increased by applying cadaver-like makeup to his face.

The decade of the 1930s is considered a "golden age" of film production. Talented writers, actors, and comedians from the New York stage trekked to Hollywood in search of fortune and fame. To lure financially pinched customers into the theater, MGM's production head, Irving Thalberg, conceived the idea of putting several of his studio's top stars into a single film in order to create an extravaganza with irresistible box-office appeal. The result was *Grand Hotel*, released in April 1932. The glamorous Swedish actress Greta Garbo was yoked with Joan Crawford, John and Lionel Barrymore, and others from MGM's stable of stars in this blockbuster film. Shrewdly promoted, it earned millions of dollars and set the pattern for future all-star films. Hollywood's best year was 1939. Its seven major studios produced a total of 341 films that year. Many were grade-B westerns, but the offering also included *Dark Victory* starring Bette Davis and Humphrey Bogart, John Wayne's *Stagecoach, Goodbye, Mr. Chips*, and many other notable films. This was also the year of two all-time Hollywood favorites, *Gone with the Wind* and *Wizard of Oz*. *Gone with the Wind*, a cathartic experience for the American South, holds the all-time record for box-office receipts as adjusted for inflation. (See Table 7-2.) *Wizard of Oz* made Judy Garland a cultural icon.

Greta Garbo

Table 7-2

Top Ten Films of the 20th Century
(ranked by gross receipts in 1996 dollars)

| title | year of release | est. domestic gross receipts |
|---|---|---|
| Gone with the Wind | 1939 | $859 million |
| Star Wars | 1977 | $628 million |
| The Ten Commandments | 1956 | $570 million |
| The Sound of Music | 1965 | $568 million |
| Jaws | 1975 | $557 million |
| E.T. | 1982 | $552 million |
| Doctor Zhivago | 1965 | $540 million |
| Jungle Book | 1967 | $483 million |
| Snow White | 1937 | $474 million |
| Ben-Hur | 1959 | $468 million |

Copyright, July 29, 1996, U.S. News & World Report

Offering the cheapest form of high-quality entertainment ever devised, the film industry was riding high. However, its success attracted criticism of several kinds. First, the industry came under attack from religious groups for the "immorality" of its productions and its performers' "decadent" lifestyles. The impetus for this criticism may have been comedian "Fatty" Arbuckle's arraignment for manslaughter in 1921 after an actress was found dead in Arbuckle's San Francisco hotel room following a night of orgy. To forestall Congressional action, the industry set up a committee headed by a former U.S. Postmaster General, Will Hays, to self-police its productions. The Catholic church formed a "Legion of Decency" which boycotted morally offensive films. Though ruining the career of Mae West, such measures came too late to stop Cecil B. DeMille from producing *The Sign of the Cross*, a 1932 thriller about Nero's Rome, which showed Claudette Colbert's bare breasts and a lesbian love dance. The film slyly included a moralistic message condemning such behavior. Another attack came from the U.S. Justice Department. In July 1938, its Anti-Trust Division filed suit against eight Hollywood studios and numerous executives charging restraint of trade. This move forced the studios to divest their theater holdings and change their booking arrangements.

A greater challenge to the film industry was competition from television. Annual attendance at movie theaters dropped from 80 million to 46 million in 1952 as the new technology was being introduced. Television had the unbeatable ability to deliver free entertainment into a customer's living room, but two disadvantages: its tiny screen and lack of a colored image. The film industry counterattacked with technological innovations to demonstrate its visual superiority. The first was "Cinerama", a technique of projecting color film onto three adjacent screens to create panoramic scenery. Audiences were taken on a realistic roller-coaster ride while seated in theaters. A year later, in 1953, the CinemaScope technique was unveiled using a single camera to produce crisp wide-screen images. Thousands of theaters were converted to this type of projection. A third innovation, 3-D films, enjoyed brief popularity. Viewers wearing paper glasses experienced the illusion of activity in three dimensions. The process of improving film sight and sound continued with systems such as Imax which were introduced during the 1970s.

Alfred Hitchcock

Hollywood continued to prosper in the television age, thanks to video rentals, foreign distribution, product licensing, film libraries, and made-for-television features. However, the film industry was slow to enter the business of producing shows for television. That left an opening for independent producers such as Revue Productions, which was a subsidiary of Music Corporation of America (MCA), a talent agency. Agents representing the Hollywood stars originally were forbidden to enter programming because a prohibition imposed by the Screen Actors Guild. Lew Wasserman, MCA's president, negotiated a blanket waiver from that rule with Ronald Reagan, the Guild's president. MCA went on to become a powerhouse in the television industry, producing roughly one third of NBC's shows in the late 1950s. This one-time talent agency purchased Paramount Pictures' pre-1948 films in 1958 and Universal Pictures' Hollywood studio and adjoining lots a year later. When in 1962 it attempted to acquire Decca Records, Universal Pictures' parent company, the U.S. Department of Justice filed for a restraining order. MCA had to agree to abandon its business as a talent agency to acquire Decca and Universal Pictures. The wisdom of accepting those terms was confirmed in 1990 when Wasserman negotiated MCA's sale to Matsushita for $6 billion.

So Hollywood has moved from the old studio system of producing films to a new system based on packaging creative talent. Success at the box office starts with the stars, and talent agencies control that resource. Successful filmmaking also requires finding the right script, the right director, cameramen, and music specialists. The person who can put all these elements together by his contacts, contracts, and negotiating skills becomes the real power in the film industry. An additional element in contemporary productions is the increasing reliance upon computer-generated special effects. George Lucas' 1977 *Star Wars* started a trend toward computerized films. Steven Spielberg has become Hollywood's most successful director with such hits as *E.T.* and *Jurassic Park*, which used computer technology. There was a renaissance in animated cartoons during the 1990s as the Disney Studio has produced *The Little Mermaid, Aladdin, The Lion King*, and other works appealing both to children and their parents. The creative talent which once produced a successful Broadway musical has lately gone into this kind of production.

### Radio Broadcasting

Ham operators dominated radio broadcasting during the first twenty years that the technology existed. The first commercial station, KDKA, began regular broadcasts in Pittsburgh in November 1920. Initially, profits were made in selling radio receivers. As sets were sold, additional stations became licensed for commercial broadcasting. Radio Corporation of America, headed by David Sarnoff, established the first radio network, NBC, in 1926. A Philadelphia cigar manufacturer, Sam Paley, purchased United Independent Broadcasters in 1928 and gave it to his son. William Paley renamed this fledgling network Columbia Broadcasting System. The Radio Act of 1927 regulated federal licensing of stations. Commercial operators were given exclusive use of certain frequencies for broadcasting their programs. The Federal Communications Act of 1934 established an independent agency to oversee all telecommunications. The authors of *Middletown* describe typical radio programming in the 1920s as consisting of "a Philharmonic concert, a sermon by Dr. Fosdick, or President Coolidge bidding his father farewell on election eve." Later, vaudeville-style comedy, play-by-play sports announcing, and dramatic presentations became staples of radio broadcasting in the United States.

In Great Britain, the Wireless Telegraphy Act of 1904 required all wireless transmitters and receivers to be licensed by the Post Office. This agency asked the radio manufacturers to organize themselves into a cartel to avoid the chaos thought to have developed in the United States from unrestricted broadcasting. The (British) Broadcasting Company, later known as BBC, was licensed to broadcast in 1922. Broadcasting was defined as a public utility. Under the BBC's managing director, John Reith, radio was to function as "a servant of culture", which would help to create a more unified and egalitarian society. A clause in the BBC's license forbad it "to deal with controversial matters in its programming service." Although that provision was softened in 1928, the BBC ran a tightly controlled operation which became regarded almost as an extension of the British government. Winston Churchill complained that politicians such as himself who were unacceptable to the party whips were denied access to radio. The BBC's policy was "to eliminate from (news) bulletins all crimes and tragedies that have not a national or international importance." Another policy forbad jokes about politicians, advertisements, U.S. prohibition, medical matters, and Scotsmen or Welshmen (but not Irishmen).

By the time of the 1938 Munich crisis, the BBC began to be compared unfavorably with competing models of broadcasting. The relatively wide-open news reporting in the United States gave the American public a more accurate picture of events in Europe than the government-managed radio news in Britain. In the mid 1930s, competition from two offshore commercial stations, Radio Normandie and Radio Luxembourg, forced the BBC to lighten up. For years, it had avoided "infusion of the human element" in news announcing to preserve the focus upon policy questions. That started to change in 1938. The BBC, which had not even had a news department until 1934, began to do recorded interviews and "eyewitness reports" from specially equipped cars. More entertainment features were added including the highly popular sports broadcasts. Fearing job losses, the Variety

Elsa Lanchester

Artists Federation, fearing job losses to radio, had advised its members in 1923 not to cooperate with the BBC. Used to feedback from live audiences, comedians at first found it hard to work in radio studios. The BBC struggled to find a type of music that would appeal to diverse audiences. Light music and dance music were early staples of its musical programming. Later, it included more gramophone recordings and more vaudeville or variety features.

American radio was quicker to recycle talent from the vaudeville circuit into the new medium. It gained stature from quality reporting of the European crises by foreign correspondents such as Edward R. Murrow and William Shirer. More radio sets were sold during the three-week period when Neville Chamberlain met Hitler in Munich than in any other comparable period. *The Nation* said then that radio had become America's dominant system of news communication. In October 1938, its power was confirmed  when Orson Wells and his Mercury Theater company broadcast a radio play based on H.G. Wells' *The War of the Worlds*. The play consisted of faked news reports about a Martian space ship landing in New Jersey. Simulated news flashes were interspersed with weird noises and then a period of prolonged silence. A mile-long traffic jam was created as panic-stricken New Yorkers tried to flee the city. Radio was an ideal medium for fast-breaking news and interviews exemplified by the famed newspaper columnist, Walter Winchell, who turned celebrity gossip into a minor industry. It showcased wisecracking comedians such as Jack Benny and Bob Hope, and presented imaginative dramas such as *The Shadow* or *The Lone Ranger* which gave it a reputation of being "theater of the mind."

## Television

During radio's heyday in the 1930s, David Sarnoff and his RCA engineers were engaged in patent battles with Philo Farnsworth, inventor of electronic television, for rights to this technology. Sarnoff unveiled RCA's system of commercial television at the 1939 New York World Fair only for World War II to interrupt its introduction. The Federal Communications Commission assigned the VHF (very high frequency) bands to commercial television, which supported only twelve channels nationwide. CBS pushed for delay of further development of VHF broadcasting in favor of color-television broadcasting on the much broader UHF (ultra-high frequency) band. The television industry stagnated during this period of technical uncertainly. When the FCC denied CBS's petition in April 1947, the FCC promptly received sixty new applications for stations and sales of VHF sets increased. Only 60,000 sets were in use that year, two thirds of them in New York City. About half were owned by affluent individuals, and half by bars serving a predominantly male clientele. The bar audience preferred news and sports programming. Because of scarce resources, there was a tendency to recycle talent and materials from radio to commercial television and recreate vaudeville in the form of comedy-variety shows.

Both NBC and CBS financed their early television operations from profits earned in radio. In addition, RCA made money from manufacturing television sets. Commercial television fought Hollywood's attempt to create an entertainment alternative in the form of large-screen television placed in movie theaters. It successfully opposed pay-television schemes brought before regulatory agencies. The Hollywood film companies were not allowed to own television stations. The scarcity of VHF licenses and an FCC-imposed moratorium on permits for station construction between 1948 and 1952 put the commercial-television industry in the driver's seat in negotiating both with advertisers and producers of programming. Advertisers, no longer the sole sponsors of programs, conceded their licensing to the television networks while retaining certain rights to censor programming content with respect to subjects, characters, and language. From program producers, the networks demanded and received ownership and syndication rights for the shows in exchange for giving them a network time slot. The success of *I Love Lucy* and *Dragnet* during the 1952 season brought increased attention to filmed productions. That led to syndication of show reruns, especially in foreign markets.

In the mid 1950s, U.S. television audiences moved from an upscale clientele to include more lower- and middle-class viewers. More than half of Americans who purchased television sets in 1950 financed them on credit. "TV is becoming the poor man's theater", a journalist observed. While original plays such as Paddy Chayevsky's *Marty* were shown on commercial television in the early 1950s, network executives soon realized that continuity of programming increased audience size. The popular western, *Gunsmoke*, ran from 1956 to 1975. *Bonanza* aired from 1960 to 1973. Soap operas had been developed for midday radio audiences during the 1930s as a means of selling soap powder to women. Commercial television took over this format. CBS, which had started well behind NBC in the television race, roared back in the 1950s to become the top-rated network. Its chairman, William Paley, had a good sense of audience tastes. He hired star comedians such as Red Skelton, Jack Benny, and Burns and Allen from NBC radio in the late 1940s and switched them over to television in the following decade. As always, the performers' personalities were the key to attracting large audiences. Viewers grew comfortable seeing the same faces week after week on the silver screen.

CBS styled itself "the Tiffany network" because of its high-quality programming, especially in television news. Paley was a close friend and supporter of Edward R. Murrow, a journalist known for his hard-hitting investigative reporting. For instance, Murrow's expose of Sen. Joseph McCarthy in a *See It Now* program aired in March 1954 helped to turn the tide of popular opinion against this anti-communist crusader. Yet, CBS's prestigious news operation was subsidized by earnings from the more popular sitcoms, quiz shows, sports broadcasts, and action drama. The network competition for audiences brought programming down to the lowest common denominator of public taste and produced what FCC chairman, Newton Minow, in 1961 called "a vast wasteland". Academic critics called for an alternative to commercial  television. The FCC responded by reserving 242 channels, mostly on the UHF band, for educational broadcasters. The first noncommercial station went on the air in 1953, but public television languished for a decade. In 1960, only 7 percent of U.S. television sets were equipped to receive UHF signals. Then, after the quiz-show scandals on commercial television, Congress provided public subsidies for educational broadcasts and required that new television sets sold in the United States be equipped for UHF reception.

The two main commercial-television networks, NBC and CBS, were joined by ABC, the American Broadcasting Company, which was formed in the 1940s when the U.S. Department of Justice forced NBC to divest its smaller network. And, in 1986, Rupert Murdoch created the Fox Network from a group of independent stations. ABC was an also-ran until the 1970s when sponsorship of the Olympic Games and programming direction by Fred Silverman, CBS's one-time entertainment strategist, lifted it for a time into first place. In the 1980s, NBC enjoyed a resurgence of popularity under the direction of Grant Tinker, a former Hollywood producer. In 1980, Ted Turner, owner of local station WTBS-TV in Atlanta, created an all-news channel, Cable News Network, which broadcast reports of international events 24 hours a day. After losing money for five years, Turner's operation became profitable in 1985. It has become a forum by which the world's political leaders talk to each other and monitor ongoing events.

The BBC began television broadcasts to home audiences in 1936, sooner than in the United States. These were discontinued during the wartime period, but resumed operations in 1946. Queen Elizabeth II's coronation in 1953 aroused interest in this medium. In 1950, only the United States, Britain, France, and Soviet Union had regular television broadcasts. The Russians used television to "mold a Marxist-Leninist outlook and promote the political and cultural development of all the Soviet people." The French, too, tended to have politically flavored programming; many television stations were either owned by politicians or the government. The British put more emphasis on educational and cultural programs. The market-driven Americans produced television shows that appealed to wide audiences. Family-oriented shows such as *The Adventures of Ozzie and Harriet* and *Father Knows Best* were popular during the 1950s. ABC's *Disneyland* made its debut in 1954, combining Hollywood-produced entertainment with the opening of Disney's first theme park. Reruns of U.S. television shows became popular in other countries. *Gunsmoke, Rin Tin Tin,* and *The Lone Ranger* were among Mexico's Top Ten television shows. Japanese society in 1958 was described as "TV-obsessed".

Ted Turner had long wanted to buy a television network. When that effort failed, he made a deal in 1985 to purchase MGM along with its library of 3,30l films plus 1,450 additional films from the RKO and Warner libraries. High debt forced Turner to sell the MGM studio and other assets, leaving him with the film libraries for which he had paid $1.2 billion, seemingly a high price. Turner realized, however, that the film classics which he had purchased, including *Gone with the Wind* and *Casablanca,* were a unique commodity. In a maturing industry, they were like ageless stars whose service commanded a high price. Turner colorized many black-and-white films, increasing their value in syndication. He established a cable-television channel, Turner Network Television, to show the films on a regular basis. Cable television was undercutting audiences tuned to the major networks. It was creating a new niche-focused mode of entertainment. Movie reruns were an important segment of cable as were sports, news, and educational programs. MTV, a youth-centered channel presenting rock videos, revolutionized the entertainment industry with its artful editing of bizarre visual images accompanying synthesizer-enhanced music. A freewheeling question-and-answer session with two hundred young people on MTV in June 1992 helped to propel Bill Clinton to the U.S. Presidency.

Television coverage has changed the nature of political campaigning. The classic event was the first Presidential debate between Richard Nixon and John F. Kennedy in September 1960. Many who heard it on radio thought the result was a draw. However, the debate gave Kennedy's campaign a boost since, to the

75 million Americans who had watched it on television, Kennedy appeared vigorous and well-tanned while Nixon, who had refused facial makeup, seemed sickly. Kennedy had been coached to look at the audience while Nixon looked mostly at Kennedy. The lesson for subsequent candidates was that one's visual appearance on television matters as much as the words spoken. On the other hand, Richard Nixon's political resurrection in the 1960s might have been partly due to an appearance which he made on the *Tonight Show* with Jack Paar. After playing a short piece on the piano, Nixon quipped that this incident would surely doom his political future since, after Harry Truman, "Republicans can't stand to see another piano player in the White House." George Bush came off as a more engaging, likable candidate than Michael Dukakis in the 1988 candidate debates. Though Dukakis' verbal proficiency was high, his body language suggested lack of emotion.

Television news has gravitated towards the cult of the anchor man. The avuncular Walter Cronkite, CBS's news anchor, was known as "the most trusted man in America." Political conservatives charged that Cronkite, a liberal, was able to slant the news by the intonations in his voice or by raising his eyebrows in a certain way. News organizations developed a format by which public officials communicated with the public through sound bites selected by television editors. They dodged questions posed by reporters such as Sam Donaldson known for ferocity of attack. In this tough environment, the most that political candidates could expect from news coverage would be to present an attractive visual image and avoid making gaffes. News editors controlled what part of their taped appearances the public would be allowed to see. Network commentators and pundits put a spin on its interpretation. The only way that a candidate could guarantee that his message would reach the public in its original state would be to purchase time for a paid commercial. However, television commercials were expensive, and the cost of running media campaigns has forced politicians to devote more time to fundraising and cater increasingly to well-funded interest groups.

Television has become a force in shaping social and political attitudes. Whether it was the Army-McCarthy hearings in the 1950s, the Vietnam war in the 1960s, the Watergate hearings in the 1970s, the clash between Clarence Thomas and Anita Hill in the 1980s, or the O.J. Simpson trial in the 1990s, television coverage has created a national morality play which polarizes the public along ideological or demographic lines. Its programming reflects the fact that sponsors want primarily to attract female viewers between the ages of 25 and 54 because they are prime shoppers for the kinds of products advertised in television commercials. Therefore, much of the programming that appears both in prime time and during the day is calculated to appeal to women. Women are shown in strong professional roles, often matching wits with men and winning. A male ghetto on television is found in the weekend sports programs. With respect to racial stereotypes, the days of Stepin Fetchet have given way to shows presenting confident black males often in military or police roles. On the other hand, the national preoccupation with the Clarence Thomas-Anita Hill conflict or O.J. Simpson's murder trial may have continued a long-standing tradition of white Americans viewing blacks as sources of amusement.

The distinction between news and entertainment is increasingly blurred. The news shows want higher ratings and entertainment-like features deliver them. So local television coverage tends to focus on crime, scandals, accidents, and other emotionally charged events. Tabloid journalism and talk shows such as Jerry Springer's specialize in revealing personally embarrassing and lurid conflicts. The new "reality-based" television programs such as *A Current Affair* or *Inside Edition* are cheaper to produce than sitcoms because some of the work can be done by regular news staff. Partly, however, such shows reflect the current disposition to trash celebrities. That may be a reaction to their contrived nature. The entertainment world is populated by a galaxy of young, physically attractive men and women who behave in a sure-footed way. Yet, the viewing public is aware that this world is essentially illusory. There may be a discrepancy between the public image and actual lives of those performers beheld at a distance in theaters or on the silver screen.

People grow hungry for personal information, especially when their idols betray human frailties. NBC's *Tonight Show* and its clones have offered a venue for interviewing celebrities.

## Sports Broadcasts

An important type of entertainment is the presentation of artificial but unscripted events where a spectator does not know their outcome while they are taking place. Athletic contests illustrate this type of entertainment. The first televised game may have been BBC's broadcast of a tennis match at Wimbledon on June 21, 1937. Only 2,000 well-heeled Londoners owned television sets at that time. The pictures were blurred. The BBC persuaded the Football Association to permit a telecast of the soccer match between England and Scotland held on April 9, 1938. There was a concern that broadcasting this game would conflict with attendance at some of the lesser sporting events in the London area. Sports broadcasting in those days also faced the challenge of unreliable equipment. The technicians hooked up the camera with thick cable which sometimes became disconnected, causing a sudden blackout. NBC kept two cameras on the fifty yard line at football games to guard against that possibility. Inadequate lighting was another obstacle. Even so, sports programming was a staple of early television because it was cheap. The networks, which lacked the resources to fill all their time slots with credible programs, paid little for this type of ready-made entertainment. It was common for saloon keepers to lure customers by offering televised wrestling or boxing matches.

Televised sports make successful entertainment because they combine a visually exciting spectacle with human drama. Each contest creates immediate winners and losers. Their physical strain and fatigue elicit a strong emotional response. After ABC sponsored the 1972 Olympics, it jumped from third to first place in the ratings. ABC executives realized that exclusive sports coverage was the key to network supremacy. While the 1972 Olympics in Munich commanded unusual attention because of the terrorist kidnappings, the television editors shrewdly focused upon individual athletes such as Olga Korbut to build human interest. They highlighted the ice skating and gymnastics routines. ABC's sports director, Roone Arledge, developed many of the techniques used in sports broadcasting today such as slow motion shots, instant replays, computerized graphics, and the practice of panning the stadium crowd to establish a sense of kinship with television viewers. *Monday Night Football* with Don Meredith and Howard Cosell affirmed the importance of personality, the commentators' as well as the athletes', in sports broadcasting. Cosell himself said: "There is no damn way you can go up against Liz Taylor and Doris Day in prime-time TV and present sports as just  sports."

The way to involve audiences personally was to convert athletic events into stories about the athletes. For instance, after the South African runner Zola Budd accidentally tripped Mary Decker-Slaney during a race at the 1984 Olympics, sports broadcasters billed their subsequent appearance together at the Olympics as a "grudge match". NBC's coverage of the 1998 Winter Olympics in Nagano, Japan, seemed to be more a collection of documentaries about the athletes' lives than reports of the competitions themselves. A favorite trick of sports broadcasters is the so-called "honey shot" - letting the camera linger for a moment upon an especially attractive female spectator in the stands to discourage the predominantly male viewers from switching channels. Sports figures have become frequent guests on talk shows, quiz shows, and other television programs. Their celebrity status allows them to command higher salaries and secure lucrative product endorsements. That has, in turn, put the spotlight on the money involved in professional sports, caused ticket prices to increase, and created pressure for team owners to demand public subsidies for building new and larger stadiums. Television money has changed the nature of sports from being a recreational pastime to big-time entertainment.

## Gambling

A characteristic of television entertainment is that it concentrates mass attention upon a particular event. The trick is to make money from that situation. One way is to insert paid commercial messages next to the programming. Another is to tie entertainment directly to the process of spending money. If many people in a large audience each contribute small sums of money, their pooled contributions can finance a large payout to the winner of a gambling event. Because the outcome is unscripted, each person who places a bet has a small but real chance of winning the big prize. There is something within an otherwise rational individual which convinces him or her that betting money on games of chance with certifiably unfavorable odds is fun. Gambling experts refer to "the heat" - an irresistible feeling that one must continue placing bets to recoup past losses or continue a winning streak. In any event, the proprietors of gambling activities set the payouts at a level which assures a healthy profit margin for themselves. While individual fortunes are being won and lost in the games, the house always wins.

Gambling has long been tied to sporting events. More Americans attend horse races each year than attend professional baseball, basketball, and football games combined. An even more popular form of gambling is the lottery. A lottery run by the Continental Congress helped to fund the American revolution. Another supplied funds to build the city of Washington. Lotteries were abolished in Great Britain in 1826. A crackdown on them occurred in the United States during the 1830s. Congress closed interstate commerce to lottery materials in 1895. However, lotteries were revived in the 20th century to fund charitable projects. The Irish Sweepstakes, organized in 1930, used gambling proceeds to operate hospitals. The states of New Hampshire and New York established lotteries during the 1960s to support the public schools. Today all but two U.S. states, Utah and Hawaii, have legalized gambling in one form or another. The biggest gambling state is, of course, Nevada, where such activities were legalized in 1931. Much of the betting here takes place in casinos where card tables, slot machines, and wheels of fortune fill the rooms and line the halls.

Gambling was legalized in Nevada in the same year that construction of the Hoover Dam began. Construction workers who came to nearby Las Vegas to spend their paychecks were exposed to this activity. Nellis Air Force Base was not far away. The city's first full-fledged resort hotel, El Rancho Vegas, opened on U.S. Highway 91 in April 1941. Three other resorts - the Last Frontier, Flamingo, and Thunderbird - soon appeared. Las Vegas acquired a reputation as a frontier town where gambling was legal. The Hollywood connection began when Clara Bow (the "It Girl") and her husband, Rex Bell, bought a large ranch just outside town. Well-known film personalities were frequent visitors. In 1946, a gangster with Hollywood ties named "Bugsy" Siegel oversaw construction of the "Fabulous Flamingo" Hotel. Suspected of embezzling money from this project, he was killed a year later. However, Siegel's vision of a big-time center of gambling and entertainment survived. Jimmy Durante became the Flamingo's first headline performer. Lena Horne, Sophie Tucker, Dean Martin and Jerry Lewis, and Ella Fitzgerald were among the entertainers who worked Las Vegas during that period. The downtown gaming clubs along Fremont Street came to be known as "Glitter Gulch".

Gambling was initially the main attraction of Las Vegas resort hotels, and entertainment merely an adjunct. However, competition among the hotels forced their managers to upgrade the live entertainment. Celebrity performers were the lure that enticed gambling customers from the other hotels. Casino executives evaluated how each headline performer affected the casino "drop" - its gambling profits - and paid accordingly for the next engagement. This sometimes resulted in huge paychecks for Las Vegas performers while nightclubs in places without gambling could not afford to book their acts. Patrons of Las Vegas casinos could expect to find a concentration of big-name entertainers such as Frank Sinatra or Sammy Davis Jr. A memorable event took place in November 1956 when Liberace and Elvis Presley performed an impromptu role-reversing duet. Presley put on Liberace's glittering jacket, assuming for the first time an image which he and countless Elvis impersonators have made famous. Las Vegas also became the site of major sporting events such as the Tournament of Champions golf event and several heavyweight-championship boxing matches.

Gambling is today America's most popular form of adult entertainment. The number of Americans who visit casinos has doubled in the past five years. More than 31 million people a year visit Las Vegas as tourists. America's fastest-growing major city, it has eleven of the world's twelve largest hotels. The amount of money bet annually in the United States exceeds the combined amount which Americans spend for automobiles and housing. Despite misgivings, the gambling juggernaut continues in part because many of those who are charged with guarding community well-being are themselves in on the take. State lotteries are widely used as substitutes for taxation; they seem to lawmakers like sources of "easy money". Indian tribes, whose casinos represent the industry's fastest growing segment, sometimes refer to gambling as "the return of the buffalo". Today's owners of Las Vegas resort hotels are no longer mobsters but large corporations and pension funds. In two years, $6 billion of new construction has taken place in Las Vegas to build such monumental attractions as "New York, New York". In ten years, some say, there will be no more controversy about gambling. "Gaming", as industry spokesmen prefer to call it, will merge with other activities to provide "one-stop shopping" for persons seeking entertainment.

It may be that a cluster of entertainment activities, including gambling and pornographic shows and, perhaps, prostitution and drugs, may emerge in Las Vegas and similar places under the heading of "adult entertainment". If not controlled by organized crime, these legalized activities will be managed by hard-nosed business types, oblivious to their social effect. Meanwhile, another cluster of activities, centering in a place like Disneyland, might provide "family entertainment." This would be entertainment suitable for children or, as they say, "for children of all ages." When Disneyland first opened in 1954, an article in *Reader's Digest* suggested that Disney had pulled off the entertainment industry's first "triple play" in adding a theme park to a top-rated television show and a hugely successful movie business. (Since then, this company has acquired a professional sports team and a major television network.) Both Las Vegas and Disneyland are "virtual cities", created by the culture of mass entertainment. Where once entertainment events required special places such as auditoriums or fairs to assemble the crowds, the process has come full circle in that mythical places like Disneyland have been created of images broadcast everywhere.

## Narrowcasting

The television broadcasting industry, which has dominated the U.S. entertainment culture, shows signs of losing its cultural grip. The top three television networks in the United States - CBS, ABC, and NBC - held 85 percent of the prime-time audience when the 1980s began. By the end of the decade, only 67 percent of prime-time audiences were watching those programs. The percentage then dropped to 54 percent in the summer of 1992, and, by the summer of 1997, to 40 percent. In 1997, almost as many Americans were watching cable-television shows as those on the big networks. Competition from cable television, the new Fox network, and personal computers have combined to produce serious erosion of audiences for network television, CivIV's form of empire. The average U.S. household owns two to three television sets and receives more than forty different channels. Eighty percent own VCRs. Ninety-four percent have remote controls. The ability to switch channels is as easy as pushing a button while one reclines on a sofa.

Cable television offers dozens of different channels catering to specialized interests. Web sites number in the hundreds of thousands. With so many more people watching such spectacles on their television or computer screen, the trend has been to move from radio and television broadcasting toward what some have called "narrowcasting". Entertainment is being pitched more narrowly to segments of the viewing public which share certain interests. Advertisers benefit from this trend because they can reach audiences known to be interested in their type of product. Their message can go out to groups of likely buyers without having to pay the higher broadcast rates. This trend toward narrowcasting may, in part, represent public reaction to the dumbed-down culture of commercial television. People are bored with the one-size-fits-all programming. They want variety tailored to their particular interests. Partly, however, it may reflect the changing nature of communications technology. Computers have become more important. The computer adds an interactive capability to communications. Allowing multilateral contact among individuals, it is the ultimate specialized communicator.

The trend is to give individuals exactly the kind of entertainment that they want. What viewers choose, in turn, drives marketing strategies to develop programming content and sell products to the various audiences. The computer is an important tool in this process because it allows entertainment executives and advertisers to track individual preferences. Data from viewer surveys and product sales are collected in computer files and then analyzed. This information becomes a basis for creating demographic profiles to be used in marketing campaigns. Individuals fitting a profile are included in the target audience for a particular sales message. Because the message is tailored to known attitudes of the group, the sender can be reasonably sure that it will strike a sympathetic chord. This is where commercial advertising is headed. We are no longer one people, able to be reached through broadcast messages, but a population segmented by demographic identity and personal interest. The sellers of products communicate separately with each known type. In this brave new society, we are defined individually by the mailing lists that include our names.

## Computer-Generated Entertainment

The computer's ability to store aural and visual images and change them in desired ways has taken entertainment to the next level. Digital samplers can create music by modifying sounds stored in the form of numerical codes on a floppy disk. By altering the codes for previously recorded sounds, this device can raise or lower the pitch, speed up or slow down rhythms, insert new musical segments, or overlay the sampled sounds to give an orchestral effect. The music is clearer than what synthesizers used to produce. Likewise, computer-generated graphics have revolutionized filmmaking. For example, technicians working on a keyboard with a five-second clip from *Interview with the Vampire* which shows Tom Cruise bending over to bite his next victim can alter details such as the color of blood smeared on Cruise's face and the size of his fangs to increase the sense of horror. Real-life actors and actresses have become models for cartoon characters, giving them a more realistic appearance. Ever since George Lucas' *Star Wars*, Hollywood filmmakers have successfully used computerized images to create scenes that could never be shot by camera. Action pictures relying upon such special effects have become some of today's biggest box-office hits.

Taking entertainment a step further, computer technicians have developed a technology called "virtual reality" to produce images that change in response to the viewer's physical movements. In the 1980s, a firm in California called VPL Research invented a set of goggles and gloves linked to a computer. If the viewer turned his head sideways, sensors inside the goggles would relay that information to the computer which would then create images in the goggles reflecting the changed scenery. Finger movements inside the gloves to simulate firing a gun might send imaginary bullets to a target on the screen. VPL Research's DataSuit, resembling an aviator's jump suit, was lined with more than fifty different sensors attached by fiber-optic wiring to a computer, which allowed visual images to change following some action on the actor/viewer's part. Unlike previous technologies which merely recorded sense impressions, computers can alter them to achieve this life-like effect.

During the 1990s, interactive entertainment became a feature of theme parks and shopping malls across the United States. This industry already earns more revenue from youngsters dropping quarters into machines than first-run movies do. The realistic action games are an outgrowth of military flight-simulation technology. The BATTLETECH center, which opened in Chicago in August 1990, was an early application to popular entertainment. Visitors to the center played a combat game on virtual-reality terrains by manipulating buttons and switches on control panels. English entrepreneurs have created a similar role-playing game based on "Dungeons & Dragons", featuring mythical characters in a medieval setting. "Merlin's Magical Motion Machine" at the Excalibur Hotel in Las Vegas takes audiences on imaginary high-speed train and roller-coaster rides. Its seats are equipped with lock-down safety bars. The "Star Tours" ride is Disneyland's most popular attraction. Blockbuster Entertainment Corp., the video-rental giant, has branched out into the area of creating "high-tech adult playgrounds" which take customers on virtual-reality tours of city streets. A firm called LunaCorp. has even proposed placing a dune buggy on the Moon's surface which customers at a theme park on earth might operate by remote control.

# Part III

**Chapter Eight**

# IMPACT OF CULTURAL TECHNOLOGIES UPON PUBLIC EXPERIENCE

## A Conversation with Socrates

One can think of cultural technologies as a way to amplify personal experience. Personal experience begins with a face-to-face conversation. Let us suppose that, as an impressionable young man or woman, you are sitting across the table from an intellectually inspiring person such as Socrates. In top form, he is discussing life's purpose with a thoughtful intensity that keeps your attention riveted on each word. As you listen to Socrates' arguments and respond to his questions, certain issues in your life suddenly become clear. You have transformative insights. You are fairly bursting with excitement over these ideas. Then the conversation ends. You shake hands with Socrates, rise, and leave the table. As you leave, Socrates' words are still ringing in your ears. Many of his thoughts remain with you. You know that you have just had an extraordinary experience and want to retain its inspiration for as long as possible.

What you immediately have is your own memory of the experience. But memory fades fast. So you take out pencil and paper and write down as much of the conversation as you can recall. You try to reconstruct parts of the conversation. Perhaps you can remember some of Socrates' actual words. After you are done, you have a written record of your experience. This can later be used to revive its memory. Although this record presents the conversation in an abbreviated form, it captures some of the ideas, phrases, and illustrative examples that you thought were important. Picking it up five or ten years later, you will be reminded of certain details that might otherwise have been lost. Any other literate person, though lacking personal experience of the event, would have an idea of your encounter with Socrates from reading this written account. Writing, as a cultural technology, has here achieved two results. First, it has preserved your recollection of the experience. Second, it has passed knowledge of the experience to another person. Metaphorically, one can say that your writing has extended the experience in time and in space.

Plato actually sat, if not across the table from Socrates, at his feet or in a nearby place as he engaged in philosophical discussions with citizens of Athenians. Plato's *Dialogues* consist of quotations attributed to Socrates and his conversation partners, supplemented by narrative descriptions which place the discussions in a dramatic setting. Although their accuracy is limited by the author's powers of recollection, the conversations seem lifelike. One would suppose that they faithfully represent experiences that happened more than twenty-four hundred years ago. Socrates' conversations have, then, an impressive temporal extension as a result of Plato's writing. Spatially, the conversations have been extended to millions of readers through copied manuscripts and printed texts. Many more people have "eavesdropped" on Socrates' conversations through the *Dialogues* than would physically have been possible when those discussions originally took place.

Written language is well suited to expression of ideas. What it cannot do well is preserve the sensuous aspect of an experience. Part of your inspiration in talking with Socrates might have come from observing his facial gestures, inflections of his voice, and his general physical appearance. Some other cultural technology would be needed to extend that part of memory. The discovery of electricity and advancements in techniques for recording aural and visual images through electromagnetic impulses or chemical reactions have produced a new set of cultural technologies that capture images of sensory experience. For example, a photographer equipped with a camera might have taken pictures of Socrates' face at particular points in the conversation. Because the meaning of speech is conveyed partly through facial gestures,

Socrates

it would add something to the remembered experience to be able to visualize the speaker's face. In this case, a visual image of Socrates would be extended in time as the words had been through Plato's writing.

One can imagine other ways that modern technology might have extended the experience of talking with Socrates:

* If someone had placed a tape recorder on the table where Socrates sat, humanity would have had a permanent record of the sounds that came out of the discussion. It would then have become possible to know the exact words which Socrates spoke as well as inflections in his voice, significant pauses, and other aural elements that conveyed subliminal meanings. This technology represents both an improvement upon Plato's memory of words and a way to pick up on part of the sensory experience.

* If a film crew or someone equipped with a camcorder had stood near the table and shot the entire conversation, then humanity would have had a permanent record of both the aural

and visual parts of the experience. The facial expressions and other body language might additionally have been preserved.

* If a microphone had been placed on top of the table, then the sound of the conversation could have been transmitted to a loud speaker in another room where a large number of people could listen to it while seated comfortably.

* If a speaker telephone had been placed on the table, the conversation might have been heard by someone hundreds of miles away listening to it through a telephone receiver.

* If the conversation had been broadcast by a radio transmitter, then a much larger group of people living within range of the broadcast might have listened to it in the comfort of their homes.

* If the conversation had been broadcast by a television transmitter, then an equally large number of persons equipped with television sets might have experienced both the sights and sounds of the conversation with Socrates.

In this context, nothing beats the experience of actually sitting down with Socrates and having a face-to-face conversation. The disadvantage is that, apart from one's personal memory, the experience is lost once the conversation ends. The cultural technologies extend memory or expand the range of the experience to other people. One should note, however, that none of the above-mentioned technologies permit two-way communication with Socrates. We can read Socrates' words as printed in the *Dialogues*, but we cannot inject our own comments or questions into the conversation. We can view Socrates' image in a videotape, but not affect the scene ourselves.

Only computer technology has the capability of transcending this limitation. Potentially, it can allow human spectators to engage in interactive discussions with intelligent machines. If a computer's memory replicated the knowledge held in Socrates' brain, then everyone who now lives or will ever live could experience something approaching a real two-way conversation with this great sage.

## Qualitative Changes in an Expression

The substitution of an experience captured in an artificial medium of expression for the real experience has at least three consequences. First, it extends the image in time and space. It allows the image to be received by an enlarged group of people. The image can belong to entire communities, not just the individuals who experienced it directly. Second, the expression of an experience through a particular medium changes the nature of the experience. The distinct qualities inherent in the medium color the type of experience that is received. The medium itself affects content. Third, an image or experience which is captured in an artificial medium becomes subject to editing. Generally, the changed image represents an improvement on the original. On the other hand, artificially improved images produce a distorted kind of experience.

Regarding the first effect, one sees that, because the amplification of an image allows it to reach many more people, it becomes the basis of a public experience. The cultural technology creates a world apart from what individuals directly experience. Activities of persons inhabiting the uppermost levels of society are brought into public view. History records experiences at this level. It is what we read in the newspapers or see on television, representing events of public life. At a lower level, societies consist of individuals interacting personally with other individuals. As people become aware of events in the wider society, their perspectives of community broaden from immediate personal experiences to events affecting neighborhoods, cities, nations, and the world. Each level of society has its own public life. At the higher levels, where history takes place, people experience events almost entirely through cultural technologies which mediate between them and historical figures.

In our illustration of the conversation with Socrates, we have assumed that the media merely amplify an experience. The cultural technologies extend an image in time and space without alteration. In other words, when something is recorded in an expansive medium of communication, the quantity of an experience is changed but not the quality. That assumption is incorrect. With increased quantity often comes a change in quality. One type of change has to do with the nature of the medium in which the image is expressed. For example, the world of book learning is quite different from the world of commercial radio. Print culture brings out the logical, rational side of an experience. Cultures arising from the electronic media bring out its emotional, rhythmic aspect. Therefore, you would not expect to find a discussion of world history like this one broadcast on a radio station even though, theoretically, an announcer might read the same words on the air. A group of media scholars, led by Marshall McLuhan, has emphasized the essential connection between what and how something is communicated. That connection is expressed in McLuhan's famous aphorism: "The medium is the message."

There is a type of qualitative change which has to do with increased quantity per se. Experiences which take place on a personal level have a different feel than those broadcast through a medium. The one is artificial while the other is real. The artificial experiences transmitted by cultural technologies, are, in a sense, "better" than the real ones. Consider a homespun example. If your cultural horizon extends no farther than the family, the most that you can hope to experience culturally would be to hear Aunt Alice play a Chopin piece on the piano in her living room. But if you are tuned to network television, then you can expect to hear the same piece played by a world-renowned concert pianist. Because the television networks attract large audiences and earn commensurate advertising revenues, they can afford to hire the very best performers for their programs. Industry pioneers such as David Sarnoff and Lord Reith of the BBC thought that this meant broadcasting works of high culture - every night, something from the New York Philharmonic Orchestra or the Vienna State Opera. Even if network television went in a different direction, its programs are at least carefully crafted. Real-life, down-to-earth, amateurish, cheap entertainment does not appear here.

Ordinary life contains its share of sloppiness and confusion. Events drag on to a boring length. In the world of television entertainment, routine imperfections can be avoided by hiring the best producers and performers and by editing out mistakes. Its world can be filled with entertainment routines and personalities of proven popular appeal. This world presents a hothouse culture of quickly ripening styles and of beautiful women and smart, high-energy men in glamorous situations. No one would confuse Show Biz with the humdrum lives which most of us live. The economics of television broadcasting provides the resources for a more energetic and sparkling kind of existence than what one would normally experience. Similarly, the fact that print technology multiplies written images so many times reduces the per-unit cost of publishing books. This means that the authors who are published can afford to linger over their choice of words, loading them with extra insight and care. The manuscript which goes to print will be the product of many revisions. The literary world will thus become a place of unnatural sensibilities where artistry has ripened into exquisite expression and perhaps created hidden levels of symbolic meaning.

What holds art back from pushing toward an esoteric extreme is the fact that, if it is to appeal to a large number of people, its expressions must relate to their world of experience. Ordinary people, not artistic geniuses, are the ultimate arbiters of popular culture. The first impulse of television producers was to present critically acclaimed dramatic works or entertainment extravaganzas with fancy chorus lines and expensive costuming. But the people did not want this for their regular fare. They wanted *I Love Lucy* and *The Honeymooners*, featuring clutsy-looking comic performers in familiar routines. Believable, if stereotypical, personalities have become the staple of television culture. One might suppose that carefully edited programs achieve a consistently higher level of quality than unedited or live programs and, therefore, that all entertainment will eventually gravitate towards that mode. But that assumption forgets the importance of believability in cultural presentations. Live programs appear to be more spontaneous and real.

From a historical perspective, the fact that a single author or performer can communicate directly with a multitude of people means that larger communities can be formed which share a common consciousness. Societies without writing necessarily exist in village-sized communities. Kingdoms controlling much territory require a means of communicating with greater numbers of people. So the introduction of written language goes hand in hand with the formation of larger-sized political units that are hierarchically organized. Through such a medium, emperors can issue commands to their far-flung subjects. So also the introduction of printing vastly increased the amount of news and information available to the masses, which is a prerequisite for democratic government. If it is true that each cultural technology adds a certain flavoring to public experience, then the fact that these technologies were invented and introduced at different times in history means that the subsequent periods were differently flavored. Human culture was different when only handwritten messages existed than it was when the technologies of printing and electronic communication came into common use.

Changing cultural technologies create changing modes of public experience. Therefore, the successive introduction of new cultural technologies at particular times in history mark the beginning of new civilizations. Each will be shaped by the mix of technologies then acting upon the culture. The interior consciousness of human communities will be affected by innate qualities in each medium or mix of media that project its public life. Historical epochs, being periods of consistent cultural flavoring and theme, will tend to follow the succession of technologies by which their messages are expressed and through whose lens their events are perceived.

## A Series of Cultural Technologies

"If it is speech that marks man off from the beast," wrote Sir Ellis Minns, a British archeologist, "the invention of writing and its improvement into a practical system may fairly be taken as the step leading to full civilization." Speech is the principal means of communication in personal life; writing, in the larger life of communities. (At least, that was true before the days of telephones, radio, and television.) Spoken language is by far the most important cultural technology. Its technique is taught quite competently in informal settings within the home. Nearly every human tribe has a spoken language. Most individuals learn to speak by a certain age. It is not so with writing. This technology was invented only five or six thousand years ago, and many persons, if not tribes, have remained illiterate. Unlike speech, the arts of reading and writing are usually learned in a class-room setting. Literacy appears to be an essential distinguishing feature between civilizations and primitive societies.

Cultural technologies, as opposed to the mechanical arts, have to do with expressing and communicating thoughts, images, words, numbers, mental perceptions and feelings. Spoken language could take place without the use of tools, but writing requires some implement to leave symbolic markings in a smooth and impressionable material. Nearly every civilized society developed a system of writing. Some societies copied the technique from its original source (which was Mesopotamia) but others also acquired it either through independent invention or some unknown cultural exchange. The dates when the various societies acquired writing are a matter of historical fact, limited to our extent of knowledge. Before writing, societies had cultures based on perpetuating their tribal memories by word of mouth. Afterwards, other cultural technologies were invented which represent improvements on basic writing or techniques for encoding sensuous images in chemical patterns or electromagnetic impulses or waves.

Not all technological inventions are of a magnitude to sway history. This book proposes five types of cultural technologies for the purpose of defining historical change. The five categories include the following:

(1) Writing: We mean here writing in a primitive form - that is, pre-alphabetic script. Visual representation has advanced beyond the stage of drawing to symbolize ideas. Each symbol represents an idea corresponding to a spoken word. The symbol represents the word as a whole, not a phonetic ele-

ment. Written language began with the use of such ideograms by Sumerian and Egyptian scribes in the 4th millennium B.C.

(2) Alphabetic writing: This was a new scheme of writing in which words are comprised of letters corresponding to phonetic elements. The letters are arranged in the same order as their sounds in the spoken words. A person who knows the sound associated with each letter can "sound out" a word phonetically and learn its meaning from prior knowledge of speech. Alphabetic scripts came into common use in the Middle East, Greece, and India during the 1st millennium B.C.

(3) Printing: While the alphabetic structure of written language remained unchanged, an advancement was made in the method of reproducing script. Printing presses were able to produce multiple copies of texts far more efficiently and cheaply than manuscript copyists could. This type of machine "writes" an entire page of text when inked type touches the paper. Johann Gutenberg's invention of an improved printing technique in the mid 15th century A.D. brought printed literature to Europe.

(4) Electronic communication: This category includes various inventions including the photograph, telegraph, telephone, cinema, tape and video recording, radio, and television. Such devices capture visual or aural images (including spoken words) in a medium sensitive to light or sound by transforming sense impressions into chemical reactions, electrical impulses, or changes in electromagnetic field. The patterns are stored in the medium in such a way that they can later be retrieved. Some devices transmit images electromagnetically over a long distance through metal wires or air waves. These technologies were developed by European or American inventors during the 19th and 20th centuries.

(5) Computers: Computers also capture, store, and transmit images in an electromagnetic medium. Additionally, they break down images and information, manipulate data, and produce informational or sensory output customized to the user. Computers apply mathematical and logical processes to data manipulation. They permit two-way communication with users. This type of machine was mainly developed during the second half of the 20th century.

## The Prehistoric Culture of Memory

The period of time before writing was invented we call "prehistoric" partly because we lack enduring records of humanity's internal experience. Human beings have lived on earth for many thousands of years, but only for the last six thousand years or so have written records been kept of their activities. One can imagine how prehistoric man might have lived from stone tools, bones, and other remains found at excavated sites. Written language allows archeologists and historians to acquire a fuller picture of life in long-lost societies. To a large extent, our knowledge and view of various people's historical importance depend upon the volume and quality of literature which these people handed down to posterity. We know little of the pre-Aryan peoples of India and next to nothing of their history because their script remains undeciphered.

The preliterate age extends back to a time when, one would suppose, man lived largely by instinct, which is a sort of knowledge stored in the genes. Cultural knowledge was passed down from one generation to the next in the form of stories, chants, prayers, and other constructs of spoken language, often presented in a ritualistic context. A child learns speech from a parent, who has likewise learned from a parent, and so on. Memory is a natural structure which holds this knowledge together. What we today regard as sublime poetry was once a device to support memory. The poems of Homer were composed in dactylic hexameter, with six stressed syllables in each line. This rhythmic arrangement helped to remember elements in the poetic repertoire. The Homeric epics were not a fixed structure of words as in modern poetry, but a set of improvisations variously recited by the different bards. Holding in memory an inventory of metric formulae associated with characters in the story, the  reciters would each produce their own version of the poem in correct meter during its performance. So each bard who recited the poems would create them anew.

While preliterate peoples also communicated through visual images, those images did not advance to a level of symbolic abstraction. Paintings of animals, geometric patterns, and human likenesses dating back tens of thousands of years have been found in caves around the world. Their purpose was probably related to rituals or symbolic magic rather than to communicating verbal messages. Notches carved in animal bones perhaps 30,000 years ago may have represented numbers. A precursor of written language would be the use of marked objects as mnemonic aids to keep track of complex information. The Incas of Peru used a device called "quipus", which consisted of knotted cords or threads of different colors and lengths strung from a cross bar. The Iroquois Indians had a type of belt called "wam-

pum" upon which stories were recorded through pictures in the colored beads. This belt doubled as a medium of monetary exchange. Other peoples have reinforced their memory through the use of notched sticks, knotted handkerchiefs or leather straps, and stringed beads or shells.

Several ancient peoples attributed the invention of writing to a god or some divinely inspired person in the past. The Egyptians credited the god Thoth, or Theuth. A passage in Plato's *Phaedrus* tells how an Egyptian king named Thamus discussed with Theuth which of his cultural inventions ought to be made available to mankind. When Thamus suggested the art of writing, Theuth said, "Here, O King, is a branch of learning that will make the people of Egypt wiser and improve their memories." But Thamus, the king, replied that Theuth's recommendation of

Thoth

writing had "declared the very opposite of its true effect. If men learn this, it will implant forgetfulness in their souls, they will cease to exercise memory because they rely on that which is written, calling things to remembrance no longer from within themselves, but by means of external marks. What you have discovered is a recipe not for memory, but for reminder."

The Greeks in Plato's time were on the frontier between oral and written culture. Their use of writing therefore carried over something of the function to support memory. Arnold Toynbee observed that "in the Graeco-Roman world, the written word had a function that was not unlike that of the typescript which a speaker is required to have in front of him at Broadcasting House when he is talking over the radio. Like the present-day broadcaster's typescript, the Graeco-Roman 'book' was really a system of mnemonics for conjuring up winged words, and not a book in our sense of something intended for reading to oneself." In contrast, the Aramaean and Hebrew people had been continuously literate since the 10th century B.C. Their sacred literature drew from still more ancient sources in Babylonian and Sumerian culture.  Therefore, Toynbee continued, "in the Syrian world to which the Jews belonged, a book was certainly not regarded as a mere mnemonic aid to human discourse. It was revered as the revealed word of God: a sacred object, in which every jot and tittle on the written page had a magical potency and therefore an immeasurable importance."

## Two Opinions of Illiteracy

The best way to understand a preliterate or illiterate culture may be to see it through the eyes of someone who has experienced life in both worlds. Jean Leung is a Chinese-American journalist whose mother grew up in China before girls from poor families were taught to read and write. She wrote about the ways that her illiterate mother coped with life in a modern society. Most adults in our society take literacy skills for granted. However, an illiterate person has to make countless adjustments and compensations to get by. Of herself, Leung wrote: "I bless the fact that my ability to read has brought so many new worlds to me ... and opened up my mind."

How might life be in a literate society for someone who cannot read or write? "When was the last time you wrote out a list of things to do?," Leung asked. "Now try to imagine being unable to use a written record to cue yourself. In the grocery store my mother does not zero in on certain items. Instead, she wanders through the aisles, relying on the displays to prompt her into remembering what she needs to buy. Picture organizing your life strictly on memory. My mother has had to break her life into routines. Sunrises are not just beautiful sights to my mother - they are her measurement of time. Every seventh sunrise means her granddaughter will be at church. The next brings another cycle. Since so much of an illiterate's memory is used up by daily living, very little of it is free for conceptual thinking. Creativity becomes impaired. Every change in life takes up more of that precious memory. Illiterates are conservative, wary of any change that will have to be remembered. Moving the bus stop two blocks away may make it accessible to more people, but it is an irritant to my mother. The same with stores opening or closing."

Martín Prechtel was once a Mayan shaman in Guatemala. In a book about his experiences, he described life in a village governed by oral culture and tradition. Prechtel's perspective on literacy is reminiscent of the Egyptian king Thamus who argued that writing would "implant forgetfulness" in the soul. "Mayans," wrote Prechtel, "know that people writing things down, not so much to remember them, but to ensure they don't have to. This gives people a choice to remember things when they feel like it. But to the Tzutujil Maya ... to forget something sacred was to dishonor it. We didn't want that choice, so nothing real was permitted to be committed to writing."

As Mayan traditionalists saw the world, the Gods had created four other worlds before creating a fifth world, the Earth Fruit, which was a natural paradise where man lived. Each child born into the village passed through the separate layers of existence as a pair of deities, an Old Man and an Old Woman, assembled the parts of its existence, uttering magical words and phrases which "became the very things they described. The Gods spoke the world into life by continuously repeating their names." This fifth world was "so delicious that they (the Gods) desire it. A spiritual contract between the people of the village and the Gods said that they would keep life coming to us if we promised to send them remembrance ... (By rituals, prayers, food, and

creative works) we learned not to forget the Gods ... The Gods gave us life so that we could remember them, to keep them alive. The Gods of all layers ate remembrance ... A forgotten God was an angry God, or a dead God. In either case, the life sap would stop flowing, and all this life would be as if it never existed. We would cease. All our rituals in the village, whether personal or public, were memory feasts for the spirits. Being remembered was their food."

idol at Copán

Written language was a way of fixing knowledge permanently in the culture so that it need not be attended further. Remembrance of the Gods, on the other hand, required continual attendance, even as the God themselves created and sustained life "by repeating the sacred names of life over and over again." So, Prechtel observed, an ancient culture such as the Mayan "has to be reinvented, reinvested annually by putting the tribe through the actual trials and experiences that their ancestors went through. The human being as a race was remade each year and infused with the stories and particular sounds that make it all live." Unlike literate cultures of the West, "Mayan tradition is not concerned with progressing to a glorious future. The Gods had already achieved that, and we were living in it! We were concerned with maintaining a glorious present dedicated to feeding what gave us this life in a remembering way ... The House of the World, like our village huts and our human bodies, no matter how magnificent, is not built to last very long. Because of this, all life must be regularly renewed. To do this, the villagers come together once a year at least, to work on putting back together someone's hut, talking, laughing, feasting, and helping wherever they can in a gradual, graceful way."

Literacy and language are related to the type of society found in a land. Literate cultures attract a growing fund of knowledge which can be used to build machines and change the natural order. Numerical literacy makes it possible to keep track of private property. Warlords can build political empires. Such a society, exhibiting great power, is capable of civilized "progress". If, however, the society is devoted to maintaining itself according to time-tested ways of divine spirit, then an oral culture forces people to participate actively in the rituals of remembrance. This communal task of remembering, which civilization regards as a waste of effort, gives meaning and purpose to life. So these "primitive" people become spiritually rich though their outward condition suggests backwardness. If progress is measured in lethal wars and degradation of the natural environment, then civilized people would do well to suspend judgment about which type of society is better. After Martín Prechtel left his Mayan village, 1,800 of its inhabitants were killed in the Guatemalan civil war. "Atitlán," he wrote, " is no longer the Belly Button of the World, but an overpopulated village of rival Christians struggling for food and money to buy things they never before knew they needed."

## Ideographic Writing

In his book *Of Water and the Spirit*, Malidoma Somé describes the experience of moving between preliterate and literate cultures. As a small boy in west Africa, he had been taken from his parents to attend a school run by French priests. There he learned to read and write and become versed in European culture. While in school, Malidoma came to feel that "the capacity to carve visible speech was like an initiation into a secret practice ... The God from across the sea was a learned person who bequeathed literacy on his believers." Returning to his native village as a teenager, Malidoma recognized that literacy had made him an alien among his own people. "People (in my village) understood my kind of literacy as the business of whites and nontribal people," he explained. "Even worse, they understood literacy as an eviction of a soul from its body - the taking over of a body by another spirit ... To my people, to be literate meant to possessed by this devil of brutality ... The ability to read and write ... made the literate person the bearer of a terrible epidemic ... an alien form of magic." Even so, the Dagara villagers asked Malidoma to write letters for them to friends living in distant cities.

For better or for worse, habits of literacy change the mind. While something is obviously gained, something else is given up. The mind becomes less keen in its immediate perceptions. With its tight grasp of abstractions, literate consciousness becomes ignorant or forgetful in other areas. One too much into this kind of thinking can become an "absentminded professor." Plato admitted that the whole world mocks the philosopher because of "his ignorance in matters of daily life ... he is unaware what his next-door neighbor is doing ... the whole rabble will join the maid-servants in laughing at him, as from inexperience he walks blindly and stumbles into every pitfall. His terrible clumsiness makes him seem so stupid." When book learning is pushed too hard upon children, their mental agility suffers. In India, observed a computer engineer from that country, "there is so much emphasis on academic prowess ... (that) by the time the kid reaches the fifth or sixth grade, his imagination is killed out of him." The Chinese sage, Lao-tse, thought that learned men made poor heads of state because "the more acts of crafty dexterity men possess, the more do strange contrivances appear ... I would make the people return to the use of knotted cords."

Yet, literacy also brings increased ability to organize information and make correct judgments about certain things. It gives a way to access the vast store of knowledge accumulated from the past and communicate that knowledge to others. From the beginning, the scribe has been a specialist in this technique of

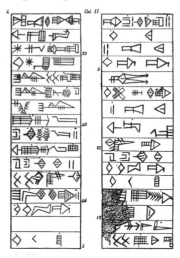

inscription on votive vases
of king Lugalzaggisi

expressing thoughts through visual symbols. That was especially true when writing was ideographic. Ideographic writing was an occupation for professionals. Its type of script uses a unique symbol to represent each spoken word. Chinese writing, for instance, contains 45,000 different symbols, of which 9,000 or so are regularly used. Each symbol must be learned and remembered separately. While the human mind easily acquires a large spoken vocabulary, it may take a student several years of study to learn to write the same words. With alphabetic writing, on the other hand, written language is structured to follow speech. Only twenty-six letters are sufficient to represent all the vowel and consonant sounds in English. This brings a huge savings in memory and learning time.

Therefore, societies such as the ancient Sumerian, Egyptian, or Chinese, whose writing never advanced beyond the ideographic stage, tended to develop a class of professional scribes. Needing to be supported through an prolonged period of training, these scribes were attached to institutions which could afford to bear the expense. This kind of writing did not produce a reading public. Its purpose was to preserve knowledge, not to converse or amuse. A relatively small number of scribes employed written language to record information useful to political or religious bureaucracies. Sumerian scribes produced clay tablets recording commercial statistics such as the daily feeding of pigs, man-days of labor, land size, and grain receipts. Their cuneiform script was also used to record mathematical procedures, grammatical rules, lists of medical remedies, and other kinds of practical knowledge. No doubt, use of this cultural technology helped to coordinate public works such as the maintenance of irrigation ditches and canals. The Egyptian cult of the dead involved reciting daily prayers that would enable the dead Pharaoh and his followers to spring back to life. These charms were later written on the interior walls of the tombs so that, if the prayers were neglected, Pharaoh in death could recite the revivifying formulae himself.

Written language went hand in hand with the development of imperial government. Once political rulers controlled large and diverse populations, tribal customs no longer sufficed to maintain the social order. The monarch needed to rule through written laws. He needed records of tax collections. Scribes were needed to deliver messages to his commanders in battle or to regional administrators. Ideographic writing, while difficult to master, had the advantage of providing a common written language for nations such as China which include people of many dialects. Literati from all parts of the empire who could not understand each other's speech could communicate through writing. The Chinese nation could possess a common written culture. A disadvantage was that, because literate persons enjoyed a monopoly over the written-down knowledge, there tended to be an abusive accumulation of power in the hands of scribes, priests, and royal administrators. The Mandarin class attached to the Chinese imperial court took power away from the more ancient class of aristocrats. Trained in the Confucian classics, these scholars shamelessly rigged the affairs of government to their own advantage. Many became hereditary landowners who exploited the peasantry by collecting excessive rents.

How Alphabetic Writing Might Have Inspired
Advancements in Philosophy and Religion

Alphabetic writing was invented by Semitic peoples in the 2nd millennium B.C. Some believe that it was derived from Egyptian demotic writing, a priestly shorthand. The Kenite people who lived on the outskirts of Egyptian society in the Sinai peninsula may have been first to use it. In the book of *Exodus* they are called "Midianites". Moses lived among them for a number of years. The peoples of Canaan and Phoenicia had fully developed alphabets (minus letters representing the vowels) perhaps as early as the time of the Hebrew patriarchs. An alphabetic script was widely used in David's kingdom, around 1000 B.C. The Phoenician alphabet was later copied by the Greeks, who added letters for vowel sounds. The literature that was produced in Judaea and Greece in those years had a major impact upon western culture. "The five or six hundred years that followed the transfer of the phonetic alphabet from the Phoenicians to the Greeks was one of the most creative periods in man's existence," wrote Robert Logan in *The Alphabet Effect*. " Within this short period there appeared many of the elements of Western civilization - abstract science, formal logic, axiomatic geometry, rational philosophy, and representational art."

Hebrew script (1489 A.D.)

Unlike its ideographic predecessor, alphabetic writing was a script for practical persons such as merchants. They were men of quick intelligence who had seen much of the world. Anyone could figure out the meaning of words from the sounds of a relatively small number of letters. The relative ease of learning alphabetic script meant that its use was not limited to professional scribes. The alphabet became a force for democratizing knowledge. In India, for instance, Brahmin priests had turned themselves into a privileged class through their control of memorized rituals. A semi-alphabetic script, Brahmi, was introduced there during a period of commercial contact with mideastern peoples in the 7th century B.C. The religious revolution that took place in India during the 6th century B.C. represented a protest against the elaborate rituals and sacrifices controlled by the priests. Both Buddha and Mahavira offered salvation through personal enlightenment to all persons, regardless of birth, who were devoted to following the way of truth.

Western religion was likewise transformed when alphabetic literacy came to the Hebrew people. Moses might have acquired this skill during his years of royal upbringing in Egypt or his sojourn among the Midianite people. After leading the Hebrews out of Egypt, he brought to them a set of tablets upon which God's moral instructions had been inscribed. The "Ten Commandments" were a core of written law for the Hebrew nation. Its people acquired the conception of God as an abstract or spiritual being rather than a graven image. God was a being known primarily through scripture. He was a character in a story who had personally spoken with the Patriarchs and with Moses. Now this same God had become the author of written laws. Because the Hebrews were among the first people to acquire the skill of writing, they developed a sense of cultural and moral superiority. In *Deuteronomy* 17, God instructed future kings of Israel "not (to) acquire many wives ... (nor) acquire great quantities of silver and gold" as other nations' kings did. Instead, "he ( king of Israel) shall make a copy of this law in a book ... He shall keep it by him and read from it all his life, so that he may learn to fear the Lord his God."

Christianity and Islam were also scripturally based. Jesus' earthly career was the product of a tradition associated with Jewish religious writers. His Messianic mission derived from that script. So literature and life were engaged in a dialogue that shaped future history. A dramatic moment occurred when Jesus read a scroll in the synagogue at Nazareth upon which Isaiah's prophecy was written concerning the year of the Lord's favor. He then made this statement: "Today, in your very hearing, this text has come true." (Luke 4:18-21) While Jesus himself left no written works, the Gospel writers pieced together a narrative of his sayings and activities in a hauntingly beautiful piece of literature. In the Gospel of *John*, Jesus is personified as God's "Word" or the preexistent Logos underlying cosmic order and purpose. Public readings from the Bible continue to be an important part of Christian worship.

The Islamic religion began with a sense of ethnic inferiority because the Arabs were an illiterate people. It represented an attempt to bring Arabic religion up to the cultural level of the

Christian and Jewish religions. The prophet Mohammed, then an illiterate merchant, received his first revelation at the age of forty. One night, the archangel Gabriel appeared to him in a dream issuing a command: "Read". Mohammed protested "I am no reader". Gabriel then repeated: "Read in the name of the Lord who created man of blood coagulated. Read! Thy Lord is the most beneficent who taught by the Pen." After further commands, the angel dictated to Mohammed over a period of years the divine message which has been recorded in the *Koran*. By tradition, the *Koran* was a transcription or copy of a tablet in Heaven. Someone else might have written it down on palm leaves as Mohammed recited the words from ecstatic visions. But Mohammed, from his travels, was familiar with the content of Biblical scriptures. He honored Jews and Christians as "peoples of the book". Significantly, many of Mohammed's early followers were students of Harb, who had popularized writing among the Quraysh aristocracy in Mecca. The *Koran* itself brought literacy to the Arabs.

So much of the world's important religious literature was produced in a period of transition between oral and written cultures. As the *Koran* originated in a society newly exposed to writing, so too the philosophical revolution that took place in the middle part of the first millennium B.C. reflects the fresh onslaught of alphabetic scripts. The first Hebrew literature was produced at the beginning of the millennium. Then, a few centuries later, came Zoroaster, Buddha, Confucius, Pythagoras, Socrates, and other great thinkers of that age. No other historical period has produced such an intense concentration of philosophically inspired persons. With the exception of Confucius, they all lived in a place and time when alphabetic writing was being introduced to society. Despite differences in their teaching, the great philosophers and religious thinkers who then lived shared a common view in the value that they attached to goodness and truth. They placed moral virtue above worldly power. The written word was yet a novelty and so were these ideas.

From a western perspective, Plato was the central figure in this intellectual movement. For all their variety, Plato's philosophical insights boiled down to a single idea: it was the idea of an idea. Plato studied ideas as if they were things. He sought to know the nature of their being. Plato perceived that ideas, as opposed to natural objects, had a special kind of being. They were universal and imperishable beings of an unmixed quality. Over the years, Plato's philosophy has taken on mysterious meanings. Platonic forms seem to float somewhere above the world, eternally present though absent and unseen. It is possible to take a simpler view of the matter. An idea, or a Platonic form, is simply a word. The form or idea of justice is what the word "justice" means. In one respect, of course, a word is a visual symbol. Plato was not concerned with the word's physical appearance as much as its reference to something else. In the *Dialogues*, Socrates was often probing the meaning of words, seeking a true definition. "What is justice?", "What is courage?", he would ask. The answerer would cite instances of justice or courage, as if to suggest a pattern. It was the being of that pattern which most interested Plato. The pattern was an abstract idea which the word expressed.

Keep in mind that Greek society, in contrast to Judaic society, had been literate for a relatively short time when these inquiries were made. One can see how a preoccupation with ideas such as Plato's might have arisen in a society that had recently become literate. Written words, being novelties, were objects of curiosity. Greek thinkers for some time had been asking philosophical questions about nature. They had been inquiring what was the basic "stuff" of which the world was made. It was understandable, then, that someone like Socrates might turn his attention to words and ask about the nature of their being. Of course, words had been around for a long time as a part of spoken language. Why did not philosophers study them as elements of speech? The answer may lie in the fact that it is not as convenient to examine spoken words as it is written ones. Words, once spoken, vanish from the scene. They are gone the moment they are uttered, leaving only an aural impression upon memory. Words written on paper or carved in stone have a more palpable existence. They seem to be like physical objects. These words stay in place long enough that a person can examine them. They have durability. Since these written words appear to be fixed objects, a philosopher might ask: "What kind of thing is this?"

Alphabetic writing increased the general level of literacy in the society so that intellectually active and curious persons from many walks of life became exposed to written language. There was a clash of viewpoints not found in temple environments. In addition, the alphabet encouraged analytical thinking because, to convert speech phonetically into writing, one must identify the successive sounds, associate each with a letter, and recombine them into words. Logan has observed that "the constant repetition of the process of phonemic analysis of a spoken words, every time it is written in an alphabetic form, subliminally promotes the skills of analysis and matching that are critical for the development of scientific and logical thinking." Also, "the linking together of ... letters to form words provided a model for the linking together of ideas to form a logical argument." Freed of the need to follow a poetic story line to express knowledge, prose writings could follow the flow of logical arguments. For purposes of classification, the letters of the alphabet in their conventional sequence allowed words to be conveniently sorted, which is a requirement of dictionaries and other reference materials. Writings on paper presented detached and objective expressions which were impartially available to readers.

### Printing and the Individual Author

The technology of printing came to Europe in the 15th century A.D. as a result of two inventions that had originated in China. One was cheap paper, and the other movable type. The Europeans were able to exploit this technology more effectively than the Chinese because their written languages were based on the alphabetic system. The small number of alphabetic letters in their script made it economical to mass-produce and reuse the type fonts created for each letter. Initially, printers did what the manuscript copyists had done, except more cheaply. Their cheaper production costs allowed them to undercut the copyists on price. Printing was, therefore, a threat to their employment. Because numerous printed sheets were produced from the same plate, printers had an incentive to check the texts more closely. Aldus Manutius, an Italian publisher of the late 15th century, hired scholars to check manuscripts for his pocket-sized editions of classical writings. He also employed proofreaders. Printers could afford to prepare the textual materials with some care. This new capability reinforced the inclination of Renaissance scholars to maintain the integrity of original texts.

Chinese literature was less amenable to printing by movable type. Initially, it was printed in a solid page. The ideographic nature of the writing called for skilled penmanship. Calligraphy became an art form by which individual writers might distinguish themselves. Stone tablets housed in a Confucian temple at Xi'an exhibit writings of several well-known scholars. The stone carvings, transcribed from paper, display different calligraphic styles. Writers have imitated these models over the years. The steles thus served to standardize writing in a pre-typographic culture. Printing downgrades the calligraphic aspect of individual writing. Its fonts present standardized scripts in a nearly perfect form. The words appear in a uniform style and are evenly spaced within the lines. The vertical margins are straight. Paragraphs are indented. Serifs at the top and bottom of letters carry the eye horizontally across the page. All is arranged visually to afford quick and comfortable reading. Previously, it was customary to read written manuscripts aloud to increase their comprehensibility. Printed literature permits silent reading. Scholars can work more efficiently.

Printing has brought an advancement in standardizing languages. Printed dictionaries exhibit the proper spellings and meanings of words. Literature has become an expression of national culture. With a growing tendency for authors to write in vernacular tongues, the different European languages each acquired a body of literature which helped to stabilize the language. Printing also served to increase and diffuse scientific knowledge. It fostered a fragmented, classified, more carefully analyzed view of the world. Regularly published journals speeded up the process of exchanging scientific information. The greater care in preparing printed texts suited the scientists' need to observe nature carefully and report their observations in meticulous detail. Printed literature helped to preserve knowledge by spreading it to a wider audience. Publication in quantity meant that a work would never be lost. As books became more plentiful, scholars no longer had to wander about between scattered locations to find them. Freed of the task of copying manuscripts, they could devote their time to pursuits of greater scholarly worth.

Before printing, people did not even know the year in which they were living. Books were so valuable that they were chained to desks. Cheap printed literature liberated humanity from ignorance and uniformity of thought. Not just wealthy people or

chained books

clerics had access to books. Where the manuscript culture had largely been confined to monasteries, universities, and royal courts, printing was pitched at a broader audience. Anyone who could read might purchase its product. No longer needing a patron for financial support, a publisher could stay in business as long as he could sell the merchandise profitably. The market would support books of many kinds. Printing reinforced the contemporaneous trend of making literature available to people in their own tongue. That gave a boost to self-education. Prospective scholars no longer had to learn a second language (Latin) before reading scholarly materials. Printed books spurred a demand for universal education. Printed newspapers spread information about current events through the community. An educated and informed citizenry was in a better position to defend its rights against abusive government. A further consequence of the printing revolution was the rise of parliamentary government and democracy, in which public opinion has played a critical role.

In Roman society, the aristocratic class had benefited from the lack of public literacy. The rich could afford private messengers or correspondents to carry letters to each other. Often cheated in dealings with them, the common people demanded that the Twelve Laws of Rome be written down. Julius Caesar, who was a champion of the poor, posted the proceedings of the Roman Senate on the Senate door. Due to a lack of open communications, the Greek and Roman experiments with democracy failed. Democratic government succeeded in post-Renaissance Europe because printed literature had produced an informed public. There were now communications media through which popular sentiments could be effectively expressed. Both religious and political leaders reacted negatively to their threatened loss of authority. Filippo di Strata tried to persuade the Venetian Senate to outlaw printing. "The press is a whore, the pen is a virgin," he exclaimed. Though kings and bishops tried to censor subversive writings, it was a losing battle. Illegal print shops sprang up ready to supply what people wanted. Eventually, the authorities were forced to hire their own writers and printers to court public opinion.

As Buddhism armed with alphabetic script had once challenged the Hindu caste system, so the Protestant Reformation used printed literature to challenge the authority of the Roman church. The medieval church exercised worldly power by controlling the Christian sacraments which were believed necessary for personal salvation. Its teachings were transmitted to individual worshipers through oral formulae recited during the Mass. The Bible itself was written in Latin. When pre-Reformation reformers such as John Wycliffe and John Huss translated the Bible into popular tongues, the church condemned them as heretics. The invention of printing gave another Biblical translator, Martin Luther, a more powerful position from which to challenge church authority. Within a month, all of Europe had heard of his posting the "Ninety-five Theses" on the door of the Wittenberg castle church. Luther and his supporters flooded Europe with printed religious propaganda. Printing made it possible for each believer to own a Bible written in his own language. The Protestants encouraged believers to base their faith upon scriptures which they themselves had read rather than upon sacraments of the church. Religion became a matter of individual conscience and belief.

In a philosophical age, people reckon by means of generalities. Generalities are such that a single concept covers many situations. This allows a certain economy to be achieved in the use of memory. Writings on paper hold diverse elements together by the physical unity of the paper itself. A checklist, for instance, reminds one of all the different steps to be taken though they may have no inherent relationship to each other. It gives an artificial unity to those elements by virtue of inclusion on the same piece of paper. Their association does not need to be remembered. Printed literature holds structures of words together in this way. Their unity is found in the authorship of the writing. Because of the extra care taken in preparing and reproducing printed texts, one can be sure that they faithfully represent what the author actually wrote. This becomes important in the modern cult of the author. We see authors as creative persons who exhibit unique insight in their choice of words and themes to express a certain vision of the world. They have an artistic talent manifested in the intricacies and nuances of their expression which is called personal style. If the exact structure of words could not be preserved on paper, it would serve no purpose to value such things.

During the Middle Ages, authorship was unimportant. Medieval writers borrowed freely from each other. Manuscript copying was a communal work in which the writers not only copied other people's writings but added to them. There was little attempt to identify the authors or titles of written works. In a tradition dating back to Babylon, manuscripts were identified by the opening words of the text. Printing brought greater attention to authors. Books began to have title pages which disclosed the authors' names. Copyright laws established a proprietary interest in written works. Plagiarism, or copying and publishing someone else's writings without attribution, became a legal concern. Because print technology made it possible to preserve texts with unprecedented fidelity, an author's unique manner of expression gained recognition within the culture. The words of poems would be quoted exactly as the poet had written them. Because their personal creative expressions were considered to be valuable, writers and musicians became heroes of the age. It would not have been possible to have a cult of the author if an author's words were regularly garbled or copied imperfectly.

However, the tradition of communal writing has continued in what may be the most important product of the print culture: newspapers. These began with individual correspondence as when one person writes another a letter narrating personal events. Letters of more general interest became the basis of newsletters. Soon a clientele of interested persons awaited the communication. The technology of printing made it economical to produce a large number of copies. Soon general newsletters or newspapers appeared. The English journalists, Addison and

monk copyist

Steele, developed a new style of writing in their weekly publication, *Tatler and Spectator*, which is called equitone. This means maintaining a single perspective and tone throughout the newspaper. The individual journalists all wrote in the same crisp and objective way. When enough readers were attracted to these publications, it became possible to persuade businesses to place advertisements. And that, in turn, has revolutionized the art of selling commercial products. Printing created the space for a new kind of public experience to take place.

## Impact of the Electronic Image

The epoch of electronic communication embraces a group of cultural technologies which have as their object recording or transmitting sensuous images. It may be helpful to put them into three categories based on their periods of invention. The photograph and the telegraph, invented during the 1830s and 1840s, came in the first wave. Three devices invented during the 1870s - the phonograph, motion-picture machine, and telephone - represent the second wave of inventions. Thomas Edison is as-

sociated with them. Finally, in the third wave, radio and television were developed during  the first four decades of the 20th
century. Certain inventions - photography, motion pictures, and
television - pertain to the sense of sight, while the phonograph,
telephone, and radio pertain to hearing. The telegraph, telephone,
radio, and television communicate messages or images over long
distances. Photography and telegraphy predate the electronic
technologies, but we put them here with the other inventions
because of their similar nature.

While printed literature had long included woodcut or
blockprint illustrations, photography broke into the new business of producing sensuous images by machine. The process of
photoengraving, which converted photographic images into
etchings on a metal plate, began to be used in the 1880s to reproduce these images in newspapers. Newspaper pictures were especially popular with immigrant groups who did not speak English well. The related technologies of lithography and chromolithography, introduced earlier, added another pictorial element to the print culture. Telegraphy led to national and international news reporting. If one examines newspapers of Civil
War vintage, one finds that many articles consist of telegraphed
dispatches from the battlefront. Taken in combination with
printed newspapers, these two first-wave inventions were well
suited for conveying exotic images and reports from distant
places. The urban masses could be entertained by pictures and
descriptive texts concerning life in the Wild West, or in equatorial Africa, or in European high society.

Because portrait and landscape painting belonged to a prestigious tradition, the early photographers sometimes touched
up their works to make them appear more artistic. This attempt
to imitate painting gave way to a new school of natural photography about the time of World War I. Ironically, the camera's
superior ability to produce visual images won over some of its
human competitors. The"Impressionist" school of painting popular in France and other countries at the turn of the century abandoned Renaissance ideals of form and shape. Its vision was instead expressed in discontinuous dabs of color. "He is only an
eye - but what an eye!", they said of Claude Monet. Monet's

technique, like the camera's, was to let rays of colored light strike the canvas where they would and not try to express forms. So, in general, the artistic culture that emerged in the early part of the 20th century was disconnected and disjointed. It was lacking in a sense of traditional harmony.

When we come to the second wave of cultural inventions, motion is added to pictures. Sound recordings trace the vibrations of music or of the human voice as projected through time. The human voice makes a powerful cultural impression. Combined with music, it produces a mysterious and profound emotional effect. Edison's phonograph and motion-picture machine were first to capture human personality in this expressive mode. As printing had captured and preserved a writer's selection of words, so the technologies of sound recording and motion pictures were able to record and preserve a performer's voice and visual appearance. The public began to track personality as it came across in sensuous ways. The individual performers, with their unique personalities, became cultural commodities. Soon sound recordings were purchased not because the music was written by a famous composer but because the singer was in demand. Once film audiences were exposed to the actors' visual images, a star system developed in Hollywood. If there had not been a medium to capture the performers' sensuous qualities, the writers and composers would have remained the chief objects of attention and acclaim.

Marilyn Monroe

While it merely transmitted words in coded form, the electric telegraph was the first technology to offer instantaneous communication between distant places. With overhead wires running along railroad tracks, it improved the process of train dispatching. The tighter train schedules dictated that standard time zones be established in different parts of the United States. The telegraph allowed quicker business dealings between goods wholesalers located in large cities and retailers dispersed to rural areas. Previously those retailers had to make periodic trips to the city to place orders for goods. George Orwell claimed that the telegraph contributed to the growth of bureaucracy because provincial administrators, no longer free to make their own decisions, had to check everything with headquarters. Britain's empire builders were reduced to clerks by this device.

When the telephone came along, individuals at home could communicate instantaneously with friends and neighbors. They had quick access to police and fire protection. This new household device eased the social isolation of women, especially those living in rural areas. Some objected to its invasion of privacy. Robert Lewis Stevenson wrote a letter complaining about the wisdom of admitting "this interesting instrument ... into our bed and board ... bleating like a deserted infant." However, most people seemed to like the social convenience. The telephone sat quietly on a table until its moment of use, disturbing the peace only when an acquaintance wished to talk. Lately, however, the availability of cell phones, voice mail, answering machines, and other accessories have made it possible for individuals to take calls no matter where they may be. Some have complained of lifestyles dominated by "an endless stream of phone calls about insignificant nonsense." This has disrupted the rhythm of activity and quiet which human beings may need to maintain their sanity.

Radio and television, in the third wave of cultural invention, combine long-distance communication with images of sight and sound extended in time. Because air time is precious, they typically deliver a carefully considered message to their vast and scattered audience. Commercial advertising makes it possible to offer this service for free. Network broadcasting created a new national culture. The radio became the family clock; living routines were rearranged to make time for favorite programs. Radio brought a sense of community to the broadcast area. National broadcasts undermined regional dialects in bringing a familiar voice into millions of households. When television burst upon the scene in the 1950s, a visual component was added. At first, its promoters claimed that television would bring families together because the viewers might entertain themselves at home. Then it was said that this medium had great educational potential. Soon enough, it became clear that television was mainly a powerful seller of commercial products. Television created brand-name images that made people want to purchase the advertised products in stores.

The small desert community of Essex, California, illustrates how life changes when people move into the television age. Until 1977, Essex was beyond the range of television signals. Then someone donated a cable device which allowed Essex residents to receive programming from a station in Phoenix, Arizona. Before the cable hookup, people in Essex entertained themselves with "books, games, neighborly visits, Wednesday night square dances (and) Thursday night movies at the school house." Afterwards, town people read fewer books and magazines. They scheduled their work around television programs. The Thursday night movies were discontinued. Teenagers instead became aware of big-city fads. Where they had once looked up to outdoor types such as park rangers, kids now idolized television and rock stars. Some girls, deciding against early marriage, thought they might wish to pursue professional careers like the female lawyers and executives they saw on television. While Essex residents disliked the brassy commercials, television proved to be a powerful force in persuading them to buy products. A woman remarked: " I just had to see if the Ball Park franks really popped ... and I'm trying to think of an excuse to go to Phoenix so I can eat at one of those restaurants I see on television with the sizzling steaks."

Because they provide high-quality or, at least, highly popular entertainment to people without charge, radio and television, especially television, offer something like an ultimate cultural experience. Their performances become immediately available in the comfort and privacy of one's home whenever one wants them. It is seductively easy to use these devices - just flick on the power switch and turn to a station. Many people depend on this entertainment to get through the day. (The only apparent disadvantage is having to endure the commercials and adhere to a time schedule when the programs are aired. For the determined consumer, tape recorders or VCRs can overcome these obstacles.) Statistics show that television sets are on for an average of seven hours a day in U.S. households. Watching television can therefore take up a large portion of the waking time available in a person's life not otherwise reserved. Television programs can become a kind of life substitute. Educators worry that prolonged television viewing may undermine children's literacy skills. It may cause adults to discontinue book reading as a recreational pastime, fostering an unimaginative, flaccid state of mind.

Media experts point out that television induces a trace-like condition in viewers. The eye has to defocus a bit to transform the flashing lines into coherent images. This relaxes some people and puts them into a state of pleasurable passivity. In other words, it turns them into "couch potatoes". Radio drama, at least, required some viewer participation in imagining characters and events. Television provides both the aural and visual components of experience. The viewer seems to be staring through a 25-inch peephole at someone else's life. This type of experience does not require periods of mental concentration as book reading does. It fosters a short attention span. A study found that television shows, including the commercials, required 39 attention shifts in thirty minutes. Television newscasters learn to break things up with frequent humor. One might question the wisdom of gaining life experiences vicariously. Though the concept of television is routinely trashed, many people continue watching it. One might say, paraphrasing Churchill, that television is the worst form of entertainment except for the other kinds.

## A Clash of Political Messages

In the 1920s, European society was becoming acquainted with new technologies which extended the human voice such as radio broadcasting. One who used them quite effectively for political purposes was Adolf Hitler. He built up a large following by delivering impassioned, hate-filled speeches in rented halls. Later, Hitler's message was distributed to even larger audiences through radio broadcasts and propagandistic films. Hitler insisted that the spoken word was superior to the written word in molding popular opinion. Leon Trotsky later took up the other side of the argument. A Russian Jew who had played a key role in the Bolshevik Revolution, Trotsky stressed the role of Marxist literature in winning over the masses to the communist cause.

Hitler's contention was that, while printed literature enjoyed cultural prestige, it was worthless in terms of persuading masses of people. "(A)ll great, world-shaking events have been brought about, not by written matter, but by the spoken word," he wrote. "Many will more readily accept a pictorial presentation than read an article of any length."  Public speaking was more effective than written arguments because "the speaker gets a continuous correction of his speech from the crowd ... A speaker can read from the facial expression of his audience whether they understand what he is saying ... (and) ... to what extent he has convinced them." A writer, on the other hand, "does not know his audience at all ... (so he keeps) his arguments entirely general ... (and in the process) loses psychological subtlety." The political success of Bolshevism would appear to be an exception, Hitler conceded. "What gives Marxism its astonishing power over the great masses is by no means the formal written work of the Jewish intellectual world, but rather the enormous oratorical propaganda wave which took possession of the masses ... The Marxist press is written by agitators."

One of those Marxist agitators, Leon Trotsky, disagreed. "Hitler's judgment is doubtless determined in large measure by the fact that he cannot write," he observed. "Marx and Engels acquired millions of followers without resorting throughout their life to the art of oratory ... An orator does not generate writers. On the contrary, a great writer may inspire thousands of orators ... Lenin became the head of a powerful and influential party before he had the opportunity to turn to the masses with the living word ... As a mass orator Lenin did not appear on the scene until 1917, and then only for a short period ... He came to power not as an orator, but above all as a writer, as an instructor of the propagandists who had trained his cadres, including also the cadres of orators."

In fact, Lenin considered motion pictures to be the most powerful medium so he nationalized the Russian film industry. After World War II, American communists tried to infiltrate Hollywood but were opposed by the president of the Screen Actors Guild, Ronald Reagan. A former newspaper editor (as was Karl Marx), Lenin saw radio as "a newspaper without paper and without boundaries." He did not appreciate its new capabilities. Because of their preoccupation with cinema, the Soviet leaders let the Russian radio industry develop largely without state interference until the late 1920s. The Nazis, on the other hand, made radio a prime vehicle for political propaganda. Radio sets sold in Germany could only receive two stations. In Britain and the United States, political influence in radio broadcasting was minimal. Franklin D. Roosevelt used radio effectively in his "fireside chats" with the American people. U.S. Presidents have addressed the nation on radio and television during national emergencies. Lord Reith, founder of the British Broadcasting System, believed that the purpose of radio was to promote education and moral improvement. Radio, he said, was "a servant of culture." In the United States, it was used mostly for entertainment.

When Thomas Edison invented the phonograph in the late 1870s, he considered it to be a "telephone repeater". In other words, it would record in permanent form what was said over the telephone. Those 19th Century types who encountered electric or electronic communication devices for the first time tended to foresee practical uses for them. They thought in terms of scientific or business applications. Entertainment, however, best utilized the capabilities of these new media. "Failure to foresee the phonograph as a means of entertainment was really a failure to grasp the electric revolution in general," wrote Marshall McLuhan. "In our time we are reconciled to the phonograph as a toy and solace; but press, radio, and TV have also acquired the same dimension of entertainment. Meanwhile, entertainment pushed to an extreme becomes the main form of business and politics." The market-driven radio and television industries in the United States moved quickly in the direction of popular entertainment. The electronic media were allowed to fulfill their innate possibilities.

In contrast, Soviet society was under the thumb of a dictatorship which lived by past ideals. For the most part, this society stuck to a literate culture that was quite recognizable in terms of 19th century styles and themes. While western society was veering off from that course into popular entertainment, Soviet writers, artists, musicians, dancers, and poets continued to create and perform in traditional ways. The Soviet leaders were stiff and unsmiling individuals who read lengthy speeches at the party Congresses. Television newscasts gave the appearance of being informational briefings. There was none of the personal sensuality and lightheartedness that western media types displayed. In 1994, the *Wall Street Journal* half-humorously reported that Soviet editors of a computer magazine had rejected some advertisements from U.S. firms on the grounds that the proposed copy "did not contain enough technical information for their readers." These editors were following an honest but, to western tastes, quaint notion of what commercial advertising ought to be. They were still selling the steak rather than its sizzle.

When change came in 1989, it was not ideology but electronic culture which overcame the Soviet system. Commentators have pointed out that eastern European cities within range of western television stations - Leipzig in East Germany and Timisoara in Romania - were early hotbeds of resistance to communist political regimes. Popular opinion followed a simple principle of television advertising: I see it; therefore, I want it. Peoples in the East wanted the various things that they saw on western television. The Soviet society was also relaxing somewhat. Films like Little Vera openly mocked communism. Mikhail Gorbachev and his stylish wife, Raisa, appeared to be more like a western political couple than their predecessors. Western-style rock groups were becoming active in East bloc nations. The pro-democracy movement in Mongolia started with a rock n' roll song by a two-man band called "Honk" which criticized the state bureaucracy. Soviet television helped to foment rebellion by reporting rebellious incidents in eastern Europe. Fax machines, photocopiers, and Internet connections also spread the word. Ronald Reagan said of communism's fall: "Our computer technology left them bewildered and behind, paper societies in an electronic age."

## The New Ideal of Rhythm

"Sell the sizzle, not the steak" is a well-known adage of the modern advertising age - a lesson which the Soviet computer-magazine editors did not comprehend. To sell sizzle involves a different kind of persuasion than in the traditional sense; for there are two kinds. One type of persuasion speaks to the intellect, setting up fact to meet fact, argument to overcome argument. Its procedure establishes truth which persuades the listener because he recognizes its universal claims. (This is selling the steak.) The other type speaks directly to a person. It is less a set of arguments than an enchanted vision which persuades by motion and sight. This type of persuasion sets forth an inviting dance which makes the viewer want to forget himself and join in. It lays out a rhythmic movement in which he finds a place to submerge himself. (This is selling the sizzle.) The culture of printed literature persuades by the first method; the culture of electronic media, by the second.

Society's values traditionally have come from philosophers and religious teachers who present concepts such as goodness and truth. The goal is to conform as much as possible to those ideals. While doing so, it is important to be steadfast in character, for goodness is often defined in the breach. A righteous person is a person without sin, who has held to the straight and narrow his whole life through. In the new culture, which developed through the electronic media, constancy of character does not matter so much. The emphasis is upon making a good performance while one is on camera. What happens off camera is of less concern. The singer wants to be up for the performance. So does the athlete who is preparing for an important game. The performance will require skills that have been developed as habits to support a particular set of motions. However, one's mental attitude going into the performance also makes a big difference as to whether or not it goes well.

When athletes play well, they sometimes say that they were "in the groove" or "in the zone". We will say that these peak performers have "rhythm". Rhythm is the graceful quality found in beautiful music. It is the magic in a tennis game where everything has "clicked". Television talk-show hosts who are sparkling with wit and have rapport with their guests exemplify rhythm, as do comedians when telling their best jokes. The performance of rhythm is a strictly personal matter. Some have it and some do not. Some are able to deliver rhythm on cue. Some are not. By and large, the electronic media are in the business of furnishing rhythmic personalities to the public, whether in music, sports, conversation, or comic performance. They want persons who can deliver this elusive element; and, for the person who can, they pay well.

The old book culture maintained that knowledge was the key to performance. If a person correctly understood the principles of something, he could apply them to achieve the desired result. Rhythm seems to operate by a different mechanism. Even if a concert musician knows the music thoroughly, he can never be sure of giving a good performance when he goes out on stage. Because giving an excellent performance is important yet is essentially uncontrollable, many performers develop "stage fright". With knowledge, one can study something until it is learned. With writing, one can mull words over for a long time until the right one comes to mind. But when one must deliver rhythmic performance to a live audience or on network television, one has only a single chance to perform. That puts immense pressure on the performer. When he or she rises to the occasion, audiences know it. They appreciate what has been accomplished.

The old philosophical culture held that will power was the key to successful execution. Mind needed to discipline the body to behave in a certain way. Will was a matter of strengthening one's resolve. It was a matter of applying mental perseverance over time. Rhythm, however, cannot be achieved by willful effort. The performer will often choke if he tries to improve a performance by tightening up or consciously forcing a correct routine. Rhythmic performance is more a matter of trusting one's instincts and letting go. Some performers use drugs or alcohol to relieve their inhibitions and loosen up. Some employ a small beginning ritual. Prior visualization of the routine helps to put many performers in a mood to perform well without thinking. Coaches and sports psychologists can help with this aspect of the sport. The athlete himself should not have to think about what he is doing, just perform. His mind, ideally, should be blank.

Rhythm does not come in a steady state of high performance, but in periods of intense effort followed by relaxation. Unlike steadfast virtues, rhythm involves a controlled flow of energy over a period of time. The hard part is usually the beginning. Once the energy flow has started in the right way, rhythm can be maintained seemingly without effort. Indeed, effortless activity is an important characteristic of performance in this mode. Rhythmic performance is natural and easy. But sometimes it will not come, no matter what a person does. As they say in show business: "When you're hot, you're hot; when you're not, you're not." Rhythm has its ups and downs. That is what makes rhythm so different than the beautiful works of literate culture. The kind of perfection that is found in the classics of literature and art may be too brittle for live performance. Rhythm needs a certain looseness to develop. So this idea of rigorous perfection has largely disappeared from the culture of electronic recording and communication. They say it's better to be lucky than good.

### Computer Links

While the full extent of computer technology is yet to be revealed, we do know that this medium offers a new way of organizing and presenting information. With printed literature, a person starts reading at the beginning of a text, continues through the text in a fixed order, and finally reaches the end. The author determines the sequence by which the reader becomes aware of the materials. Whatever information the text contains will be exposed in a prearranged sequence, presumably designed for maximum intelligibility. Except for occasional flipping of pages back and forth to indulge idle thoughts, the reader sticks to the course set out in the script. The same is true of electronic recordings. The creative artist presents a series of images that flow in a certain order, broken only by the ability to fast-forward or reverse tapes. Computer menus, on the other hand, offer several options for moving to the next place. One clicks on an icon that seems interesting and is transported immediately to a new field of information. The viewer decides where to go next. This utter freedom to choose the path for viewing information within a system represents a departure from sequentially-based methods of exposing knowledge.

Theodor H. Nelson coined the word "hypertext" for expressions that allow persons to read nonsequentially as suits their own purposes. Reading in hypertext is based on associative rather than sequential thinking. Nodes and links, which are points of connection between related elements, form a bridge between different portions of text. It is like following the allusions to Homer, Dante, or another author in John Milton's *Paradise Lost*; the computer lets readers call up the referenced texts electronically by clicking on icons. This arrangement suits readers who wish to browse casually through texts as well as those who want to find particular information without reading through a lengthy text. There is an artistry in designing a system to connect the different files and an art to navigating effectively in these informational waters.

The Greek philosophers discovered the concept of generality which links abstractions with specifics. Hypertext can place texts in a similar relationship to each other. Menu-linked layers of text let readers progress from general discussions to specific ones. The more general discussion would cover an entire field of knowledge, while, at various points, electronic links would connect readers to more detailed presentations of the same subject. World history, too, is suited to this type of treatment. A short overview of historical events might be connected to a much larger collection of writings that expand upon each incident or topic. Ultimately, historical writings lead to stories of individual lives which affected events on those "higher" levels. Newspapers make use of hypertext to provide supplemental information relating to the published articles. Scientific reports can also be organized in this way. One can foresee the construction of enormous electronic encyclopedias whose texts embrace the bulk of human knowledge. They might be, for the computer civilization, like the great pyramids of Gizah.

## Chapter Nine

# A SHORT HISTORY OF CULTURAL TECHNOLOGIES

---

### How Writing Began

M ost historians agree that the Sumerian people of ancient Mesopotamia were first to develop the technology of writing. They made that cultural invention during the
4th millennium B.C. Egyptian hieroglyphic writing, though
roughly contemporaneous, is believed to have been derived from
the Sumerian script some time later because it appeared suddenly in a developed form. The Sumerians and Egyptians used
a script based on pictorial symbols, later mixed with phonetic
elements. Three other peoples - the pre-Aryan peoples of the
Indus valley, the Chinese, and Mayans of Central America - seem
to have developed pictorial and phonetic writing more or less
independently. The as yet undeciphered script of the Harappan
civilization was used by people in northwest India during the

3rd millennium B.C. The oldest Chinese inscriptions date back to the 14th century B.C. The Mayan people invented their system of writing at some time before the 3rd century A.D. Crude pictures and mnemonic devices such as knotted ropes or notched sticks predate the use of written language. The pictures became simplified and stylized, and then associated with ideas. Then came phonetic associations with speech.

The Sumerians were a commercial people and writing was developed to serve that end. Sumerian merchants and traders needed to record quantities of goods. They used baked clay tokens of a distinctive shape, two to three centimeters in length, to represent quantities of commodities such as grain, livestock, labor, and land. Each token represented both a quantity and type of commodity. For example , a "ban" ( 6 liters) of wheat required a different kind of token than a "bariga" (36 liters) of wheat, or a ban of barley, or a jar of oil. There were 200 different kinds of tokens in common use. Accountants placed these tokens inside a bowl or pouch. Later, they put the tokens inside sealed clay envelopes to increase security. To be able to tell what was inside, the accountants marked the outside of the envelopes. One marking identified the owner and another represented the tokens that were held inside. Before long, the Sumerian merchants realized that it was unnecessary to place actual tokens inside the envelopes; the external markings were a sufficient record. Having dispensed with hollow envelopes, Sumerian scribes began to use clay tablets laid on their backs as a writing material. This medium took an inscription from pressing a straight-edged stylus made of reed or bone into wet clay before it was baked.

Accountants in the Middle East had been using baked clay tokens for centuries before they made several conceptual changes that transformed this system of commercial recording into written language. The breakthrough came in separating quantities from commodities. The token for a ban of wheat was made to symbolize the number one. The token for a bariga of wheat was made to symbolize the number ten. Abstract numbers were now isolated from the quantity-commodity compounds. The next step was to place the numerical symbol next to a symbol representing another type of commodity. For instance, the token for a bariga of wheat (meaning ten) might be impressed next to a token representing a jar of oil. This combination of symbols could represent either a bariga of wheat plus a jar of oil or ten jars of oil. The Sumerians overcame this confusion by representing the jar of oil with a special symbol that was cut into the clay with a stylus when it was meant to accompany a number. Once symbolic incisions had replaced the baked-clay tokens, it became possible to employ a much larger number of symbols for both numbers and words. Each pictorial symbol represented a numerical or verbal concept.

Originally, the incised symbols were pictograms or ideographic representations of physical objects. Their own linear image presents the shape of the represented object. For example, the symbol for sun might be a circle with a dot in the middle. The hieroglyphic symbol of an eye was two concave horizontal lines with a half circle hanging down from the top - i.e., the drawing of an eye. While pictograms can express natural objects, they are less able to represent abstract concepts, proper names, or parts of speech such as pronouns, conjunctions, and prepositions. The next step, then, was to express such words through association with one or more ideograms that had a natural reference. For example, the picture of an eye with dropping tears has been used to express the idea of sorrow. A circle representing the sun can also mean day because each day starts with a sun rise. Sometimes several pictographic signs were combined to create a new ideogram. The Chinese character for "word" is a combination of characters representing the mouth and vapor. The Sumerian symbols of a woman and a mountain used together represented a female slave. That is because slaves in Mesopotamia customarily came from tribal peoples living in the surrounding mountainous region.

Another approach was to associate pictorial symbols with abstract words which had the same spoken sound as a word that could be visually represented. In other words, an ideogram could represent both a word of concrete reference and its homonym. For example, the symbol for the number four (4) might represent the preposition "for" or, perhaps, "fore" as in "foresight". The reference to syllabic sounds - e.g., the "fore" in "foresight" - offered a means of extending ideographic writing to words that could not be visualized. Sumerian speech contained many polysyllabic words with short syllables found in other words. That condition favored use of a technique known as "rebus writing". A rebus is a multi-syllable word with pictographs for each syllable. For example, the name of a well-known palace, "Buckingham", contains three syllables: buck, king, and ham. Three pictographs representing a male deer, a monarch, and porcine meat would be its rebus symbol. Another kind of symbol, called a "determinative", helped to distinguish between words that have the same sound but different meanings. For example, the Sumerians used the same spoken word, "ti", to mean both an arrow and life. If a V lying on its side (>) represents the arrow and the determinative sign is an apostrophe, the word for life might be written: >'

Most systems of ideographic writing are heavy with homonymic references. Chinese speech consists entirely of monosyllabic words. A syllabic sound can have ten or more different meanings. Spoken Chinese extends its range of meaning through tone and context. The meaning of a word depends upon the musical tone or pitch in the speaker's voice and its position in sentences. The large number of homonyms in spoken Chinese makes it easy to apply pictorial symbols to abstract words. Nine-tenths of Chinese characters have been created from phonetic associations with the words of spoken language. Often determinants are added to the ideograms to avoid confusion. Many phonetic symbols found in modern Chinese writing reflect the sounds of long-forgotten speech. This script has changed little in more than two thousand years as spoken dialects have come and gone. Modern Chinese writing, like ancient Sumerian script, represents, in Toynbee's words, "an illogical and clumsy use of ideograms and phonemes side by side."

In the case of Sumerian writing, the phonetic base of words was complicated by the fact that the Akkadian conquerors of Sumer grafted their own spoken language upon Sumerian script. While words written in this script meant the same thing in both Akkadian and Sumerian speech, Akkadian speakers could not longer recognize the homonymic associations. Their script included a mixture of ideographic words and words representing Sumerian syllabic symbols. For instance, the cuneiform symbol for mouth was pronounced "ka" in Sumerian and "pum" in Akkadian. When appearing with a determinative, however, this symbol referred to the syllabic sound "ka". This dual system of writing meant that nearly every sign had several different pronunciations and meanings. To resolve the ambiguities, the Akkadians used determinative signs to indicate classes of objects as well as phonetic values. Eventually they moved towards a type of syllabic writing in which sixty written symbols represented the syllables of all words in Akkadian speech. The syllables each contained a single sound with a particular consonant and vowel mix.

A purely phonetic script disengages pictorial elements from the idea content of words. The written symbols instead stand for sounds in spoken words. This type of script can be either syllabic or alphabetic. With syllabic writing, each symbol represents the sound of a syllable. For example, the word "syllable" itself has three syllables sounding like "sill", "ah", "bull". The three sounds would each be represented by a pictorial symbol. They would be positioned in the same sequence as in the spoken word. The other possibility is alphabetic writing. Here the written symbols represent the pure elements of sounds in speech. These sounds correspond to letters of the alphabet. Syllabic writing represents an intermediate stage between ideographic and alphabetic writing. The Japanese have two syllabic scripts which were adapted from Chinese in the 8th or 9th centuries A.D. One, the kata kana, is used for formal documents and scholarly works. It has about 50 written symbols and may not be strictly syllabic. The other type, hira gana, is found in newspapers and popular literature. There are about 300 symbols in this syllabary, but only 100 in common use. The script developed for the Korean language is another example of syllabic writing.

## Diffusion of Ideographic Writing

Most ancient peoples had a "transitional" script which was in the process of evolving from an ideographic or mixed system into syllabic or alphabetic writing. In addition to ideograms, Egyptian hieroglyphic writing contained phonetic symbols representing the consonant root of words. Because the 24 consonant signs covered the entire range of Egyptian speech, some see this as a prototype of alphabetic writing. From the beginning, the pictorially elaborate hieroglyphic writing was accompanied by a short-hand or cursive script known as hieratic writing which priests used for correspondence. A later version, demotic writing, was developed for popular use. The Minoan society on Crete borrowed its still undeciphered "Linear-A" script from the Egyptian and Sumero-Akkadian civilizations during the 17th century B.C. Mycenaean Greeks who seized Crete around 1450 B.C. developed their "Linear-B" syllabic script in imitation of the Minoan. The Assyrians simplified Sumerian cuneiform script, reducing it to 570 symbols of which 300 were frequently used. The early Persian cuneiform script, influenced by the Aramaic alphabet, consisted of 41 mostly phonetic symbols. Chinese writing, while ideographic, is also a transitional script.

The scribes of Sumero-Akkadian society produced clay tablets recording commercial transactions and other types of messages. Over half a million such tablets have been found. The strokes cut with a stylus were thicker on one end than the other, so that they resembled a triangular sliver or wedge. Scribes imprinted the wedge-shaped or "cuneiform" messages in horizontal rows, moving from left to right. That kind of writing spread from Mesopotamia to neighboring lands whose peoples adapted cuneiform writing to their own spoken language. Sumerian script expressing Akkadian speech became an international language during the 2nd millennium B.C. Even Egyptian pharaohs used it when communicating with rulers of their satellite states in Syria and Palestine. Hammurabi, a Babylonian king who compiled a famous code of laws, simplified this script in the 18th century,

B.C. His reign saw important advances in mathematics, astronomy, banking, and other areas. Sumero-Akkadian-Babylonian civilization continued to dominate the cultural and commercial life of the Middle East long after this empire disappeared. Cuneiform writing began to disappear in the 5th century B.C. as the spoken Babylonian language fell into disuse.

The ancient Sumerian script or its Babylonian derivative inspired the written languages of the Hittites, Elamites, Kassites, Assyrians, and other Middle Eastern peoples. While written Chinese shows a certain structural similarity with the Sumerian script, evidence of direct influence in this case is less convincing. There are, for instance, no signs had in common by the two scripts. Chinese tradition attributes the invention of writing to two "gods", Ts'ang Chieh and Chü Sung, who were secretaries to Huang-ti, a legendary emperor of the 3rd millennium B.C. Ts'ang Chieh invented a set of diagrams used in divination, called "pa kua", consisting of three broken or unbroken horizontal lines that represented basic elements of nature. Chu Sung invented a system of knots to aid memory. These two inventions, plus hand gestures, tally-sticks, and ritual symbols, may have developed into the early Chinese characters during the first half of the 2nd millennium B.C. The ta chuan or "great seal" characters appear in a book written in the 9th century B.C. The "small seal" or hsiao chuan characters were introduced by Li Ssu, a minister of the first Ch'in emperor in the 3rd century B.C. The li shu, a simpler script developed then to draft documents related to prisoners, is the prototype for most modern Chinese scripts.

When the Spanish conquistadors entered Mexico in 1519 A.D., they found that the Aztecs had an ideographic script which was used mainly for religious purposes. Archbishop Zumárraga ordered most of the "devilish scrolls" destroyed. Aztec writing was highly pictographic but had some phonetic elements. The Spaniards found in the jungles of the Yucatán peninsula and elsewhere evidences of the still older Mayan civilization, which had flourished in the first half of the 1st millennium A.D. The Mayans, too, had an ideographic script, which, in its use of cartouches, resembles Egyptian hieroglyphics. Intolerant Christian priests again destroyed manuscripts written in this language. Today, only fourteen Aztec and three Mayan manuscripts remain. The writing has been only partially deciphered. Most is known about the Mayan and Aztec calendars and numerical systems. The Aztecs and Toltecs probably derived their scripts from the Mayans. The origin of the Mayan script is unknown. A superficial comparison of scripts may suggest contact with the ancient civilization of Egypt - as ideographic inscriptions on Easter Island suggest contact with the Indus Valley civilization - but such explanations are speculative.

Linguistic scholars made rapid progress in deciphering ancient scripts during the 19th Century. In addition to Egyptian hieroglyphics, the knowledge of several cuneiform scripts was revived. They include the early Persian, neo-Elamite, Babylonian, and Sumerian languages. (It is ironic that the Mayan script remains undeciphered since it continued to be understood until the late 17th century.) The choice of writing medium affects the quantity of ancient documents available. While the Sumerians wrote on clay tablets, Egyptian scribes preferred papyrus, a paper-like material made from the stalks of plants that grew in the Nile delta. A technique of writing on parchment, or the untanned skins of animals, was developed at Pergamon in Turkey. Diviners of the Shang dynasty in China inscribed their prophecies on bones and tortoise shells. Some of the most durable writings are inscriptions in stone monuments. Darius I of Persia ordered a proclamation to be carved in three languages on a stone-faced cliff in Behistan. The Indian emperor Asoka erected inscribed more than thirty-five stone slabs, or stele, to promote Buddhist teachings. A cache of more than one thousand baked-clay tablets and fragments which are five to six thousand years old has been found at Uruk in southern Iraq.

Babylonian
cylinders

## Alphabetic Writing

We have seen how the technique of expressing words in a visual form progressed from pictograms to ideographic writing including phonetic elements, and then to a syllabic script. Alphabetic writing is the final step in this process. The sounds within the syllables of spoken language are broken down into pure elements. The word "word", for example, is spelled W-O-R-D. Each successive letter represents a sound heard sequentially when someone pronounces that word. The alphabet itself is a complete listing of the written letters. The Hebrews associated each alphabetic letter with the first sound of a word in their spoken language. The Greeks, from whom the English alphabet is derived, copied the Phoenician and Hebrew system of writing.

There is a faint pictorial reference in this lettering scheme, as Richard Hathaway explains:

"A is alpha from the Hebrew aleph, meaning an ox head

B is beta from beth, the house

C and G are gamma from gimel, the camel

D is delta from daleth, the door

H is eta from kheth, the fence.

I and J are Greek iota from yod, the hand

K is kappa from kaph, the palm of the hand

M is mu from mem, the water

N is nu from nun, the fish

P is pi from pe, the mouth

R is rho from resh, the head

S is sigma from shin, the teeth."

If you turn capital "A" upside down, you can still see the ox's head with its horns sticking up, though the eyes and nostrils are omitted.

Both the Hebrews and Greeks also used alphabetic letters as numbers. The first nine letters of the alphabet represented the successive numerals from one to nine. The next nine were the numerals multiplied by ten: 10, 20, 30, 40, etc. This association has given rise to schemes found in the Jewish cabala and elsewhere which attach symbolic significance to the numerical total of letters in certain words, especially proper names. The Book of *Revelation* declares, for instance, that the number of the beast, a man's name, will equal six hundred and sixty-six. An occult art of linguistic analysis and interpretation known as gematria studies ancient texts seeking mystical illumination from the numbers associated with words. The Romans also used letters to designate numbers but limited them to the following: I, V, X, L, C, D, and M. The modern scheme of numbers, divorced from alphabetic lettering, came from India via the Moslems. They are known as Arabic numerals.

We consider alphabetic writing to be more advanced than ideographic or syllabic writing because it achieves significant economies in the use of symbols to express words. Ideographic scripts require as many different visual symbols as there are words in a dictionary. For syllabic scripts, one might need several hundred symbols for the associated sounds. Alphabetic writing expresses the entire range of spoken language in between 20 and 30 letters. The alphabet allows each written word to be "sounded out" phonetically to discover its meaning. It is easy to learn the relatively small number of associations between letters and sounds. On the other hand, as John Logan has pointed out, there are "hidden lessons" which need to be learned in converting sounds into visual signs, coding and decoding information, and ordering words alphabetically. All things considered, it takes children in North America about as much time to learn to read and write in the English language as it does Chinese students to learn the 1,000 basic characters in their ideographic script. Both sets of students typically begin to study reading when they enter school at the age of five and have achieved literacy skills three years later.

The earliest alphabetic scripts did not run in a consistent direction. Some scripts were written in vertical columns. Some moved along horizontal lines. The Phoenician script was read horizontally from right to left. The Ethiopian and Greek scripts, in contrast, went from left to right. Some peoples' writing followed the "boustrophedon" pattern, moving from right to left on one line and from left to right in the next. This term is derived from a Greek word which means "turning like oxen in ploughing." Boustrophedon inscriptions are found on the walls of temples in southern Arabia. A person can read them while walking in one direction and then, at the end of the line, pick up the next line without having to walk back to a starting point. By the mid 11th century, B.C., alphabetic writing had become more stable. Most scripts settled on movement in a horizontal direction. Pictorial features gradually disappeared as the lettering became more stylized. Alphabets beginning with the Ugarit in the 14th century B.C. appeared with their letters arranged in a certain order. Our word "alphabet" comes from "alpha" and "beta", which are the first two letters in the Greek alphabet.

## Spread of Alphabetic Scripts

Alphabetic writing began with scripts invented by Semitic peoples inhabiting Syria, Palestine, and the Sinai peninsula during the 2nd millennium, B.C. Documents written in such scripts have been found at the Serabit el Khadem temple in the Sinai and at nearby copper mines which are dated to approximately 1500 B.C. Because certain of the alphabetic letters resemble symbols used by Egyptian scribes, some scholars suspect Egyptian influence. This "proto-Sinaitic" or "proto-Canaanite" writing is believed to be the ancestor of all alphabetic scripts. It followed an acrostic principle by which the sound of the first consonant in a word becomes the sound of the letter itself. For example, the pictorial symbol for dog might represent the letter "D". Next, symbols representing the other consonants in the word were written in order of their respective sounds. The word "dog" might be spelled by placing symbols representing a dog, an owl, and a goat together in sequence, except that the early Semitic alphabets contained only consonants and no vowels. The proto-

| MEANING | OUTLINE CHARACTER, B. C. 4500 | ARCHAIC CUNEIFORM, B. C. 2500 | ASSYRIAN, B. C. 700 | LATE BABYLONIAN, B. C. 500 |
|---------|------|------|------|------|
| The sun | | | | |
| God, heaven | | | | |
| Mountain | | | | |
| Man | | | | |
| Ox | | | | |
| Fish | | | | |

development of cuneiform scripts

| PHŒNICIAN | ANCIENT GREEK | LATER GREEK | ENGLIS |
|-----------|---------------|-------------|--------|
| | | | A |
| | | | B |
| | | | C |
| | | | D |
| | | | E |
| | | | F |
| | | | Z |

development of alphabetic scripts

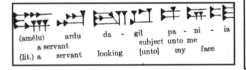

(amêlu)    ardu    da – gil    pa – ni – ia
a servant        subject unto me
(lit.) a    servant    looking    [unto]    my    face

from Annals of Sennacherib
(Assyrian script)

from Code of Manu
(Indian script)

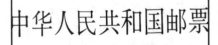

Chinese script

Greek script

Sinaitic or proto-Canaanite alphabets had twenty-two letters for consonant sounds in their languages.

The original alphabet, the proto-Canaanite, evolved into the Phoenician and proto-Arabic alphabets around 1300 B.C. The Aramaic alphabet evolved from the same source at a later date. The proto-Arabic alphabet gave rise to scripts used in southern Arabia and Ethiopia. Phoenician writing, which is closely related to early Hebrew, passed its alphabetic system along to the Greeks. The Greeks may have received the Phoenician alphabet around 1050 B.C., although some historians believe that the transfer took place as late as in the 8th century B.C. Alphabetic writing was a kind of shorthand suited to the needs of merchants and traders. The mercantile class, more than any other, helped to spread this new technique. Two peoples, the Phoenicians and Aramaeans, were its principal carriers. The Phoenicians were ultimately the source of all alphabetic scripts adopted by nations west of Syria. Those used in Syria and places to the east were based on the Aramaic script.

The Phoenicians were a Semitic people given to commercial navigation. Their principal cities were Tyre and Sidon, in Asia Minor, and Carthage in North Africa. They were the first civilized people to set sail in the Atlantic ocean. The Phoenician script was widely used in the Mediterranean region for more than a millennium. Its derivatives include the scripts used in Phoenicia proper (Lebanon) and in colonies on the islands of Cyprus, Sardinia, Malta, and Sicily, as well as in the coastal cities of Marseilles and Carthage. The so-called "Punic" script was used in Carthage until the Romans destroyed this city-state in 146 B.C. Phoenician writing became extinct in the 3rd century A.D. Legend has it that the Greek alphabet was adapted from the Phoenician by Cadmus of Thebes, who lived in Phoenicia for many years. The Greek alphabet had both an eastern and western branch. The classical Greek alphabet, consisting of 24 letters, came from the eastern branch. In 403 B.C., the Ionic script used in Miletus was officially adopted in Athens. The other Greek city-states came around to this version during the next half century. From the western branch emerged the Etruscan and Latin alphabets, and, through them, most of the alphabetic systems associated with European languages.

When the Greeks acquired Phoenician writing, they made a modification to the alphabet which greatly increased its appeal. The Phoenician and other Semitic alphabets had consisted exclusively of consonant letters. Words in those languages were written with the consonant letters (usually three) forming their base. Sometimes an unstressed aspirant consonant, used like a vowel, would be added to resolve ambiguities. The Greeks converted the unstressed Hebrew letters aleph, hey, yod, ayin, and vav into vowels equivalent to a, e, i, o, and u. They also added two new vowels, eta ("a" as in fate) and omega ("o" as in open), and three new consonants found in Greek but not any of the Semitic languages. These were theta ("th"), phi ("ph" or "f"), and psi ("ps" as in lips). The Greek alphabet thus offered a complete selection of sounds spoken in that language, so that words might be written without ambiguity. The Latin alphabet contains most of the Greek letters but shortened them for convenience. Alpha became "a", beta "b", gamma "c", etc. In addition, the Romans inserted a new letter "g" into the alphabet to replace "z", and later reintroduced "y" and "z".

Meanwhile, another family of alphabetic scripts was entering lands to the east. While the Phoenicians traded in ports bordering the Mediterranean sea, their Semitic cousins, the Aramaeans, brought merchandise overland along mideastern caravan routes. The Aramaean people, originally from northern Arabia, had settled in Syria during the 12th century, B.C. and established fortified towns, the most important of which was Damascus. That group of city-states came in conflict with the expanding Assyrian empire. Damascus fell in 732 B.C. To control conquered peoples, the Assyrians had a policy of removing them from their homeland and resettling them elsewhere in the empire. This cruel practice worked to the advantage of Aramaean culture. Aramaeans became the dominant traders within the Assyrian empire. Knowledge of their language spread. Aramaic writing had become the dominant script in the Middle East by the end of the 7th century, B.C. The Assyrians were conquered by the Medes and Babylonians, who were, in turn, conquered by the Persians. So influential was Aramaic writing by this time that it replaced cuneiform writing as the official script of the Achaemenian Persian empire.

Though it had existed since the 10th century B.C., Aramaic writing did not become historically important until after the Aramaean states in Syria ceased to exist. Then its commercial prominence gave it an advantage. Even after Alexander the Great officially dumped it in favor of Greek, Aramaic speech continued to be the vernacular language of most peoples living in the Middle East. Jesus, for instance, spoke this language. The Aramaic alphabet was the parent of several later scripts, including classical Hebrew, Nabataean-Sinaitic-Arabic, Palmyrene, Syriac-Nestorian, Mandaean, and Manichaean. Some were used by oriental Christian churches. The Arabic script, in which the *Koran* is written, developed from Nabataean writing at the end of the 4th century, A.D. Pahlavi, a Persian script developed in the 2nd century B.C., was used in the Parthian and Sasanian empires. A related alphabet known as Avesta is associated with Zoroastrian sacred literature. Aramaean traders also had contact with India, especially during the Persian occupancy of lands in the Indus valley. Two Indian scripts of the 1st millennium B.C., Brahmi and Kharoshthi, are derivatives of Aramaic.

As trade follows the flag, so it is said that systems of alphabetic writing follow religions. The Latin alphabet, associated with the Roman Catholic church, is today the most widely used alphabet in the world. The Arabic alphabet, second most widely used, prevails in places where the Islamic religion is dominant. Syriac, an offshoot of Aramaic writing, was the script of Christians at Antioch. It split into two branches after the Council of Ephesus in 431 A.D. The Eastern branch became associated with Nestorian Christianity, and the Western branch with the Egyptian Coptics. The Nestorian script traveled east to India, China, and Central Asia through an active missionary corps, influencing the Sogdian and Uighur alphabetic languages. The Jacobite script, named after a Monophysite Christian bishop, was used in Syria, Egypt, and Abyssinia. There was also a Manichaean alphabet associated with the Manichaean religion. The later split between eastern and western Christianity brought a corresponding split in the use of alphabetic scripts. Those nations which embraced the Greek Orthodox faith also adopted the Cyrillic script. They include Bulgaria, Serbia, Russia, and the Ukraine. On the other hand, the Poles, Czechs, Croats, and Slovenes, who were Roman Catholics, adopted Latin-based scripts.

Modern Hebrew is more closely related to Aramaic writing than to the Hebrew script used in pre-exilic times. Likewise, the writing of the pre-Aryan civilization of the Indus valley is unrelated to Kharoshthi or Brahmi. The emperor Asoka left over 35 stone inscriptions in these alphabetic scripts, promoting his political and religious (Buddhist) views. Brahmi, which may first have appeared in the 7th or 6th century B.C., was the script used by Brahman priests for writing in the ancient Sanskrit language. After the Mauryan empire disintegrated, this script acquired many regional variations. The Hindu revival beginning in the 1st century B.C. produced a sacred literature in Sanskrit. Buddhist and Jainist documents were written in vernacular languages, or "Prakrit", especially the Pali dialect. The Gupta dynasty, which existed between the 4th and 6th centuries A.D., coincides with the golden age of Hindu culture. Its written language was a prototype for most Indian scripts, as well as those in Tibet, Ceylon, and other neighboring countries. The North Indian Nagari or Deva-nagari script, developed in the 7th century A.D., is the ancestor of Bengali, Kaithi, and other scripts. The South Indian Kanarese and Teluga scripts date from the 5th and 9th centuries A.D. respectively. The Grantha script of southeast India is the ancestor of Old Javanese and Khmer (Cambodian) writing.

Greek writing is the ancestor of all European alphabetic scripts. Classical Greek, based upon the Ionic alphabet, gave rise to cursive, uncial (large rounded letters), and, later, minuscule scripts in the opening centuries of the Christian era. From Greek uncial writing came two scripts used by Slavic peoples, Glagolitic and Cyrillic, both introduced by St. Cyril in the 9th century A.D. Western Greek writing was a model for the Etruscan and Latin scripts. The Etruscan people who controlled northern Italy between the 8th and 5th centuries, B.C. may have acquired an alphabetic script from Greek sources during the 8th century. The

Romans developed their Latin alphabet in the following century. It was likely of Etruscan and Greek origin. The Greek colony of Cumae near Naples was a principal transfer point for passing the Greek alphabet to Italian peoples. Latin was, of course, the language of the Roman empire. As such, it spread far and wide. The modern scripts of Europe are adaptations of the Latin alphabet to European languages. To its Latin parent, the English alphabet added the letters J and U during the 17th and 18th centuries A.D., and the letter W during the middle ages. U and V were once the same letter, as were I and J. W, with an antecedent in the runic alphabet, is related to U and V.

## Printing

Printing may have originated in the Sumerian use of cylinder seals to make impressions in clay. In China, religious pilgrims made ink rubbings of Buddhist texts that were inscribed in stone pillars. By the 6th century, A.D., Chinese engravers had mastered the art of wood-block printing. This involved a process of transferring inked writing from paper to a wood surface and then cutting away the uninked portions to leave the script in relief. To print, the cut wood block was inked and covered with a sheet of paper which was rubbed on the back with a brush. This technology helped to meet a demand for Buddhist and Taoist literature during the T'ang dynasty (618-906 A.D.). In the 11th century, A.D., a Chinese alchemist named Pi Sheng invented a method of printing with movable type. He fastened the type font to a metal plate with an amalgam of glue and clay that was baked to harden the attachment. The reusable font could later be removed by reheating the plate. A Chinese magistrate in the 14th century published a book on the history of technology which used more than 60,000 characters carved from wood. In the early 15th century, a Korean king ordered 100,000 pieces of type to be cast in bronze. Korea became the center of print technology until it spread to Europe later in the century.

Europe launched the print revolution rather than Asia because European alphabetic writing was better suited to the use of movable type than the ideographic Chinese or syllabic Korean or Japanese scripts. The relatively small number of alphabetic letters made it possible to cast reusable metal type in molds at a low cost. It is believed that Uighur Turks living in a region just west of China brought Asian typographical knowledge to the Moslems who then passed it along to the Europeans. Islamic society also gave Europe another technology which the Chinese had developed: paper manufacturing. Its invention may date to the 2nd century A.D. In 751 A.D., Moslems in Samarkand repelled an attack by Chinese soldiers and took some prisoners. Among them was a group of skilled papermakers. However, the Moslems did not themselves embrace a print culture because their religion would not allow the words of Allah to be reproduced artificially. (The Islamic ban on printing was not lifted until the 19th century.) Paper, which took print better than parchment, may have entered Europe during the 12th century from Moorish Spain or through Italian ports that had active trade relations with the Islamic world. Italy soon became a center of paper manufacturing and related arts.

The abundance of cheap paper fed a growing market for literature produced by manuscript copyists. There was a demand for Bibles, prayer books, and other religious literature. University students had need of scholarly texts produced by the stationarii. Works written in living or vernacular languages catered to popular interests. Dante's *Divine Comedy* and Boccaccio's *Decameron* pioneered that genre during the 14th century A.D. Approximately ten thousand copyists or scribes were employed in Europe to serve these various markets. Europeans began printing with wood blocks in the late 14th century. Initially, their purpose was to produce the large capital letters which began medieval texts. The engravers then included accompanying religious pictures and short passages of text. As their engraving skills improved, the quality of the lettering increased to the point that the text became more important than the ornamental features. Wood-block printers produced short books called "donats" in the early 15th century. A Dutch printer named Laurens Janzoon, also known as Koster, printed a book of prayers, titled *Speculum Humanae Salvationis*, in 1428 A.D., using wooden fonts. Printers soon preferred to use lead type for the letters because numerous castings could be produced from the same die and they were more durable than wood.

Historians generally credit the invention of printing in Europe to Johann Gutenberg of Mainz, Germany, who printed a Latin-language Bible using movable type and his own press. Gutenberg, a member of the goldsmiths' guild in Strasbourg, began experimenting secretly with the new techniques in the 1430s while earning a living from cutting jewels and producing mirrors. However, the prolonged experiments cost money and Gutenberg was forced to borrow from friends and business associates to continue this work. In 1450, he borrowed 800 guilders from Johann Fust, a wealthy financier. He pledged his tools and printing

printing press

equipment as collateral. Gutenberg completed production of the Mazarin *Bible* in 1454. Its printing brought together a number of technical innovations including a new kind of mold for casting type, a type-metal alloy, an improved press, and oil-based ink. Fust promptly filed a lawsuit against Gutenberg to recover his money. The court ordered Gutenberg to repay Fust's loans plus compound interest. While sale of the printed Bibles would have amply covered this amount, Fust was allowed to seize the type for the Bible and a Psalter and some of Gutenberg's printing equipment. With the help of a son-in-law who had been Gutenberg's assistant, Fust himself set up shop as a printer.

Despite Fust's claims to the contrary, Gutenberg belatedly received credit for inventions that launched the age of printing. He may not have been the first to print with movable type but he did perfect the chief elements needed to make this technology commercially successful. Gutenberg mass-produced reusable lead-alloy type fonts from soft-metal dies and a mold. He also developed his own handpress that allowed large sheets of paper to be printed. His printing press, adapted from a wine press, combined a fixed lower plate with an upper surface, or platen, that could be moved up or down by turning a small bar in the worm screw. The type font were individually arranged in lines along a wooden strip and locked in place. After printing, the fonts were disassembled and put back into the type case. Around 1475, steel dies replaced the bronze or brass dies used to produce the copper matrices. A sliding or rolling bed was introduced to allow the form to be withdrawn and reinked after each sheet was printed. Improvements in the worm screw allowed the platen to be raised and lowered more quickly and evenly. Eventually the wooden presses were replaced by ones made of metal. Rotary cylinders with revolving lines of type replaced stationary presses.

Johann Fust and his family became Europe's first publisher. Fust sold printed Bibles in Paris at one fifth their normal price, causing panic among professional copyists. By the end of the 15th century, an estimated 20 million copies of 35,000 different books had been printed. Thanks to Gutenberg and his successors, common people could afford to own their own copies of the Bible. Printing presses churned out religious pamphlets that fed controversy between Protestant and Catholic partisans. William Tyndale, an Englishman who had visited Martin Luther in Wittenberg, produced his own English-language translation of the *Bible*. This offended England's King Henry VIII. Tyndale was condemned of heresy and put to death. Two years later, Henry issued his own English-language Bible as a means of bolstering his authority after the rupture with Rome. The king put his own name and picture on a front page. A thoughtful group of 17th century Europeans, weary of religious hatred, began to study the natural world. Pierre Bayle's scientific newsletter, *Nouvelles de la République des Lettres*, began publication in 1684. Improved postal services allowed individuals sharing a common interest to engage in regular correspondence. This led to printed newsletters and then to general-interest newspapers.

The great expansion of European printed literature and correspondence among scholarly individuals broke down barriers between religions or nations to create an international "Republic of Letters". The Dutch humanist, Erasmus of Rotterdam, was first to take full advantage of the print technology. In 1516, he published a new Latin-language version of the New Testament based upon an original translation from the Greek. Erasmus is today better known for his witty commentaries. Like Voltaire, he had friends throughout Europe and used his contacts to promote intellectual and religious tolerance.The quickening interest in vernacular languages produced a crop of first-rate national poets such as William Shakespeare and John Milton, rivaling those who wrote in classical languages. Essayists such as Montaigne, dramatists such as Molière, and philosophers such as Descartes or John Locke, exploited possibilities of the print medium. French prose literature became a model for the European literary culture during the 17th century. It was crisp and precise, stating its themes in simple sentences rather than torturous aggregations of subordinate clauses.

Erasmus

Printing became a tool for organizing knowledge in Diderot's *Encyclopedia* and Samuel Johnson's *Dictionary of the English Language*. It helped to spread new political ideas as expressed in Thomas Paine's *Common Sense*, the *Declaration of Independence*, and *Declaration of the Rights of Man*. Perhaps the most popular application of this technology in the early days was to produce almanacs for farmers, seamen, and others. These almanacs gave astrologically propitious times for planting crops or heading out to sea. They included other kinds of information in their filler space. *Poor Richard's Almanac* is famous for its pithy sayings and advice for successful living. Besides publishing books, the early print shops reproduced government proclamations, ships' manifests and bills of lading, popular ballads, and weekly newspapers. Printed pamphlets distributed in Germany encouraged people to emigrate to Pennsylvania. Handbills advertising products for sale lured customers into stores from off the street. The Sears catalog, introduced in 1896, was so successful in selling sewing machines and other products that it killed the general store. Many Americans, especially in rural areas, learned to read from this book.

Daily newspapers first appeared in Europe during the 18th century. The first daily newspaper in England, the *Daily Courant*, began publication in 1702. Noah Webster's *Minerva*, begun in 1793, was New York's first such publication. Many of the weekly papers were mouthpieces for political parties; however the future lay with mass-circulation newspapers. Cheap wood-pulp paper began to be used for printing newspapers in the 1860s. Photoengraving, lithography, and stereotypical printing made it possible to combine pictures or cartoons with the text, increasing reader interest. To boost circulation, Joseph Pulitzer's *New York World* pioneered the use of large-type headlines, sections for comics and sports, and a Sunday supplement. It pitched content to flatter or interest the common man. Violent or sensational events became staples of news reporting. Technologically, power-driven rotary presses which printed on continuous rolls of paper helped to speed newspaper production. Ottmar Mergenthaler invented a linotype typesetting machine featuring a keyboard similar to a typewriter's which was installed at the *New York Tribune* in 1886. Teletype printers took stories from the wire services.

## Photography

Photography was the first in a series of cultural technologies which conveyed sensuous images rather than words. It began with the camera obscura, a device which projects light through a pin hole to produce an inverted image on the inside surface of a box or darkened room. Giovanni Battista della Porta discussed the concept in a book published in 1553. Johann Heinrich Schulze discovered in 1727 that exposure to sunlight darkens solutions of silver nitrate. In 1802, Sir Humphry Davy and Thomas Wedgwood produced visual "silhouettes" by placing objects on paper soaked in silver nitrate and then exposing it to light. A French chemist, Joseph Nicéphore Niepce, conducted experiments in transferring camera-obscura images to glass coated with silver chloride. In 1816, he printed on paper the world's first photographic negative. A decade later, he imprinted a positive image on a metal plate. Niepce teamed up with another Frenchman, Louis Daguerre, to perfect this process. After Niepce's death in 1833, Daguerre developed a method of producing positive images on silver plates. His "daguerreotypes" became a way to make inexpensive portraits.

The principle of black-and-white photography is that light which is focused upon a plate or paper surface coated with silver bromide leaves a visual pattern reflecting the degree of exposure in various places. A chemical reaction turning the silver-bromide crystals into silver occurs in spots more intensely exposed to light. Unexposed spots on the plate retain the silver-bromide coating. A negative is produced when the silver bromide is dissolved with sodium thiosulfate, leaving undissolved silver. The image from this negative projected upon photographic paper produces a positive, in which dark and light spots from the negative are reversed. To sharpen the image, the camera focuses incoming light upon the coated surface of the negative through a lens. A shutter opens and closes the diaphragm, controlling the amount of light to be admitted. Shutter speed and aperture width control the amount of light allowed to strike the film. Film sensitive to light of various colors produces negatives from which color prints can be made.

The daguerreotype portrait of the 1840s popularized the new technique of photography. The first such picture made in the United States required a half-hour exposure. Photographic techniques improved in subsequent decades as better lenses and more sensitive coatings were invented and as the wet collodion process was applied to photographic plates. Daguerreotype artists roamed the country on riverboats or in specially equipped cars making portraits in each town. In the 1860s, Matthew Brady and his assistants photographed scenes from the U.S. Civil War. George Eastman introduced roll film in 1888 which applied a gelatinous and chemical coating to paper. His later substitution of celluloid for the paper backing created film for the motion-picture industry. Color film first appeared in the 1930s. An MIT professor, Harold Edgerton, invented the electronic flash tube in 1938 to replace flash powder and bulbs. Photographic realism overtook the news profession in the 1930s and 1940s as newspapers and magazines increasingly used photographs to illustrate their stories.

## The Telegraph

The electric telegraph began the modern age of telecommunications. The French physicist André Marie Ampère first had the idea of sending messages with electricity. His writings inspired an American painter and pioneer of photography, Samuel F.B. Morse, to experiment along those lines. In 1844, Morse gave a practical demonstration of an electric telegraph to members of the U.S. Congress. He sent the message, "What hath God wrought", from Washington to Baltimore. This message was sent in "Morse code", in which each letter of the alphabet corresponds to a set of dots and dashes - short or long buzzing sounds - produced by activating and relaxing an electric circuit. The telegraph depends upon an electric circuit in which a single copper wire forms one part of the circuit and the earth another.

Samuel F.B. Morse

An electromagnet in the receiver alternately makes and breaks the circuit as electricity passes through the wire. Patterns of electrical engagement initiated at one end of the wire are received at the other end as audible sounds.

Morse's invention accompanied the development of railroads during the 19th century. The telegraph machine allowed large military operations to be coordinated effectively from headquarters. Later enhancements allowed several different messages to be sent through the wires at the same time. In 1872, J.B. Stearns invented a "duplex" telegraphy system, which allowed two messages to be sent through the same set of wires. Thomas A. Edison, whose career began as a telegraph operator, invented a "quadruplex" system in 1874. Automatic telegraphy became available with the use of punched paper strips. A copper cable capable of carrying telegraphed messages between continents was laid across the North Atlantic ocean in 1866. By 1902, telegraphic cables, primarily owned by the British, crisscrossed most of the earth's oceans and seas, including the Pacific. Then, suddenly, this wire-based technology became less important as radio communication appeared.

## The Telephone

The telegraph, like ideographic writing, was a device for experts who had learned a specialized code. The next cultural invention, the telephone, was like alphabetic writing. Because the messages were delivered in spoken language, it became a means of popular expression. The invention of the telephone is attributed to Alexander Graham Bell, a Scottish-born teacher of deaf children then living in Boston. However, Elisha Gray invented a similar device about the same time. On March 10, 1876, Bell was working on his project in an attic workshop when he spilled sulfuric acid over his clothes. "Mr. Watson, come here, I want you," he called to his assistant in the basement. Watson heard Bell's voice coming from the wire. He rushed upstairs with great excitement to deliver the news. Later that year, Bell exhibited what he termed a "talking wire" at the Centennial Exhibition in Philadelphia. Emperor Dom Pedro of Brazil stopped by to see Bell's exhibit. As Bell spoke into the transmitter, the emperor listened at the other end of the wire. "My God, it speaks!," the emperor exclaimed. Bell's invention became the hit of the exhibition.

Alexander G. Bell

The telephone operates according to the principle that sound waves emitted by the human voice can produce an electrical current whose impulse patterns express acoustical qualities in the originating speech. Bell's invention consisted of a diaphragm - a thin plate of soft iron - which vibrated like an ear drum in waves of varying intensity and frequency. These vibrations affected the magnetic field of a nearby bar magnet, which, in turn, induced a current in wire wrapped around the bar. A receiver, at the other end, picked up the electric signals and converted them back into sound by a reverse process. The current received by this device created a fluctuating magnetic field which caused its diaphragm

to vibrate in the same way as the transmitter's. Thus, the same sound might be heard as was spoken at the other end of the wire. Within a year, Thomas Edison and two other Americans invented an improved transmitter, the microphone, which used grains of loosely packed carbon instead of bar magnets.

Bell's telephone

Today, more than three out of four U.S. households have telephones. Switchboard operations are highly automated. The telephone lines carry more than voice signals. Computer data can now be transmitted through these lines to distant computers. Written text can be transmitted between fax machines. The era of the video telephone may be approaching. To meet the greatly increased demand for images and information transmitted by telephone, communications companies have installed several coast-to-coast networks of fiber-optic cable during the past twenty years. Glass fibers carry information more efficiently in the form of light signals than electrical impulses through copper wire. Moreover, the technique of sending light down each strand of fiber in closely spaced wavelengths allows the cable to carry signals on many different channels, further increasing its carrying capacity. In addition, wave bands have been reserved for cellular phones, pagers, and personal communication devices exploiting the new wireless technologies. Individuals can place or take calls nearly anywhere. As telephone service is linked to computers and satellite transmissions, communications experts have suggested that "in the future, all roads lead to the telephone."

## Sound Recording

Thomas Edison, America's best-known inventor, created the first phonograph machine in 1877. Working with an assistant, Edison sang "Mary had a little lamb" in a loud voice into a rotating cylinder covered with tin foil. The sound of his voice agitated a needle attached to the cylinder which produced quivering grooves in the tin foil. The cut grooves reproduced the original sound when a needle was later drawn across the rotating cylinder. Another inventor, Emile Berliner, brought out an improved version of the phonograph in 1888 which he called a "gramophone". This was a flat disk with spiraling grooves of uniform depth and lateral variation. Its advantage was that an unlimited number of duplicates could be made from a matrix. Berliner sold his gramophone records from a mail-order catalog. By 1895, he had 100 different disks in the catalog, each with a four-minute recording of music taken from operas or John Philip Sousa marches. The range of frequencies was limited, and the sound quality erratic. This type of record was played on a turntable with a spring-driven motor that needed to be rewound each time. Wooden or steel needles ran in the grooves.

Thomas Edison

Sound recordings were a popular type of entertainment in the penny arcades of the 1890s. Edison manufactured a coin-operated machine which cost a penny to play. Electric record players offered improved convenience and sound quality. A crystal in the playing arm converted mechanical vibrations from the record into voltages that were fed into an audio amplifier. Voice patterns from the phonograph were then converted into electrical impulses which recreated the sound. As automatic record changers were developed and recordings improved, increasing numbers of phonograph records were sold to consumers reflecting the musical interests and styles of the times. The juke box, placed in bars and restaurants, became popular in the 1930s. "Top

40" lists of the most popular recorded songs were showcased on radio stations across the country. The 78 r.p.m. records gave way to 45 r.p.m. disks with single hits on each side, and to the longer-

Edison's phonograph

playing albums with multiple selections. Recorded music became an integral part of the fast-paced, youth-oriented American lifestyle.

Meanwhile, the technology was changing as more sound recordings were issued on tape. The technology of tape recording began with Valdemar Poulsen's discovery in 1898 that a steel wire retains part of its magnetic flux when drawn across an induction coil in which electrical impulses from sound vibrations had created a fluctuating magnetic field. Poulsen, a Danish inventor, built a device called a "telegraphone" to capture and replay the magnetized sounds. In the 1930s, the German chemical companies IG Farben and AEG developed magnetic tape which offered better sound quality than wire. American scientists seized a few of their "magnetophones" after World War II and studied the technology. That knowledge was put to use in building tape recorders for sale to commercial radio stations. The consumer market did not take off until the 1960s when tapes became available in the form of cartridges and cassettes. Phillips Electronics NV brought out the cassette tape player in 1963. Eight-track players briefly became popular. In recent years, the tape-based technology has given way to compact disks featuring digitalized recordings.

### Motion Pictures

Thomas Edison, who is credited with inventing motion pictures, regarded this technology as an extension of photography. Cinematic film is indeed nothing more than a series of still pictures shown in quick succession to create the illusion of motion. In 1824, Peter Mark Roget, the author of *Roget's Thesaurus*, wrote a paper noting that visual impressions from a scene linger after the picture changes. If a number of pictures are shown rapidly one after another, they will seem to blend together in an image of continuous motion. Several photographers experimented with this effect during the 19th century. Eadweard Muybridge and J.D. Isaacs took a series of photographs with electrically controlled shutters which recorded race horses in motion. When these pictures were mounted on a revolving disk, the horses seemed to move. A device based on this principle, the zoetrope, was a popular toy for many years. Muybridge's photographic studies of human beings and animals in motion may have been the inspiration for Edison's experiments with motion pictures which were likely done by his assistant, William Dickson.

Edison's "kinetoscope", invented in 1888, consisted of a large box with a screen inside. Still photographs were attached to a cylinder rotating behind the screen. The viewer looked through a small hole to see moving objects. An early venue for Edison's invention was the peepshow in penny arcades. His films were also shown during interludes between vaudeville shows. In 1893, Edison developed a new type of machine which used celluloid film. "Kinetoscope parlors", devoted exclusively to this new medium, were established in Ottawa, New York City, and other cities in the following year. For a nickel, the viewer could watch thirteen seconds of animated entertainment on fifty feet of film. Several inventors found a way to project pictures onto an exterior screen. The Latham family of New York City invented a projection device called the "Eidoloscope" in 1895. Seven months later, Auguste and Louis Lumière showed their first film to Parisian audiences using an improved projector, the "Cinématographe". Within weeks, the Lumière brothers were drawing 2,500 people a night to this new type of entertainment.

The first films were simple spectacles of motion. "Fred Ott's sneeze" was the title of a kinetoscope production from Edison's studio in West Orange, New Jersey. The Lumière brothers' film

the sneeze

showed children horsing around, workers punching out on a time clock, and a train pulling into the station. A single stationary camera recorded outdoor scenes in direct sun light. Around the turn of the century, film makers began to experiment with the dramatic potential of the new medium. A French director, George Méliés, was first to create motion pictures that followed a story line. His *Cinderella* and *Trip to the Moon* employed photographic tricks. In 1903, Edwin S. Porter produced *The Great Train Robbery*, featuring "Bronco Billy" Anderson. Not only did this production involve more advanced editing techniques, but it also was the first time that an actor became a "star". In 1908, a group of independent film makers began working in southern California. That was because an association of companies holding patent rights to this technology were attempting to keep unlicensed companies out of business. The unlicensed operators wanted to be near the Mexican border in case U.S. courts imposed an injunction against them.

The era of silent films produced a rich crop of celebrities including Charlie Chaplin, Mary Pickford, and John Barrymore. By 1908, the roles of actor, director, camera operator, screen writer, and laboratory technician had become separate functions. Film was now shot in lighted studios. Animated cartoons, which had first appeared in 1906, became popular in the following decade. Hand tinting added coloration to films. Experiments done at the time of World War I added sound to the visual component. By converting sound into light beams that could be recorded on film, the oscilloscope made it possible to synchronize sight and sound. The first "talking picture" was Warner Brother's *The Jazz Singer*, which opened in New York City in October 1927. Walt Disney's talking cartoon *Steamboat Willie*, featuring Mickey Mouse, came out in the following year. Nearly every major studio converted to talking pictures within two years of its introduction. The 1930s and 1940s were a golden age of Hollywood filmmaking as large studios such as MGM, Warner Brothers,

Paramount Pictures, and Universal turned out a steady stream of motion pictures aimed at mass audiences.

As tape recordings and compact disks have replaced the phonograph record, so videotapes have increasingly been used to record visual motion. The first videotape recorders were produced in the 1950s. Ampex Corporation began selling them to television stations in 1956. Consumer videocassette recorders (VCRs) came along in 1976 when Sony introduced its Betamax machine. Including a television set, this device cost over $2,000. As the Betamax and VHS formats competed for dominance, prices came down and videocassette recorders grew in popularity. In 1983, the U.S. Supreme Court settled a lawsuit brought by Disney and MCI against Sony alleging that home taping of television shows infringed upon their copyright. Its ruling in favor of Sony gave further impetus to this practice and to VCR sales. Having failed to stop videotape recordings, film producers set up departments to distribute copies of their own films. A new industry was created to rent or sell videos to individuals for viewing in their homes.

## Radio

The radio is an electronic device which receives audio signals from electromagnetic waves. Commercial radio uses waves in a frequency range between 550 and 1,600 kilocycles per second. To produce radio signals, a microphone converts sound waves into electrical impulses which are then amplified and used to modulate carrier waves created by an oscillator circuit in the transmitter. (Modulation means to create waves in various patterns of frequency, amplitude or phase which carry information.) The modulated waves, again amplified, are directed to an antenna which converts them into electromagnetic waves that travel through space. At the other end of the transmission, antennae attached to a radio receiver catch some of the waves that have bounced down from the ionosphere. If the receiver is tuned to the same frequency as the waves, it will amplify the signal, remove the modulations, and feed the signal into a loud speaker that converts its electrical impulses back into sound.

In 1873, a Scottish physicist, James Clerk Maxwell, published a treatise which included a set of mathematical equations to describe the nature of electromagnetic waves. Fifteen years later, Heinrich Hertz built a device to generate radio waves. Guglielmo Marconi gave the first practical demonstration of radio communication in 1895. He used Hertz's spark coil to transmit the letter "S" in Morse code and a coherer invented by Edouard Branly to receive this message a mile away on his family's estate near Bologna, Italy. Marconi worked on improving this equipment until he was able to send a message across the Atlantic ocean in 1901. Three years later, Sir John A. Fleming built the first vacuum tube to detect radio waves electronically. Lee De Forest's "audion" tube, which placed a wire between the filament and plate, offered a way to amplify them. In 1913, Edwin H. Armstrong patented the circuit for a regenerative receiver which, improving upon the audion, fed the radio signal back through the tube several times so that it oscillated with more power and could send long-range signals. Armstrong's second great invention, the superheterodyne receiver, mixed the voltage from the incoming signal with that from a built-in oscillator so that clear signals were heard at particular frequency settings.

During its first twenty years, radio was a toy for amateur operators. It proved useful in detecting distress signals from ships on the ocean. David Sarnoff became famous as a wireless operator who took telegraphed messages from the Titanic. In 1920, a ham operator in Pittsburgh named Frank Conrad began broadcasting baseball scores and recorded music to his fellow operators. A local store provided free records in exchange for being mentioned in the broadcasts. When a Pittsburgh department store ran a newspaper advertisement offering to sell radio receivers, a Westinghouse vice president saw a business opportunity in manufacturing this product. Westinghouse's "cats-whisker" crystal radio sets sold for $25. To stimulate product demand, the company set up the world's first commercial radio station in Pittsburgh with the call letters KDKA. This station began regular broadcasts on November 2, 1920, starting with a report of returns from that year's national election. A successor to the Marconi Wireless Company, the Radio Corporation of America (RCA), was established in 1921 to market radio receivers. In 1926, RCA organized the first radio network, National Broadcasting Company.

The three great pioneers of commercial radio - Lee De Forest, Edwin H. Armstrong, and David Sarnoff - were a contentious bunch who frequently battled each other in the courts. De Forest sued Armstrong for patent infringement in 1915, winning on appeal twenty years later. As general manager of RCA, David Sarnoff was an early champion of Armstrong's inventions who later became an implacable foe. To deal with the problem of static, Armstrong worked for eight years to develop a radio system whose signals were based on frequency modulation (FM) instead of amplitude modulation (AM). He set up an experimental laboratory atop the Empire State Building in New York City where he was able to complete this work in 1933. Armstrong established his own "Yankee network" for FM broadcasting. Sarnoff, who was not eager to scrap millions of AM radio sets, had Armstrong evicted. Sarnoff also lobbied the Federal Communications Commission to reserve the FM frequencies for a new device, television, which his company was developing. In 1954, Armstrong committed suicide by jumping from a 13th floor apartment window.

Charles Laughton

## Television

Television uses a technology which broadcasts both aural and visual images on electromagnetic waves. Television waves occupy frequencies in a range between 54 and 216 megacycles per second (VHF) and between 470 and 890 megacycles per second (UHF). They have among the longest wave lengths in the electromagnetic spectrum. To create pictures, an electronic scanner passes across a plate coated with a photosensitive material with a zigzag motion covering 525 lines thirty times a second. The plate consists of a thin sheet of mica coated with a silver-cesium compound and backed with a metallic conductor. Light hits the cells in this mosaic at various intensities causing each cell to emit electrons and retain a positive charge. The scanner, passing its beam across the cells, produces an electrical signal as it releases the charge. This signal passes through an amplifier and goes out in carrier waves. The broadcast signals are picked up by antennae in the television receiver. To reconstruct images, an electron beam scans the fluorescent face of a cathode-ray tube line by line, causing the individual cells to glow in a visual pattern. As thirty still pictures per second flash across the screen, persistence of vision creates the illusion of motion.

An Irish telegraph operator named Joseph May first noticed that sunlight affected the electrical resistance of instruments made of selenium. That discovery, made in 1861, led to experiments with the electrical conductivity of selenium. In 1884, a German inventor named Paul Nipkow received a patent for a selenium-based television device with a mechanical scanner. It consisted of a pair of perforated disks, one at either end of the transmission, which rotated at a constant speed. Light from the subject passed through the moving holes to hit selenium cells and be changed into electrical signals. The disk at the receiving end converted electricity back to light, which could be viewed through an eye piece. In 1897, Karl Ferdinand Braun invented the cold cathode ray or "Braun" tube which allowed images to be produced by non-mechanical means. An Englishman, Campbell Swinton, proposed in 1908 that "distant electric vision" was possible using cathode-ray tubes at both ends. Experimenters in Germany, Russia, and France worked to develop a practical model of this system. In St. Petersburg, Professor Boris Rozing of the Technological Institute had already applied for a patent on a system that used two mirror drums to scan and dissect the image and a cathode-ray tube to receive it. An engineering student named Vladimir Zworykin assisted in this work.

In the United States, an alliance was formed between General Electric, AT&T, and Westinghouse Electric after World War

I to pool patent interests related to radio. Television research also took place under their sponsorship. Westinghouse and General Electric supported research by Charles F. Jenkins, who had invented the motion-picture projector in 1895. In 1922, he applied for a patent on a device that transmitted wireless pictures with prismatic rings as a scanner. In 1923, John Logie Baird filed a patent application in London for a television system using a Nipkow disk. Vladimir Zworykin, now working for Westinghouse Electric, then filed a patent for an all-electric system using a Braun tube as receiver and an improved camera tube. Baird gave a three-week demonstration of television broadcasting at Selfridge's Department Store in April 1925. Later that year, Zworykin demonstrated his all-electric system to a group of Westinghouse Electric executives. Picture quality was poor, and the executives ordered Zworykin to "work on something more useful." Edouard Belin demonstrated a device using cathode-ray tubes to three French officials in 1926. In 1927, an Idaho farm boy turned inventor, Philo T. Farnsworth, patented the world's most advanced television camera tube. He called it an "image dissector".

Radio Corporation of America (RCA), a General Electric subsidiary, redoubled its efforts to perfect a television system after AT&T's research laboratories demonstrated television transmission between New York City and Washington, D.C. in April 1927. The picture quality was good, even with mechanical equipment. RCA's vice president, David Sarnoff, sent Vladimir Zworykin on a trip to Europe to inspect work done there to develop television. Zworykin was most impressed with the system developed by Edouard Belin and associates in France. He thought that their cathode-ray tube, with a few adjustments, might solve the problem of television reception. Back in Pittsburgh, Zworykin pitched this hopeful message to his superiors at Westinghouse. They were not interested. He then met with Sarnoff, who pledged $100,000 to support Zworykin's research efforts. Now working for Sarnoff, Zworykin hired Belin's chief engineer, Gregory Ogloblunsky, and together they built a 7-inch cathode-ray picture tube called a "kinescope". Zworykin then turned his attention to the camera tube. The best equipment was Philo Farnsworth's image dissector. Zworykin visited Farnsworth in San Francisco and was shown everything. Sarnoff personally offered to buy out Farnsworth for $100,000, but Farnsworth declined. Zworykin then developed his own camera tube employing some of Farnsworth's concepts.

Zworykin filed a patent application for this "iconoscope" in November 1931 but delayed its announcement. In 1934, Farnsworth gave a public demonstration of electronic television at the Franklin Institute in Philadelphia. In the following year, the U.S. Patent Office awarded him "priority of invention" for his

1936 demonstration of
experimental television

television system. RCA refused to pay royalties. Farnsworth began broadcasting to a small audience from a Philadelphia suburb in 1936. Meanwhile, a new holding company had been formed in England, called Electric and Musical Industries Ltd. (EMI), which was partially owned by RCA. When EMI applied for permission to begin broadcasting in 1933, it brought a strong reaction from Baird Television Ltd., which had been doing an experimental broadcast for the BBC since 1929. The General Post Office and BBC established a commission of inquiry. It ultimately decided to establish a television service in London, utilizing technical apparatus from both companies. The London Television Service began regular broadcasts in November 1936. Its success prompted Sarnoff to start broadcasts in the United States. The first such event took place at the 1939 New York World Fair. World War II intervened. Although RCA by then had started to pay royalties to Farnsworth, his patents expired in 1946. Farnsworth then quit the business. RCA had the U.S. television business to itself.

In the United States, the Federal Communications Commission (FCC) was given the authority to regulate commercial broadcasting. It granted licenses to commercial stations to broadcast on certain frequencies. Sarnoff's firm had created the first radio network, NBC, in 1926. The second network, Columbia Broadcasting System (CBS), was formed two years later from a string of independent radio stations owned by William Paley, son of a Philadelphia cigar manufacturer. Its successful radio programs featuring comedians such as Jack Benny and Red Skelton earned big profits. Paley's ambition after World War II was to beat NBC in radio competition. NBC had a commanding technical lead in television. Television broadcasting was then restricted to frequencies in the VHF band, which were only enough to support twelve channels nationwide. Paley petitioned the FCC to reserve frequencies in the UHF band for a system of color television which CBS hoped to develop. When the FCC denied CBS's petition in April 1947, it clarified industry standards and started a rush of applications for commercial broadcast stations. The FCC then froze permits to construct television stations for four years. The scarcity of VHF licenses created a seller's market for television advertising and a buyer's market for programming.

At first, advertising agencies representing corporate sponsors controlled the programs that appeared on television. Moving away from single sponsorship of the programs, advertisers gave up the right to license programs while reserving the right to censor objectionable materials. The television networks, principally CBS and NBC, negotiated with independent production companies for ownership of the programs in exchange for a slot in prime-time broadcasts. *Texaco Star Theater* hosted by Milton Berle dominated early television audiences. Then came the sitcom, of which *I Love Lucy* was a notable example. This comedy series starring Lucille Ball and her husband, Desi Arnaz, made effective use of television's visual potential. Shows began to be taped, permitting reruns. After the quiz-show scandals of the mid 1950s, the networks turned to Hollywood for programming content. As U.S. commercial television became concentrated in three major networks, viewers wanting greater variety subscribed to cable-television services. In 1980, Ted Turner's Cable News Network began broadcasting live news reports from around the world 24 hours a day. Since 1991, western-style television has come to the masses of Asia through satellite broadcasts and cable television. The STAR network reaches 38 countries with a combined population of 2.7 billion people.

## Computers

The computer differs fundamentally from other electronically based cultural technologies in its ability not only to record images and information but manipulate them in desired ways. Modern computers are a collection of electronic components and peripheral devices that perform the following functions: (1) They enter data into the system. (2) They store the data in memory. (3) They control the computer's own operation. (4) They perform processing operations as the data is manipulated. (5) They exhibit the results of the manipulation externally. The most common method of entering data is to type letters and numerals on a keyboard. Attached printers or video monitors (cathode-ray tubes) output the results of computation. The computer's memory consists of electromagnetic codings on a coated disk inside the processing unit. Its operating system is a software program - codings in a symbolic language - which controls the machine's processing activities. Additionally, the system may accept other canned or customized programs that perform functions such as word processing, spreadsheet creation, or graphics.

The computer's invention comes from a tradition of improved calculating machines. John Napier, discoverer of logarithms, published a work in 1617 which proposed a new way to multiply and divide using mechanical "rods" or "bones". The French philosopher, Blaise Pascal, built a calculating machine with geared wheels in 1642 to help in his father's business. In 1671, Gottfried W. von Leibnitz built a machine based on binary arithmetic that could calculate square roots. Meant to compute astronomical tables, it was called the "stepped reckoner" because calculations were performed by rotating a drum with stepped teeth which represented numerals through variation in length. Commercial calculators were introduced in the 19th century. In 1820, Charles X. Thomas built a machine following Leibnitz's design that was the first to be used successfully in business.

Another machine performed arithmetical calculations by rotating wheels with retractable pins which protruded through a plate at particular numerical settings.

Unlike calculating machines, computers can perform operations that depend on meeting certain conditions. One of the first machines with that capability was the Jacquard loom, invented in 1801. Joseph Marie Jacquard, a French weaver, developed a technique to weave designs automatically in cloth. Holes punched in cards controlled the loom's operation. An English inventor, Charles Babbage, was impressed with a portrait of Jacquard that had been created by a process requiring twenty-four thousand cards. Babbage is credited with inventing in 1835 the world's first digital computer. Called the "Analytical Engine", it had one deck of punched cards for the data and another deck to control the operating routine. Plungers passed through holes in the cards to feed data into the program. The computer's memory consisted of fifty counter wheels to store numerical information. The machine permitted conditional transfers ("if statements") by which a comparison of numbers directed the operation to other points in the processing routine. There were also iterative loops or subroutines ("do loops") like those in modern computer programs. Although Babbage did not build a working model of this machine, he did produce drawings which showed all its components.

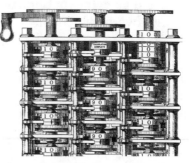

Babbage's machine

In 1886, a statistician named Herman Hollerith had the idea that a machine fed with punched cards might compile data collected in the U.S. census. He built such a machine for the 1890 census which allowed its work to be done in one third the time that the previous census had required. Hollerith's machine held the punched cards above trays filled with mercury. When metal pins dropped through holes to reach the mercury, it completed an electrical circuit and added to the count. Certain positions in the cards held information indicating characteristics of the population. These fields were tabulated separately as cards passed through the machine. While similar to Babbage's "Analytical Engine", Hollerith's invention used an electrical sensing device instead of mechanical feelers. In 1911, Hollerith and others formed a company which later became International Business Machines (IBM).

The computer would not have been possible were it not for the work of George Boole, an English mathematician and logician. Boole's *Treatise on Differential Equations*, published in 1859, presented the concepts of Boolean algebra. This system holds that a proposition of logic can have only two values: true or false. Likewise, in binary arithmetic the digits of any whole number can be represented by one or zero. An American philosopher, Charles Sanders Peirce, realized in 1867 that the values represented in Boolean algebra could be expressed mechanically by "on" and "off" positions in switches built into an electrical circuit. That meant that someone could design a circuit according to the Boolean scheme which either stopped or passed electrical current depending upon whether the switch was open or closed. Such a circuit might perform both arithmetical and logical calculations. In 1937, George Stibitz of Bell Telephone Laboratories connected some batteries, wires, and lights on top of his kitchen table and gave the first practical demonstration of an electrical circuit governed by Boole's principles.

The modern era of computing began at the time of World War II. Starting in 1939, IBM engineers worked with Professor Howard Aiken of Harvard to develop a fully automated electromechanical calculator controlled by punched paper tape. This machine, the "Mark I", performed arithmetic computations and could check table references. It was a machine with wheels like Babbage's except that electrical impulses controlled the switches. The first all-purpose electronic computer was the "Electronic Numerical Integrator and Calculator" (ENIAC) which two electrical-engineering professors at the University of Pennsylvania, John Mauchly and J. Presper Eckert, built with vacuum tubes instead of electro-mechanical switches. Its purpose was to compute firing tables for aiming artillery at German troops. The ENIAC computer could calculate in several minutes what might take a man equipped with a calculator forty hours. This machine consisted of a collection of 8-foot high cabinets, weighing 50 tons, which were filled with trays containing wired circuits and vacuum tubes. Work on the ENIAC was completed in February 1946 - too late to help in the war effort. Across the Atlantic, however, the British built a computer called "Colossus" which was used to break the German code.

A chance meeting at a railroad station between Herman Goldstine, the U.S. Army's liaison with the ENIAC project, and John von Neumann, a mathematician at the Institute of Advanced Studies in Princeton, brought von Neumann's immense talents to the design of computer architecture. In 1946, von Neumann, Goldstine, and Arthur Burks published a paper, *Preliminary Discussion of the Logical Design of an Electronic Computing Instrument*, presenting the concept of a computing machine in which both data and operating instructions were stored. Computer technicians no longer had to rewire the machine when new instructions were issued. This paper also discussed how computers might perform mathematical or logical calculations through step-by-step processing routines. Several universities built machines employing the von Neumann architecture. However, the technical challenge of computers is not limited to designing and maintaining hardware. Software is also a factor. Initially, computer programmers had to write detailed instructions in binary code which the machine could recognize. In the early 1950s, Grace Hopper of UNIVAC developed a "compiler" which would translate short, English-like statements into the machine language. A team at IBM developed the FORTRAN language for scientific programming applications.

Computers were first used for scientific research and large-scale government undertakings. UNIVAC I, developed by ENIAC's inventors and Remington Rand engineers, was sold to the U.S. Census Bureau to help with the 1950 census. Federal research laboratories at Los Alamos and Livermore needed massive computing power to develop the hydrogen bomb. The U.S. space program spurred a demand for more advanced technology during the 1960s and 1970s. In the 1950s, the two largest computer manufacturers, Remington Rand and IBM, decided to abandon the scientific market in order to develop computers for business. IBM became dominant in that lucrative field, producing large "mainframe" computers that could handle payrolls, billing, and production processes. Control Data Corporation became the leading producer of "supercomputers" for scientific work. However, federal aid to universities for computer research dwindled in the aftermath of the Vietnam war. In 1971, Control Data's principal computer designer, Seymour Cray, formed his own company to build supercomputers. Cray Research built the largest and fastest computers until the era of massive parallel processing.

Processing speed drove computer development during this time. The faster that computers could handle the calculations, the more computing power these machines had and the broader their range of applications. Speed is defined in terms of "clock period", which is the shortest time it takes the computer to do a simple operation. The number of operations which a computer can perform in a second is called a "flop". Howard Aiken's Mark I computer could multiply two numbers in three seconds, so it had a clock period of 0.3 flops. The ENIAC computer, which used vacuum tubes for switches, had a clock period of 400 flops - 1,200 times faster. When transistors were substituted for vacuum tubes in the CDC 7600 computer, the clock period increased to ten million flops (or 10 megaflops). As Table 9-1 indicates,

|  |  | | Table 9-1 |
| --- | --- | --- | --- |
| | Advances in Computer Switching Speed | | |
| time period | switching technology | calculations per second | computer models |
| 1939-1946 | electromagnetic relays | 0.3 | Mark I |
| 1946-1961 | vacuum tube | 400 to $10^5$ | ENIAC, UNIVAC |
| 1961-1976 | transistor | $10^6$ to $10^8$ | LARC, CDC 7600 |
| 1976-1990 | integrated circuits | $10^8$ to $10^{10}$ | Cray-1, X-MP |
| 1990 - | microprocessors | $10^{10}$ to $10^{12}$ | Delta, CM-5 |

Source: *Supercomputing and the Transformation of Science* by Kaufman. Copyright 1993 by W.H. Freeman and Co. Used with permission.

computer speed increased enormously as new technologies of switching were introduced. Integrated circuits, invented at Texas Instruments in 1959, further increased speed by using miniature circuits. Flat transistors and wiring were embedded on small slices of silicon called "chips". Intel Corporation's invention of the microprocessor in 1971 provided integrated circuits with all the elements of a computer. Since then, as a rule of thumb, processing speed with microprocessors has doubled every 18 months.

The microprocessor, which is "a computer on a chip", led to the revolution in personal computers that began in the late 1970s. The first working model of a personal computer was created at the Palo Alto Research Center in California. Here icon-based menus were developed for computer screens. In 1980, Dan Bricklin and Dan Fylstra wrote the software for VisiCalc, the first electronic spreadsheet for personal computers, meant to be used on the Apple II computer. In 1981, IBM brought out its own version of a personal computer licensing its DOS operating system from a small company called Microsoft. The Pac-Man video game became popular. The Lotus 1-2-3 spreadsheet for IBM and IBM-compatible machines came out in 1983. Apple Computer made a comeback in the following year with its popular Macintosh, a user-friendly machine with a mouse. Then, in 1985, Microsoft brought out the first version of Windows, also with icons and a mouse. Lotus introduced a program called Notes in 1990 which allowed computers to exchange documents. Microsoft increased its dominance of the computer-software field by licensing the MS-DOS operating system - about 90% of the world's computers use it - and bringing out improved versions of Windows and other products.

The recent trend has been toward computer networks. In the late 1960s, a team at the University of Illinois hooked up 64 identical Burroughs computers in parallel to create the ILLIAC IV machine. Processing in parallel with several smaller machines gives the same speeds as a larger machine while allowing better access to the system. IBM is promoting the concept of "network computers" to replace personal computers in offices. The terminals are cheaper and system upgrades do not have to be installed on each machine. While computer networks began in an office setting, they soon spread to the home. In the 1980s, the French postal and telegraph service decided to hook up the entire nation to a computer information base. Millions of Americans subscribed to online services such as Prodigy, CompuServe, or America Online which gave them similar access. Computer users became aware of belonging to a limitless network of users, both individual and institutional, in all parts of the world. This system became known as the Internet.

The Internet started in 1969 when the Pentagon contracted with a consulting firm in Cambridge, Massachusetts, called BBN to construct the ARPANET network. In 1972, a BBN engineer named Ray Tomlinson sent the first E-mail message using @ in the address. Initially ARPANET connected computers at four large universities on the west coast. As computers at other universities and research centers were added, the system evolved into several commercial subnetworks. The World Wide Web began in 1991. Today, the Internet has grown into a global network that links more than 120 million computers. This system in the aggregate is so large and chaotic that new kinds of software have been developed to allow users to navigate in its "cyberspace". Websites have been set up to focus communities of interest.

**Chapter Ten**

# USING HISTORY
# TO PREDICT THE FUTURE

## Why History Does Not Repeat Itself

If history repeats itself, the past indicates the future. A common approach to prediction is to extrapolate from current trends. Events presently observed are carried to a logical conclusion. Therefore, the futurist needs to know what is happening in today's society. He should be in touch with the creative centers where new ideas or products are hatched. If one wants to know, for instance, how American automobiles may look in three years, a good place to visit might be the styling offices at Ford or General Motors. One must use intuition and common sense to imagine how today's innovations will play out in future society. There is always an element of uncertainty in any apparent movement towards an end. If, on the other hand, history does not repeat itself, then all bets are off. This type of reasoning will be of little use.

Lord Acton's maxim, "Power corrupts" , describes processes that drive historical events. Because of corrupt tendencies inherent in any organization, history does not move in a straight line. Corrupting power brings progress to a halt in each line of development. The correction must come from another direction.

Bureaucracy is the name of an organization advancing toward a state of corrupted power. Any enterprise which succeeds in its purposes develops an organization that has power. This organization works through a structure of persons placed in functional positions. Individuals at the top of the hierarchy exercise power over persons in the lower ranks. The organization itself exercises power in the larger society. So long as those managing the organization remain true to its purposes, the organization will remain healthy and strong. But power is a much-coveted object. The quest to acquire or retain power within a bureaucratic organization becomes a new purpose which subverts the original one. So power corrupts.

As a general rule of bureaucracies, it would seem that any organized effort tends in time to become disorderly and corrupt. Where an organization once had a clear purpose, that purpose becomes confused while developing a material structure to achieve it. With material development comes a shift of attention away from external purposes and toward the appeasement of internal power. Persons within the organization become aware of the personal concerns of those holding superior power. A bureaucratic mentality develops in which clear expressions of purpose give way to a devious process of decision and thought, sensitive to the power structure, its personalities, and their special needs.

One can see that historical change might be driven by tendencies for the society to become something other than what it once was. Worldly endeavors which once exhibited strong purpose develop blockages of spirit. Powerful institutions become centers of coercion and deceit. They wage wars and burn people at the stake. Absolute power, such as Caligula's, invites such depravity that it cannot be allowed to continue. Unless a reformer arises internally, the cure for this corruption can only come from outside the circle of power. Here people are freer to speak and think the truth; and that makes them strong. So, when a society becomes clogged with coercive decisions and arrogant lies, it is time for a new message to be delivered from outside the powerful class. The conventional wisdom then becomes ripe to be challenged. The spiritual energy flows in a direction other than in the past.

Organized society contains the seed of its own destruction. The future gravitates not towards this but a positive end. Courage, not wisdom, is on the cutting edge of change. Courageous acts, almost by definition, are performed in the face of real difficulty, which in this context means to oppose abusive power. Therefore, historical change quite often goes against what might be predicted from an assessment of current strength. The world moves away from developed realities toward the invisible idea. It comes to resemble more what is not than what was in the past. Civilizations tend eventually to move away from themselves. In fact, the tendency of historical epochs is for the flow of events to reverse their original direction.

It should be evident that the most awesome power to coerce worldly affairs in favor of its own perpetuated existence fails to sway the course of history. Time and time again, historical events run counter to this power. Human intelligence is too weak to prevent errors from entering into society even if one had total powers of enforcement. The safest strategy, then, is to build society in such a way that errors can be corrected if they appear. The society should contain pockets of slack, or purposes running counter to the prevailing purposes, so that a source of opposition can be found to corrupted power and this can be brought to bear against abuse. Malignancies that would be fatal in a single trunk will not destroy societies having a pluralistic power structure. That is why totalitarian systems of governance do not last.

## Prediction through Analogy with Previous Cultures

Desiring to know the future of world civilization, one might think it contradictory to use history for that purpose if the future does not resemble the past. Profound breaks will occur in the flow of historical events. Prediction of them is problematic. We call these breaks "apocalypse" or "revolution." Curiously, the early prophets of apocalypse combined attempts at prediction with a kind of literary deception designed to gain credence for their views. The writer did not publish prophecies under his own name but under that of a well-known religious personality from the past. "In the classical apocalypse," wrote Albert Schweitzer, "the alleged writer undertakes to predict the course of history from his own day in the remote past to the age in which the real writer lives, as something glimpsed in a series of visions, and rounds it off with visions of the final age. Since the reader can establish the accuracy of the prophecies of past events, it is hoped that he will come to be convinced that the events still to come will occur as foreseen."

Another approach is to regard human culture as resembling organic entities whose experiences follow a life cycle. The major discontinuities of world history are associated with the birth of new civilizations. The civilizations, once born, move through a sequence of events which can to some degree be predicted by analogy with previous civilizations. Because their history is known, the next phases of the present culture can be anticipated with reference to corresponding points in that earlier development. While it is true that the future unfolds in new and unexpected ways, there may be a general congruence of events between the future and past in the same way that a child's expectations of future life might follow the parents' experience. Even in the crib, the child would be expected to have a future of growth, maturity, and decay. If we apply this model to cultures, the definition of the culture becomes critical. Without a clear definition, the lifelike patterns of historical experience could be interpreted any number of ways.

Oswald Spengler suggested such a technique of historical prediction which was modeled after Goethe's conception of "living nature." In *Decline of the West*, he wrote: "Every Culture passes through the age-phases of the individual man. Each has its childhood, youth, manhood and old age. It is a young and trembling soul, heavy with misgivings, that reveals itself in the morning of Romanesque and Gothic ... Childhood speaks to us also ... out of early-Homeric Doric, out of early-Christian art and out of the works of the Old Kingdom in Egypt that began with the Fourth Dynasty ... The more nearly a Culture approaches the noon culmination of its being, the more virile, austere, controlled, intense the form-language it has secured for itself,

Cologne cathedral

the more assured its sense of its own power, the clearer its lineaments ... Still later ... fragrant with the sweetness of late October days, come the Cnidian Aphrodite and the Hall of the Maidens in the Erechtheum, the arabesques on Saracen horseshoe-arches, the Zwinger of Dresden, Watteau, Mozart. At last, in the grey dawn of Civilization, the fire in the soul dies down. The dwindling powers rise to one more, half-successful, effort of creation, and produce the Classicism that is common to all dying Cultures."

Spengler took note of great intellects such as Goethe and Frederick the Great who moved "with perfect assurance" among historical analogies. "Thus, he (Frederick the Great) compares the French to the Macedonians under Philip and the Germans to the Greeks. 'Even now,' he says, 'the Thermopylae of Germany, Alsace and Lorraine, are in the hands of Philip,' therein exactly characterizing the policy of Cardinal Fleury. We find him drawing parallels also between the policies of the Houses of Habsburg and Bourbon and the proscriptions of Antony and of Octavius." Yet, for the most part, these were flashes of historical intuition. Spengler's aim was "to work out a method" to solve the problems of history: "Analogies, insofar as they laid bare the organic structure of history, might be a blessing to historical thought. Their technique, developing under the influence of a comprehensive idea, would surely eventuate in inevitable conclusions..." Such a technique he called the "morphology of world-history."

This technique has a practical benefit when predictions are made based on morphological comparisons between different civilizations. Spengler's "decline of the west" involved such a prediction concerning the late 19th and early 20th century culture of western Europe and America in relation to the cultures of Greece and Rome. "Let it be realized," he wrote, "that the nineteenth and twentieth centuries, hitherto looked on as the highest point of an ascending straight line of world-history, are in reality a stage of life which may be observed in every Culture that has ripened to its limit ... Considered in the spirit of analogy, this period appears as chronologically parallel - 'contemporary' in our special sense - with the phase of Hellenism, and its present culmination, marked by the World War, corresponds with the transition from the Hellenistic to the Roman age. Rome, with its rigorous realism ... will always give us, working as we must by analogies, the key to understanding our future. The break of destiny that we express by hyphenating the words 'Greeks-Romans' is occurring for us also."

Spengler has been much criticized for his assertion of iron-clad parallels between events happening in different cultures. Biological processes may have a looser causal connection than physical motions. As it turned out, the future of the West in the 20th century scarcely resembled patterns found in histories of the Roman empire. Writing at the dawn of the entertainment age, Spengler failed to anticipate "pop culture." His predictions were rooted too much in a *Civili* mentality. Yet, though Spengler's specific predictions were off base, his analogical approach at least offers a means of dealing with historical uncertainty. If current trends cannot be trusted, congruent points in cultural lifecycles may point a way to the future. Arguing by analogy with historically known events, would-be prophets of present and future societies can anticipate what might happen from a general knowledge of past civilizations. The same inner dynamic applies to human culture in all epochs.

## Some Observations of Past Civilization

World history provides definite clues to the future of society. Some of the developmental patterns to be gleaned from past societies include the following:

(1) that when a major new cultural technology appears in society, it marks the beginning of a new civilization. This is the birth phase of its life cycle.

(2) that a new civilization brings new institutions of power. Certain functions become organized within their structure which once took place informally. These institutions assert political and cultural dominance.

(3) that there is a connection between the dominant institutions in a civilization and its triggering cultural technology. Inherent qualities in this technology shape the ensuing civilization.

(4) that the new civilizations bring new types of belief and new models of personality.

(5) that, over the course of an epoch, the cultural dynamic produces a change in values. Themes that prevailed at the beginning of an epoch give way to their opposite as the epoch comes to an end.

## Movements to the Opposite

With respect to the last point, one trend that we saw, for instance, at the beginning of CivI was increased concentration of military and political power. Rulers of the city-states went to war against each other to expand their territories. The large empires in the Middle East fought ferociously. Entire nations were uprooted from their ancestral lands. After centuries of unrelieved carnage, Octavian achieved total power in Roman society. As the emperor Augustus, he then renounced further territorial conquest. Around this time, a child was born in a manger to parents complying with an imperial census. He became known as the "Prince of Peace." Jesus taught that in God's kingdom the meek would inherit the earth. The last would be first, and the first last. This humble king, wearing a crown of thorns, was put to death on a cross. Yet, the next civilization belonged entirely to him.

At the beginning of CivII, the focus of thought was upon ideas, the "word", or what the Apostle Paul called "things unseen." Visual representations of God were considered idolatrous. The early Christians admired ascetic personalities like St. Anthony. They were pacifists who refused to participate in Roman military service. Then the Christian church became Rome's state religion. The Papacy became a surviving center of power. Toward the end of CivII, Popes were ordering European princes to undertake military expeditions against Moslem rulers of the Holy Land. The Papal state hired mercenary soldiers to protect its territorial domain. It rebuilt St. Peter's church, employing some of world history's best-known artists. This new emphasis upon beauty, wealth, and power was the antithesis of early Christian values.

CivIII began, during the Renaissance, with a type of artistic expression that exhibited wholeness of visual forms. Giotto's works pointed the way to a new style of realistic painting whose colors and shapes suggested palpable objects. This epoch also began with the transcendent power of European princes. Then, in the 19th century, the newly invented technology of photography allowed machines to produce a more accurate representation of visual scenes than a human artist might hope to achieve. Inspired by the camera, Impressionist painters abandoned attempts to create the image of shapely objects and instead placed colored dots on the canvas as rays of light might strike the eye. This break with tradition led to other schools of experimental art - cubism, surrealism, Dada - around the time of World War I. This was an art without beauty or form in a traditional sense. It produced a fragmented view of the world. The great war that occurred at the end of CivIII brought the collapse of the German, Russian, and Austro-Hungarian monarchies and the Turkish Ottoman empire.

CivIV started out with the entertainment industry being a sideshow. In America, white society took delight in mimicking the song-and-dance routines of Negro slaves. Exotic circus-like spectacles attracted gawking customers. Set against a tradition of academic pretentiousness, popular culture won people's affections. It was good-humored and safe. As this type of entertainment prospered, however, the business aspect became more important. Movies, radio, and television produced quantifiable audiences which could be tapped by advertisers. In time the fun went out of the entertainment business. Cold product calculations drove what was allowed to be heard and seen. The threat of large corporations defending their intellectual property rights stood behind innocent-looking cartoon figures. In the aftermath of the Civil Rights movement, the depiction of blacks in U.S. popular entertainment was guided increasingly by political correctness, mandating favorable treatment. Here, too, the pendulum had swung in the opposite direction.

### Synchronized Political Leadership

With respect to models of personality, all civilizations, starting with the first, have had political leaders. Those leaders who have risen to the level of historical greatness have tended to take on the flavoring of the personalities associated with their age. The principal requirement of a political leader is to be a skilled military commander, administrator, or lawgiver. In addition, the great kings and emperors of CivII have had a taste for philosophy or a gift for divine revelation. Those in CivIII have sometimes been talented writers. Some in CivIV have had an entertainment background.

Besides being an effective general, Alexander the Great was well versed in philosophy and Homeric literature. A student of Aristotle, he actively promoted the philosophically-based Greek culture. The Indian emperor Asoka is known for promoting the Buddhist religion. One of Rome's "wise emperors", Marcus Aurelius, was a philosopher of some note. His *Meditations* are still widely read. The prophet Mohammed was, of course, a communicator of divine messages as well as a skillful military and political leader. The renowned Mogul emperor, Akbar the Great, invented his own religion.

In CivIII, two of the greatest U.S. Presidents, Thomas Jefferson and Abraham Lincoln, are known for their mastery of written language. Jefferson composed the *Declaration of Independence*, and Lincoln the *Gettysburg Address*. Their reputation for greatness depends, in part, upon their skill in finding the right words to express democratic ideals. Frederick the Great was a master of French prose writing. Winston Churchill is known for his eloquent speeches in the House of Commons in the darkest hours of World War II. John F. Kennedy's Presidential reputation is bolstered by often-quoted lines from his Inaugural Address.

In CivIV, one of the most effective political leaders was Ronald Reagan, who was a film star and television host before he entered politics. John F. Kennedy was also a telegenic personality. Bill Clinton, a saxophone player, connected with youthful audiences on MTV. Jesse Ventura, the first Reform Party candidate to be elected governor of a U.S. state, became famous as a professional wrestler.

If some day in the future a computer nerd becomes elected President, history may record another political leader in synch with his age.

There are, of course, some political leaders whose accomplishments were ill-timed for the age in which they lived. Lenin, a philosopher, lived towards the end of CivIII; his religious-political empire no longer stands. Pharaoh Ikhnaton may have been ahead of his time; his religious innovations were promptly undone after his death. The emperor Nero was a self-styled artist. Adolf Hitler painted landscapes before he became a politician. Neither of these talents added any luster to their historical reputations.

A memorable photograph shows Richard Nixon, political leader of the Free World, shaking hands with Elvis Presley, the "king" of rock 'n roll music. It was one of those moments when the top representatives of two different civilizations came face to face. When England's Princess Di perished in a car crash in 1997, a bitter confrontation took place between the royal household and the press. Diana's brother, Lord Spencer, accused the paparazzi of precipitating her death by pursuing Diana too aggressively. There was an immediate popular reaction against the press. The tabloid press soon counterattacked with headlines suggesting that Queen Elizabeth and other

Nixon meets Elvis

royals were taking Diana's death too dispassionately. "Where is the queen?," blared one headline. "Your people are suffering, speak to us, ma'am," said another. Soon people were complaining of the Queen's coldness, and she had to go on television to reassure the public that she truly cared. Curiously, the same rash of stories brought out the fact that, privately, members of the royal family referred to themselves as "the firm", which is an epochally correct way of referring to the monarchy in a commercial age.

## Effect of Changing Civilizations

A lesson of history may be that powerful institutions become coercive and brutal while seeking to retain that power. Typically, this happens at the end of the epoch in which they were the dominant force in society. Then other institutions arise from the margins of society to assume dominance in the next epoch. The creative impetus passes to a new sector.

When the first civilization gave way to the second, philosophers presented a moral critique of government. Idea-based religion took its place in society alongside government as an institution of power. When the second civilization gave way to the third, Popes and Holy Roman Emperors were engaged in a costly and ferocious power struggle. Christians were fighting Moslems. Protestants were fighting Catholics. In that context, the money-lender gained leverage in society. Secular learning gained new support. When the third civilization gave way to the fourth, humanity had just experienced two world wars brought on by economic rivalries and hostile ideologies. The high culture had become self-congratulatory. Ideas taken too serious had sown anger and strife. Therefore, the public turned to lighthearted pursuits. Mass entertainment became the order of the day. Now, as we start to move into the fifth historical epoch, a reaction may be taking place against an entertainment culture which shows signs of becoming overblown.

Curiously, the arrival of a new civilization also brings a change in institutions developed two epochs earlier. Such institutions undergo a major transformation giving impetus to democratization:

First, we compare the religious institutions transformed by philosophy in the second epoch with religion as practiced in prehistoric times. Prehistoric or primitive religion, controlled by hereditary priesthoods, is ritualistic, nonscriptural, and nature-centered. World religion is creedal, scripturally based, and centered in ideas of God. Membership is open to all believers, and a meritocratic process determines the hierarchy. The democratic impulse is seen most clearly in early Buddhism challenging the Brahman priests.

Next, imperial government, which had dominated CivI, was similarly transformed during the third historical epoch. Despite repeated attempts, no monarch was able to reunite European peoples in an enduring empire. Later, monarchy itself was replaced by democratic government. The will of the people became, in theory at least, the new political master.

Finally, world religion, product of CivII, has come under a subtle attack during the fourth historical epoch as the entertainment culture has discredited serious thinking. Television-induced consumerism has created a materialistic attitude which prefers "things seen" to promises of Heaven. The religiously motivated person, or indeed anyone with strong ideological convictions, comes across in this culture as a sinister, cult-like figure.

If the pattern holds true to form, one would expect that the arrival of CivV might transform institutions developed in the third historical epoch. Chief among them would be secular education and commerce. A process of democratization might affect those institutions.

## Some Questions About This Process

Civilizations are not living creatures with clearly developed, observable bodies but unifying patterns which historians have found in the mass of recorded experience. Each may see a different cultural pattern in the mass of facts. Spengler quotes Goethe as saying on the eve of the Battle of Valmy in September 1792: "Here and now begins a new epoch of world history, and you, gentlemen, can say that you 'were there.'" There can be no doubt that the first movements of the French armies towards their eventual conquest of Europe were historically important; but whether this marked the beginning of a new epoch of world history is another matter. This book does not regard events happening in the year 1792 as being pivotal to human history. Historians have associated epochal break-points as well with such experiences as the Industrial Revolution, the emergence of democratic government, the rise of empirical science, and economic globalization. All these are, of course, important events though perhaps not definitive of new epochs in world history.

This book must offer a defense of its scheme. What makes cultural technologies supremely important in the determination of new historical epochs? An answer is that these communicative technologies shape public experience. They have a certain causal connection with institutions which exert power in the society and "make its history", so to speak. Historical experience partakes of their flavoring. If this be true, then the first invention and widespread use of a major new cultural technology marks the beginning of a new civilization and, by implication, the end of an old one. Since computers embody such a technology which has only recently appeared, we know that we are in the midst of a significant cultural shift. The challenge is to predict what will come next.

Change is a fact of every time and place. The question is whether the changes which people observe mark the beginning of a profound and irreversible cultural shift - i.e., a new civilization - or are evidence of mere fluctuation. A dogmatic history such as this helps to reach a decision; but is the decision correct? In defense, it should be said that the conclusions reached in this book are generally in line with historical consensus. Most historians regard the period of the 6th and 5th centuries, B.C., as being pivotal to human history; and, again, the period of the Italian Renaissance during the 14th and 15th centuries, A.D., is thought to be historically significant. This book envisions that those times marked the beginnings of CivII and CivIII respectively. It should also be said that they were accompanied by particular circumstances which were not present at other times, working to inspire creative change. They will be discussed later in this chapter.

## A Connection with Social Structures

First, let us consider the causal impact of cultural technologies upon the society and its culture. This book advances the theory that the introduction of new cultural technologies in society **causes** new civilizations to appear. To assert a causal relationship between two things, one should be able to demonstrate, first, that the cause appeared earlier in time than the effect, though not too much earlier, and in approximately the same place or involving the same set of objects. Second, there should be some logical connection between cause and effect which seems to explain how the one affected the other. In this case, we are suggesting that the invention and widespread use of a new cultural technology precedes the arrival of a new civilization and that the technology exhibits characteristics which relate to elements of the impacted civilization. The cause - the cultural technology

- is quite clear. Each was invented in a particular time and place by historical persons. The effect - the civilization - is harder to place.

A change in the dominant mode of communication changes the nature of public experience and, with it, the type of society. "Eventually social structures come to imitate or replay the patterns by which these dominant (cultural) technologies are organized," wrote Robert Logan. In his view, for instance, the perception of written language brought a different brain-wave pattern into play than is found in television viewing. "The left-brain patterns of rationality, logic, linearity, sequence, mathematics, and analysis are characteristic of the literate mode of communication ... The right-brain patterns of intuition, analogy, pattern recognition, nonlinearity, simultaneity, and holism are associated with both the oral and electric information modes of communication. Left-brain literacy information patterns favor specialism while the right-brain patterns of oral and electric information tend more to a multidisciplinary approach."

The invention of ideographic writing is related to the rise of imperial government. The purpose of training scribes was to supply literate administrators for the temple and palace bureaucracies. At this point, literacy was restricted to a small number of professionals. Society needed only to have information recorded once in a form from which it could later be retrieved. Ideographic writing was too difficult for mass instruction. Only a large bureaucracy could afford to train individuals in this art. Written language, in the hands of a few, was capable of supplying a communications link between numerous people engaged in the same enterprise. Government could exercise control over a vast territory and send a consistent message to diverse communities. The writings could be delivered from royal headquarters to places throughout the empire. This supported a system of taxation and law.

Alphabetic writing was easier to learn. As more persons in society became literate, the culture changed. The escape of literacy from a professional elite to the masses was accompanied by a democratization of religion, especially in India. General literacy produced an increase in philosophical awareness. Logan explained: "Perhaps the most striking effect of the alphabet was the great number of new abstractions that appeared almost simultaneously. All spoken words are abstractions of the things they represent. The written word is a further abstraction of the spoken word, and phonetic letters give it an even greater abstraction than ideographs or pictographs. The use of the alphabet thus involves a double level of abstraction ... The impact of alphabetic writing can be traced by noting the increase in abstract thought and language that occurred as Greek literature progressed from Homer to Hesiod to the pre-Socratic philosophers and then to Plato and Aristotle ... Under the influence of alphabetic literacy, Greek writers created the vocabulary of abstract thought that is still in use to this day, notions such as body, matter, essence ... Ideas such as truth, beauty, justice, and reason took on new meanings and became the subject of a new type of discourse."

Printing multiplied copies of the same text. Printed literature became articles of commerce. The extra care that went into preparation of texts was well-suited to scholarly pursuits, including science. Printing accelerated the dissemination of knowledge and supported a system of universal education. It elevated the individual author or artist to the status of cultural hero. Most significantly, it transformed personal correspondence into newsletters and newspapers that circulated among a larger circle of readers. Printed newspapers and periodicals created a sense of instant history. Their communication constituted an ongoing spectacle of events in real time connecting individuals to activities in the uppermost levels of society. Democratic government became possible when the multitudes of citizens became informed about political issues and personalities. The newspapers also became vehicles for commercial advertising. This revolutionized the way that the producers and sellers of products communicated with their customers. A consumer mass market was created for various kinds of manufactured goods containing new and improved features.

The technologies of electric or electronic communications that appeared in the 19th century took over some of the newspapers' function in presenting an ongoing spectacle of public events.

However, their ability to convey the sensuous detail of persons personalized the spectacle. People became interested in it not to gather information but to be entertained. Radio and television broadcasts introduced a stream of exciting or amusing new persons into the household, interrupting daily living routines. People settled back to enjoy a substitute experience at certain times of the day or week. As millions of people were all experiencing the same thing, the content of radio or television programming became the society's common culture. The commercial advertising connected with the programs became its most powerful selling force. Certainly the communications technologies which present this big show are related to the entertainment culture: they gather its audience.

## Some Anomalies

If one assumes that cultural technologies are the determining factor behind civilizations, then one is led to the following conclusions:

Any society which uses an ideographic or pre-alphabetic script belongs to CivI.

A society which uses alphabetic script in hand-written rather than printed texts belongs to CivII.

A society which has printed literature but not electrical or electronic communication belongs to CivIII.

A society which has embraced electronic entertainment but not the culture of computers belongs to CivIV.

When the computer culture becomes fully developed, that will be CivV.

By and large, this scheme applies to societies in the times after the invention of particular cultural technologies. However, it is possible for a society to neglect or refuse to implement a technology that has become available elsewhere in the world. In that case, our scheme would assign its culture to the civilization associated with the earlier form of communication.

An example of that situation would be the civilization of Far Eastern peoples. The first Chinese city-states appeared around 1900 B.C., and they developed a system of writing not long after that. Yet, the Chinese have never adopted an alphabetic script. Neither have the neighboring Korean and Japanese people. If one accepts the association between cultural technologies and civilizations, one would have to conclude that the Chinese civilization (together with its Japanese and Korean satellites) belongs to CivI. Some would say that this indicates cultural backwardness. On the other hand, Chinese culture has always seemed rather sophisticated to western peoples. This book takes the position that, because they failed to adopt alphabetic writing, the Chinese and their neighbors have remained in the first civilization for thousands of years. A corroborating fact is that Chinese society has long been dominated by imperial government, which is the characteristic institution of that civilization in its mature phase. The philosophical revolution of the 6th century B.C. failed to produce an indigenous world religion in China.

Islamic society, an outstanding example of world religious culture, likewise failed to advance from the second to the third civilization because it rejected the technology of printing. A combination of religious opposition and cultural arrogance blocked the introduction of printing presses in the Ottoman empire. Although a Turkish press began operations in 1726, it was shut down in 1742 after printing less than twenty books. After Islamic governments sent students to the West to acquire technical training in the early 19th century, the ban on printing was relaxed. Soon numerous books were translated into Arabic, Turkish, and Persian, and newspapers appeared in Islamic countries. Three and a half centuries of delay had cost these Mid Eastern peoples a wealth of secular learning while preserving the intensity of their religion.

An example of a society failing to advance from the third to the fourth civilization may be that of the Soviet Union, which, until its fall in the 1990s, was wedded to a rigidly literate mentality and to 19th century cultural forms. That situation has already been discussed.

An example of a society failing to advance from prehistoric culture to that of basic literacy may have been the society of India before Buddha's time. The Indus Valley culture had possessed an ideographic script until its demise around 1800 B.C. The Indian people were then without writing for more than a thousand years during Vedic times. However, this was also a period of cultural ferment when the poems and hymns of Aryan culture were developed in oral form. It left a foundation for primitive religion with its rituals and pluralistic deities. Literacy reappeared shortly before the time of the religious reformers, Buddha and Mahavira. This injection of philosophy into the Indian religious tradition created a world religion, Buddhism, and pushed the earlier Hindu religion in the same direction.

Another way of looking at this situation would be to say that certain civilizations have failed to "advance" to the next stage because of their own perfection. Societies which have come into a particular civilization relatively late in the historical process tend to acquire a more perfect version of that civilization than ones which adopt it sooner. They cling to the civilization more tenaciously.

The first Chinese emperor, Shih Hwang-ti, unified China in 221 B.C., nearly three millennia after King Narmer of Upper Egypt had established the first Pharaonic dynasty. The pattern of imperial government which he and his Han successors established then lasted for another two millennia. Islam was the last of the three principal world religions to appear. Philosophy characterized this type of religion early in its historical cycle, but spiritual empire, including warfare, characterized it in a later stage. Islam's prophet, Mohammed, shows less of the philosopher and more of the spiritual official than Buddha or Jesus. He was himself a successful military leader and head of state. The Marxist-Leninist state established in Russia was a product of late CivIII thought. Marx and Lenin were both newspaper editors early in their political careers who later wrote scholarly books. The society which was created in the image of their thought reflected the coerciveness, anger, and intellectual arrogance of these two university-educated men.

World history focuses upon the first introduction of a technology, giving the impression that this innovation spreads evenly over the world. However, we have seen that the different societies on earth have adopted new cultural technologies at different times. We have also seen that a society can retain an older technology beyond its period of common use. Finally, it should be noted that, when a new cultural technology is introduced in society, the previous ones do not disappear. People still produce handwritten letters in an age of printed literature. They still read books and newspapers in an age of free television programming. Institutions that arose during the first or the second historical epoch can still be found in contemporary society. It is, therefore, a mistake to suppose that historical epochs suddenly begin or end on particular dates and that the cultural scenery abruptly changes. Rather, the beginning of those new periods are marked by the addition of something. The society fills up with an even greater variety of cultural practices.

### The Timing of New Civilizations

If one contends that the introduction of a new cultural technology causes a new civilization, then timing becomes critically important. One should recognize, however, that the date when a cultural technology was invented may be less significant than the date when its cultural influence was first felt. We need to have a sense of when the technology became widely used in the society in order to know when it became culturally influential. How much of a delay was there between the invention or first appearance of a new cultural technology and the time when it took effect in the society? The answer is often unclear.

The easy part is to determine the date when the technology was invented. Ideographic writing first appeared in Mesopotamia around 3300 B.C. It came to other Middle Eastern societies

## Table 10-1

### Alphabetic Scripts

| type of writing | what people | when began | derived from which script |
|---|---|---|---|
| North Semitic | Semitic | 16th B.C. | Egyptian demotic |
| Phoenician | Phoenician | 13th B.C. | North Semitic |
| Hebrew (old) | Hebrew | 11th B.C. | North Semitic |
| Greek | Greek | 11th B.C. | Phoenician |
| Aramaic | Aramaeans | 10th B.C. | North Semitic |
| South Semitic | Yemen | 8th B.C. | North Semitic |
| Etruscan | Etruscan | 8th B.C. | Greek |
| Latin | Roman | 7th B.C. | Greek/ Etruscan |
| Brahmi | Indian | 6th B.C. | Aramaic |
| Hebrew (new) | Jewish | 3rd B.C. | Aramaic |
| Kharoshthi | Indian | 3rd B.C. | Aramaic |
| Pahlavi | Persian | 3rd B.C. | Aramaic |
| Nabataean | Nabataean | 2nd B.C. | Aramaic |
| Meroitic | Nubian | 2nd B.C. | Egyptian |
| Syriac | Syrian | 1st A.D. | Aramaic |
| Coptic | Egyptian | 2nd A.D. | Greek |
| Runic | Celtic | 3rd A.D. | Etruscan |
| Gupta | Indian | 4th A.D. | Brahmi |
| Armenian | Armenian | 5th A.D. | Aramaic |
| Arabic | Arab | 5th A.D. | Nabataean |
| Grantha | Indian | 5th A.D. | Gupta |
| Deva-nagari | Indian | 7th A.D. | Gupta |
| Tibetan | Tibetan | 7th A.D. | Gupta |
| Kavi | Javan | 8th A.D. | Grantha |
| Glagolitic | Moravian | 9th A.D. | Greek |
| Cyrillic | Slavic | 9th A.D. | Greek uncial |

Source: *Philosophical Library, Inc., New York*

and to China at various times during the 3rd and 2nd millennia B.C. Table 10-1 gives approximate dates when alphabetic scripts were introduced to societies around the world. The dates shown here are based on information in David Diringer's book, *The Alphabet*. Crude though they might be, this information provides a set of temporal parameters for the first two civilizations: Civ I could not have appeared in Egypt or Mesopotamia before the middle of the 4th millennium B.C. In India, China, and Crete, it came centuries later. Civ II could not have appeared in Phoenicia or Palestine before the 13th to 11th centuries B.C., in Italy before the 8th century B.C., in India before the 6th century B.C., in Arabia before the 5th century A.D., or in Java before the 8th century A.D.

Robert Logan has estimated that "(i)t took about five hundred years for literacy to take hold of the Greek mind, and a similar period elapsed between the introduction and widespread use of literacy among the Hebrews." If alphabetic writing was introduced to the Hebrews and Greeks in the 11th century B.C., then this statement would imply that its cultural effect was first felt during the 6th century B.C. in Greece and Judaea. Solon, Pythagoras, Thales of Miletus, Heraclitus, Jeremiah, Ezekiel, and Second Isaiah are some who lived in that century.

A society's rate of literacy would be an indicator of how strongly written language affected its culture. People must know how to read and write before literature can have a direct impact. On the other hand, a literate elite can influence the views of many others without reading skills. Because their religion emphasized scripture, the ancient Hebrews may have been the first people to attain basic literacy. Only a small minority of Greeks in Socrates' time could read or write. A reading public arose for the first time during the Hellenistic period. The amount of literature available greatly increased in Aristotle's time and especially after Ptolemy I established the great library at Alexandria. At its peak, this library contained more than 700,000 scrolls. Starting with Latin translations of Greek writings, Roman aristocrats in the 3rd century B.C. began to assemble private libraries. The imperial bureaucracy employed numerous scribes for administrative purposes. When the western part of the Roman empire fell to Germanic invaders, this apparatus collapsed. With it went the need for writing. It is estimated that the literacy rate in Europe dropped to between 1 and 2 percent by the year 1000.

The Christian church kept European literacy alive through the "Dark Ages". In the 5th century A.D., the Benedictine abbot Cassiodorus ordered his monks to collect Greek and Latin manuscripts. Church administration continued to use written documents. The cathedral schools started by Charlemagne in the 9th century A.D. revived the tradition of scholarship. The need for books by university students, the emergence of law and other learned professions, and the translation of the Bible and other texts from Latin into popular languages caused literacy rates to climb sharply in the period between 1200 and 1400 A.D. Paper meanwhile became cheaper and more plentiful thanks to technologies imported from the Islamic world. However, the greatest spur to literacy was the invention of the printing press. By 1700 A.D., literacy rates in Europe had increased to between 30 and 40 percent. Universal elementary-school education brought the rate to above 50 percent in 1850, and above 90% in 1930.

| Table 10-2 Percentage of Literacy by Nation (reported 1983 or 1984) | |
|---|---|
| Nation | Literacy Rate |
| Japan | 100 |
| United Kingdom | 100 |
| Germany | 100 |
| Australia | 100 |
| U.S.S.R. | 100 |
| France | 99 |
| Italy | 97 |
| Canada | 96 |
| United States | 96 |
| Argentina | 96 |
| South Korea | 93 |
| Yugoslavia | 91 |
| Mexico | 90 |
| Colombia | 88 |
| Venezuela | 87 |
| Philippines | 86 |
| Vietnam | 84 |
| South Africa | 79 |
| Brazil | 78 |
| Turkey | 74 |
| Indonesia | 74 |
| Iran | 51 |
| Algeria | 49 |
| Egypt | 45 |
| Nigeria | 42 |
| Bangladesh | 33 |
| Pakistan | 26 |

*World Facts and Figures* by Victor Showers. Copyright 1989 John Wiley & Sons. Reprinted by permission of John Wiley & Sons.

UNESCO assumes that it takes four years of schooling to teach basic literacy skills. To meet that standard would require that a society reach a certain level of affluence and commitment to formal education. A UNESCO survey published in 1978 estimated that 70 percent of Africans, 60 percent of Indians and other residents of south Asia, and 30 percent of Latin Americans were illiterate in 1970. Rates of illiteracy were officially less than 5 percent among residents of North America, Europe, the Soviet Union, Japan and South Korea. Table 10-2 gives comparative literacy rates by nation in 1988.

To assess the cultural impact of technologies since printing, we must follow a different approach. Most technologies of electronic communication transmit their messages in spoken language. Nearly everyone can understand those messages without additional education. The question then becomes, instead of skills, how many people possess the equipment needed to receive its type of communication. For instance, the number of people owning radio sets indicates the potential size of the radio

Table 10-3

Rates of Telephones, Radios, and Televisions in Use in Several Countries

(rates per 1,000 inhabitants)

| nation | telephone | radio | television |
|--------|-----------|-------|------------|
| U.S.A. | 771 | 2042 | 790 |
| Canada | 668 | 761 | 463 |
| West Germany | 572 | 401 | 360 |
| Australia | 538 | 1300 | 423 |
| France | 537 | 859 | 375 |
| United Kingdom | 523 | 993 | 479 |
| Japan | 513 | 713 | 556 |
| Italy | 405 | 250 | 243 |
| Spain | 350 | 286 | 258 |
| South Korea | 149 | 451 | 178 |
| Yugoslavia | 123 | 238 | 303 |
| South Africa | 113 | 282 | 75 |
| U.S.S.R. | 107 | 514 | 308 |
| Argentina | 105 | 540 | 199 |
| Mexico | 86 | 291 | 111 |
| Brazil | 76 | 386 | 127 |
| Colombia | 73 | 141 | 105 |
| Turkey | 55 | 119 | 115 |
| Chile | 54 | 304 | 116 |
| Iran | 51 | 178 | 55 |
| Philippines | 15 | 45 | 26 |
| Egypt | 12 | 174 | 44 |
| Nigeria | 8 | 79 | 5 |
| Pakistan | 5 | 77 | 12 |
| China | 5 | 69 | 7 |
| India | 4 | 62 | 3 |
| Indonesia | 4 | 140 | 2 |
| Bangladesh | 2 | 8 | 2 |

*World Facts and Figures* by Victor Showers. Copyright 1989 John Wiley & Sons. Reprinted by permission of John Wiley & Sons.

audience, which, in turn, suggests the importance of radio to the culture. The same is true of television and personal computers. Table 10-3 compares percentages of radio and television ownership in several nations during 1988. While a majority of people in industrialized countries owned such devices, the rate dropped to less than 20 percent in nations such as China, India, Pakistan, Nigeria, and Bangladesh. Since literacy rates were higher in those nations, one would assume that many people read books and newspapers for relaxation. Alternatively, listening to the radio or watching television might be a communal experience.

Statistics showing annual sales of particular kinds of communication devices suggest their cultural impact upon societies in particular places and times. Tables 10-4 through 10-6 show the number of telephones, radio receivers, and television sets in use in the United States during certain years. In each case there was a period of "take off" in the sale and use of the device. For all its success at the 1876 Centennial Exhibition, the telephone experienced slow commercial development. Barely more than a million Americans subscribed to telephone service at the end of the 19th century. Then, because of a reform in rate charges, the service took off. Nearly one American in ten was connected to telephone service when World War I began. For radio, the take-off period occurred in the decade between 1923 and 1933. For television, it was during the 1950s. The technology had been ready for a decade but World War II upset the timetable of commercial exploitation. Cable-television subscriptions took off in the 1980s. Fifty nine percent of U.S. households

| Table 10-4 | |
|---|---|
| Telephones in Use in the United States, 1880 to 1975 | |
| (in thousands) | |
| year | telephones in use |
| 1880 | 60 |
| 1890 | 228 |
| 1895 | 340 |
| 1900 | 1,356 |
| 1905 | 4,127 |
| 1910 | 7,635 |
| 1915 | 10,524 |
| 1920 | 13,273 |
| 1925 | 16,875 |
| 1930 | 20,103 |
| 1940 | 21,928 |
| 1945 | 27,867 |
| 1950 | 43,709 |
| 1955 | 56,243 |
| 1960 | 74,342 |
| 1965 | 93,656 |
| 1970 | 120,218 |
| 1975 | 149,008 |

*International Historical Statistics*, Gale Research Co., 1983

Table 10-5

Radios in Use
in the United States,
1922 to 1975
(in thousands)

| year | sets in use |
|------|-------------|
| 1922 | 60 |
| 1924 | 1,250 |
| 1925 | 2,750 |
| 1927 | 6,750 |
| 1930 | 13,750 |
| 1933 | 19,250 |
| 1935 | 21,456 |
| 1940 | 28,500 |
| 1945 | 33,000 |
| 1950 | 41,000 |
| 1955 | 46,000 |
| 1960 | 50,000 |
| 1970 | 62,000 |
| 1975 | 73,000 |

*International Historical Statistics*, Gale Research Co., 1983

with television sets subscribed to cable in 1990, compared with 22.6 percent in 1980. For the personal computer, the first burst of sales occurred during the same decade. There were 2.3 million computers in use in 1980. That grew to 50 million in 1990, and 90 million in 1995.

Anecdotal and statistical evidence from Robert and Helen Lynd's *Middletown* suggests the impact of phonographs, telephones, motion pictures, and radio on life in a hypothetical mid-sized American community in the 1920s. The phonograph, which was still a curiosity in 1900, was then owned by 59 percent of American families. Twenty-three percent of working-class families had bought phonograph records in the preceding year. About 46 percent of "Middletown" families owned telephones, including most of its business class. Motion pictures had largely replaced live shows in the opera house, popular in the 1890s, and had cut into lodge attendance. Between half and three quarters of Middletown's population attended one or more movies in July 1923. About 12 percent of the business class and 6 percent of the working class owned radios. Radio listening was by then the most popular activity in homes, cutting into reading and movie going.

Table 10-6

Television Sets in Use
in the United States,
1947 to 1975
(in thousands)

| year | sets in use |
|------|-------------|
| 1947 | 14 |
| 1948 | 172 |
| 1949 | 940 |
| 1950 | 3,900 |
| 1951 | 10,000 |
| 1952 | 15,000 |
| 1953 | 20,000 |
| 1954 | 26,000 |
| 1955 | 31,000 |
| 1960 | 46,000 |
| 1965 | 53,000 |
| 1970 | 60,000 |
| 1975 | 73,000 |

*International Historical Statistics*, Gale Research Co., 1983

One notes that the lag time between the invention of a cultural technology and its implementation in society has progressively shortened with each civilization. Where alphabetic literacy took five hundred years to penetrate the Hebrew and Greek societies, more than half of Americans owned phonographs within fifty years after this device was invented. Personal computers appear to be gaining acceptance at an even faster rate. In 1998, about 41 percent of U.S. households owned home computers. This degree of market penetration represents phenomenal growth for a technology which began in the late 1970s. It took radio 37 years to reach 50 million households; television, 23 years; and cable television, 15 years. Experts predict that the Internet will take another five to seven years to reach that level.

Another anomalous situation concerns the timing of the third epoch. If this epoch began with the invention of printing, one would expect to find a change in the culture at a later time. Instead, a rather dramatic cultural change took place in the century **preceding** Gutenberg's invention. The 14th and 15th centuries are considered to cover the period of the Italian Renaissance, yet Gutenberg printed his first book in Germany during the second half of the 15th century. Clearly the invention of printing did not cause the Renaissance. Some have proposed a connection between the two events on the basis of reinforcing previous trends. Robert Logan has suggested that, unlike the revivals of European learning which took place in the 9th and 12th centuries A.D., "(t)he printing press allowed the Italian Renaissance to sustain itself ... (so that) ... the quattrocento revival could continue to gain momentum."

## The Organic Life Cycle

Civilizations, as we said, are like living creatures. They have a birth-like beginning, a period of youthful growth, a prolonged period of maturity and strength, and a time of stagnation followed by terminal decline. Their birth would be associated with the reception of a new cultural technology. The youthful phase would occur when this technology, taking effect, starts to realize its creative potential by producing new forms of expression. New institutions of power are associated with them. The period of mature strength would be associated with empires which have grown from these institutions. The time of stagnation and terminal decline would involve the inevitable corruption of empires as they become preoccupied with their power and engage in coercive acts to protect it. At each point in their life cycle, civilizations resemble individual persons going through a similar process of life.

There is a dichotomy between the creative and adult phases of this development. An individual human being, while growing up, changes rapidly during the first fifteen to twenty years of life and then settles into a relatively unchanging physical state for most of life's remaining years. So civilizations experience times of unusually intense and fruitful creative activity when new technologies, new values, new thoughts, and new artistic and social forms are introduced. Such times are followed by much longer periods of stability when existing patterns are maintained. We tend to look back sentimentally upon the years of adolescence and childhood when critical growths took place within a relatively short period of time. Yet, it was for the sake of adulthood that the child underwent growth. So the phase of empire, though relatively uncreative, must be seen as the culminating stage of civilizations. Both the periods of fast and slow development are important to their history.

Oswald Spengler expressed this historical dichotomy in terms of "culture" and "civilization". Culture described society in a period of creative, youthful change. Civilization referred to the same society when it had devolved into a static condition "consist(ing) in a progressive exhaustion of forms that have become inorganic or dead." We use the terms "culture" and "civilization" interchangeably while upholding Spengler's distinction. The time of Spenglerian "culture" is indeed special, coming, as it does, right after major turning points in world history. Its creative energy holds the promise of empires to come.

When a new cultural technology is first introduced, it comes with such a rush of novelty and excitement that a burst of creative expression is released. The classic works of a culture are created in this environment. It is no accident, then, that the unsurpassed prose of Biblical writings or of Plato's or Aristotle's philosophical discourses (classics of CivII) were produced at a time when alphabetic scripts were still fresh. Likewise, wrote Toynbee, regarding CivIII: "When the vernaculars won the upper hand completely, the first effect was to give license for an exuberance that provided a hotbed for genius. An example of this in prose is Rabelais (1494-1553) and in poetry Shakespeare (1564-1616)." Besides the switch from Latin to vernacular languages, the print revolution was then sweeping across northern Europe. As for CivIV, classic films such as *Gone with the Wind* or *Wizard of Oz* were produced in the decade after motion pictures acquired sound. Elvis Presley and Buddy Holly sang "golden oldies" in the decade when recording artists first appeared on television.

Shakespeare

It may be that we only think that these pioneering artists were the best. Alternatively, it may be that others as talented were prevented from following in their uninhibited footsteps by naysaying critics attached to their cult who cut others down to size. Or, perhaps, the early original works, once expressed, exhausted the logical possibilities inherent in the medium so that subsequent works in the same vein seemed imitative. Marshall McLuhan has written that the different cultural media "evoke in us unique ratios of sense perceptions ... (which) ... alter the way we think and act ... Those who experience the first onset of a new technology, whether it be alphabet or radio, respond most emphatically because the new sense ratios set up at once by the technological dilution of eye or ear present men with a surprising new world which evokes a vigorous new 'closure' or novel pattern of interplay, among all of the senses together." Intuitively, we can associate these times of cultural fruitfulness with the youthful vitality of a new culture. They are when a civilization is entering its stage of daring, exuberant adolescence. The energies then pouring into creative expression serve to make a clean break with the previous civilization.

## Golden Cities

Historical change does not take place in the abstract. We tend to remember the start of a new civilization by its association with a "golden city" located in a time and place where the changes were culturally most productive. Most historians would agree, for example, that the Greek city-state of Athens presented an extraordinary spectacle of intellectual and artistic brilliance during the time when Pericles was its political leader. In the 15th century A.D., the Italian city of Florence was the center of a similarly lush cultural growth. Cosimo de' Medici, and his grandson, Lorenzo, were, like Pericles, prodigious statesmen and patrons of the arts. While Athenian culture of the 5th century B.C. excelled in philosophy, architecture, sculpture, and drama, Re-

the acropolis in Athens

naissance Florence is known for its architecture, sculpture, and painting. These two golden cities each arose in the period of youth for a new civilization. The cultural florescence associated with Periclean Athens marks this time in the life of CivII, as the Florentine Renaissance culture does for the following civilization.

Is there an equivalent city to represent the florescent culture of CivIV? Because this civilization was introduced by a number of inventions over a long period of time, one hardly knows where to spot its beginning. One might say, however, that the decade of the 1920s in the United States was a time of intoxicating involvement with new media. The first commercial radio station began broadcasting at the start of this decade. Phonograph machines blared music of the "Jazz Age." Paris and New York City were both cultural meccas in the 1920s. A bevy of famous writers graced the literary scene while avant-garde art found eager patrons. Keeping in mind the electronic nature of this culture, though, a better candidate for the role of "golden city" in the fourth historical epoch might be Hollywood, which is a kind of virtual city specializing in film entertainment. Or, perhaps, centers of popular music like New Orleans, Memphis, or Nashville, or New York's "Radio City", would fit that role. As for the first and fifth epochs, we know that the city of Babylon in Hammurabi's day was a culturally fruitful place and that the revolution in personal computers was hatched in a place called "Silicon Valley".

## Signs of Quickening Culture

Futurists are often proclaiming the dawn of a new age, based upon one sign or another. This book regards the introduction of new cultural technologies as a prime indicator of historical change. The times of technological innovation are reasonably clear. Greater uncertainty surrounds the period of implementation, when a technology achieves cultural impact. Even so, historians have a rough idea of when new civilizations appear from the introduction of the successive cultural technologies in particular places and times. The early periods in the development of civilizations we say are times of "quickening culture". They are times of cultural florescence, when the Shakespeares of the age briefly shine. They are times when golden cities like Athens and Florence appear in their prime. Since the major cultural technologies have penetrated the earth's societies on a staggered timetable, it may not be possible to say that a single period of years encompasses the time of cultural quickening associated with each technology. Each appears in some societies sooner than in others. Their times of invention and subsequent adoption on a broad scale vary considerably from place to place.

That said, we can predict significant historical change through the appearance of a major new cultural technology such as alphabetic writing. Such an event portends the birth of new civilizations. Particular periods of time will be stamped as times of cultural quickening when civilizations are entering their formative stage. They are set apart from periods of inconsequential fluctuation and slow growth accompanying civilizations in a later phase. Accordingly, let us assume that:

- the period of cultural quickening associated with CivI occurred in Egypt and Mesopotamia during a centuries-long period following 3100 B.C.; in India, five hundred years later; and , in China, a thousand years later.

- the period of cultural quickening associated with CivII occurred in Syria, Palestine, Greece, and India between 600 and 300 B.C.

- the period of cultural quickening associated with CivIII occurred in western Europe between 1400 and 1600 A.D.

- the period of cultural quickening associated with CivIV occurred in the United States and other industrialized nations between 1870 and 1970 A.D.

- the period of cultural quickening associated with CivV has been taking place in the industrialized nations since 1990.

We are presuming here to identify special times in world history which lead to new civilizations while other times do not. Historians could cite many cases of cultural florescence during the last six thousand years. Not all have been associated with a change in civilizations. Hammurabi's Babylon reached a cultural peak more than a millennium after civilization first appeared in that region. Christian scholarship and art flourished in Ireland between the 6th and 8th centuries A.D. as did Islamic culture a short time later. Then, of course, we have the 17th century revolution in western science, the 18th century Enlightenment, the Industrial Revolution of the early 19th century, and so on. It seems, in other words, that cultural creativity has been exercised in every period since civilization began. Yet, we are claiming a special historical distinction for places and times which followed the introduction of a new cultural technology. Were Athens and Florence, in fact, so unusual compared with Baghdad, Córdoba, Paris, and Edinburgh?

The period of empire is easy to recognize; one spots it for sheer size. The splendor of imperial Rome or China made an undeniable impression upon human consciousness then and now. A less evident situation is the seed of empire. It can easily be mistaken for something else. If we find ourselves in the midst of unsettling cultural change, we are interested to know whether the latest trend will turn out be an ephemeral event or one of history's turning points. We want to be able to recognize the genuine article of future greatness when it appears in humble origin. There may be signs marking such times of true change. There may be particular circumstances denoting the infancy of new civilizations. Besides coming at a time soon after the introduction of a new cultural technology, the quickening phase of a culture may be characterized by the following conditions:

(1) Such a period is associated with a place of political and cultural parochialism and a thriving commerce. A plurality of small states contend for dominance.

(2) This period also produces important innovations in mathematics and commercial practice.

(3) It is a time of expanded geographical horizons when perceptions of a wider world broaden understanding.

## An Environment of Parochial Contentiousness
## and Commercial Contact

Arnold Toynbee has noted that the cities of Athens in the 5th century B.C. and Florence in the 15th century A.D. shared, besides cultural brilliance, a similar geopolitical condition. Both were independent city-states having populations in a range of 50,000 to 150,000 persons. As relatively small political units, these states were vulnerable to military attack by larger neighbors. They also engaged in fratricidal wars with other states of comparable size. Having cooperated at the start of the 5th century B.C. to defeat invading Persian forces under Xerxes II, Athens and other Greek cities fought amongst themselves in the bloody Peloponnesian war and then for much of the next century until they were subdued by Philip II of Macedon. A similar situation existed in Renaissance Italy. Caught in the struggle between Popes and Holy Roman Emperors, the north Italian city-states enjoyed two centuries of independence before the region was invaded by France in 1494. Like their Greek predecessors, the Italian city states were unable or unwilling to form political associations on a larger scale. Their fate was to lose their independence to the more powerful monarchies of France, Austria, and Spain.

This pattern of contending states fits other societies that existed on the brink of a new civilization. It describes the warring Sumerian states before they were unified in the 24th century B.C. It fits the pattern of the Chinese kingdoms that were struggling for supremacy in the period when Lao-tse and Confucius lived. Northern India was split into a number of warring kingdoms at the time of Mahavira's and Buddha's religious activity. The kingdom of Magadha, where Buddha achieved enlightenment, won the military competition in the first half of the 5th century B.C. Toynbee saw a parallel between what the Greeks and Italians faced at the time of their cultural ascendancy and the situation of western Europeans in the early 20th century. The common situation was that a plurality of contending parochial states with advanced cultures were losing their political position because of failure to form a government large enough to withstand threatening foreign empires. What Macedon and Rome did to the Greeks and what European monarchies did to the Italians, the United States and Soviet Union were doing to the nations of western Europe in Toynbee's day: dwarfing them politically and militarily.

The point is that worldly pressures may inspire creative thinking. Extraordinary needs elicit unusual cultural and social solutions. In the 5th century B.C., European Greeks were under stress from the Persian empire. The Athenians and their allies repelled the Persian invasion through a valiant effort. The next half century of Greek history was culturally brilliant. Renaissance Italy faced a similar situation in pressures exerted upon western Christendom by the Ottoman Turks. In 1453 A.D., Turkish armies captured Constantinople, the last stronghold of the Byzantine Roman empire. Since the Ottoman empire blocked overland trade routes to the East, European merchants were forced to pursue alternative transportation by sea. That led to the Portuguese and Spanish voyages of discovery and European colonization of the New World. The condition of civic particularity in Italy and Greece was intellectually stimulating. The small-scale communities brought diverse cultures into close range of each other, which inspired creative comparisons of various sorts. Athens, Sparta, and the other Greek cities had their own laws and social systems. Their citizens were intensely patriotic, considering foreigners to be barbarians. A similar situation existed in Renaissance Italy.

Another stimulation comes through foreign trade. Athens in its prime was a bustling center of seaborne trade with communities along the Mediterranean and Black seas. The Greek colonies in Ionia, first to distinguish themselves in science and philosophy, were also first to develop a thriving commerce. An economic revolution occurred on the Greek mainland in the 5th century B.C. as neighboring peoples resisted the Greeks' practice of dispatching their surplus populations to colonies. With colonial expansion blocked, the Greeks had to find ways to support a growing number of people on a fixed amount of land. Their solution was to switch from mixed farming to support lo-

cal populations to a system of specialized agriculture that produced goods for export. The Greeks exported products such as
wine and olive oil and received grain and dried fish in exchange.
The black- or red-painted vases which we admire for their artistic design were export items that helped the Athenians to balance their trade.

In the 15th century A.D., northern Italy was bustling with
commerce. Italian bankers prospered from money-lending activities related to the frequent wars in this region. Venetian merchants controlled the European trade in oriental spices and silk.
Italy and other parts of Europe had sustained severe depopulation from the Bubonic plague which occurred in the mid 14th
century. At least a third of the people died. The result was to
create a labor shortage which drove up wages and left farm land
without a means of cultivation. The price of grain dropped due
to shrinking demand. In response, Italian landowners discontinued cultivation of marginally productive land, improved irrigation, and began growing specialized crops with greater profit
potential. In textiles manufacturing, low-profit goods such as
woolen cloth were abandoned in favor of more expensive silk
products. During the Renaissance period, northern Italy became
a supplier of luxury goods.

We know that the Sumerians who invented writing were a
commercially active people. The Egyptians had extensive trade
relations with peoples in southern Arabia, Nubia, Syria, and
Crete. Nineveh and Babylon, as well, were important centers of
trade. The two centuries in India which preceded the rise of Buddhism were a time of brisk expansion in manufacturing and maritime trade. Merchants traded in commodities such as jewelry,
spices, cloth, and dried fish along the southwest coast of India
as well as in Babylon, Arabia, and Egypt. The Egyptian city of
Alexandria, known as a place of religious ferment, carried on an
active trade with India and other places. Mecca was a commercial hub for Arabic peoples in the early 7th century A.D. Prior to
his religious calling, Mohammed led caravans to trade in Yemen
and Syria as agent for his wealthy wife. So it would seem that a
commercial environment does not preclude other kinds of interests; it may actually spur intellectual or spiritual questionings.

## Mathematical and Commercial Innovations

The periods of cultural quickening were also times when new techniques appeared. In addition to the technologies of written language and electronic communication, each of these periods brought forth discoveries in the field of mathematics. Each produced advances in commercial practice. The Sumerians developed a system of installment purchases. They used barley and silver as a medium of exchange. Professional moneylenders took advantage of the farmers by lending them silver to buy seed and demanding repayment of the loan at harvest time when the market price of barley was low. The ancient Egyptians developed many of our basic concepts of arithmetic and geometry including fractions. They used this mathematical knowledge to restore landmarks wiped out by floods. Egyptian plane geometry was based on generalization from particular cases.

A novel feature of the period between 600 and 400 B.C. was the use of minted coins to facilitate trade. This practice began in Lydia around 600 B.C. Lydia was a small kingdom in Turkey which had conquered most of the Asian Greek city-states. Its last king, Croesus, made the mistake of attacking the Persians, who defeated him in battle and annexed his kingdom. Before that disastrous event, Croesus had issued the first minted gold coins based on the local standard of Phocaea, a captive Greek city. Their use spread quickly through the Persian and Greek worlds. The advantage of minted coins was that the coin bore an official inscription certifying that its gold content was of a stated quantity and degree of purity. Trading became more convenient than under the previous system where the monetary medium had to be weighed and tested, or, in the case of cattle, fed. Greek thinkers of this period used deductive reasoning to increase mathematical knowledge. Thales of Miletus, who imported Egyptian geometry to Greece, was among the first to study relationships between the different parts of a geometric figure. Pythagoras, known for the Pythagorean theorem, also discovered that simple numerical ratios in the length of vibrating strings produces harmonious music.

The third period, between 1400 and 1600 A.D., saw the rapid growth of towns in Europe. They were centers of commerce and manufacturing. The medieval system of tenant farming had been replaced by a system of contract labor. Guilds regulated occupational work in the cities. Merchants' associations promoted exports of local products. New financial arrangements were developed to facilitate trade expeditions to distant places. The joint-stock company pooled the resources of several investors for large-scale enterprise. Marine insurance covered the risks of loss at sea. Banks took deposits from individuals, cashed bonds, and issued letters of credit. A Venetian monk, Fra Luca Pacioli, is credited with having invented the modern system of double-entry bookkeeping in 1494 A.D.

Several mathematical concepts and techniques which had been developed in India came to Europe via the Moslems in this period. Algebra was introduced into Italy in 1202 A.D. by Leonardo of Pisa. Arabic numerals, introduced to Europe in the 11th century A.D., were so called because Europeans acquired them from a book written in India which was translated into Arabic. The Arabs themselves never used this numbering system. There was some resistance to it because the symbol for zero (0) was easily confused with 6 and 9. However, printing removed that visual ambiguity and the new system prevailed. The technique of long division, which began to be used in the 15th century, first appeared in Calandri's arithmetic published in Florence in 1492 A.D. Mathematical practitioners of the 15th century introduced the modern notations for plus (+), minus (-), and percent (%).

from Calandri's *Arithmetica*

The fourth historical epoch, beginning in the second half of the 19th century, established the modern practice of retail shopping. The department store, which first appeared in Paris in 1852, revolutionized the way that commercial products were sold to customers. The products exhibited in store displays were sold at a fixed price. This ended the traditional haggling over prices in the market. Because retail markups were low, profits depended upon attracting prospective customers into the stores. The merchants placed paid advertisements in newspapers to interest the public in their products. Mathematical discoveries during this period challenged long-held assumptions about space and time. Non-Euclidian systems of geometry were developed by Lobachevsky, Riemann, and others during the 19th century. Albert Einstein challenged Newtonian physics with his theory of relativity. Quantum mechanics questioned spatial assumptions of experimental science. Boolean logic, formulated in 1854, provided a theoretical basis for digital processing.

## Perceptions of a Wider World

While cultural technologies are a force to shape historical experience, civilizations also change with new perceptions of the world. Societies can expand their mental horizons both by seeing the world in a different way and by traveling to previously unknown places. Historically, the scattered peoples of the world became more aware of each other as they had increased contact. Improved techniques of transportation and communication have made humanity aware of a larger world than what they knew before. Starting with their immediate environment, human beings have come to see a progressively enlarged territory supporting human culture. The Greeks called this "Oikoumenê", which means the "inhabited" part of the world. World history includes, among other things, the process of "discovering" previously unknown places on earth and the people inhabiting these places, so that the definition of Oikoumenê is broadened.

The turning points of world history have taken place in times of discovering this broader world. Once separate peoples who came in contact with each other enjoyed the stimulating effect of that experience. The earliest Sumerian, Egyptian, Indian, and Chinese societies were limited to a few city-states. None had more than a vague idea that other peoples existed. Archeologists have found no reference to Egypt in Sumerian writings before the 15th century, B.C. The separate Aztec and Inca societies were unaware of each other when the Spaniards arrived in the 16th century, A.D. With the dawning of Civl came an expansion of geographical horizons. The first Pharaonic dynasty, which united Lower and Upper Egypt, brought political and cultural unity to a land extending hundreds of miles along the Nile river. Sumerian society originally consisted of a dozen small communities within a hundred miles' radius of each other. When King Urukagina of Lagash unified this region in the 24th century B.C., he boasted of an empire stretching "from sea to sea" - from the head of the Persian Gulf to the Mediterranean sea.

Herodotus' view of the world    (438 B.C.)

The period between 600 and 400 B.C. was a time for Mediterranean peoples to explore the world. While Aramaean merchants traveled east on overland routes, sailors from Carthage visited lands along the shores of the Atlantic ocean. Carthaginian traders obtained copper from Spanish mines and tin from southwest England. In 520 B.C., a Carthaginian captain named Hanno set forth on a voyage along the west coast of Africa, reaching present-day Gambia. There his crew collected specimens of plant and animal life including some chimpanzees. Some believe that a group of Phoenician sailors commissioned by Pharaoh Necho circumnavigated the African continent in the 7th century B.C. During this period, the Greeks established colonies in southern France, Italy, Sicily, Libya, Turkey, and the Ukraine. Greek tourists frequently visited the ruins of Egypt. Herodotus, a geographer and historian of the 5th century B.C., believed the inhabited world to be a mass of land bounded, on its four corners, by India, Ethiopia, Iberia (Spain), and Scythia (Ukraine), which was penetrated by two great seas.

Herodotus' geography encompassed three of the four great Old World civilizations - China's alone being excluded. It, of course, also excluded the New World civilizations. The next epoch brought both of those areas into the scope of the known world. When the Mongols attacked Poland and Hungary in the 13th century, A.D., it brought Europe in contact with a political empire that extended eastward to the Pacific Ocean. A young Venetian named Marco Polo traveled to Peking with his father and uncle where they were warmly received by the Mongol emperor. After spending seventeen years in China, Marco Polo returned to Italy where he wrote a book about his adventures. The desire for oriental riches and the opportunity to convert numerous heathen people to Christianity inspired Columbus' attempt to reach China and Japan by sailing west. His voyage across the Atlantic Ocean led to the discovery of a new continent. Columbus mistakenly supposed that he had reached India. Geographical knowledge also expanded with the Portuguese navigator Bartholomeu Dias' voyage around the tip of southern Africa in 1488. Another Portuguese captain, Vasco da Gama, reached Calcutta by this route ten years later.

Ferdinand Magellan, a Portuguese captain employed by Spain, commanded the first voyage around the world. In September 1519, he set sail for South America with five ships. It took a year to find a passage to the Pacific ocean around southern Argentina. The expedition next headed straight across that ocean to the Philippine islands where Magellan was killed. One of his ships, the Victoria, continued to travel west through the Indian ocean and around Africa and, in September 1522, it arrived back in Portugal. This voyage demonstrated both that the earth was round, though larger than what Columbus had thought, and that it included a second hemisphere. Such explorations put all the earth's major societies in touch for the first time. In the same year that Magellan set sail, Hernando Cortés overthrew the Aztec empire in Mexico with a group of four hundred armed men. French explorers probed the interior waterways of North America, seeking a "northwest passage" to the Pacific similar to what Magellan had found in the south.

When CivIV began in the mid 19th century, there was renewed interest in geographical exploration. The Explorer's Club of London sponsored an expedition to equatorial Africa to discover the true source of the Nile. Richard Burton and John Speke discovered Lake Tanganyika in 1858. Speke went on to reach Lake Nyanza, now believed to be the Nile's source. The Mormon trek to Utah and the California Gold Rush of 1849 brought arid lands in the western part of North America in touch with the eastern population centers. Australia and New Zealand received an influx of white immigration. Admiral Matthew Perry's visit to Japan in 1853 brought that island society out of its self-imposed isolation. The completion of the Trans-Siberian railroad in 1905 opened up the interior of northwest Asia to Russian colonization. In some of the earth's last unexplored territories, Robert E. Peary traveled to the North Pole in 1909. Rival teams of explorers, led by Robert Scott and Roald Amundsen, raced to the South Pole in 1911-12. Amundsen's team was the winner. Scott and his four colleagues perished on the return trip from the Pole but left diaries.

Humanity has since moved into a new era of geophysical discovery. Advancements made in theoretical physics early in the 20th century have made people aware of new worlds at the extremities of physical magnitude. They perceived an atomic structure with protons and electrons in the tiniest particles of matter. They witnessed the destructive power of energy released from atoms when the U.S. Government exploded two atomic bombs over Japanese cities during World War II. The German V-1 and V-2 rockets used to drop bombs on English cities in that war progressed to the development of intercontinental ballistic missiles (ICBMs) which, equipped with nuclear warheads, stocked strategic arsenals during the Cold War. People living in these times were aware of how dangerously small the earth had become. Missiles launched from another hemisphere could obliterate their own city in less than an hour's time. However, the same type of missile helped to launch the space age. Rivalry between the two military superpowers, begun with the launching of Sputnik, led to a series of manned expeditions to the Moon and unmanned space probes to several planets.

The physical exposure to new worlds stretches the mind. This experiences brings forth new conceptions which might not otherwise have appeared. Because Greek intellectuals were familiar with cities besides their own, they could intelligently discuss the relative merit of different forms of government. Plato was able to imagine an ideal society as described in the *Republic*. The discovery of America inspired Sir Thomas More in 1516 to write *Utopia*; it suggested to him the possibility of a world better than his own. In 1948, the astronomer Fred Hoyle suggested that if someone could take a photograph of the earth from outer space, that image would change men's minds as never before. His prediction was fulfilled when such a photograph was taken during the Apollo flights to the Moon. The

earth viewed from space

picture of our own planet, a bluish white-streaked sphere suspended in the darkness of space, has been credited with inspiring the environmental movement. Arthur Clarke has predicted that the colonization of space will have an even greater impact upon human thinking.

## Chapter Eleven

# INTIMATIONS OF
# A FIFTH CIVILIZATION

### Shape of the Computer Age

As humanity approaches the end of the second millennium A.D., three civilizations have passed into world history, a fourth has reached the stage of maturity, and a fifth appears now on the horizon. Since this fifth civilization is still in its infancy, we do not know what its epoch will bring except that computers will be the defining cultural technology. Our expectations of this new civilization are based on analogy with other civilizations whose histories are known. They are based on past events and present trends and on reasonable projections from them. But there is also a part of the history which cannot be known at this time. Predictions of the future are notoriously inaccurate. Be forewarned that the discussion in the remainder of this chapter will attempt that very thing.

In making our historical argument, we assume that the appearance of a new dominant cultural technology - in this case, computer technology - means that a new civilization is about to emerge. Each new civilization produces new institutions in society as its sectors become further differentiated. While their functions may also have existed in earlier times, they become better organized and are incorporated within the society's power structure. The new civilization brings a new set of values, beliefs, and models of personality. There is a flow of events from previous civilizations. There are points of conflict. Values and ideas that are dominant at the beginning of the historical epoch may be overtaken by their opposite as it comes to an end.

### The Nature of Computers and Related Projections

If the new civilization will be shaped by computers, then the direction of events may be related to the nature of this shaping technology. In that regard, one can make the following statements about computers:

• Computers can perform mathematical or logical calculations with great accuracy and speed. They can handle scientific computations or business recordkeeping functions with greater proficiency than human clerks or engineers could using mechanical calculators and sheets of paper. Certain calculations become possible which would otherwise have been too difficult to make in a reasonable time.

• Computers have the ability to keep track of numerous facts about individual persons and make lists of individuals who share certain characteristics.

• Computers can communicate with other computers over telephone lines. They can access information in a limitless number of files.

- Computers can store visual and aural images and manipulate these images in desired ways. The altered images can create the illusion of an imaginary scene.

- As computer technology progresses, its cognitive capabilities may approach those of the human brain. Man's position in this world may be challenged by an equally intelligent creature of his own making.

The implications of these capabilities are many. If the cost of computers is compared with the cost of human workers who perform the same task, employers may decide to substitute investment in machines for hiring people. That decision may impact employment and social conditions. If computers can store and analyze information about individuals, that means that organizations can locate individuals more quickly and easily. More efficient marketing campaigns become possible. If computers can communicate with many other computers, the dissemination of information is greatly increased. Linked computers amount to another communications medium. If computers can create new visual and aural images, then creative expression can go beyond sense impressions captured on film or tape. This expands the possibilities of communicating for educational, business, or entertainment purposes. Finally, if computer intelligence rivals that of human beings, then the computer becomes potentially either a greatly upgraded servant or master of the human species. Human dominance of the earth is threatened. The world of science fiction comes into view.

## Employment Implications

When business firms first embraced computer technology in the 1950s, the term "automation" was used to describe its application to industrial processes. That word conjured up the image of factories which operated on automatic pilot and did not require human labor. Social theorists then wondered how human beings might find employment if the old-style jobs disappeared. At its worst, the age of computerization might bring mass unemployment and poverty. At its best, it might lead to a society which could afford to support people without working. Proponents of the more hopeful scenario foresaw that government might redirect the wealth achieved by industrial progress toward the masses of people in an expanded welfare state. Income would be disconnected from work. Another possibility was that labor unions would continue to agitate for higher wages and shorter working hours. Even if machines assumed a portion of that work which human beings once performed, human workers would still be needed in other areas of productive enterprise and could command a healthy wage on that basis. Opponents argued that such adjustments were unnecessary. On its own, the economy would develop new kinds of output to keep everyone productively engaged.

By the close of the 20th century, the following picture has emerged: Business has continued to apply computer technology at a fast pace. Corresponding improvements in labor productivity have taken place. These developments have not brought a collapse of employment. In the United States, the current level of unemployment is low by historic standards. In western Europe, expectations of employment shortfalls have been realized to a greater degree. American labor unions have largely abandoned their campaign for shorter working hours. The overtime premium, meant to discourage working longer hours, has instead become a kind of wage supplement eagerly sought by some workers. As a result, average working hours have lately increased in the United States. The idea that the government would support people without working caught on for a time, but this practice, too, has lately lost steam. Welfare reform, forcing single mothers to seek paid work, has won bipartisan support. Paid retirement continues to persuade many older persons to withdraw from the work force, but its funding mechanisms are a perennial problem.

The salvation of employment has been continued growth of Gross National Product. Productivity increases have not meant growing joblessness because dollar-denominated output has also increased. Yet, although employment numbers remain strong, wage gains for most workers have not kept pace with the gains achieved in previous years. Some in upper-level managerial and professional positions have done well while a large segment of the work force is stuck in low-wage jobs. As for the growing output, a declining share consists of goods and services which are actually useful to people. Many areas of expanding economic activity could be characterized as waste. The gambling craze which has hit the United States produces a few big winners and some prosperity in communities near the casinos, but otherwise impoverishes individuals. The drug epidemic and war on drugs contribute to an atmosphere of lawlessness combined with increased job opportunities for police officers and corrections officials. Ours is an economy increasingly driven by lax credit policies, sweepstakes promotions, the conversion of holidays into times to hawk merchandise, and excessive litigation and medical treatment.

## Modeling the Natural World

Computers have been used to model the natural world. Scientific knowledge is expressed in the form of mathematical equations that express relationships in nature. To become useful, this knowledge must be applied to real situations. Computer users in the scientific community have developed techniques of simulating natural conditions by observing and measuring conditions in various places and assigning numerical values to spatial locations for the relevant variables. For instance, data pertaining to temperature, humidity, and wind velocity, collected in several places, can be assembled in the computer to create the picture of an approaching thunderstorm. Calculation of scientific equations helps to predict how these various elements will interact and show how, in its entirety, the storm will develop over a period of time. Weather predictions, in turn, give advance warning of dangerous conditions. The damage can be minimized by taking timely action. Powerful computers are needed to record the large quantities of data and make the calculations in time to furnish a useful result.

Much scientific experimentation pertains to the worlds of the very large or very small. To make sense of events on that scale, the computer must convert mathematical data into visual images that will suggest something to human intelligence. Astronomers, for instance, have collected a wealth of data from electromagnetic radiation coming from distant places in the cosmos. Events which take place in this realm happen too slowly to register a perceptible change. The computer can speed up the process to show what will become visible after many years. Some of this information can be used to test theories of how the universe might have originated. There is an equally compelling need for structural models to make sense of phenomena on the submicroscopic level. If it were not for supercomputers, the emerging science of genetics could not absorb all the information that has become available about the chemical structure of the DNA and RNA molecules. These molecules, which govern all life processes, contain millions of genes in a particular sequence.

Computer simulations can demonstrate the effect of changes in a structural model much more easily and cheaply than if tests were performed on a physical model. They have revolutionized the design of commercial products ranging from jet aircraft to tooth brushes. Industrial designers once had to fit physical prototypes with sensing devices to measure stress and strain. Now they can observe stress changes with a few clicks of the keyboard as they play with a computer model. When the MacGregor Golf Company wanted to find the best design for a new golf club made of titanium, they tested a simulation on a Cray Y-MP supercomputer. The result was that additional slots and teeth were cut to stiffen the club and improve its aerodynamics. The automobile industry has used computer simulations to conduct crash tests on cars. Dow Chemical has used computers to test the absorbency of disposable diapers. Aircraft manufacturers observe the flow of air around variously shaped objects shown on a computer screen to pick a shape that minimizes turbulence. Computer models can be viewed as if in three-dimensional space.

They can be rotated or displayed in a way which reveals their interior structure.

The new technology of Geographic Information Systems (GIS) embeds computerized information in maps. Each geographical location is identified not only by its spatial coordinates but by topological features and nonphysical characteristics such as ownership or political jurisdiction. The computer's ability to combine information allows maps to be drawn with differently colored areas to represent significant conditions. For instance, a GIS cartographer might show in red all parcels of land in Lafayette County, Mississippi, used primarily for farming which were owned by persons over 50 years of age. Presumably a map of this sort might interest a salesman who specialized in selling products to elderly farmers. Algorithms can be written to direct an automobile at a satellite-detected location to a particular street address. Orbiting satellites equipped with cameras sensitive to radiation of various wavelengths can send data back to earth which indicates the type of vegetation found in particular regions. Special-purpose maps can be created from this information to illustrate, for instance, the effect of drought in nations which furnish certain agricultural commodities.

The graphic capability of computers depends upon digitalized information which can be manipulated to produce various effects. In that respect, it differs from earlier technologies which transformed visual images into electromagnetic impulses without changing the image. Computer graphics have cut the cost of film production while greatly expanding the range of visual possibilities. Computers can create images of objects that never existed. Cartoon characters can be "morphed" into human actors, and vice versa. Realistic-looking scenery can be created for imaginary situations such as the destruction of entire cities or warfare conducted in outer space. Some of today's most popular films depend heavily upon computer animation. Action adventures such as *Terminator II* and *Independence Day* have dazzled audiences with vistas once scarcely imaginable. Daniel Hillis, a former computer-industry executive working at Disney, has said: "Just as the space program was the big driver of (computer) technology at one time, the new driver is the entertainment industry."

## Selling by Computer

Computers have transformed the arts of advertising and selling commercial products. Their ability to collect and analyze data pertaining to individual customer preferences has changed the paradigm of advertising strategy. David L. Milenthal, chairman of HMS Partners, explained that the purpose of advertising was previously to strengthen brand name or "to develop a far-reaching, creative brand personality for our products and services. Once that personality was developed and securely 'branded' into the consumer's consciousness, we would use whatever funds were left to develop slightly more focused messages..." Now computer data bases allow advertisers to "identify and define individual customers", especially those who tend to spend more money. "We are moving from the era of shotgun-style 'mass marketing'," said Milenthal, "into a new millennium of 'customerization' in which we have finally unlocked the key to actually knowing - not just predicting - the message and combination of communication vehicles that can best reach our clients' customers."

The new marketing approach is driven by two requirements. First, the message must be honed to suit the prospective customers' individual preferences. Second, the subsequent marketing effort must involve enough people for the marketer to be able to take advantage of economies of scale in communicating with customers. The only way to meet these conflicting requirements is to identify narrowly focused personality types within a large customer pool. Sophisticated marketers with access to computer data bases can pull off this feat. Banks, utilities, telemarketers, direct-mail specialists, and other businesses having a large customer base are the types of firms which make use of customer-profiling techniques. The average American receives 553 pieces of unsolicited or "junk" mail each year from organizations that use targeted mailing lists. Each dollar spent in direct-mail solicitation typically brings back ten dollars in sales.

This approach is twice as effective as spending for television commercials. Therefore, the volume of junk mail is expected to triple in the next decade. To be successful, however, the direct-mail advertiser must pay attention to detail in designing the letters and, above all, mail to the right list. Skilled analysis of computer data provides the information needed to do that well.

Fingerhut Companies, Inc., a large direct-mail retailer, mails out 130 different catalogs to computer-defined groups of customers. A mailing never goes out to less than 10,000 persons but the list can be as large as a million. Through an operation known as "data mining", the company's marketing experts analyze 3,500 variables representing its customer base with an eye to segregating individuals by groups with similar buying habits. This analysis helps Fingerhut predict how particular customers will respond to direct-mail campaigns. A software feature instructs the computer to search through the data file to find interesting but previously unknown relationships between customer variables which may reveal a propensity to buy certain products. Fingerhut uses this information to decide which customers should receive which catalogs and how many catalogs to print. It may cost the company $400 to $900 to print and mail 1,000 catalogs. Even a slight improvement in accuracy in defining the target audience reaps a huge benefit in increased sales and profitability.

Because of its potential to send electronic messages to a large audience, the Internet is being viewed as a promising medium to advertise commercial products. The trick is to lure viewers to a Website where the advertisements are displayed. With so many different Websites to choose from, users can log on to sites representing highly specialized interests. Those who maintain or advertise on the Websites can be assured that their messages will reach a highly targeted audience. Costs can be kept to a minimum. Another advantage of computer-based communication is that the senders of messages can track the responses automatically. They can painlessly create a data base to record consumer preferences. Advertisers will know precisely how many and what types of people saw a commercial message and which of them purchased the product. IBM has worked with the sporting-goods retailer, L.L. Bean, and others to develop a catalog-like display on the Internet. Its software package includes order placement, shipping, and billing for products purchased online.

While less than half of today's Websites are profitable, businesses advertise on the Internet because this market is expected to expand enormously in the years ahead. Annual sales on the Internet are expected to rise from between $7 billion and $13 billion in 1998 to $41 billion in 2002 and perhaps $103 billion in 2003. America Online, which had 13.5 million paying subscribers in August 1998, reports that 48% of them made online purchases, up from 42% that January. In 1998, Internet commerce was becoming dominated by three firms: America Online, Yahoo!, and Microsoft. Like an electronic shopping mall, Yahoo! alone offered more than two million products from 27,000 different stores. Online sales are expected to overtake catalog sales in 1999. Driving this surge in E-commerce are the fact that personal computer prices and connection times are dropping, Web pages are becoming easier to use, and fragmentation of markets is being overcome by large Web sites and better search engines. Because of high processing costs and privacy concerns associated with credit cards, several firms have explored new methods of payment using digital money or smart cards.

The most popular products purchased online to date are computer hardware, travel tickets, and books. Online merchants are able to customize advertisements to the consumer. For example, someone who orders a book from Amazon.com may receive a message recommending another book which other customers who fit a similar buying profile have enjoyed. He or she may consider this "permission advertising" (which is "anticipated, personal, and relevant") to be helpful rather than intrusive. Search engines called shopping "bots" (robots) allow customers to look through numerous Websites in search of the lowest price for particular products. They can order the products online or else use this information to haggle with conventional merchants. While one would suppose that consumers might prefer to do their own shopping for food at supermarkets, a firm called Streamline in Boston takes grocery orders on the Internet and delivers to the household for a flat $30 per month. Customers save an average of four hours' personal time for each order placed. While they cannot squeeze peaches or Charmin on the Internet, customers can read ingredient labels. Streamline's founder predicts that people will eventually do the bulk of their shopping through electronic clearinghouses.

When journalists describe the promise of computer technology, they tend to overlook some of the more useful applications in favor of the frivolous. They have reported, for instance, that computerized sensing devices in Bill Gates' mansion automatically turn the lights on and off or play a person's favorite music as he walks from room to room. A more compelling need would be for computers to liberate humanity from the knowledge requirement that comes with purchasing and maintaining technically sophisticated machines. Karl Marx once said that for capitalistic markets to function properly customers needed to possess an "encyclopedic" knowledge of products and prices. An untrained housewife is supposed to know something about each of thousands of products and monitor their constantly changing schedules of prices. The knowledge crunch becomes acute in a society whose ease and convenience depends upon a host of highly technical products such as electrical appliances, automobiles, and building supplies. One needs access to a huge source of information both to shop intelligently in this environment and properly maintain the products after they are purchased.

A solution has been to build knowledge into the products themselves. Microprocessors embedded in the products can hold technical information that can be used to guide consumer applications or pinpoint repair problems. For example, diagnostic circuitry in a photocopying machine tells the user what is causing the machine to malfunction and where corrective action needs to be taken. Instead of calling a service technician, an office worker can fix the paper jam by following simple instructions. If a refrigerator malfunctions, a device attached to the machine can communicate with the manufacturer's Website to receive pertinent information. Microprocessors control 83 percent of the functions in new models of cars including fuel-injection and braking systems. These miniature computers work to optimize performance in each area. There is also a move to install microchips in ordinary household appliances to maximize energy efficiency. Electric and gas utilities have installed home servers to control such devices as furnaces and air conditioners, which adjust them automatically to the right temperature settings and eliminate the need for meter readers.

If computers can monitor the operation of machines and signal when something unusual needs to be done, their human owner can safely forget about all but the machine's intended function. Computers will tell the user when preventive maintenance is due. If a device is dangerously overheated, it will shut down automatically. Magnetic bumps or strips embedded in the machine may contain information like that in a repair manual. Downloaded to a personal computer, they might provide easy-to-follow instructions in a menu-like format. No longer would consumers need to search for an owner's manual which might have been thrown out or misplaced. Whirlpool, which spends an average of $50 on each warranty service call, saves a considerable sum of money when information downloaded to the Internet tells the service technician which repair parts to bring. "You haven't seen anything yet," a *Wall Street Journal* article exclaimed. "Plug a constellation of devices into the Internet and the myriad gadgets of everyday life will get smarter and more useful. When people hook up their PCs to the World Wide Web, they transform glorified typewriters into windows on a world of information."

## Education and Training

Many children in the United States are exposed to computers in day-care facilities. Computer instruction becomes better organized in kindergarten and first grade. Games like Putt-Putt show preschoolers how adults handle daily living routines. The Mario Brothers' typing game teaches typing skills. There are games to teach the ABC's and games to teach math. Children learn about geography while playing detective in a game which sends them out on investigative assignments. In the early 1980s, educators began to develop a type of instruction that linked the Apple II computer to video playback machines. The idea was that, like video games, these computer-based systems would teach skills or convey knowledge as a by-product of entertainment. Students would work alone at the terminals on an assignment. If they failed to complete the assignment in time, a buzzer would sound which would alert a roving teacher to the fact that these individuals needed extra help. Some computer exercises functioned like tests which required students to remember information and immediately correct wrong answers. The computer blends sights, sounds, and texts into a set of expressions which can be customized to suit the individual's learning style. Today, on average, U.S. schools have one computer per 7.8 students. Nine out of ten schools are hooked to the Internet.

In some situations, computer-based teaching has replaced traditional modes of instruction. Generally this takes place when real-life training would be too expensive or dangerous to offer on a regular basis. For example, jet pilots are normally trained in flight simulators which display appropriate visual scenery while a student pilot works the control panel. Virtual-reality machines have helped to train police officers to make the right split-second decisions when considering whether or not to shoot an armed suspect. Inexperienced surgeons can make their learning mistakes while operating on virtual rather than real patients. The U.S. Army developed the SIMNET system to allow as many as one thousand persons at a time to engaged in a simulated tank battle. Students at the Fort Knox Armor School learn military teamwork and artillery skills on computer-controlled equipment instead of tearing up nearby terrain. In virtual-reality machines, sensors attached to the viewer's body send signals to the computer that change the scenery in response to bodily motions. If one's head turns to the left, a new panorama will appear on the screen. The experience of watching electronic images respond to one's own physical movement enhances the illusion that one is participating in an actual event.

Computer technicians have been experimenting with an application known as "augmented reality" which supplies work-related knowledge in real time. The workers wear glasses upon which diagrams, parts lists, and instructions are projected while they are performing work. Boeing thinks that this technology will help aircraft engine mechanics do their jobs more skillfully. The transparent glasses permit both real-life vision and computer-generated images such as the engine's interior view. A type of software known as "electronic performance support systems" (EPSS) is being used by some U.S. companies to help lightly trained workers perform complex technical work. This software automates much of the knowledge used in job routines and provides on-the-spot instructions for human workers to figure out the rest. The National Association of Security Dealers has a program, CornerStone, which helps perform an audit of a securities firm. It takes an auditor through the major procedures step by step disclosing key ratios that might indicate securities violations. NASD estimates that use of CornerStone has cut average training time for employees from 2 1/2 years to one year. PricewaterhouseCoopers, a public-accounting firm, has used EPSS to train consultants. This software is especially good at mastering arcane detail.

As computer applications such as EPSS find their way to the business world, more relatively inexperienced job applicants may become qualified to fill technical and professional positions. That will increase the pool of applicants competing for a given position, which, with fixed demand, would tend to depress the wage offering. The adage, "what you earn is a function of what you can learn", may become less apt. Predictably, the wage differential between workers with and without college degrees - currently 50 percent - will narrow as the knowledge which a prospective employee brings to the job becomes less critical. The narrowing of the wage gap may, in turn, dampen young people's interest in continuing their educations. And so, computerized work may weaken one of the main foundations of the third civilization, which is the use of education to advance oneself in a career. Computers may do to the college-educated worker of the 21st century what industrial and office machines did to the high-school graduate early in the 20th century: Remove the element of personal knowledge and skill from jobs and make the working person a tender of machines.

## Prediction by Analogy

Past civilizations, which have already run their course, can suggest the future of existing civilizations. The foregoing discussion has been based upon extrapolation from current trends. Events may or may not unfold as predicted. Now, in the remaining part of this chapter, we will follow up on the idea that the arrival of a new civilization brings changes to institutions formed both in the previous epoch and two epochs earlier. The fifth civilization, driven by computer technology, will shake the foundations of the current society in ways as yet unseen. If the past is any indication, one can anticipate that, on one hand, the news and entertainment media and, on the other, institutions of commerce and education will be caught in the vortex of fundamental change. Already a reaction seems to be taking place against empires of the entertainment culture. Broadcast entertainment is dissolving into a myriad of specialized communications. Bearing in mind that the creative energies of CivIV are not yet fully spent, this book speculates how those events will ultimately play. With respect to the second area of prediction, one can look to a transformation of institutions associated with CivIII. A profound democratization may affect institutions dating back to Renaissance times. While the discussion is speculative, we can at least focus upon areas of expected change.

## New Ways of Deciding
## to Buy Consumer Products

A person's material needs are met by consumer products placed on the market. Each consumer must decide for himself or herself which products, among many, to buy. In making that decision, three considerations need to be addressed: (1) The product should meet the consumer's needs as closely as possible. (2) The product should carry the lowest possible price. (3) The product should be convenient to purchase and deliver. Under the current system, product decisionmaking is influenced by paid advertisements in the media, by product displays in stores, and by other devices which attract attention as a person may be thinking of other things. Computer technology allows information about products to come to the consumer when he or she is focused on their need. This is a more intelligent way to buy products. The process serves the consumer rather than purveyors of merchandise.

The thought that a person needs to buy a particular product to suit a certain purpose in life normally arises from habits of upbringing. Such needs and wants arise from observation of others and from information obtained by word of mouth. In addition, paid commercials in the entertainment media plant ideas about branded products in relation to personal lifestyle. Such an approach to consumer buying is mostly hit-or-miss. A better approach might be to present information on Websites which address particular areas of life experience. Knowledge presented on the Internet would guide consumers to the right consumer products used in those contexts. For example, one such presentation might disclose what a homeowner needs to know to maintain the heating system in a house. The discussion would include explanations of commercial products to meet each need. Like television infomercials, these presentations would be visual and personal. Unlike the infomercials, they would not be directed towards selling any particular product but, instead, would inform consumers of the range of products available and suggest ways to choose intelligently between them. Once consumers begin to trust these various Websites, their proprietors would exercise a certain power, like that of the television networks today, in commanding people's attention.

The bewildering variety of technically advanced products suggests a need to standardize product information in computer data bases. A beginning step might be to create a universal code number which would uniquely identify each consumer product in general use today. A segment of that code might identify its manufacturer. Complete product information would become available by typing the universal code number in appropriate places on a Website. Directed to a file for the particular product, the consumer could move about clicking on topics of interest. If the product malfunctions or needs repairs, answers to simple questions about the malfunction might bring explanatory texts to the screen. To type in certain keywords would direct a person to appropriate places in the text. Information downloaded from the product itself would help to narrow the search for instructions to solve the problem at hand. Computers make it possible to store in one place detailed information concerning the use, repair, technical specifications, and warranty protection about every major commercial product. Nothing needs to become lost or forgotten.

Carrying this concept a step further, one can imagine that the Internet might become a kind of electronic "Yellow Pages" to help consumers find local suppliers of products that they wished to buy. Given the name of a product or its universal product-code number, a search engine might explore the Websites of vendors in the area to learn which merchants carried the product and at what price. Each merchant might regularly upload data from the store's inventory file to its Website. The consumer's personal computer might list in ascending order of price all retail outlets within a certain geographical range which had the desired product in stock, giving their telephone numbers and street addresses. The computer might also disclose pertinent information concerning competing products. Computers linked to the Internet could thus provide a means of quick comparison shopping. This would take the guesswork out of shopping and force merchants to offer low prices in order to compete.

Another aspect of shopping is delivery of a product. How far the customer must travel to view or take possession of products becomes a factor in purchasing decisions. The computer can help to minimize this effort. Computer-based geographic information systems can relate two points on a map to a network of roads and calculate expected travel times between them. The computer knows the customer's home location and the vendor's business location from their respective telephone numbers. Given those two pieces of information, it can then calculate travel times between the vendor's and customer's locations from a file with geographical information. So customers can also do comparison shopping on the basis of delivery convenience. Once purchase transactions are entered into a computer, the information becomes available for many purposes.

Ultimately, computers may eliminate the need for individual customers to travel far from their homes to obtain merchandise. The "Streamline" model of shopping for groceries in Boston suburbs suggests a distribution method which could be applied to many other kinds of products. Instead of traveling to a store to view merchandise, place orders, and take possession of these products, customers might obtain information about products on the Internet and order the products online. The seller might arrange for delivery of products to the customer through a network of neighborhood depots. Two or three times a day, vendors might deliver ordered merchandise to trucks or vans which would make the rounds of urban neighborhoods, dropping the products off at the depots where customers could pick them up at their convenience. Besides improving transportation efficiency, this arrangement would eliminate the need for stores to carry a large inventory of goods for display purposes. The whole apparatus of contemporary retailing, including stores and shopping malls, would be called into question by this new method of displaying and delivering consumer products.

At stake here is nothing less than erosion of the connection between mass entertainment and sale of commercial products which underpins CivIV. If the customer knows how to obtain online the best products at the lowest possible price, why on earth would anyone follow some other method of making product decisions? Why base purchasing decisions on impressionistic commercials about a wide range of consumer products when persons prepared to buy a certain product can go straight to the source of its information and find out exactly what they need to know? Letting television entertainment determine one's choice of consumer products makes sense only when the customer has no other place to turn. To the extent that people do their shopping on the Internet, the market will be forced to deliver a more suitable product at a more favorable price because customers will be able to compare many alternatives. Purchasing decisions can then be made free of the hoopla and hype that has characterized modern merchandising. The excessive, wasteful purchasing that arises from ignorance of product or price due to the free market's huge knowledge requirement can be kept to a minimum.

The average American living in a city with a population of one million persons must pick and choose between as many as one million different commercial products. In the face of this awesome variety, the customer must somehow find products to satisfy each want or need. Television commercials, which occupy roughly 18% of total broadcast time, push products at people who happen to be paying attention to something else. This is, at least, one way of becoming informed about consumer products. If a better way comes along, people may still watch commercial television for the sake of the free entertainment but will turn to the more sensible alternative when it comes time to buy something. Prospective advertisers, recognizing the reduced effectiveness of the commercials, will become less interested in underwriting the cost of television programs. Entertainment will then have to find some other means of financial support.

## Computerized Teaching

There is no reason why every mentally capable person in the industrialized world should not receive a high-quality education at a reasonable price. Cost should be no object. The knowledge itself is expertly presented in books. For at most several hundred dollars a year, one could own all the books that one could comfortably read and digest in any field of interest. Books can be recycled or borrowed for free from public libraries. Of course, most people need reinforcement of visual learning through classroom presentations and spoken discussions. For this part of the lesson, students could listen to audiotapes. Someone could read books aloud or retrace their themes in a recorded discussion. Better still, skilled teachers could perform on videotape. The tapes could record classroom scenes. Someone sitting in front of a large-screen, high-definition television set hooked up to a VCR would receive as much instructional experience from watching a videotape as that which could be had from attending a class. The only thing missing would be that the student could not ask the teacher any questions or be questioned. The fear of being caught unprepared would also be missing.

The element of interactivity, missing in books and videotapes, is among the computer's capabilities. This electronic machine permits two-way communication between teacher and learner. Therefore, the gap between an actual teaching experience and a taped replay can be at least partially plugged. Once a successful teaching routine is captured in a computer memory, the performance supplied by a human teacher can give way to an automated procedure. Machine-based instruction can be inexpensively reproduced and distributed to students. However, the interactive function of teaching is not well handled by machines in the current state of their technology. Especially for younger children who must be taught by spoken words and personal example, real-life teachers are better instructors than electronic gadgets with mechanical interfaces and screens. The gap may narrow as new machines are developed with improved visual capabilities and voice-recognition features. Once computer software reaches the point of permitting an intelligent conversation in the English language, the two modes of teaching may appreciably converge.

Of course, we are not yet there. The idea of parking seven-year-olds in front of personal computers where they spend hours staring at a small screen and typing in answers to clunky questions is justifiably disturbing to many people. The average computer screen presents a grainy, two-dimensional image that permits thirty degrees of vertical and forty degrees of horizontal vision. That compares with grainless, three-dimensional images seen in a normal range of 155 vertical and 185 horizontal degrees in real life. The student's interface with the computer might be a keyboard, mouse, button, knob, ball, joystick, wheel, or touch screen. Yet, technological advances in large-screen and high-resolution television will spill over into the area of computer monitors and screens. Computers which recognize spoken words will be improved and become more widely used. The technical barriers to simulating a lifelike classroom situation will, in time, be greatly reduced. Virtual-reality features will become available. A final ingredient needed to bridge the gap will be the creative vision to discover new ways of exploiting the teaching potential of computer-based technologies as D.W. Griffith once pioneered film techniques. Artist-educators of the future will surely rise to the challenge of creating an experience which is both educational and personally stimulating .

The education establishment has begun to recognize that educators who know how to teach are as valuable as skilled researchers. Larry Rudnick, an astronomy professor at the University of Minnesota, has been recognized as an effective teacher. His approach to teaching is, he said, "willingness to learn, to listen to students and to change," recognizing that different people learn in different ways. In the middle of the semester, Prof. Rudnick surveys students about his course and makes mid-course adjustments. He admits to having stolen good teaching ideas from others. His classroom performance mixes lecturing, blackboard diagrams, slide presentations, and audiotapes. The question is whether the expertise which a human teacher has acquired from classroom experience can be transferred to a computer's memory. Clearly, those types of electronic media which support the entertainment culture are insufficiently flexible to provide the tailored instruction that Prof. Rudnick and other outstanding teachers have put into their courses. Multimedia computer software does have that capability.

If teaching is to be perfected, its product must be able to be multiplied and expanded to reach larger audiences. Then resources will become available to polish its expressions to a high degree. Then we can see, on a broad scale, what type of lesson works. The need for standardized, high-quality lessons dictates that the thrust of education move beyond the human teacher to a machine-based system. The skills of an individual teacher perish when that person leaves, but teaching routines which can be stored in a computer's memory last indefinitely. The most important educational lesson is to teach children how to speak. Since parents are typically the teachers, it is critical that society allow them enough time away from work for verbal interaction regularly to take place within a family setting. The company of other children also stimulates learning by example. At higher levels of education, the computer can draw upon its limitless fund of knowledge to enrich the teaching experience. Pimentel and Teixeira have written: "Someday, teachers will be able to take students to the bottom of the ocean without leaving their classroom. Students will play with atoms and make their own molecules in VR (virtual reality) to experience chemistry, instead of just reading about it."

Conventional education is labor-intensive. A live teacher delivers a lecture to perhaps thirty students in a classroom, asks questions to see what the students have learned, and gives answers to the questions. Periodic tests tell how well the lesson has been remembered. To the extent that computer-based systems replicate the classroom experience, education is no longer limited by class size or by a teacher's capacity to deal individually with a certain number of students. All students can have access to the very best teachers and receive frequent feedback from them. Present technology requires students to type in their responses to questions or click on items appearing in a list or menu. Because computers can store information about the user's key strokes, they can monitor responses to questions and assess how well the students have learned their lessons. Testing can take place whenever students are engaged in a learning exercise, not just during official "tests". All this has the potential to revolutionize the teaching process.

## Knowledge Alienated from Workers

Today's paradigm holds that extensive education is needed to handle the intellectually more challenging kinds of work found in a technologically advanced society. Knowledge-based occupations require more education and training. That may not necessarily be the case. Because an occupation involves a large component of knowledge does not mean that a human being has to provide it. Some of the knowledge can be supplied by computers. At one time, manual labor was an element in most occupations. Power tools and equipment, which supplement or replace muscular exertions, have changed the nature of blue-collar work. Henry Ford's assembly line showed that in large-scale productions it was helpful to coordinate the flow of parts to workers who would install them on products. The parts arrived on overhead conveyor belts which dropped them onto the product as needed. Information and knowledge are today like those parts which were delivered to the assembly line. Computers are like the power tools. Employers can improve the efficiency of white-collar work by rationalizing the operation, identifying and defining the knowledge that is needed at each point, and arranging for its delivery to a worker just in time to be used.

Data-processing systems lay out the knowledge requirements for calculation by a computer. Flow charts show how one piece of information connects with another. The computer stupidly follows this scheme and the task is done. The next step, then, is to bring the human being into the flow of information processing. While doing a job, a worker knows what to do at each point in the work routine. This is knowledge become habit, born of long practice. The knowledge-laden techniques could be codified in some way. Theoretically, each person's work could be analyzed and arranged in logical steps like information in flow charts. Computers could store the required knowledge and spit it out at appropriate times, reminding an employee of what to do next. Computer output could provide complete information needed to handle the work at each stage. In that case, even an inexperienced person could do complex work with reasonable competence. Knowledge-intensive managerial or professional work may require a bit more preparation, but even this can be formulated in a work routine. Each job carries a spectral shadow, which is the knowledge supporting its performance. The computer can hold this pattern of work performance in its memory as an intangible asset, drawing upon it as needed.

If offices of the future deliver just-in-time knowledge to employees, it means that the people who work there are not required to bring the knowledge with them to their job. It means that, except for basic literacy and math skills, prior education is largely unneeded. Workers would not have to remember an entire work routine, but only enough to handle the part which the computer has brought to their attention. No doubt, higher-level work positions demand a breadth of knowledge and flexibility of thinking that do not lend themselves so well to this kind of treatment. Intellectually creative functions involve unprogrammable experimentation and intuitive solutions. Yet, though a certain part of work performance must be left to human experience, more job skills can be reduced to discrete points of knowledge than their possessors may want to admit. Besides self-interest and pride, an obstacle to computerization is that busy, important people generally do not have the time to sit down with a scribe and recall everything that they do. That would take too much self-conscious reflection. The trick is to record the knowledge of work in some effortless way while a person is doing it. Those who work with computers, for instance, leave a record of keystrokes which can be automatically retrieved.

Much of the knowledge actually required in careers is of a utilitarian variety. No one needs to know Einstein's theory of relativity or the themes of Shakespearean plays. Instead, there is a need to understand the comparative merits and technical specifications of particular commercial products or systems. Programmer analysts are hired not because they know the principles of computers as such but because they know UNIX, HTML, Windows 95, Java, or another type of software. This is a relatively unglamorous type of knowledge. Because commercial systems come and go, frontloading the knowledge into a student's mind does not make sense. While there is no question that knowledge is an essential element in performing work and that employers must pay the going rate to obtain it, it does not follow that this knowledge resides only in certain specially trained or experienced persons. The technology exists to put knowledge in a form that can be accessed by persons of mechanical talents to produce a quick transfer. Temporarily certain individuals will have this knowledge ready to go. In the long run, however, no one can claim a personal distinction on the basis of possessing knowledge. The knowledge itself is alienable from persons.

If work-related knowledge is pried loose from the persons who developed it, then the worker's position as a unique knowledge-laden commodity which fetches a certain price on the market is threatened. Who owns the knowledge to do a certain job, the employee or employer? If the employee, it is a possession that may have little use beyond the employer's enterprise. If the employer, there would seem to be little justification for paying an employee a premium wage for possessing it. As computers are increasingly used in business, more work-related knowledge will be put into a form that can be extracted from individual workers and made accessible to others. Objectified knowledge, which is removed from an employee's mind, will then seem to belong more to the employer, especially if it was acquired on company time. Possession of this knowledge would be like having use of any company-owned tool.

Some will say that the future looks bleak if working people are stripped of the one possession that gives them hope and security. If denied the ability to advance in a career through education and acquisition of superior knowledge, what do people have left? They have privileges of incumbency. Failing that, they have their humanity held in common with the managers and owners of the machines. They have their political rights which translate into the power to trump legal and business arrangements. Against the trend of contemporary political thinking, the ultimate answer must be to regard business-related knowledge as the common property of humanity. Henry Ford once said: "All so-called private fortunes are nothing less than public reserves. I have noticed that those who work exclusively for money ... do not retain it unless they continue the use of it for the public." This statement bespeaks the attitude of creative capitalism. Uncreative capitalism, of course, has a different point of view. Here business managers are tight-fisted in dealing with employees and customers but quite generous when it comes to themselves. It is not just business executives but lawyers, doctors, educators, union members, assorted administrators and professionals, and many others who exhibit tendencies of greed.

Organized labor has exerted a check upon abuses of the managerial class. However, U.S. unions are weakened by declining memberships and a failure to raise issues on behalf of the larger community. Government, too, might challenge unfettered business power. Influenced by campaign contributions and free-market ideologies, current political fashions run in another direction. Values-forming institutions such as religion and the communications media have agendas unrelated to this type of concern. Another source of hope might be the educational sector. Unlikely as it might seem, this may be a promising place to turn public opinion around on questions of responsibility. If many who occupy leading positions in our society are socially irresponsible, a certain amount of the blame can be laid at the feet of the people who educated them. The growing disparity of incomes is, in large part, product of an attitude that people are differentiated from each other by skills imparted through education. The idea that some people have much higher incomes than others because of their prolonged or specialized education or their competitive worth in the free market will be shown to be spurious once the knowledge component is rationalized.

The fact is that progress in computers and other productive technologies could open up a better life for all people. Greater production efficiency and elimination of waste could provide more abundant output while reducing the amount of human labor required to have it. The fact that we have instead chosen longer hours, greater inequality of incomes, and more waste bears witness to the selfishness of a power elite which has diverted the fruits of production improvement to its own use. Many of these people are highly educated. They are persuaded that they deserve disproportionate wealth because of economic merit. Let their claim to advancement by superior knowledge be stripped away and they may recover some humility. For, it is not just blue-collar workers who are displaced by labor-saving technologies. If education is advocated primarily as a means of economic self-advancement, then, of course, we will have managers and professionals who loot the public. They may have to do this to pay back their student loans. But if the institution is driven by a spirit of inquiry and love of truth, and if tuitions are cheaper, then its graduates accept careers that include some element of self-sacrifice. Plato's thought that students of philosophy will learn to love sublime ideas brings education back to a sound footing.

## Rethinking College

Learning has never been the entire purpose of education. Social mobility has been a factor as well. The social historian, J.C. Furnas, wrote of colleges in 19th century America: "As colleges and universities fanned out toward the Mississippi, the prestige a boy acquired from having been to college came to outweigh considerations of what he might have learned there. To have been able to send him there was the outward and visible sign of economic arrival." An upwardly mobile American might gain a certain satisfaction in sending his son to attend school with the sons of the Cabots, Vanderbilts, and Saltonstalls. Soon enough, the idea caught on that the same opportunities ought to be extended to poor but meritorious students. Soon there was a push to make a college education available to everyone. However, if social mobility is the purpose of attending college, a system of universal education is self-defeating. Not everyone in society can be upwardly mobile.

The computer, an information-crunching machine, has an infinite capacity to deliver knowledge. To the extent that computerized lessons replace live experiences in the classroom, then high-quality education is no longer limited by class size or a teacher's ability to deal individually with students. There are, then, no schools that are better than the rest. Suddenly outstanding teachers become available in every field. Like any commodity, education becomes cheap when supply exceeds demand. Computers, fulfilling their potential, have the capacity to deliver an unlimited supply of superb education. It is only through scarcity that this becomes expensive. As a rule, the capitalist system is able to meet marketplace demand for any machine-built product. So it will be possible to increase the quantity of education to meet any level of demand. That means that, in the coming age of computers, everyone who wants it can have the same brand of high-quality education. No student need ever be rejected for admission to this type of college. That being the case, the fact that someone has attended a particular institution of learning ought not to confer any competitive advantage. Education ceases to be a factor in social stratification.

Of course, some learning is required for young people to start careers. Schools will have to deliver this product in a way which can be measured and verified. Beyond that, the idea that successful completion of a four-year program of study or of a particular package of professional training is needed for success in careers is largely a myth. If it were true that an academic degree indicates mental proficiency or the "stick-to-itness" needed to compete in today's complex economic environment, then how could a college drop-out like Bill Gates go on to become the world's richest man before the age of 40 in founding and managing a firm on the cutting edge of technology? There are just too many examples like this of persons with unimpressive academic records who later amass fortunes, or make important inventions, or become effective managers in complex technical fields for educators to continue to make a plausible argument about the need for their particular service to prepare for successful performance in a career.

The more that machines can produce a high-quality educational experience, the easier it will become to transfer work-related knowledge to previously unskilled individuals. The training function will become relatively cheap. If a large number of persons are trained in the same work function, the supply of persons able to handle the function increases and, all else being equal, wages drop. That has implications for schools which have sold themselves on the basis of bestowing higher lifetime earnings upon students in exchange for acquiring an academic degree. If graduates of expensive colleges find themselves competing on an equal footing with persons who have had a cheap computer-based education, then these more expensive institutions may fail to attract the desired number of students and may themselves need to shift into a cost-cutting mode.

It costs students an average of $20,000 per year in tuition, room, and board to attend a private, four-year college in the United States, and $8,000 year for a public four-year college. Harvard charges $31,000. College tuition costs have increased twice as fast as inflation during the past two decades. The cost of higher education includes not only the direct outlay for tuition, room, and board (minus financial aid received) but also the lost opportunity to earn income during those four years and to start a career at a time of energetic, impressionable youth. In cold financial terms, the $80,000 that a student, parents, or other benefactor puts towards education at a private four-year college could provide a comfortable endowment for purchasing a house, starting a business, or weathering the inevitable job changes during a career. On the benefit side, the student who graduates from college has instant credibility with employers. In a highly competitive job environment, academic degrees may be demanded for any career position with growth potential. All too often, however, one hears of college graduates who cannot find suitable jobs despite the investment which they made in their educations. Persons with Ph.D.'s are driving taxi cabs or working as file clerks. The education process comes, of course, with no guarantees.

A growing segment of college-age youth in the United States, especially young men, has chosen not to pursue a college education but instead take advantage of the immediate opportunities for high-paying employment that exist in today's booming economy. The women, in contrast, have continued to move in lockstep toward obtaining an academic degree. As a result, 57 percent of American students who earned bachelor's degrees in 1999 were women, compared with 43 percent in 1970 and 24 percent in 1950. Young males are increasingly attracted to technical jobs which can be entered after a quick period of training yet offer a good starting salary. When some computer positions pay as much as $75,000 or $100,000 after a few years on the job, this becomes an attractive alternative to spending the same time in pursuit of an academic degree. Traditionalists predict that the males are being shortsighted and eventually the advantage of continuing one's education in terms of higher lifetime earnings will become clear. On the other hand, we could be in the midst of a paradigm shift in which traditional types of education lose both their luster and ability to deliver higher incomes.

## The Idea of a University

Predictably, colleges and universities will need to reinvent themselves to keep their place in society. They will have to try harder to appeal both to students and employers. For students, who are their immediate customers, they can offer the following improvements: First, they can reduce the cost of the educational process by applying computer and other technology to a greater extent and by setting fees and tuitions at a fair mark-up over cost. Second, they can offer teaching in a variety of sizes and shapes, as suits the students' individual needs, and confer credit accordingly. Third, they can assume continuing responsibility for their graduates' economic well-being. They can assume the additional function of representing their graduates to employers. This could take the more limited form of becoming like an employment agency which finds jobs for its clients and, once they are hired, leaves them in another's charge. More ambitiously, it could take the form of becoming the graduates' nominal employer, like a temp agency. The university might assign people to work at various businesses but retain a loose supervisory role, especially as regards training and personnel functions.

For business firms, such universities would offer several advantages: First, the more standardized curricula and evaluation procedures would make it safer for employers to hire their graduates. The schooling would be a known quantity. Second, the reduced cost of the education would ease expectations of starting salaries. Third, the universities would have a closer working relationship with employers. Having educated these graduates, they would have more intimate knowledge of an individual's educational record. That would allow them to make better referrals to positions and assure employers of obtaining more honest and accurate information. Fourth, as a temp agency, they could provide workers to businesses on a basis which is relatively free of risk. If a particular worker did not perform adequately, the university would take him back and furnish a replacement. The discharged person could go back to school for additional training or counseling and be made ready for a new assignment. Fifth, they could free businesses of handling functions such as payrolls and benefits. They could provide specialized career training.

In some respects, such a university might also assume the function of a labor union. While forswearing strikes and other contentious actions, the educational association might represent its members in their contractual relationships with employers and in formulating career plans. It might become a political force to change attitudes and promote the betterment of working people. The association might not object if employers wished to hire their graduates as employees to lock them into a more permanent relationship. Having employment responsibilities, this university would be in close touch with employers and thus be able to design courses which meet real occupational needs. The emerging practice of lifelong learning and career change would be handled with ease. Pension and vacation benefits, accrued by years of service, would become portable. Even so, this would not be a trade school or an extension of corporate training but a university. Its purpose would be to give status, place, and security to men and women currently set adrift in a sea of shifting employment requirements.

An educational institution has several functions. First and foremost would be the teaching of basic skills. Reading, writing, and arithmetic - the 3 Rs - comprise the core of skills to be taught at the elementary-school level. Such additional skills as typing, use of computers and calculating machines, personal grooming, diet and health, athletics, and public speaking are also appropriate subjects to be taught in schools. A second function, which tends to be reserved for higher levels of schooling, has to do with transmitting the community's cultural heritage. Subjects which fall into this category include history, literature, languages, science, music and art, philosophy, and law. College curricula have traditionally focused upon them. Beyond this, there is an area of learning which has to do with the soul of the institution and its individual students. It would include subjects related to personal values. Religion, ethics, and social consciousness would fall into this category. Education generally instills an appreciation for truth. Persons who are sincere and accomplished seekers of truth find an honorable place within this community. Financial endowments are established to support their labors. Hierarchies distinguish the truthseekers' accomplishments at various levels.

Beyond this, there are values of a more personal nature. The guiding principle of a values curriculum is that life's most important values are self-chosen. No educator "educates" students in what they should believe or esteem. On the other hand, a common value of any community must be to respect the boundaries of others. There should be a consensus to respect other peoples' opinions even while perhaps disagreeing with them. Another value might be to encourage each person to find a basis of self-pride. It would encourage individuals to take pride in their race, gender, religion, nationality, and social background, whatever it might be, and would give them resources to deepen their understanding of such matters. Religious teachings, if presented in an unobtrusive and respectful manner, would find acceptance in this type of pluralistic community. Values curricula should teach how to fight fairly, how to be polite, how to assert one's own legitimate interest but give way to others' legitimate concerns. It is not that people should be taught not to be selfish but that they should learn to recognize their own selfishness and accept certain limits.

### The Quest of Self-Definition

Education in the computer age can take a cue from Socrates' instruction: Know thyself. People today are quite interested in knowing who they are. That desire is manifested in the popular interest in astrological signs which are said to be associated with certain character traits. Knowledge of personal self-identity is an object of psychological testing. Such knowledge presumably helps them to pick suitable roles in real life. Direct marketers analyze customer data to develop profiles of persons likely to buy certain products. The police identify criminal suspects through profiles of persons likely to commit crimes. Each of us is on somebody's list as exhibiting a type of personality that fits in with some exploitative purpose. But people are also interested in simply knowing who they are. If one has a reasonable self-pride, there is a joy in looking into the mirror and seeing one's own reflection.

Human personality is such a fragile construct that abstractions purporting to describe it hardly belong to the realm of serious science. Psychological testing may involve the use of concepts that seem stupid or contrived. Methods used to compile test scores may themselves dictate the result. Moreover, persons taking the psychological tests may not have a clear idea of their own position with respect to some of the questions; and the quality of information obtained from such testing cannot rise above what was contributed. It may be that, in the future, psychological tests will need to involve more active participation on the part of the people being tested. The test subjects will need to search their hearts and minds to decide what type of information best indicates their own personality. It may be, for instance, that they know they like a particular song, or identify quite strongly with a particular historical figure, or are interested in a hobby. Whatever resonates most clearly within them can be a guide to constructing self-portraits.

Education can facilitate definitions of personal self-identity. With the aid of computers and other tools, it can bring together groups of like-minded individuals to explore their self-chosen ways. Any commitment of time to do or learn something pushes a person in a particular direction to become something. Individuals often want to become what they can do well and for which they may have received personal recognition. Tests, contests, and competitions, which celebrate the winners, can build self-esteem. Too often, however, education functions in a rejection mode. The fear of becoming a failure drives children to learn too much too fast. This pressure-cooker education might make sense if successful career work depended on cramming as much knowledge as possible into one's head, but not if the goal is self-discovery. For that, a person needs a solid background of childhood experience where individuality runs free. If young people are to discover where their true interests lie, they must be allowed room space to flounder and make their own mistakes. Because the impetus for self-discovery comes from within, there is something to be said for slack which loosens the reins of direction and lets children be.

The quest of self-identity presents a challenge which can be met by a sampling of experiences or by dramatic role-playing. Some virtual-reality games have prepared children to project themselves imaginatively into roles. They become lifelike characters interacting with one another on the screen. Multimedia computers make it easy to escape to a personal fantasy world which, though artificial, offers real opportunities for learning. Even without the technology, schools should be a place to experience variety before one is forced to narrow down to a specialty. It is said that success in life involves, in baseball parlance, "going with one's best pitch," and doing this with some frequency. That makes it all the more important to discover from varied experience what are one's strengths and where one's true interests lie.

## The Possibility of Catastrophe

It is possible that CivV might not turn out as this or any prediction would anticipate. The thrust of world history to date has been progress defined in terms of growth in human populations, advancing technologies, and increased wealth and knowledge. That could change if events took an unfortunate turn. For instance, even though the Cold War has ended, humanity could still be obliterated by a nuclear explosion. More than twenty-five nations are developing nuclear, biological, or chemical weapons and have ways to deliver them. Even if national governments kept the problem under control, crime syndicates or terrorist groups could acquire these weapons. Problems such as overpopulation and environmental pollution also hang over the future. The "greenhouse effect", a consequence of industrialization, could heat the earth's temperature to the point of turning habitable areas into desert while submerging others in oceanic waters. Depletion of the ozone layer could expose the human population to dangerous radiation. Raw materials upon which our way of life depends could be significantly depleted.

Technology, beneficial in the short term, has produced some disturbing long-term consequences. Medicine has brought humane relief to sick people, but it has also kept alive many persons who might otherwise have died. Their survival brings the possible birth of offspring with similar characteristics. Nature's way of flushing out genetic weaknesses within the human population is thereby nullified. Over the long term there would appear to be a race between advancing medical technology and naturally deteriorating health. A related problem is that the frequent treatment of illness with antibiotic drugs may have served to create new strains of drug-resistant viruses and germs. Some patients who are prescribed these drugs fail to take the full dose of medicine to knock out the germs. As a result, the hardiest germs survive and multiply, making the next round of illness even more difficult to treat. A strain of infection discovered recently in Japan has become resistant to vancomycin, medicine's drug of last resort. A plague based on any of these hardy microbes would be devastating.

Perverse incentives in our society also work to reduce the level of human intelligence. An advanced education, presumably reserved for the community's most intelligent persons, serves to keep intelligent young men and women from marrying at an early age. Women postpone marriage and childbearing as society encourages them to become educated and pursue a career. If the more intelligent individuals are systematically held back from contributing to the gene pool while those less intelligent breed freely, average intelligence will decline over time. The same effect is achieved by methods traditionally used to select men for military service. National governments have drafted the healthy men and rejected those with mental or physical problems. Why society would want its healthier specimens to become cannon fodder while sparing the less healthy so that they might become the next generation of parents is incomprehensible.

Foreseeably, the deterioration of human health and intelligence will continue, though perhaps at a pace too slow to have a visible impact. Advances in technological knowledge may soften the impact somewhat. But, as technology becomes more complex, human intelligence would meanwhile be weakening. Civilization may be on a collision course between these two trends. Worldly affairs may become so complicated that the intelligence to solve problems is overwhelmed. That, at least, is how humanity in its natural state might face the future. But humanity is not in a natural state; it has machines to assist in overcoming difficulties which nature has imposed. That is a new and historic factor which affects life on this planet. If, in a pessimistic scenario, human populations are ravaged by thermonuclear radiation or deadly disease, the earth might be inherited by insects, bacteria, or another type of organism. Alternatively, the next dominant species might be a race of intelligent machines.

Once before, the earth experienced massive poisoning by a species inhabiting its surface. About three billion years ago, single-cell plants which had developed a capacity for photosynthesis "polluted" the environment by releasing free oxygen into the air. New forms of animal life evolved which metabolized this oxygen and created the balance of atmospheric gases that we have today. Now, in the last two hundred years, humanity has fast been turning the earth into a waste dump. Either living species will appear which feed upon this waste, or intelligent organisms or machines immune to its deadly influence will. A possibility to be considered is that computers may lead the way to this new age. Computers may allow man to reinvent himself by altering his own DNA. Alternatively, man may himself become fused with machines.

### The Frankenstein Civilization

Medieval Jews living in an oppressive society entertained themselves with thoughts of the "golem", a creature made of clay to which rabbis had given life by uttering a charm. Rabbi Low in 16th century Prague was said to have made one, but he was forced to destroy the creature when it ran wild. Mary Wollstonecraft Shelley, wife of the English poet, wrote a book, *Frankenstein*, in which a German student who knew the secret of infusing inanimate materials with life created an artificial being. This monster turned on its creator and destroyed him. In 1921, a Czech dramatist, Karel Capek, wrote a play about a machine which tirelessly performed labor. The term, "robot", comes from that play. And so the fifth epoch begins with myths or literary works that imagine the creation of artificial human-like beings. One can call it the "Frankenstein civilization". The title suggests that man will artificially re-create himself. This could happen in several ways: Man might create a machine version of his own mind. He might re-make his own body through genetic engineering. He might create an artificial environment in which his life functions can take place.

If this epoch has a supreme moment, it will be when humanity first encounters an alien creature whose level of intelligence equals or surpasses its own. Our first thought is that humanity might encounter space aliens who came to earth in flying saucers. That is because our historical imaginations tend to be conservative; we project past experiences upon the future. Once before, at the beginning of the third epoch, Europeans encountered a previously unknown but equally intelligent race of beings. Arawak Indians greeted Columbus and his crew when they first set foot on American soil. However, this event represented merely the reconnection of two human tribes which had been separated for thousands of years. Creatures from outer space, if such exist, would likely be of a different chemical makeup. Their intelligence could be of an entirely different order. The best known evidence that these creatures exist concerns an incident that took place in 1947, when an unidentified metallic object dropped from the skies into a field near Roswell, New Mexico. Since then, numerous people have reported observations of unidentified flying objects (UFOs), flying saucers, and the like. Spokesmen for the U.S. Government have denied knowing anything about this.

Popular interest in space aliens and explorations of outer space remains strong. However, it centers in a "Star Trek" image of space travel which is backward-looking. This is the old model of sailors (acting in this case a bit like Greek philosophers) who travel the cosmic oceans in a large boat, encountering strange peoples along the way. Predictably, the human experience of space travel will be an encounter with the very large and the very slow. Except in the sphere of intra-human communications, events will not happen at a normal pace. Distances measured in light-years are beyond the range of travel in a conventional sense. Before human beings can move even a small fraction of that distance, they may have evolved into some other creature or had meaningful encounters with fast-reproducing microbes. Human life in space will likely be confined to the narrow range of places within the solar system which have low gravity and the raw materials to fashion an environment resembling conditions on earth. Scientists suspect that the planet Mars, several moons of Saturn or Jupiter, and perhaps the earth's own Moon might be suitable sites to support human colonies.

Like currents in the ocean, space travel will be affected by the gravitational configuration of celestial bodies. The locations of magnetic fields and radiation belts will also be important to human travelers. But the main question may be whether travel is even needed. Most travel is undertaken for the sake of delivering something or learning something. If the travel is intended to gather information about distant places, this can be obtained more cheaply by unmanned space probes than by human exploration. Machines which can endure conditions intolerable to man can communicate information to earth as well as human travelers can. Moreover, they do not mind one-way trips. Increasingly, communication would be taking the place of transportation. The human experience in space mainly would consist of communicating with other human beings. Human travel might involve the transportation of genetic materials for purposes of colonization or survival, to reduce the possibility that our species will become extinct.

It is unlikely that humanity will be able to survive in outer space unless machines mediate between us and nature. Machines, which Daniel Boorstin has called "the fourth kingdom" (after minerals, plants, and animals), will comprise a large part of our future whichever way history turns. Machines are today considered to be tools, subservient to the purposes of their human creator. Intelligent machines could change that model. When we imagine that moment in the fifth historical epoch when humanity meets an equally intelligent being, a scenario other than meeting space aliens is that humanity will have a significant encounter with intelligence born of his own technology. Perhaps, in a small way, that moment may already have arrived when, in May 1996, the "Big Blue" chess-playing computer developed by IBM beat Gary Kasparov, the world's top-rated human chess player, in a tournament. Computers have an advantage over human intelligence in the accuracy and speed of performing certain calculations and in their ability to preserve memory and function in a harsh environment. The human brain yet retains a huge advantage in overall processing capacity. However, computer technology is rapidly improving while the brain is stuck in a slow evolutionary drift.

The goal of some computer designers is to create a machine which thinks like a human being. They approach this challenge by simulating processes believed to take place within the brain during thought. Some psychologists believe that passing signals between two neurons strengthens the synaptic connection between those neurons. Thoughts are actually patterns of strength between particular connections. Computer engineers have written algorithms to simulate learning according to this process. Computers have plotted neural positions on a map which correspond to the brain's synaptic connections. The visual patterns bear an eerie resemblance to patterns observed on the surface of a monkey's brain when it processes sensory experience. The human brain has over one trillion neurons which may each connect with a thousand other neurons. It is, then, no easy task to simulate brain activity by keeping track of these connections and manipulating them in various ways.

Scientists have also played Frankenstein by studying and manipulating the chemical basis of human life. Its essential structure is formed by information stored in the DNA (deoxyribonucleic acid) and RNA (ribonucleic acid) molecules. These complex molecules contain two intertwining strands of genetic materials, each like a string of pearls. The "pearls", or nucleotides, are each made of a particular phosphate group and have a ringed structure called a "base". The sequence of nucleotides carries genetic information to direct the production of proteins which create cells of a living organism. The Human Genome Project is attempting to map the entire sequence of elements in a human DNA molecule. There are about three billion bases strung together in this molecule. A supercomputer is needed to keep track of the enormous quantity of data. Geneticists who have compared the DNA molecules of several different animal species have found similarities which may indicate how particular types of thinking relate to physiological functions. Roughly 70% of a human gene is identical with that of a mouse. Within the human species itself, genes are identical to one part in a thousand.

As more knowledge is obtained about the information encoded in human genes, medical technicians can selectively intervene to alter or remove parts believed responsible for health problems. Though scientists are yet unable to create new life in a test tube, they have the knowledge to use procedures such as cloning to create living organisms from preexisting genetic materials. Conceivably genetic surgery will some day create an "improved" type of human being or a new species. Humanity, possessing finite knowledge, would then be "playing God". Already scientific knowledge promises to deliver something like eternal life. Personal immortality of a sort has become available at a modest cost by storing frozen samples of a person's genetic material with a firm called GeneLink. If one wishes to preserve the genetic blueprint of a dead relative, this firm will instruct funeral directors on procedures to take a sample of flesh, before it is too late, by swabbing the deceased's mouth. Of course, personality would not come back to life unless the brain cells were preserved. However, the technology of cryogenics, which freezes the corpse so as to permit later revival, offers that.

The fifth civilization will take humanity into deeper and ever more dangerous realms of experience. One cannot now predict whether this civilization will mark the final phase of human existence or bring a further progression toward what will become a sixth and then, perhaps, a seventh or eighth epoch of world history. When the computer develops a mind of its own and, like a rebellious child, begins to go against its parents' wishes, then we will know that the era of Frankenstein is upon us. The fact that computer software can develop a so-called "virus" suggests that man-made intelligence has taken on the qualities of an independent life form. Already, human beings are dependent on machinelike appliances to augment their sense of hearing, keep their hearts beating in a regular rhythm, and replace missing limbs. Many people need daily injections of psychotropic drugs to maintain emotional stability. Such medical developments suggest that humanity's future may be to evolve into a man-machine hybrid.

World history will not end unless humanity ends. Progress and struggle will both continue. It may be that a part of the population will be Amish-like abstainers from medical treatment and their descendants may come to be valued as a pure and endangered species. Conflicts may then arise between the "artificial" and "natural" people. Or, it may be that elitist dictators will seize control of computer networks and threaten the mass of human populations in some way. On the other hand, the current trend towards fragmentation of experience may continue and confuse the historical picture. One would long for the heroic simplicity of the old days. At the juncture of man and machine, creative interactions will take place. Governments, religions, commerce, entertainment, and other yet unformed institutions will be around. Social hierarchies will continue to exist.

# Bibliography

Aristotle. Nicomachean Ethics, from *Introduction to Aristotle*, ed. Richard McKeon. New York: The Modern Library, 1947.

Beck, J. Spencer, editor. *The Variety History of Show Business*. New York: Abrams, 1993.

Brasch, Rudolph. *How Did Sports Begin: A Look at the Origins of Man at Play.* New York: McKay, 1970.

Bridgwater, William, and Kurtz, Seymour, editors. *The Columbia Encyclopedia, third edition.* New York: Columbia Univ. Press, 1968.

Bronowski, J. *The Ascent of Man.* London: British Broadcasting Co., 1976.

Chandler, Tertius. *Four Thousand Years of Urban Growth, an Historical Census*, second edition. Lewiston, NY: Edwin Mellen Press, 1987.

Clare, Israel Smith. *Illustrated Universal History: A Clear and Concise History of All Nations.* Philadelphia: J.C. McCurdy, 1878.

Clark, Kenneth. *Civilisation.* New York: Harper & Row, 1969.

Davies, Norman. *Europe: A History.* New York: Oxford University Press, 1996.

Diringer, David. *The Alphabet, a Key to the History of Mankind.* New York: Philosophical Library, 1948.

Douglas, David. "The Paris of Abelard and St. Louis", in *Cities of Destiny*, edited by Arnold Toynbee. New York: McGraw-Hill, 1967.

Durant, Will. *The Story of Civilization*. Vol. 1-4. New York: Simon & Schuster, 1954.

Furnas, J.C. *The Americans: A Social History of the United States, 1587-1914*. New York: Putnam, 1969.

Garraty, John A., and Gay, Peter, editors. *The Columbia History of the World,* Dorset Press edition. New York: Harper & Row, 1972.

Gombrich, E.H. *The Story of Art.* New York: Phardon, 1966.

Guillaume, Alfred. *Islam.* New York: Penguin, 1956.

Hamit, Francis. *Virtual Reality and the Exploration of Cyberspace*. Carmel, Ind.: Sams Publ., 1993.

Hegel, Georg Wilhelm Friedrich. *The Philosophy of History*, from *The Philosophy of Hegel*, ed. Carl J. Friedrich. New York: Modern Library, 1954.

Hitler, Adolf. *Mein Kampf.* London: Hurst and Blackett, 1939.

Hughes, Langston, and Meltzer, Milton. *Black Magic: A Pictorial History of the African American in the Performing Arts*. New York: Da Capo Press, 1990.

Huizinga, Johan. *The Waning of the Middle Ages*. New York: Doubleday Anchor, 1954.

Kaufmann, William, and Smarr, Larry, editors. *Supercomputing and the Transformation of Science*. New York: Scientific American Library, 1993

Langer, William L., editor. *An Encyclopedia of World History*. Cambridge, Mass.: Houghton Mifflin, 1952.

Lewin, Roger. *In the Age of Mankind: A Smithsonian Book of Human Evolution*. Washington, D.C.: Smithsonian Books, 1988.

Logan, Robert K. *The Alphabet Effect*. New York: William Morrow, 1986.

Lynd, Robert S. and Lynd, Helen M. Middletown: A Study in Modern American Culture. New York: Harcourt, Brace & World, 1956.

Marty, Martin E. *A Short History of Christianity*. Cleveland: Meridian Books, 1967.

McCarthy, Eugene J. and McGaughey, William. *Nonfinancial Economics: The Case for Shorter Hours of Work*. New York: Praeger, 1989.

McEvedy, Colin and Jones, Richard. *Atlas of World Population History*. Harmondsworth, NY: Penguin, 1978.

McLuhan, Marshall. *The Gutenberg Galaxy; the Making of Typographic Man*. Toronto: Univ. of Toronto Press, 1962.

—— *The Medium is the Message*. New York: Bantam, 1967.

Meyers, Philip V. *General History*. Boston: Ginn & Co., 1906

Mitchell, B.R. *International Historical Statistics, the Americas and Australasia*. Detroit: Gale Research, 1983.

Muller, Herbert J. *The Uses of the Past: Profiles of Former Societies*. New York: Oxford Univ. Press, 1957.

Newman, James R. *The World of Mathematics*, Vol. I. New York: Simon & Schuster, 1956.

Pimentel, Ken, and Teixeira, Kevin. *Virtual Reality: Through the New Looking Glass*. New York: Intel/Windcrest/McGraw-Hill, 1993.

Plato. *Republic*, from *Plato: the Collected Dialogues*, ed. Edith Hamilton & Huntington Cairns. New York: Pantheon Books, 1961.

Prechtel, Martín. *Secrets of the Talking Jaguar: A Mayan Shaman's Journey to the Heart of the Indigenous Soul*. New York: Jeremy P. Tarcher, 1998.

Samhaber, Ernst. *Merchants Make History: How Trade has Influenced the Course of History throughout the World,* translated by E. Osers. New York: John Day, 1964.

Scannell, Paddy, and Cardiff, David. *A Social History of British Broadcasting, 1922-1939*. Cambridge, Mass.: B. Blackwell, 1991.

Scarre, Chris. *Timelines of the Ancient World*, Smithsonian Institution publication. New York: Dorling Kindersley, 1993.

Schweitzer, Albert. *The Kingdom of God and Primitive Christianity*. New York: Seabury Press, 1968.

Showers, Victor. *World Facts and Figures*, third edition. New York: Wiley, 1989.

Smith, Anthony, editor. *Television, an International History*. New York: Oxford Univ. Press, 1995.

Somé, Malidoma P. *Of Water and the Spirit: Ritual, Magic, and Initiation in the Life of an African Shaman*. New York: Putnam, 1994.

Spengler, Oswald. *The Decline of the West*, abridged edition by Helmut Werner, translated by Charles Francis Atkinson. New York: Alfred A. Knopf: 1962.

Toynbee, Arnold J. *A Study of History,* abridgement in two volumes by D.C. Somervell. New York: Oxford Univ. Press, 1956.

—— *An Historian's Approach to Religion*, Gifford lectures at the University of Edinburgh, 1952-53. New York: Oxford Univ. Press, 1956.

—— *Mankind and Mother Earth, a Narrative History of the World.* New York: Oxford Univ. Press, 1976.

Trotsky, Leon. *Stalin.* New York: Stein and Day, 1967.

Wells, H.G. *The Outline of History, Being a Plain History of Life and Mankind*, in two volumes. New York: Macmillan, 1920.

\*\*\*\*\* \*\*\*\*\*\* \*\*\*\*\*

Alexander, Steve. "Data Mining". *Star Tribune*, August 17, 1997. p. 1D

Allman, William F. "Wisdom We Inherited from the Stone Age". *U.S. News & World Report*, October 24, 1994. p. 80.

Barber, John. "A Wireless World". *Star Tribune*, November 25, 1994. p. 23A

Begley, Sharon. "Could Dinosaurs Return?, Behind Jurassic Park." *Newsweek*, June 14, 1993. pp. 57-65

Brauchli, Marcus W. "Star-Struck: A Satellite TV System is Quickly Moving Asia into the Global Village". *Wall Street Journal*, May 10, 1993. p. 1.

Braudy, Leo. "In America, Fame is an Open Door", conversation with Alvin P. Sanoff. *U.S. News & World Report,* October 6, 1986.

Bulkeley, William M. "It's too bad NBC didn't have these Editors for the Olympics." *Wall Street Journal*, October 20, 1988.

Caniglia, Julie. "Cyberpunks Hate You". *City Pages*, February 10, 1993. p. 8.

Cook, William J. "Men in Blue". *U.S. News & World Report*, February 16, 1998.

Dawson, Jim. "City at the Edge of the Beginning". *Star Tribune,* November 26, 1995. p. 1A.

Fellman, Bruce. "Finding the First Farmers". *Yale Alumni Magazine*, October 1994. pp. 40-47.

Gaw, Jonathan. "Online Shoppers Mostly Just Browsing". *Star Tribune*, November 26, 1997. p. 1D.

Goldberg, Robert. "Television, Replaying the Eighties". *Wall Street Journal*, January 2, 1990.

Gorbachev, Mikhail. Address to 27th Congress of the Communist Party of the Soviet Union. Reprinted in *USA Today*, March 19, 1986. p. 5A.

Grove, Lloyd. "Dukakis' Eyebrows". *Star Tribune*, October 12, 1988. p. 19A

Grow, Doug. "Reality Bites the Dust at Olympics". *Star Tribune*, July 26, 1996. p. 2B.

Headden, Susan. "The Junk Mail Deluge". *U.S. News & World Report,* December 8, 1997. pp. 40-48.

Holstein, William J., et. al. ""Click 'til You Drop". *U.S. News & World Report,* December 7, 1998. pp. 42-53.

Holston. Noel. "'Mind' TV Series Explores the Brain". *Star Tribune*, October 12, 1988. p. 11E.

Koerner, Brendan I. "Where the Boys Aren't". *U.S. News & World Report*, February 8, 1999. pp. 47-54.

Kolata, Gina. "A Headstone, a Coffin and, Now, the DNA Bank". *New York Times*, December 24, 1996.

Krauthammer, Charles. "The Great Di Turnaround". *Time*, September 22, 1997. p. 104.

Lardner, James. "Please Don't Squeeze the Tomatoes Online". *U.S. News & World Report*, November 9, 1998. pp. 51-52.

Leff, Laurel. "TV Comes to Town; Fads and New Wants Come along with it'. *Wall Street Journal*, October 2, 1979. p. 1.

Leung, Jean Y. "Life with an Illiterate". *Wall Street Journal,* September 2, 1986.

Leyden, Peter. "On the Edge of the Digital Age". *Star Tribune*, June 11, 1995.

Longman, Phillip J. "The Janitor Stole my Job". *U.S. News & World Report*, December 1, 1997. pp. 50-52.

Lowry, Brian. "Network Difficulties". *Star Tribune*, August 13, 1997. p. 1E.

Marshall, Jonathan. "Supercharged Fiber Optics Deliver Data Faster than Ever". *Star Tribune*, August 17, 1997. p. 1E.

McGraw, Dan. "Big League Troubles". *U.S. News & World Report,* July 13, 1998. pp. 38-46.

Milenthal, David L. "Paradigm Shift is Hitting the Advertising Business". *Star Tribune*, December 11, 1995. p. 3D.

Muller, Joanne. " A Little Lesson on the History of the Internet". *Star Tribune,* September 24, 1998.

Olsen, Henry. "Tammany Technology: Soul of a New Machine". *Wall Street Journal*, October 13, 1989.

Parshall, Gerald. "The Prophets of Culture". *U.S. News & World Report,* June 1, 1998. pp. 58-71.

Raphael, Michael. "Number-crunching Behemoth Spawned Modern Computer Age". *St. Paul Pioneer Press*, February 12, 1996. p. 1.

Reagan, Ronald. "Commencement Address at Louisiana State University". *Wall Street Journal*, May 24, 1990.

Robinson, Carl. "Publishing's Electronic Future". *Publishers Weekly,*

September 6, 1993.

Rockwell, John. "Technology Altering the Basic Sounds of Western Music". *Star Tribune*, October 13, 1986. p. 5C.

Rosenkrantz, Linda. "Collectors Stroll down 'Penny Lane'. *Skyway News*, August 15, 1995.

Samuelson, Robert. "Computer Communities". *Newsweek*, December 15, 1986. p. 66.

Schulberg, Budd. "In Movies, the Writer's the Thing". *Star Tribune*, December 7, 1989.

Smetanka, Jane. "U Studies Ways to Boost the Quality of its Instruction". *Star Tribune*, November 30, 1998. p. 1

Stewart, Susan. "What Pre-fab Images Fill Kids' Daydreams". *Star Tribune*, February 27, 1995. p. 3E

Thomas, Susan G. "The Networked Family". *U.S. News & World Report*, December 1, 1997. pp. 66-86.

Tomsko, Robert. "Sampler Revolutionizes Recording and Brings Battles over Copyright". *Wall Street Journal,* November 5, 1990.

Toth, Robert J. "From Caves to Computers". *Wall Street Journal*, Special Report on Entertainment and Technology", September 15, 1995. p. 4R.

Vogelstein, Fred. "Paying for College". *U.S. News & World Report*, September 7, 1998. p. 68.

Webber, Thomas E. "Talking Toasters: Companies Gear up for Internet Boom and Things that Think". *Wall Street Journal,* August 27, 1998. p. 1 & 6.

Welch, Michael. "Long Live Rock". *City Pages*, April 4, 1988. p. 13.

Welsch, Chris. "Is Tourism the Devil's Bargain?". *Star Tribune*, July

23, 1998. p. 22A.

Zoglin, Richard. "The Show-and-Sell Machine". *Time*, May 1, 1989.

\*\*\*\*\* \*\*\*\*\* \*\*\*\*\*

*ABC Nightline:* "What's Become of Hollywood?", March 28, 1989; "Lucille Ball Dies", April 26, 1989.

*Academic American Encyclopedia*. Danbury, Conn.: Grolier, 1997. p. 368, 775.

*Encyclopedia Americana, International Edition*, Vol. 9. Danbury, CT: Grolier, 1996. pp. 643-652.

*Encyclopedia Britannica*. New York: William Benton, 1971.

Forbes: *American Heritage Special Report*, July 24, 1989. p. 20.

*History*, China Handbook Series. Beijing: Foreign Language Press, 1982.

*Personal Report for the Executive*: "Hooked on TV", June 1988.

*Star Tribune*: February 15, 1994, p. 7A; November 18, 1994, p. 1D; June 10, 1996, p. 4D; August 19, 1996, p. 7D; October 1, 1996, p. 1E

*St. Paul Pioneer Press*: February 20, 1989, p. 2E; November 28, 1989. p. 6A.

*Time*: June 17, 1996, p. 83.

*U.S. News & World Report*: June 19, 1995, p. 46.

*Wall Street Journal*: July 3, 1984, p. 18; January 23, 1990, p. 1; January 24, 1990, p. 1; February 1, 1990, p. 1

# Index

## A

A Current Affair 320
A Study of History 32
Aaron, brother of Moses 50
Abbas, founder of Abbasid dynasty 218
Abbas I, Safavi emperor of Persia 223
Abbasid caliphate 197, 217–220, 221–223
Abbasid revolution (750 A.D.) 217, 220–221
Abd ar-Rahman, founder of Ummayad Iberian state 218
Abel, son of Adam and Eve 34
Abélard, Peter, professor of theology 81, 238
"abortive" civilizations 32
Abraham, Hebrew patriarch 24
absolute power 277, 420
absolute reality, worship of 94–95, 115
abstractions 349, 352, 373, 377, 434, 495
Abu Bakr, Mohammed's successor 216–217
Abu Hureya 142
Abyssinia 200, 222, 389
academic critics 317
academic degree 490–491
academic records 490
academic tradition, western 80–82
Academy (Plato's) 96, 109
academy of Jewish studies 196
accounting 376, 476
Achaean Greeks 150
Achaemenian dynasty of Persia 151, 167, 212, 389
Achilles, Greek warrior 107
acrostic principle of alphabets 385
Act of Union (1439) 164
acting methods 305
action drama 316, 328, 469

Actium, battle of 156
Acton, Lord, John Emerick Edward Dalberg-Acton 420
actors and actresses 126, 132, 328, 404, 469
Actors' Equity Association 305
Adam, first man (Genesis) 23
Addison (Joseph) and Steele (Richard), editors 361
administration 217, 257
    corrupt imperial 233
    Islamic 232
    of Roman church 441
    Turkish 224
Admiral Dot, circus performer 85
admission to colleges 489
adolescence 446, 448
Adrianople 158
Adriatic sea 243
adult entertainment 325–326
advancements in philosophy and religion 351–355
Adventures of Ozzie and Harriet 318
advertisements 457, 477
    customized 472
advertisers 315, 327, 427, 470–471, 481
advertising 87–89, 91, 129, 304, 338, 361, 369, 370, 395, 406, 411, 470
AEG, German chemical company 402
Aetolian Confederation (Greek) 152, 154
Afghanistan 151, 165, 174–175, 223, 225, 232
Africa 141, 153, 161, 217, 222, 243, 247, 251, 253, 258, 275, 283, 362, 442, 458–459
    early kingdoms 145
African Company 299
"African Roscius" 299
Afshar dynasty of Persia and India 223
age-phases of the individual man 423
Aghlabid Arabs in Tunisia 220
agora (market) 152
Agra, India 223
agrarian reform 179
agriculture 56, 85, 94, 100–101, 181, 395

# I

# K

# O

**X**

**Y**

# Z